ELIZABETH'S IRISH WARS

ELIZABETH'S IRISH WARS

by

CYRIL FALLS

*With seven Illustrations
and a Map*

CONSTABLE · LONDON

First published in 1950
This edition published in Great Britain 1996
by Constable and Company Limited
3 The Lanchesters, 162 Fulham Palace Road
London W6 9ER
Copyright © 1950 Cyril Falls
Paperback edition 1997
ISBN 0 09 477220 7
Printed in Great Britain by

A CIP catalogue record for this book
is available from the British Library

To
THE DUKE OF ALBA

PREFACE

THE wars in Ireland in the reign of Queen Elizabeth have been neglected by historians. Writers of general history have had relatively little to say about them, and writers of military history less still. Fortescue showed in his *History of the British Army* that they did not interest him; Oman in his *Art of War in the Sixteenth Century* scarcely mentioned them, except to express his opinion that the one Elizabethan soldier with a capacity for high command was Lord Mountjoy and that he was 'wasted' in the Irish wars. It might have been expected that Irish historians would fill the void, that they would glorify the exploits of their countrymen who opposed the alien oppressor and shook his power. This has not been the case. Attempts have been made to establish Hugh O'Neill, Earl of Tyrone, as military genius and patriot, but the literature devoted to him is neither bulky nor notable in quality. It has been the practice to regard the Irish wars as a series of obscure and savage combats and skirmishes in bog and forest, dull in themselves and of no particular significance.

It was not the view of the chief English actors that these wars lacked significance, any more than it was that of European observers. It is natural that Spanish and Scottish correspondence should contain frequent references to revolt in Ireland and to English difficulties there, but they are found also in French and Venetian. The governors and soldiers sent to Ireland by the Queen did not doubt the importance of their tasks, though they often disliked them and begged for recall, being conscious of how easily a good reputation might be buried there. Queen Elizabeth's viceroys were generally able and often of high military capacity. Sussex—whom she inherited from her sister Mary—Sidney, Fitzwilliam, Perrott, and Essex were remarkable figures. If Essex appears inferior in calibre to the rest, as well as to Russell and Burgh, we must remember that he was the Queen's favourite and the greatest man in the kingdom, so that in sending him to Ireland she sent what she held to be her best. Mountjoy, the last of her viceroys, may perhaps be ranked as the greatest English soldier of the period.

Many of the foremost professional soldiers served in Ireland. Sir William Pelham and Sir George Carew were most capable fighting

men. Sir Richard Bingham, that fierce flail of Connaught, saw half
a century of service, campaigned with the Spaniards at Saint-
Quentin in 1557 when England and Spain were allied, and is believed to have fought in the Spanish fleet at Lepanto in 1571. The
Norris brothers, Sir John, Sir Thomas, and Sir Henry, were re-
nowned warriors, and John's exploits on the Continent were world-
famous; yet he could win but small distinction in Ireland.

The security of Ireland was a matter of moment to England,
particularly before the crowns of England and Scotland had been
united by the accession to the former of James I and VI, when a
hostile power had some prospect of obtaining support in Scotland
for its designs against England, and Irish rebels could hire Scottish
mercenaries and buy Scottish arms and powder. After the outbreak
of open war with Spain, the danger became acute. Spain possessed
one great advantage when opposing English rule in Ireland in that
the normal winds from the south-west would bear Spanish fleets
swiftly and at most seasons to the British Isles, while rendering it
difficult for English fleets to intercept them. Command of the sea
becomes a relative phrase when applied to a situation in which the
fleets of one belligerent and their accompanying transports may
evade those of its foe and plant an army on its soil. This danger
hardly touched England itself, because the bulk of the population
was by then loyal, and a very powerful army would have been
required to overcome its defences; Philip II envisaged the conquest
of England only by means of a strong army transported from his
territories in the Low Countries under cover of his fleet and largely
by boats. But it affected Ireland, where the population was of another
race and the greater part of it was potentially hostile to England and
favourable to Spain. The Spaniards were capable of carrying, all the
way from their home ports to Irish harbours, an army big enough to
swing the balance in Ireland against the power of the English
Crown. Their disadvantage was that the Irish never succeeded in
winning a good port for their use.

It may be argued that, if such a force could reach Ireland, it could
not be maintained there unless the Spanish fleet were strong enough
to insure the passage of supplies and reinforcements, and that the
Spaniards, if they did not occupy the whole country speedily, could
not hope to prevent fresh English forces from landing on the east
coast and in the long run attaining numerical superiority. Then too,
modern students realize how heavily Spain was handicapped for
war with England because the former's Mediterranean commit-

ments resulted in only a portion of her fleet being suitable for naval warfare in the Atlantic and hindered her in absorbing the new methods of oceanic warfare. All this is true; but in both Ireland and England it appeared to the authorities that there was a risk of the Spaniards establishing themselves in Ireland. Their presence there would not only have constituted a threat to England from close quarters, but would also have afforded advantage to Spain in her struggle to control the routes to the Americas.

Ireland, linked to Spain by refugee Irish soldiers and sailors in Spanish armies and navies, by refugee bishops and priests in Spanish cities, by commercial intercourse which made Irish pilots familiar with Spanish and Portuguese harbours—and Spanish pilots to some extent familiar with those of Ireland—was a weak point in the English armament. Observant Englishmen sometimes considered that Ireland's safety was neglected for the Continental expeditions. Sir Walter Raleigh wrote to Sir Robert Cecil: 'We are so busied and dandled in these French wars, which are endless, as we forget the defence next the heart.' Years earlier the Jesuit David Wolf reminded Philip II of a proverb: 'He that will England win, let him in Ireland begin.'[1]

Anxiety was most acute during the period when the Armada was awaited because it was thought probable that the Spaniards would land a force in Ireland. After the Armada had been dispersed and some of its remnants had been driven on to the Irish coast either by the elements or by the need of food and water, the presence of dispirited and starving Spanish soldiers and crews greatly perturbed the Queen and Lord Burghley. The Privy Council warned Lord Deputy Fitzwilliam not to risk a defeat or to fight the Spaniards except at an advantage. At the same time, it contemplated sending over another 2,000 men to deal with the supposed Spanish menace. It took on to the English pay-roll retainers of the native Ulster lords, on whom it ordinarily looked with suspicion and whom it was continually seeking to disarm.[2] The slaughter of virtually helpless men by Fitzwilliam and his lieutenants, which sheds so ugly a light upon the honour of English arms, can be set down to nervousness at the prospect of contact between the Spanish troops and the native Irish.

Apart from the Armada, there were constant reports of expeditions fitting out which might be destined for Ireland. And even when

[1] *Salisbury Papers*, Pt. IX, p. 310. *C.S.P. Roman*, Vol. II, pp. 151-68.
[2] S. P. Ireland, Vol. XXXVI, 52.

there was little question of an expedition, individual ships bringing arms and munitions might greatly strengthen a rebel leader or induce a chief who had been hanging in the balance to come out against the Government. It was possible for such vessels to lie for several days in some of the western inlets of the sea before reports of their presence reached Dublin, though it must be acknowledged that the Government generally possessed an Irish agent to send the news without loss of time.

If it be a misapprehension to despise Irish warfare as unimportant, it is still wider of the mark to regard it as easy. It was, in fact, more difficult than Continental warfare because, while it might occasionally include episodes of a type usual on the Continent, it was more often of a very different nature. The efficient commander had to be ready to fight either in the Continental style or in the Irish skirmishing style. In the latter case his obvious difficulties were tactical, but he was also always faced by the overmastering strategic difficulty of war in such a country that, apart from the enemy's troops, who were extremely elusive, there was no obvious objective the loss of which would ruin the enemy. It will be related how remunerative objectives were devised. The characteristic Irish style made high demands upon the commander's eye for country, his skill in minor tactics, his system of intelligence and knowledge of the enemy's habits and methods, his courage, fortitude, vigilance, speed of thought, and ability to maintain a supply system in the field in country where it might be necessary to lay down hurdles in order to pass vehicles over heavy ground or even impossible to employ vehicles at all. Irish warfare was an art which some men who had won fame in other theatres took long to learn or never fully acquired. It was also arduous in the extreme. The fighting man lived hard, if not miserably—'all the soldiers in Christendom must give place in that to the soldier of Ireland', said Sir William Pelham, who had plenty of experience of other wars.

The strategic problem of Ireland in relation to England is eternal. It had appeared before the Elizabethan age, though not in so serious a form, when France temporarily interested herself in Irish affairs. It reappeared at the end of the seventeenth century, when French arms supported in Ireland a king who had been driven from the English throne. It reappeared at the end of the eighteenth century, in the wars of the French Revolution, when the last battle against the land forces of a foreign invader was fought at Ballinamuck. It reappeared in the First World War in the early twentieth century, and once more, as very important issue, in the Second World War. It influences the attitude of British governments to the partition of Ireland and reinforces the plea of Northern Ireland to remain a part of the United Kingdom. The dependence of Great Britain upon supplies carried across the Atlantic has increased the strategic significance of Ireland. And behind this lies the inescapable truth that Ireland alone, however friendly an Ireland she may be, cannot successfully defend herself against invasion by a major power.

Elizabeth's Irish wars were not, then, unimportant, and they illustrate an English embarrassment which still exists. Whether Irish warfare be in itself as uninteresting as previous historians have apparently concluded is a question which must be left to the reader to answer. Many of the personages who appear in it are impressive. Its background, the dissolution of a Celtic community in contact with a Teutonic influenced by Roman law and ideas, is pathetic. These pages will at least make it clear that the conduct of the wars became more systematic than the historians have generally admitted. While at first sight—and some of these historians did not spare the subject a second glance—the maintenance of English power in Ireland appears to have been achieved by purposeless slaughter, accompanied by indecision, waste, and corruption, policies were in fact worked out, though they were not always steadily pursued, and remarkable advances in efficiency and organization took place.

These policies may not have been profound or far-sighted; they were practical and of short range. The qualifications, the doubts, the moral qualms, the generosity, of modern England in similar circumstances did not trouble Elizabethan heads. It was enough for them to accept the principles of authority without question and to meet opposition to them as they appeared. Posterity would have to meet its problems in its turn.

They sought an immediate goal and reached it. Spain was defeated in Ireland as on the seas. Elizabeth handed over to her successor an Ireland in part depopulated, hungry, devastated, and sullen, but pacified and constituting no further danger for long years to come. In the warfare of arms and of will, the English—with their Irish allies—had prevailed. The rebellion of the Earl of Tyrone, by far the most dangerous of all and led by a man who recognized the King of Spain as King of Ireland, had been broken. Wild and inaccessible regions, above all in Ulster, not held hitherto and in a few cases hardly visited by Englishmen for many a long year, had been brought under the control of forts. Elizabeth had won the fight, against Spain and revolt in Ireland. The Queen 'in her deep and declining age did seal up the rest of all her worthy acts with this accomplishment, as if she had thought that her task would be unfinished, and tomb unfurnished, if there could not be deservedly engraven thereon, "PACATA HIBERNIA" '.

*   *   *

The dates are given in old style, but taking the year as beginning on 1 January. The Spaniards, of course, used the new style of the Gregorian calendar introduced in 1582. There is, however, a slight complication in Irish correspondence as regards this matter. The old style was official and used normally by Irish and English alike. The mayor of a town employed it as a matter of course. On the other hand, the Irish chiefs in revolt adopted the new style on what are now called ideological grounds, because it was the work of the Papacy. When they wrote to Spain, in which case the scribes were nearly always priests, they used new style. On occasions when dates in or appended to letters in new style are quoted, they are given as they appear, with the letters 'n.s.' in brackets beside them.

I have usually anglicized Irish names, proper and common. Even the majority of Irish readers might not recognize Tyrone in 'Tir Eoghain'. And though there has been a cult for signatures in Celtic form in recent times there are very few people who sign themselves 'Maguidhir' out of all the thousands of Maguires, McGuires, or even McGwires. There may be less justification for using *bonaghts* in place of *buannadha* for mercenaries; but I have found the former used by people who did not recognize the Celtic spelling.

I have to thank Mr. C. T. Atkinson, who has been kind enough to read my chapters and has given me useful advice. I am grateful also to Mr. A. L. Rowse for some helpful suggestions and most of all for his evocation of Elizabethan spirit and motives. During a visit to Spain I received valuable aid from Spanish authorities, especially the Historical Service of the Army, its Director, Colonel José Vidal Colmena, and one of his officers, Captain Vázquez.

C. F.

ALL SOULS COLLEGE

CONTENTS

ILLUSTRATIONS

CHAPTER I

IRELAND UNDER ELIZABETH

IN the time of Queen Elizabeth Ireland differed sharply from the England to which it was united by the person of its sovereign and which provided its administrators. Irish civilization lagged behind that of England, yet this fact is far from sufficing to explain the gulf between the two countries. This gulf was wider than the distance by which English civilization was ahead of Irish because Irish was moving along different lines. There were elements of strength and beauty, with here and there the touch of genius, in Irish civilization, but they bore no relation to the magnificent blossom of English civilization in the Elizabethan age. The two stood on different planes, and it is the differences in kind rather than the differences in quality which best repay consideration, because the former are not in dispute, whereas the latter depend largely upon the point of view. A strong antipathy existed between the two cultures because there was scarcely a point of contact between their traditions, their ideals, their art, their jurisprudence or their social life.

This antipathy is to be found at its full strength only where Irish culture was pure and unmingled with that of England. It is tempting and usual, but an over-simplification, to regard the conflict solely as one between Saxon and Hibernian, English and Celtic, culture. It was so mainly, but not entirely. In point of fact, the English had made a deep impression upon Ireland, and though this had been almost effaced in some districts where it had once been sharp, it had not been entirely eradicated. Indeed, Tudor policy had done something to restore it.

There was a steady gradation from the Irish herdsman in Tyrone, living in the community known as the 'creaght', moving with the cattle from one pasture to another—'a very idle life and a fit nursery for a thief', as Edmund Spenser thought—through the man of County Cork, through the dweller in the English Pale, through the Dubliner, and up to a great Anglo-Irish nobleman like the Earl of Ormonde or the Earl of Kildare. Each was marked to a greater degree than the one before by English influence. The

Tyrone herdsman was untouched by it. He spoke no English and was unaffected by English habits; indeed, he might not have laid eyes upon an Englishman because the creaght was if possible sent into a hill fastness when an English expedition penetrated deeply into Ulster. The Cork man at least saw the English on the roads and knew something of their way of life. The Palesman was in frequent contact with the English, and in many cases had English blood in his veins and bore an English name. He had adopted English customs so far as to wash his shirt four or five times a year. The Dubliner was also probably of English descent; he lived in the shadow of the Castle, where dwelt the Queen's Lord Deputy, and, if the latter were as popular as Sidney, turned out to give him a cheer in the street; he was a lawyer arguing before a judge who might be an Anglo-Irishman like himself; he was a merchant, a caterer, a sea captain sailing to Holyhead or Bristol. And Ormonde was a man of English culture, who had been educated in England, had been smiled upon by the Queen, had won the friendship of her minister, William Cecil, Lord Burghley, professed the Protestant faith in her reign, and yet lost little of the vast prestige and popularity which attached to the house of Butler.

It is at least a defensible proposition that Ireland might have become as closely united with England as Wales was or as Scotland was to be but for the failure of the Reformation in Ireland. Its effects were disastrous for the Church in that country, since they enfeebled and disorganized Roman Catholicism without establishing Protestantism, except nominally, in its stead. Any slight progress made by the reformed Church had been reversed for ever by the Marian reaction. Under Henry VIII the greater nobility, including even the O'Neill of Tyrone and the O'Donnell of Tyrconnell, had 'abjured the Pope'; but this was merely for their personal advantage and did not touch their subjects. There had been a period when a large proportion of the inhabitants of a few considerable towns had attended Protestant churches, but it had passed. The monasteries had been dissolved, though a number survived, either tolerated because they lacked property or situated in remote parts. The great men, Norman, English, and Irish, had not scrupled to join in the scramble for their lands, and Queen Mary had not ventured to restore them when she re-established the Roman Catholic faith. English bishops appointed to Irish sees virtually never spoke the language of their flocks.

On the accession of Elizabeth a number of bishops made enigmatic

statements of adherence to the reformed Church, the significance
of which is matter for dispute. Latin Masses were celebrated at the
beginning of the reign, even in the cathedrals of Dublin. At the
solemn installation of the Earl of Sussex, Elizabeth's first viceroy,
the Mass was followed by the Litany and *Te Deum* in English. Some
bishops who accepted the Queen's supremacy probably did not
adopt uniformity of worship. Those under the patronage of the
northern chiefs—Clogher, Dromore, Derry, Kilmore, Raphoe—
were not summoned to the first Elizabethan Parliament. On the
other hand, the Archbishop of Dublin, Hugh Curwen, Lord
Chancellor in 1559, who had been selected by Mary to restore
Roman Catholicism, went over to Protestantism clearly and without
reservation under her sister.[1] The fact that he and more than one of
his successors held these double offices suggests that in their ghostly
functions they were not overburdened with work.

Different as were the circumstances and sentiments of the two
countries, the ecclesiastical policies followed in each were somewhat
similar, though the results were contrary. The Queen and her
advisers, clerical and lay, began by leaving matters of doctrine in a
vague state, so that there should be a gentle and scarcely noticeable
transition from Catholicism to Protestantism. It was a subtle policy,
but was presently divined by Rome, and in both countries the
Papacy challenged it. The differences must be made clear; Catholicism must proclaim itself and accept the sacrifices involved. There must
be martyrs. 'The more you cut us down, the more we grow; the seed
is the blood of the Christians', the boast of Tertullian, became a pre-
cept of Catholic policy. It failed in England, but succeeded in Ireland.

Rome's counter-offensive in Ireland, as so often, took the form of
despatching to the country a number of travelling friars, a large
proportion of them Jesuits. These preachers and missioners, generally
Irishmen, but occasionally Englishmen, educated in England in the
reign of Mary, in Flanders or in Spain later on, were far superior in
learning, ability, and respectability of life to the clergy displaced
from their benefices and the monks. They helped to maintain those
who had clung to the old Church in their faith and to bring back to
it many who had temporarily left the fold. They were found at the
elbows of the great lords, but they did not fear the hardships of the
fern or the bog. They were the scribes of the illiterate, who included
many powerful chieftains, and from that it was but a short step
towards becoming their political advisers too. They formed a sort

[1] Ronan, *The Reformation in Ireland under Elizabeth*, pp. 6–24.

of cement which united nationalism with religion against the Queen and her Lord Deputy.

It was not only at home that Irish churchmen played a prominent part in opposition to England. A number of them dwelt abroad, in Spain or the Spanish Netherlands, a few in Rome. When war broke out between England and Spain, their influence became of high importance. At the end of the reign the titular Archbishop of Armagh and Primate of All Ireland, Peter Lombard, lived in Rome. A titular Archbishop of Dublin took refuge in Spain. But in the Irish north the Papal Bishop of Derry was reported to be riding about 'with pomp and company from place to place as it was accustomed in Queen Mary's days'.

Trade with Spain provided another link with that country unfavourable to English interests even while Spain and England remained nominally at peace. Elizabethan Ireland exported timber, hides, furs, and a little linen; but fish, shipped in salt to Spain, was the biggest export, while Spanish wines were normally the biggest import. If the Government regarded this trade with suspicion it was because of the belief that it tended to foster rebellion in Ireland. There was no repression of the intercourse. No trade restrictions, but for a few imposed by the Irish Parliament, existed. England under Elizabeth was, in this matter at least, easier-going than in later years. Nor were Irish Catholics subject to economic disabilities. None the less, trade with Spain constituted a danger. Apart from its effect upon Anglo-Irish relations, it made Spanish pilots acquainted with the chief Irish ports. After the outbreak of war it did not entirely cease, and was then, of course, accompanied by greater perils, though it had the advantage that Irish sea captains brought back valuable information, especially about concentrations of Spanish ships of war at Cadiz, Lisbon, or Coruña.

The machinery of government was relatively simple. At the head stood the viceroy, bearing the title of Lord Deputy, or in exceptional cases the higher one of Lord Lieutenant. There had been several Anglo-Irish viceroys in the past, but the practice of appointing Irishmen was discontinued by Elizabeth. In a reign of forty-four years there were eleven viceroyalties, averaging four years apiece, not taking into account several interludes. There were, however, only nine viceroys, since two were given two terms of office. The successive viceroys were the Earl of Sussex, Sir Henry Sidney, Sir William Fitzwilliam, Sir Henry Sidney, Lord Grey de Wilton, Sir John Perrott, Sir William Fitzwilliam, Sir William Russell, Lord

Burgh, the Earl of Essex, and Lord Mountjoy, of whom Sussex and Essex bore the title of Lord Lieutenant and the rest that of Lord Deputy. It was deeply impressed upon the representative of the Crown that his office was sacred. He was solemnly installed by the Archbishop of Dublin and was handed the sword which was the symbol of his authority and without which he could not act; in fact, his viceroyalty commenced from the moment when it was placed in his hands. He possessed wide powers, including that of conferring knighthoods. Sometimes the Queen would turn in fury upon a Lord Deputy who had granted too many—largely because her economical spirit dreaded that they would become suitors for money or office to support their positions—but she did not disavow them. These men had been touched with her sword and bidden to rise by her own appointed representative and mouthpiece. The Lord Deputy could proclaim a man to be a traitor or issue to him a pardon by letters patent under the Great Seal. He could levy forces and had in fact most of the prerogatives of royalty, except that of coining money. Again, however much the Queen might object, she would not go back upon his word.

The Lord Deputy was assisted by a Council, chosen in England. This included the Lord Chancellor, the Chief Justice, the Treasurer at Wars, the Marshal of the Army, and generally one or two great noblemen, such as the Earls of Ormonde and Kildare. Lord Deputy and Council were in effect the Government, to an even greater extent than Queen and Privy Council were the Government of England because Parliaments played a smaller part in Ireland, which had only a trifling revenue of its own and where the Government had to be continually subsidized from England. Parliament, not being needed to grant subsidies, met at rare intervals for some special purpose, such as (under Sussex) to restore the Protestant religion, (under Sidney) to extinguish the title of the O'Neill, (under Perrott) for the attainder of the Lords Desmond and Baltinglas. The Secretary of the Council was a most important official, who might be called a civil servant. He and the Treasurer represented elements which, through longer experience, might be most helpful to the Lord Deputy, but occasionally thwarted him and intrigued against him. When a President of Munster was appointed he was also given a Council, together with a Chief Justice. The experiment of creating a presidency in Connaught failed, and thereafter, until the end of the reign, the officer commanding the troops in that province was designated Governor.

The only civil subordinates of the Government were the sheriffs of counties and the mayors or sovereigns of corporate towns. Until, however, a district had been shired there was no sheriff, and if a county became deeply involved in revolt the sheriff might be driven out or shut up in a fortress where he could not function. Ormonde, and Desmond before his rebellion, possessed special powers in their countries, and these might be partially extended to other noblemen, as to the Earl of Thomond in the latter part of the reign. Until the appointment of a Chief Justice of Munster, all the judges resided and held their courts in Dublin. The circuit system had been introduced, but, as will appear from what follows, could be applied only locally and in favourable times, though generally in the English Pale.

The Pale consisted of the shires of Dublin, Meath, Westmeath, Kildare, and Louth. In unsettled times it was the only part of the country, outside the generally loyal corporate towns, where the Queen's writ ran. It had been organized and controlled since English rule was established in Ireland, and, if its fortunes fluctuated, it was always possible to restore order after incursions into the Pale by Irish rebels. The lords and gentry of the Pale were generally of Norman descent, Catholics, to a certain degree hibernicized, but less so than the descendants of the early English settlers in other parts. Normally, they supported the Government, and raised their swords-men and tenants at least for the defence of the Pale, though not enthusiastic about venturing far beyond its limits.

Wicklow was not part of the Pale. It had never been settled, and its mountains were almost impossible to control. In the glens of this tangled country the O'Byrnes remained unsubdued, and often raided the Pale. A night's march would take them to the gates of the capital. Thus Dublin, sometimes regarded as the centre of the Pale, was rather a frontier city, where constant watchfulness was called for.

On the other hand, there had been a sort of extension of the Pale in the counties of Leix and Offaly, Queen's County and King's County—the Queen and King in whose honour they had been renamed being Mary and her consort Philip II of Spain. A colonization scheme had been inaugurated in the reign of Mary after the suppression of the revolt of the Irish overlords, the O'Moores and O'Connors, in the reign of Edward VI. By the terms of their grants, the new landlords undertook to maintain their principal residences on their estates, to use the English language and dress, to take no Irish tenants and employ no Irishmen except those born in their county, to part with none of their lands without the consent of the Queen's Lord Deputy, and to acknowledge that any females of their families marrying Irishmen should forfeit their jointures or dowers. This colonization of Leix and Offaly, completed in the reign of Elizabeth, had widened English influence, but its foundation was far from solid, and the parts of the counties left in native hands were nearly always on the edge of rebellion.

Outside Leinster the power of English law varied with that of English arms. It is sometimes pretended that the Queen's rule extended no farther than Leinster or even beyond the accepted boundaries of the Pale, but this is an unsatisfactory generalization. There were, as will appear later in this narrative, periods when it was effective over a great part of Munster. For some years before Tyrone's rebellion in the latter part of Elizabeth's reign Connaught was almost completely tranquil, though actual control was less effective. In Ulster Shane O'Neill and later his second cousin Tirlagh Luineach O'Neill and his nephew Hugh O'Neill, Earl of Tyrone, kept out English influence and power throughout the reign, and the last-named was not finally subdued until the Queen lay on her deathbed; but even in Ulster there were intervals of relative quietude during which English penetration became less difficult. Naturally, this penetration was chiefly into the shires bordering on the Pale, Armagh and Monaghan. Down cannot be included because of the barrier of the Mourne Mountains, and Cavan ('the Brenny O'Reilly') formed part of the province of Connaught at the accession of Elizabeth. But in those quieter days the garrisons in Newry, Armagh, and Monaghan town were undisturbed. The castle of Carrickfergus, on the Antrim shore of Belfast Lough, was always held by the forces of the Crown.[1]

Yet Ulster, certainly apart from Armagh and Monaghan, was the least touched by English influences of the four provinces of Ireland. In all the others the chieftains, Butlers, Fitzgeralds, Burkes or de Burghs, were in the main the descendants of English or Anglo-Norman invaders, and sometimes purely Irish families, such as the O'Brians, had been partly anglicized. The old settlers might have become almost indistinguishable from the Irish in mode of life, in habits, and in dress; but some faint gleam of their past seems to have endured within them—very faint sometimes, hardly perceptible

---

[1] The areas are described as counties and given their county names for convenience, but they were not shired, or made counties, till 1584, in the deputyship of Perrott.

even to themselves, but a minute relic, a hint, a reminder of a different ancestry. And this germ could in some instances be revived and enlarged by royal patronage, by a title from the fount of honour. They might be the leaders of dangerous revolt, as were the Fitzgeralds of both branches, Kildare and Desmond, but they could be, and had occasionally been, reclaimed.

There remained no great lords or chieftains of English descent in Ulster. In Down, in the country round Strangford Lough—the Great Ards to the north, the strip of the Little Ards to the east, Lecale to the south—a few Norman names such as Jordan and Savage were still to be found, but their holders were no longer figures of import-ance; they were at the mercy of stronger native chieftains, to whom they paid the 'black rent' of submission. The Ulster lords were pure, or in the Elizabethan phrase 'mere', Irish.[1] Throughout the reign very few of them learnt or desired to speak English. One man alone, Hugh O'Neill, second Earl of Tyrone, had lived in England and acquired English 'civility'. He had been brought up at the seat of the Sidneys, Penshurst, partly for his own safety and partly as an experiment, in the hope that the O'Neill influence would be bent to the side of the Government. That experiment appeared to have succeeded when he first returned to Ireland, but it failed in the end, as it did not fail with the holders of the Clanrickarde and Thomond peerages.

The O'Neill of Tyrone, the head of which family had been ennobled by Henry VIII, occupied in Ulster a position for which there was no equivalent in the other provinces. As the O'Neill he claimed an overlordship established by Shane. His paramountcy was not acknowledged by the greatest of his rivals, the O'Donnell of Tyrconnell, but it amounted to something which impressed the minds of the people of Ulster, of all Ireland, of the Government, and even of the Spaniards. He was incontestably the greatest power in Ulster, even when the title of the O'Neill was held by a man of relatively little energy, like Tirlagh Luineach. And this Irish para-mountcy was one of the features of Irish life which the Queen's Government was chiefly anxious to abolish, with all that it stood for —and what it stood for must be described later. It was symbolized by the title of 'the O'Neill', which to the people of Ireland was far more significant than that of Earl of Tyrone. Occasionally a modern

[1] Contrary to general opinion, there was nothing pejorative in the expression 'mere Irish'. On occasion a contemporary is to be found speaking of the soldiers in a company as all 'mere English'.

historian is found asserting that the Government called upon Tyrone to renounce the name of O'Neill. That is a misapprehension. The Government did not desire to abolish the family name; it did not demand, for instance, that Tyrone's sons should be called by any other. It demanded that he, the head of the family and the holder of a peerage from the Crown, should abjure the title of the O'Neill, with its conflicting pretensions.

Tyrone has been called above the head of the family, not the head of the clan. There must be some doubt as to the propriety of using that word with application to Ireland. Because the County Tyrone is called O'Neill's Country, Tyrconnell O'Donnell's Country, Fermanagh Maguire's Country, Monaghah MacMahon's Country, this means only that the families named were predominant and that each furnished his 'country' with its ruling chieftain, not that the country was by any means solely inhabited by the family of his name. Of those mentioned above the MacMahons probably provided the highest percentage bearing the principal name. In Fermanagh were to be found McCuskers, Flanagans, McCafferys, and many others. Some might have hereditary functions, as the O'Bristans, who were Brehons, or judges, and the Cassidys, who for nearly two centuries, from 1320 to 1504, were physicians to the Maguires.[1] It may be added that in Scotland, where the clan system possessed greater reality than in Ireland, it is a fallacy, fostered by romantic sentiment, to picture the whole clan areas as peopled by members of the main clan. Cantyre, closely linked with Ulster and its affairs, was the country of the MacDonalds, but the greater landholders under them included MacKays and many other families.

Another feature of Ulster life and in less degree that of all Ireland is the settlement of men of Scottish descent and the visits of Scottish mercenaries to serve the chiefs in war. On the Antrim coast above all there was a permanent Scottish settlement and at the same time a constant coming and going of Scots across the narrow waters dividing the two countries. These Scots were primarily MacDonalds from Cantyre and the western islands, but by no means wholly of that clan. The settlement of the coast strip, 'the Glynns' of Antrim, dated from the beginning of the fifteenth century. The MacDonalds also constituted one of the most important families of mercenaries, the *gallóglaigh* (anglicized to gallowglasses), who had begun to enter the country in order to take service with the Irish chiefs in the mid-thirteenth century and had remained as their hereditary

[1] M'Kenna, *Devenish*, p. 126.

henchmen.[1] These two types of Scots, the Antrim settlers and the gallowglasses, exercised a great effect upon Ireland and Anglo-Irish relations, the former chiefly in north-east Ulster, the latter all over the country, though in the province of Leinster, where they were not numerous, to but a small degree. Finally, under the Tudors, another wave of Scots mercenaries came over, chiefly to serve the Ulster lords. These did not settle. They were mercenaries hired for a season or a campaign and returned home when their term was over. Much more remains to be said about the Scots as a military factor. They have to be mentioned here in passing as an element in Irish social life.

The general Irish social system was patriarchal. The chief was, or had once been, a little king. He possessed a demesne, great or small according to his power, which was regarded as his property, which was farmed by his own tenants, unfree and hardly beyond the status of serfs, and which provided his household with its means of subsistence. Outside the demesne he did not possess the soil of his territory, which was peopled by families at least theoretically free, but who paid him a rent in some form, generally that of cattle, and had to submit to the billeting of his soldiers upon their land. The whole constituted the *tuath*, or lordship, of such a chief. The *tuatha* were, in fact, small, self-contained states, not 'clans' founded on kinship.[2]

The system was, however, complicated by the varying power of the chief. He might stand at the head of a single lordship. A more common feature was that of a superior chief with a number of secondary chiefs dependent upon him, each possessing a lordship such as that described above, but owing allegiance to the overlord, so that there was a group of lordships, making up what the English observers called the overlord's 'country'. These secondary chiefs were the great chief's *oir rioghtha*, which was anglicized as 'urraghts' or 'urriaghts' by English writers of the Elizabethan age. Purists may object to the translation of 'vassals', which is not exact; perhaps 'dependents' is closer. The vassals, besides maintaining their own soldiers, would commonly have to support those of the overlord.[3] Finally, as has already been indicated, the O'Neill in Ulster held an even higher position than other great overlords or chiefs of 'countries' because he pretended to a suzerainty over those in this situation.

[1] Hayes-McCoy, *Scots Mercenary Forces in Ireland*, p. 22.
[2] MacNeill, *Early Irish Laws*, p. 94.
[3] The military system is described in detail in Chapter IV, devoted to the Irish armies in the wars of the Elizabethan age.

The order was aristocratic, and it is as fallacious to suppose it communistic as it is to confuse it with feudalism.

It is again fallacious to regard Celtic society as static, something which can be examined and accepted, as is an exhibit under a glass case in a museum, as a representation of the thing itself fixed for once and all. In a brilliant passage a student of Celtic civilization shows the type of development which was going on under the Tudors, to be arrested by the overthrow of the Irish at the battle of Kinsale.

'It has become common to speak of "Celtic Ireland" as a kind of personified abstraction, the theory of which was rudely broken in upon at Kinsale, and to consider the Irish scheme of life and institutionalism as an unchanging whole ... its incidents and organization presenting nothing new as the centuries passed. If this were so, then Kinsale would have been no tragedy, for it would merely have averted stagnation. The tragedy lay in this, that the defeat of the Irish at Kinsale arrested an institutional development which had been going on steadily through the centuries, slowly at first, when the Scandinavian and Norman invasions had brought about the inevitable retrogression, speedily then with the winning over of the Norman settlers to Gaelicism, and with increasing force during the sixteenth century when the power of the great lords, both native and adoptive, grew apace and ushered in the aristocratic phase of Irish evolution. This last was the keynote of development during the Tudor period. It might upon superficial consideration be assumed that this tendency towards the concentration of despotic power in the hands of a nobility was a retrogression. But it was not so: it was a development, a legitimate stage in the growth of national society, and the traditional freemen could never hope to enjoy to the full at a later stage the political fruits of their early social training as the mass of the nation without first passing through a period of subjection at the hands of the lords. This was the tragedy of Kinsale, a tragedy of arrested development, and this was also the reason why the war of Tyrone and O'Donnell was not a war for the political freedom of Ireland, for Ireland as an entity had not yet emerged in the sense of the new conception of the nation-state, but a war for freedom to continue natural development.'[1]

The only possible qualification to this analysis is that the Norman settlers were not wholly won over to Gaelicism, that they frequently retained, for example, English usage in the matter of inheritance,

[1] Hayes-McCoy, *Scots Mercenary Forces in Ireland*, p. 304.

and that, though the little men, the Barretts, Cusacks, Lynches 'and sundry English surnames now degenerate' whom Lord Deputy Sidney met in Galway, had gone or been forced over, even they were still 'lamenting their devastation', while the great men still kept the memory and some of the traditions of their Anglo-Norman past.[1] It may also be worth while bearing in mind the sentiments of those by whom this 'legitimate stage in the growth of national society' was not viewed as objectively as by the historian. When the power of the O'Neill was broken the English were deafened with the complaints of men who asserted that he had deprived them of their rights as freeholders and made them his tenants at will. Some actually fled from him into the Pale. Great vassals, such as O'Cahan with regard to Tyrone, and O'Dogherty with regard to O'Donnell, denied that they could legally be considered to be such. If Irish civilization was not crystallized, it was consequently subject to the constitutional problems and controversies of other civilizations.

From time immemorial it is established that 'the succession to an Irish dynasty was normally elective, but that eligibility was confined to the royal kindred'.[2] This does not involve in itself the full system of tanistry, since that includes election before the kingship becomes vacant, but tanistry appears in later times, without becoming universal. The tanist was the successor; he might be called, in an idiom foreign to Ireland, the 'crown prince', and exacted his own tribute or 'cuttings' from the country.[3] Theoretically, no system could be sounder in such a community, since it put at the head of the lordship the member of the princely house best fitted to rule, passing over weaklings and the immature. In practice it was another matter. It encouraged claimants belonging to the chief's family to band together the largest possible number of fighting men, to assassinate their rivals and to prey upon the latter's lands. Even if the succession were decided only on the occurrence of a vacancy—perhaps indeed most of all then—the struggle for the lordship was the curse of the country. So thought the Earl of Sussex, the Queen's first viceroy, a man of great ability and also of experience, since, when he wrote in 1562, he had served her in that capacity for three years, after serving her sister Mary for four.

'The election to the captainship of the country', said Sussex, 'is the cause why the Irishmen do keep great numbers of idle men of war, that thereby they might be the stronger, hoping by their

[1] *Carew Cal.*, Vol. II, p. 49.   [2] MacNeill, *Celtic Ireland*, p. 114.
[3] Joyce, *Social History*, Vol. I, p. 45.

strength to be elected captain upon a vacation. These men of war, being brought up and fed with idleness, cannot be restrained in time of peace from stealing and a number of other enormities. To maintain them in this life they have finding and expense upon the country, whereby be brought in coyne, livery, bonaght, and all other Irish exactions, which be the only grounds and causes of all the uncivil and detestable disorders of that realm and of the licentious disobedience to the Prince.'[1]

Even if the tanist were accepted, he might think it well to throw his weight about in order to prove his strength and fitness for war. The 'first adventure of a young lord', regarded almost as a ceremony, celebrated in glowing terms by the poet, hymned by the harper, glorified by the scribe, who delights in recording how it was rued by widows and fatherless children, was to raid his neighbour's cattle in order to bring on a fight. This convention, in fact, rendered internal strife and disorder within the lordship commoner and more dreadful than external wars.[2] Raiding with sword and fire involved no moral obloquy. Grave and tonsured annalists record that such and such a chief 'burnt the country entirely', and when they come to his death tell us how virtuous he was and that his loss was 'a great calamity'. Their annals, indeed, when not concerned with genealogies, are chiefly a record of 'preys', and they manifestly look upon an accomplished raider as we look upon a hard rider to hounds.[3]

How this laudation of raiding appeared to a contemporary English observer is shown in an amusing piece of doggerel:

> Now when their guts be full,
>   Then comes the pastime in;
> The bard and harper melody
>   Unto them do begin.
> This bard he doth report
>   The noble conquests done,
> And eke in rimes shows forth at large
>   The glory thereby won.
> Thus he at random runneth,
>   He pricks the rebels on,
> And shows by such eternal deeds
>   Their honour lies upon.
> And more to stir them up
>   To prosecute their ill,
> What great renown their fathers got
>   They show by riming skill.

[1] *Carew Cal.*, Vol. I, p. 348. For 'coyne, livery, and bonaght', see Chapter IV.
[2] MacNeill, *Celtic Ireland*, pp. 122–3.   [3] *Annals of Lough Cé, passim.*

> And they most gladsome are
> To hear of parents' name,
> As how by spoiling honest men
> They won such endless fame.
> Wherefor like graceless grafts
> Sprung from a wicked tree
> They grow through daily exercise
> To all iniquity.[1]

It is all a question of the point of view.

A word must be added about the custom of gavelkind, the fresh division of the land of a group on the death of its head, though opinion and evidence are conflicting as to the extent to which it was practised. The latest theories are against the view that whole territories were periodically redistributed. So far, however, as it was practised—and there is clear evidence that it was on occasion—its effect was to disinterest the holder in the state of his land and to bring about undue subdivision. The wars, however, by preventing the rapid growth of population, prevented the latter tendency from operating as unfavourably as would otherwise have been the case.

Even where not influenced by English practice, as it was with most Anglo-Irish families, a third mode of inheritance, by descent from father to son, is to be found in Ireland. But English practice in this respect had assumed importance before Elizabeth came to the throne. Her father, Henry VIII, had initiated the policy known as that of 'Surrender and Regrant'. His intention was that the great lords should surrender their lands to the Crown and receive them back again from it in the capacity of feudatories, by letters patent. This would afford some guarantee of their loyalty, since their lands would be forfeit to the Crown if they proved themselves disloyal. Knowledge of Irish tenure was at this time very vague among the English—much more so than after Elizabeth's reign, when Sir John Davies studied it intelligently—so that, while no injustice to the secondary chieftains was intended, it sometimes occurred, they becoming simply tenants of land which had become the property of the overlords. These latter did not scruple to avail themselves of the opportunity. Under Henry VIII the policy of Surrender and Regrant did not go very far, and it was neglected under Edward VI and Mary; but it was continued by Elizabeth, and by that time there were Anglo-Irish lawyers ready to advise noble clients to obtain grants of exclusive ownership, even in the lands of freeholders.[2]

[1] Derricke, *The Image of Ireland.*
[2] W. F. T. Butler, *Gleanings from Irish History*, p. 217.

To consolidate the process, both Henry VIII and Elizabeth bestowed titles on some of the great chiefs. Con O'Neill of Tyrone became Earl of Tyrone. The head of the O'Brians was created Earl of Thomond. Ulick de Burgh, or Burke, of Connaught was made Earl of Clanrickarde—and if this family was by origin Norman, it had in the fourteenth century repudiated the law of primogeniture and adopted the system of tanistry, so that in practice there was little difference in the experiment.[1] A large number of baronies were also created.

These new titles put their holders upon the same footing as an Anglo-Irish nobleman like the Earl of Ormonde. Henceforth the titles and the lands that went with them must by English law pass by right of primogeniture. On the Ormonde estates there was no dispute about the matter, but the principle was in some cases fiercely opposed. This conflict between English and Irish systems of tenure and inheritance, in fact, represented the strongest collision of ideas in Ireland under Elizabeth, stronger than that between English rule and Irish nationalism. Some of the chiefs strove to make the best of both principles and to be at once absolute owners, holding their lands as grantees from the Crown as their personal property, and at the same time exercising all the privileges of an Irish chief.

The English disliked and despised the native Irish law of the Brehons as much as they misunderstood it.[2] When the famous Attorney-General, Sir John Davies, gained a remarkable grip upon it, he continued to dislike but not to despise it, and he paid tribute to Irish love of justice. *Breitheamph*, anglicized as Brehon, means a judge. The Brehons, generally hereditary holders of their office, held courts for the trial of both civil and criminal cases. The remarkable feature of the criminal side is that it was law virtually without sanctions, since there existed no machinery to enforce the decisions; but they were prevented from becoming farcical in this respect because the normal penalty for a killing on a raid—which English law would have treated as murder—was a fine paid to the victim's family. Here the decision was generally accepted, as it was in civil cases, largely concerned with succession and tenure. Brehon law was, in fact, remarkably pure ancient Aryan law, untouched by Roman.

[1] Hayes-McCoy, *Scots Mercenary Forces in Ireland*, p. 8.
[2] According to the greatest Irish authority on the subject, they do so still. Professor MacNeill (*Early Irish Laws*, p. 81) points out that written Irish law is in fact the decisions of schools of law, whereas Sir Henry Maine supposed it to be a record of customary law.

It had been to a great extent adopted by the Anglo-Irish.[1] Now, however, it was doomed, though it was to survive into the reign of James I.

Elizabethan Ireland was both an agricultural and a pastoral country. Tillage was of a crude kind, half a dozen garrans, or Irish cobs, with no harness on them, being tied by the tails abreast to a cross-bar on a small plough. The English strove again and again to abolish this custom. It is tempting to suppose, in view of their traditionally greater dislike of cruelty to animals than of cruelty to human beings, that there was an element of sentiment in their efforts; but this tradition hardly extends as far back as the sixteenth century. They were not successful. In 1613, James I, reproving a party of recusant delegates in the Council Chamber for their procedure in the Irish Parliament of that year, remarks in his heavily jocular way: 'It went untowardly, like your Irish ploughs.' And Pynnar in his survey of the Plantation of Ulster in 1618, when he comes to the estate of an Irish grantee in Cavan, notes with a sort of grim despair, 'and all his tenants do plough by the tail'.[2] Nevertheless, considerable crops were raised, when the process was not disturbed by civil war or rebellion.

Then, as now, Ireland was a great cattle country. Wealth was largely counted in terms of cattle and they were the chief spoils of war. Captain William Mostyn, a soldier with twenty-seven years' experience of Ireland, estimated in 1598 that there were 120,000 milch kine in Tyrone alone, and that there would be thrice as many barren kine and other cattle. He declared that he had seen Hugh Roe O'Donnell, Ireland's champion cattle-raider, prey 30,000 in a morning.[3] The estimate for Tyrone may well be exaggerated, but the number was still enormous.[4] Great herds of brood mares, swine, and goats also existed. Sheep were plentiful in some districts, and 'muttons' as well as cattle were the prey of the marauder. The stout, rough Irish friezes were on occasion bought to clothe the royal troops.

The creaght may be said to have amounted to a social unit. With the herd there moved from pasture to pasture a little community

---

[1] *Catholic Encyclopædia*, Vol. II.   [2] Falls, *The Birth of Ulster*, pp. 209, 215.
[3] *C.S.P. Ireland*, Vol. CCII (Pt. 3), 185.
[4] On the eve of the Second World War the cattle population of the six counties of Northern Ireland was rather under 750,000. It is to be noted, however, that Tyrone was far larger in 1598 than it is now, including about one-third of the present Co. Londonderry, and that the proportion of pasture was high.

of cowmen with their families, building for themselves temporary huts of sods and branches of trees. In summer, pedlars with pack-horses moved among the creaghts, selling them such necessities as were not provided by the cattle themselves. This system was of great advantage to an Irish lord at war with the Government, since it enabled him to feed rapidly-moving forces with cattle on the hoof. But its control required high organization, and a chief could not always lay his hand upon a particular creaght at short notice. This is proved by an incident in the celebrated 'Flight of the Earls' in 1607. When the Earl of Tyrone fled from Ireland he was forced to leave behind his young son because his creaghting foster-parents were not to be found.[1] The creaght and its possibilities furnished a major strategic problem. If it could make use of the best pasture when it was 'weak'—that is, after the winter—the lord was furnished with the means for a long and perhaps distant campaign. If it could be confined to the mountains, he was proportionately handicapped.

With all this seeming plenty, the country was unsuited to the maintenance of any but the smallest English army. In the viceroyalty of Perrott, after the Desmond rebellion, when relations were not unfriendly, when the threat of the Armada had not begun to over-shadow the country, and when the garrison numbered only about 2,000, there was relatively little difficulty, and then the farmer, certainly in the Pale, was so well off 'as the poorest of them all did scorn to take any money for meat or drink from any traveller, much less from the soldiers'. The same was true under Fitzwilliam.[2] But at the height of Tyrone's rebellion, with 15,000 troops or more in the country, with that country largely devastated, it was another matter. At no time was any 'furniture' or equipment worth counting to be obtained locally. Even the horses, though popular as hacks, were not up to the weight of English cavalrymen, so that chargers had to be imported. Ireland's lack of resources constituted as heavy a drain upon England as the number of men required for the English forces or the dysentery and malaria which wasted them away.

Despite the qualifications already set out, the main conflict can be described as one between a State of the Renaissance and one of the Dark Ages. All the English influences which have been men-tioned must be regarded as English outposts in a foreign land. The tug-of-war was between the English who sought to win the chiefs and the latter's own people, led by their priests as well as by their instincts, who sought to win them back to an ill-defined but still

[1] Falls, *The Birth of Ulster*, p. 118.   [2] *C.S.P. Ireland*, Vol. CCII (Pt. 2), 108.

very potent nationalism. The odds were against the Irish because the English Renaissance State to which they were opposed was competent and well-organized, ahead of its time, though at the start of Elizabeth's reign hardly even abreast of it for prosecuting war. The balance was nearly squared because of the other strains, the Continental expeditions and the war with Spain, which England had to face, the Crown's lack of money, and the personal parsimony of Queen Elizabeth. It was finally swung over again to the English side by the qualities of the English soldier and the skill of men like Sir George Carew and Sir Henry Docwra, who enlisted the Irish to fight the Irish. There was hardly a moment, except perhaps after the battle of the Yellow Ford, when the English were entirely isolated from Irish aid—and then the English cause was saved by the devotion and persistence of an Anglo-Irish nobleman, the Earl of Ormonde.

Such was the land which Queen Elizabeth laboured to bring into complete subjection throughout her long reign, from the time when she ascended the throne to find herself confronted by the man whom she stigmatized as 'a false, perjured, seditious and pernicious conspirer, rebel, and traitor'—Shane O'Neill.

NOTE

QUEEN ELIZABETH'S IRISH VICEROYS

Sussex, Thomas Radcliffe, Earl of (formerly Queen Mary's Viceroy, first as Lord Fitzwalter), Lord Deputy 1559, Lord Lieutenant 1560	1559
Sidney, Sir Henry, Lord Deputy	1566
Fitzwilliam, Sir William, Lord Deputy	1571
Sidney, Sir Henry, Lord Deputy	1575
Grey de Wilton, Arthur, Lord, Lord Deputy . . .	1580
Perrott, Sir John, Lord Deputy	1584
Fitzwilliam, Sir William, Lord Deputy	1588
Russell, Sir William, Lord Deputy	1594
Burgh, Thomas, Lord, Lord Deputy	1597
Essex, Robert Devereux, Earl of, Lord Lieutenant . .	1599
Mountjoy, Charles Blount, Lord, Lord Deputy (created Earl of Devonshire and appointed Lord Lieutenant by James I)	1600

CHAPTER II

ELIZABETHAN ARMIES IN IRELAND

'BUT since of late Elizabeth and later James came in', there were great changes in the art and conduct and equipment of war. And because they came to this country from outside and were introduced gradually and against the grain, they brought with them an unwelcome foreign atmosphere which acted as one more dissolvent of the old England. Not only, as Sir John Fortescue notes, had complicated drill and manœuvres superseded the pleasant, almost medieval, week-end shooting at the butts, a sport as well as training for war, but the dependence upon Continental-trained bravos had given the new professionalism a disagreeable appearance. 'The acknowledged leaders in hundred and parish and shire gave place to experts trained in foreign schools, men who swaggered about in plumed hats and velvet doublets and extravagant hose, swearing strange oaths of mingled blasphemy taught by Spanish Catholics and Lutheran landsknechts.'[1] Their jargon was seamed with Spanish, German, Dutch, and French military words and phrases. They lectured insufferably, 'in one long insolent crow of military superiority'. But by their harangues on the drill-ground and their books they set things moving in what would else have been, in matters military, a frigidly conservative nation.

An army of the Elizabethan age was highly organized and increasingly so as the reign progressed. If it were large, the commander would have at his disposal a General of the Foot and a Lieutenant-General of the Horse. The Marshal appointed the camping-places, punished abuses and corrected disorders, having a Provost-Marshal under him for the latter purposes. The Serjeant-Major-General (from which title descends that of our Major-General) drew up the forces for battle. The Scout-Master was responsible for reconnaissance. The functions of the Forage-Master are explained by his title, while the Carriage-Master was the transport officer of later days. In the wars of Ireland, where armies were small and more than one expedition might be in progress at any time, the hierarchy

[1] Fortescue, *British Army*, Vol. I, p. 129.

could not be maintained. Thus the Marshal and the Serjeant-Major might each hold independent commands.

Certain high officials would accompany an expeditionary force abroad, but in Ireland would have their headquarters in Dublin. The most important was the Treasurer at Wars, responsible for the receipt and disbursement of military funds. The Master of the Ordnance handled matters of artillery, munitions, and fortification, his subordinate being the Master Gunner. The Muster-Master had to check establishments, and in those dishonest days his chief duty was to discover how many men for whom the units drew pay were actually present with them.

A regiment was commanded by a colonel, but the name rarely occurs in Ireland before the rebellion of Tyrone in the concluding years of Elizabeth's reign, when larger royal forces were employed. In any case the regiment was not in the modern sense a 'unit'. The self-contained and self-supporting 'unit', for records, pay, and rations, and in most cases tactically, was the company, a term gradually replacing the looser, old-fashioned 'band'. Only in a few instances, and those mostly after the viceroyalty of Burgh, who died in 1597, did a regiment as such come over from England to Ireland. Otherwise, when one was required for a particular purpose, it was made up by joining together a number of companies. Its strength varied, but 500—that is, five companies—was about normal.

The company of foot was occasionally 150 or even 200 strong, but 100 was the normal strength. It was commanded by a captain, the other officers being a lieutenant and an ensign or ancient. There were two serjeants, a drummer—who gave signals by taps—perhaps a fifer, and on occasion a surgeon. The officers were provided with cobs. The band of horse was nominally fifty strong. There were both light and heavy horse, but the latter were not used in Ireland; in fact, the fully armoured heavy horseman with a long lance had disappeared before the end of the reign, to be replaced by the 'demi-lance'.[1] The light horseman was heavier than any foe he would have to meet—even if the Spaniards came they would bring only saddles for their cavalry and obtain horses locally—and none too mobile for the work he would have to do. The man carried a light lance, or 'horseman's staff', and pistols, or else a sword and a long pistol or petronel. The English cavalry could commonly break up a body of Irish foot if the latter would stand, but a force of trained and disciplined pikemen, such as Tyrone formed, was

[1] Oman, *Art of War in the Sixteenth Century*, p. 386.

virtually impenetrable to cavalry. On the Continent, therefore, the practice had arisen of cavalry wheeling across the front of a body of pikemen and firing its pistols in succession. If it succeeded in opening gaps in the ranks, it might charge in before they could be closed. Before Tyrone's rebellion—and against the forces raised by other Irish leaders while that rebellion was in progress—the English cavalry gained successes at almost incredible odds. It was thus always worth while maintaining at a proportion of about one-eighth of the strength of the infantry, despite the disadvantage at which it fought in the great bogs and woodlands of Elizabethan Ireland and the higher cost. Cavalrymen were supposed to be chosen from men who could ride, yet the captains sometimes complained of receiving very bad riders. Elizabethan England was not so much a nation of horsemen as might be imagined.

Each cavalry trooper was commonly accompanied by an Irish boy on a garran, or native hackney, and had to keep him out of his pay. The horseboys, who foraged for their masters and cleaned their armour, were the pest of their fellow countrymen and brought odium upon the English army. A humane man, William Lyon, Bishop of Ross in Carbery, said of these young ruffians at the time of the Desmond rebellion, that they 'go out into the country for the compass of three or four miles and fetch in horse-loads of corn of the poor people day by day, they having no other sustenance to relieve them and their families than their little corn, about which they have taken great pains and travail, and, if they come to rescue it from the horse-boys, they fall upon them and beat them and cut them in the heads, most lamentable to see. . . . Amongst the heathen there is no such wicked soldiers'.[1]

In roadless Ireland artillery was an encumbrance rather than an asset to a field army. It played no important part in open warfare as in the great Continental battles of much earlier days, such as Marignano. A saker, firing a shot of about 6 pounds' weight, accompanied the army defeated near Armagh in 1598, and had to be abandoned in the retreat with a broken wheel, the few lighter guns being saved. When, during Sir Cahir O'Dogherty's revolt in the reign of James I, it was desired to batter in two castles on the Donegal coast held by his adherents, a demi-culverin, about a 9-pounder, was sent round by sea for the purpose rather than by a shorter land route. The value of cannon to the royal army was none the less very great. Given time and plenty of shot, it would break up

[1] *C.S.P. Ireland*, Vol. XCV, II (i).

the rough masonry of the Irish castles. The consequence was that Tyrone, going into rebellion, destroyed his own fortresses, thereby saving the army much trouble. A few of the best castles in Ireland were virtually impervious to a demi-culverin, and there is no record of the use of anything bigger in Ireland except for the fixed fortifications established at points of paramount importance, such as Cork, during the attack on the fort of the Italian invaders in 1580, the siege of Kinsale, and the capture of Dunboy Castle, knocked to pieces by a demi-cannon and two culverins within a few hours. Some of the heavier pieces employed were ships' guns.

The firearms carried by the individual soldier were of much greater importance. The chief technical military interest of the reign is to be found in their development, increasing use, and methods of handling. The arquebus, harquebus, or hackbut long preceded the reign of Elizabeth. It was in fact based upon an invention of the fifteenth century, a cock through which was passed a coil of 'match', which could be kept smouldering. The pulling of a trigger brought the cock down upon a little pan containing powder, and the firing of this powder exploded the larger charge within the barrel.[1] The harquebus was a rough, extremely inaccurate, and clumsy weapon, small in bore and firing a light bullet. It was, however, portable; in fact, the Spanish Army Museum contains a harquebus lighter than the Mauser, model 1893, once the weapon of the Spanish army. The improved form, known as the musket and invented in 1546 or 1547, with greatly increased range and accuracy and a heavier ball, was longer and heavier. It is said that the Duke of Alva was the first to adapt the musket to field warfare. Before his expedition to the Netherlands in 1567 he 'added to each company of harquebusiers 15 musketeers. Hitherto the heavy muskets could be discharged only in siege warfare, supported on a wooden tripod; but the Duke adapted them to the use of a field army, so that they could be carried on the shoulders of the soldiers and supported on a forked stake of his invention'.[2]

Here England was inclined to be backward and even reactionary and to cling to the long bow, with which such great successes had been won, after more up-to-date nations had abandoned its foreign equivalent, the cross bow. The attempt to do so was useless, if only because the sport of shooting at the butts was going out. Bishop

---

[1] Oman, *Art of War in the Sixteenth Century*, p. 80.
[2] Ossorio, *Vida y Hazanas de Don Fernando . . . Duque de Alba*, p. 346. *Armamento de los Ejercitos de Carlos V*, pp. 20–2.

Hugh Latimer regretted that England had 'taken up whoring in towns instead of shooting in the fields, a wondrous thing that so excellent a gift of God should be so little esteemed'. A muster book of a date shortly after Elizabeth's accession to the throne shows harquebusiers and archers in about equal numbers in companies, serving in Ireland: forty harquebusiers to forty-six archers in one, forty-eight harquebusiers to thirty-eight archers in a second, fifty-one harquebusiers to fifty archers in a third.[1] There is occasional mention of mounted archers. It does not appear that the armament of troops in Ireland was notably inferior to that of those employed in the continental campaigns, and as late as 1585 we find a company of archers serving under Leicester in the Low Countries, though that was a rarity and worthy of remark. Very different is the return of a Border muster of the previous year, which classifies these troops as 2,500 billmen, 2,500 archers, 827 with jack and spear (pike), and 1,547 with spear only.[2] There is no mention of harquebusiers or 'shot' of any kind. And this was the year in which a force of 2,400 Scottish mercenaries, arriving in Ulster to aid the rebels, contained 500 shot as against 1,100 bowmen.[3]

After the complete disappearance of the bow, firearms increased at the expense of pikes. In a levy upon the City of London for the expedition to Normandy in 1589, the 'shot' were to number 400, the pikes 600.[4] In a levy for Ireland in 1596, early in the period of Tyrone's rebellion, the 'shot' were to amount to one half of the total, one in four of these being armed with the heavy musket, fired from a rest, and the other three with the lighter caliver; the other half were to be pikemen, equipped with corselets, and a few halberdiers.[5] In 1598 two reinforcements sent to Ireland contained, as to the first, the proportion of twenty muskets, fifty calivers, twenty-four pikes, and, as to the second, thirty muskets, forty calivers, twenty-four pikes, in each case out of 100 men.[6] The six unaccounted for were 'dead pays', of which something more must be said later. In general it would appear that, where Ireland was concerned, it was the tendency not only to increase firearms as against pikes but also to increase the light calivers as against the heavy muskets, doubtless because the former were better suited to the operations. In 1600, in the time of Elizabeth's last viceroy, Mountjoy, the Ordnance

---

[1] *C.S.P. Ireland*, Vol. III, 47 (i).
[2] *Cal. Border Papers*, 1584. (The bill was a type of halberd.)
[3] *C.S.P. Ireland*, Vol. CXI, 70.   [4] *A.P.C.*, Vol. XVIII, p. 88.
[5] *A.P.C.*, Vol. XXV, p. 262.   [6] *A.P.C.*, Vol. XXIX, pp. 94 and 238.

Officers in London were ordered to prepare for despatch to Ireland, among other equipment and stores, 1,000 calivers as against only one hundred muskets.[1]

It is to be noted that the pikemen wore corselets, whereas the musketeers did not because more mobility was required of them. Sancho de Londoño, a celebrated Spanish writer of the age, whose work was dedicated to the Duke of Alva, stated that, for every 300 men, there should be forty pikemen without armour except for a steel cap, to accompany the musketeers in manœuvre.[2] In 1600 Arthur Chichester, later to be the famous viceroy of the Plantation of Ulster, asked to have a company of 100 men armed in the proportion of seventy with calivers and thirty with pikes, and the pikemen to wear no armour. He was clearly contemplating raids from his fortress of Carrickfergus to be carried out swiftly, and therefore wanted to dispense not only with the pikemen's armour, but also with the heavy muskets fired from rests.

Armour, like the bow, was gradually passing out of use, though it was to survive its old enemy for a long time to come. On setting forth upon Continental expeditions, the captains of companies sometimes told their men to throw away their poldrons (shoulder-pieces) and other accessories, as useless encumbrances.[3] The portraits of noblemen and commanders in full armour, with visored helmet lying on a table or held by a page, which appear as late as the American War of Independence, are somewhat deceptive. They are show portraits, and the armour may bear no closer relation to the realities of warfare than the plump, winged cherubs who hold wreaths of laurels above the heads of the wearers. Yet it was still the general practice until long after the Elizabethan age for the pikemen to wear steel caps, breast-plates, and back-pieces, possibly cuisses protecting the thighs. The same was true of the cavalry, even the light horse employed in Ireland.

The Elizabethan armies in Ireland were recruited in various ways. The militia, which descended from the *fyrd* of Anglo-Saxon days, was being reorganized, and constitutionally it was a matter of doubt whether it could be employed in Ireland, though it frequently was. Another source of man-power was the volunteer, and he was the best, but more likely to be attracted by Continental than by Irish war. The bulk of the troops were pressed men or conscripts. The sheriffs at the beginning of the reign, the lord lieutenants later, were

[1] *A.P.C.*, Vol. XXX, p. 374.   [2] Londoño, *Disciplina Militar*, p. 30.
[3] Grose, *Military Antiquities*, Vol. II, p. 322.

allotted quotas, which they filled in great part by picking up un-employed and vagabonds at the fairs or any other 'loose persons' they desired to be rid of. On this subject the Privy Council was constantly admonishing the local authorities, without much result.[1]

Then there were the Irish, under which heading must be included the gallowglasses of Scottish descent, cheap but not always reliable soldiers. They were recruited for more than one reason: because they were cheap, because they knew the country, and because, after heavy losses in battle or from sickness, it was sometimes necessary to fill the ranks quickly, and the Irish were at hand when perhaps English reinforcements were not. The factor of cheapness proved a fatal temptation to the roguery of the captains. They would fill up the ranks with Irish—in the case of the cavalry, the miserable horseboys already mentioned—pay them a pittance, draw full pay for them, and put the balance in their pockets. Some were alleged to encourage their English soldiers to desert in order to replace them with such profitable substitutes. Yet a great deal of the recruitment of Irishmen was unavoidable, and without it whole companies would have disappeared.

In the early years of Elizabeth it was decided not to allow more than five or six Irishmen to serve in each company of the royal troops.[2] The Irish on the Government's pay roll, apart from this handful, then served in a separate body, with its own 'General of the Kerne'. Thus, in 1574, when the total of the garrison in Ireland was 1,928, it consisted of 415 horse, 1,288 foot, and 225 Irish kerne.[3] Later in the reign the number of Irish in the regular forces increased enormously, with results which were often unhappy. Lord Deputy Burgh, appointed in 1597, was the first to recruit them wholesale, but he could not help doing so, because his English companies melted away in the war with the Ulster lords, and under his bold leadership there were no unfortunate incidents. Once the Irish were in, there was no safe way of getting rid of them except by normal wastage; otherwise they provided more trained men for Tyrone.

Under the best commanders the Irish fought gallantly, but in times of adversity they were apt to desert to the enemy. At their worst, the enlisted men, drawing the Queen's pay, even if at cut rates, were more to be depended on than the levies of many of the loyal chiefs, temporarily and locally hosted and known as the 'rising' or 'rising out'. 'In this service', writes Sir Richard Bingham,

[1] Recruiting and administration are treated fully in Chapter III.
[2] *Carew Cal.*, Vol. I, p. 355 (1563).   [3] *Carew Cal.*, Vol. I, p. 460.

after his victory over the Scots on the Moy in 1586, 'I had none but such as were in Her Majesty's pay; for I turned home all the rising out, for that they did me no good at the meeting of Collooney. And I would I had never had any of them; for they were very troublesome and put me to great charges.'[1] Yet the majority of Bingham's regular troops were Irish, and they could not have shown more dash and determination than they did.

The drawing up of forces, foot especially, in battle array was apt to be a long business, but it is a mistake to suppose that considerable thought was not applied to it or that means to expedite the process were not sought. Mathematical treatises on the subject were published in England, as in other countries. Elaborate tables were prepared to provide ready reckoners giving the number of ranks to be formed from various numbers of men with various numbers in each rank.[2] The sort of problem that arose is thus set out by a senior officer of the day. There are, he supposes, three regiments containing respectively 280, 320, and 600 pikes. The general orders them to be drawn up on a front the triple of the flank. If they are regarded as a single mass, then each rank will consist of sixty pikemen and there will be twenty ranks, giving a total of 1,200 pikemen. But in order that the sergeant-major may perform the evolution quickly, he will number off the body in 'maniples' of five to seven men or perhaps in 'maniples' of as many ranks as the front has soldiers, and these bodies, which we might call sections or platoons, will wheel into their allotted places. Let us suppose the general keeps the units separate. His three regiments will be drawn up as follows:

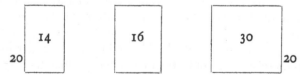

If the troops are raw, the writer prefers to see them drawn up in one mass; if, however, they are reliable and experienced there should be several 'battles'.[3]

Another authority is more explicit. Two squares side by side; three squares, two side by side and the third in support in the centre; or four squares in pairs, two in front and two in support—such

[1] C.S.P. Ireland, Vol. CXXVI, 34.
[2] Styward, The Pathway to Martial Discipline, p. 112.
[3] Digges, An Arithmetical Warlike Treatise, p. 225.

formations, with the pikes in each square winged with 'shot', are, he considers, the strongest possible. But the mass, small or large, need not necessarily be formed in a true square. A square formed from 800 men, taking the nearest square root, will have twenty-eight men in a rank and twenty-eight ranks; if a broad square is desired, there will be forty men in a rank and twenty ranks; in a 'base' square fifty men in a rank and sixteen ranks. The last-named formation will probably be adopted when there exists protection for the flank, such as a hedge or ditch.

The same writer, Barnaby Rich, who served in Ireland, has what may be called his own patent, a cross square, as below, with 'p' for pikeman, 'o' for shot, 'h' for halberdier, and 'A' for the ensign.

```
ooooopppppooooo
ooooopppppooooo
ooooopppppooooo
ooooopppppooooo
ooooopppppooooo
ppppppppppppppp
pppppphhhppppppp
pppppphAhppppppp
pppppphhhppppppp
ppppppppppppppp
ooooopppppooooo
ooooopppppooooo
ooooopppppooooo
ooooopppppooooo
ooooopppppooooo
```

It will be observed that there are only eight halberdiers to guard the colours. This would seem to be a highly artificial formation, possibly effective for the defensive pure and simple, but not otherwise.

He also informs us, however, that the formation need not be a square or parellelogram. It may be a triangle. To meet a triangle, the formation known as a shear was useful, since it outflanked the opposing force and also developed a greater volume of fire than a square, thus:

A saw formation would have an advantage of a similar nature over a shear, thus:

Rich, writing in 1587, remarks that he need not mention the old English weapons, bow and brown bill; the bow was already set aside.[1] The pike was considered a nobler weapon than the firearm. Even a prince's son, first following the career of arms, might hold it honourable to trail a pike.[2] In the Spanish army, we learn from Londoño and others, a number of the nobility and gentry served in the infantry. They were accorded the privilege of riding-horses for their own use, with the aid of which they could carry messages and help along soldiers wearied out on the march, and a proportion of extra pack-horses for their possessions. This might seem to moderns likely to be prejudicial to discipline, but it was considered of the highest value to attract such volunteers. They were 'the nerve of the infantry'. And the Duke of Alva himself, one of the sternest disciplinarians, as he was the greatest soldier, of the age, was always happy to see plenty of the young nobility in the ranks of his armies, encouraging the troops and learning the trade. 'I am resolved to grant them all the privileges they desire', he wrote to Philip II from Flanders of the gentry who flocked to join his colours, 'for there is nothing more important than to have this type of man in the army and not leave it to farm-hands and lackeys'.[3]

'I have seen', writes an authority of the reign of James I, 'when in the necessity of affairs and when the approach of the enemy hath awakened a double regard to present dangers, that these voluntary gentlemen have been more diligent in watches and more severe in performing all manner of duties than any mercenary soldier whatsoever.' He acknowledges, however, that volunteers in excessive numbers become a nuisance and recommends commanders to limit them strictly.[4]

Digges, writing in 1579, eight years before Rich, did not like to

---

[1] Rich, *A Pathway to Military Practice.*
[2] Digges, *An Arithmetical Warlike Treatise,* p. 121.
[3] Londoño, *Disciplina Militar,* p. 43. Duke of Alba, *The Great Duke of Alba as a Public Servant,* p. 18.
[4] Markham, *Epistles of War,* p. 26.

see the proportion of musketeers raised to anything like that suggested by the latter in his cross square. 'The massy battles of pikes', he said, should be empaled with three or four ranks of musketeers, but no more than could be protected by the pikemen. A certain number of muskets, he suggested, should be charged with small shot in place of a single bullet, to deal with horses and men at close quarters, and never discharged at more than one hundred paces. Musketeers should be taught to fire from a kneeling position—on the right knee of course. In this attitude they could be protected by pikemen. It would also be possible for two ranks to fire volleys simultaneously, the first kneeling, the second standing, thereby recovering some of the advantages lost with the abandonment of the long bow.

A force of infantry was drawn up in battle order with the standards—not really regimental standards, but bearing the arms of the captains—in the centre protected by a handful of halberdiers. Apart from this core, gay with colour, the centre was composed of pikemen. On either flank were the troops armed with missile weapons, archers on either side of the pikemen, musketeers outside the archers, and when the archers had disappeared the musketeers (with whom we here include calivermen) became the sole troops flanking the pikemen. The pike was about 15 feet in length, with a long steel collar attached to the head, so that it could not be hacked off by a mounted swordsman. The pikemen might be drawn up in a square with intervals left open, and through these the skirmishing musketeers could be smoothly and quickly withdrawn if driven in by superior force. Bowmen, before they became obsolete, might be employed in conjunction with the musketeers to skirmish in front of the main body. In 1581, however, when it was still thought worth while to discuss the bow, 'though archers be not as heretofore they have been', the commander was advised to station the bulk of the musketeers with the advanced guard and the bulk of the archers with the rear guard.[1] The musketeers, in handling their clumsy weapons, went through a series of movements by comparison with which the most complicated kinds of drill in more modern times appear simplicity itself.

The English soldier fought under grave handicaps in Ireland. He was generally a pressed man, and therefore far from being a picked man. Sometimes he was a criminal. 'We disburden the prison of thieves, we rob the taverns and alehouses of toss-pots and ruffians;

[1] Styward, *The Pathway to Martial Discipline*, pp. 77, 96.

we scour both town and country of rogues and vagabonds', remarks a soldier of these wars.[1] His pay was usually in arrears. He was frequently left short of supplies, and though there was normally ample meat on the hoof in Ireland, there was little else. Even the butter was rancid. The climate was wet and feverish. He had to deal with an elusive enemy, who seldom stood up to face him for long, but had extraordinary powers of endurance and generally knew every foot of the country. In the great bogs, where the Englishmen's main anxiety was to avoid being drowned, the Irish kerne hopped like a goat from one firm tussock to another. When an Irish force seemed to be enveloped and at the mercy of the Queen's army, it would steal away by some bridle-path in the night, and the following day the baffled Englishmen would see the smoke of its raids rising twenty miles or more away. Passages through woodland were in particular attended by deadly peril, since at any moment a flight of arrows might descend upon the column, or, later on—for the Irish took to firearms only a little more slowly than the royal army —a volley of shot. The whole service was unsatisfactory because there was little to show for it and few objectives for which the enemy could be forced to fight.

In these circumstances the soldier sometimes lost heart. He became mutinous, apathetic, or cowardly, and the reverses suffered by royal armies were always due to his failure to live up to his normal standards. When left short of pay he treated the inhabitants savagely. When the wars were at their worst and the greatest number of men were pressed, he deserted whenever he found a chance to do so— after the muster in his own shire; on the road to Chester or Bristol or Plymouth; at the port, where an unfavourable wind might detain him for two or three weeks and give him an excellent opportunity to escape; even at the Irish port, where it was often possible to get aboard a vessel homeward bound. Occasionally he went over to the rebels, but this habit was mainly confined to the Irish.

Sometimes it was thought wise to ship his equipment and neces-saries—a word used by Elizabethan soldiers and not obsolete yet— separately in order to prevent him from selling them. On other occasions his coat would be carted to the English port of embarkation in case he ran away in it.[2] It is not always possible to decide when it was due to those responsible for fitting him out or by his own fault that he went to Ireland half naked, but the effect was deplorable. In 1596 ten horsemen came to the Surveyor-General of the Musters at

[1] Rich, *A Pathway to Military Practice.*   [2] A.P.C., Vol. XXIX, p. 120 (1598).

Chester and told him they had no shirts, doublets, or stockings. He explained to Burghley that he had not noted the fact when they were on parade because their armour and coats covered their bodies and their riding-boots covered their legs. Their conductor, needless to say, said they had sold their clothes. It would be interesting to know the truth, because this party of horse was raised by the Bishop of Gloucester and was part of a contingent raised by and at the expense of the fathers of the Church.[1]

Who can be astonished at these failings? The man was torn from his home to go to a land he loathed on reputation and hated worse still on sight. When warfare was brisk he might get no training at all and be sent straight off to fight a tough enemy. He was possibly cheated of his dues by his captain and kept in arrears of pay by his Queen. He must have learnt from common talk how few came back from these wars; for if the enemy did not end a man sickness would. The Low Countries might be wet and cold, but how pleasant were the winter quarters in snug, well-built towns by comparison with winter in some miserable camp or dirty hamlet in Ireland!

The astonishing thing is how excellent the English soldier was under competent leadership, how brave and enduring, how ready to take on the enemy, Irish, Scot, or even Spaniard, at long odds, how regularly he was successful, what a mere handful of English troops normally sufficed to hold down a turbulent country where there was always some disaffection, frequent rebellion, and most men went armed. It is to be doubted whether English soldiers were ever successfully called upon for greater endurance than they were by Mountjoy, but it is the numbers who fought in the wars before Tyrone's rebellion that make the most notable reading. In 1559, when Shane O'Neill was in revolt, the regular troops, apart fom Irish kerne, numbered 1,150—326 horse and 824 foot. In 1562 the return of strength was 1,100. In 1569 it was 1,483, at a time when there were estimated to be 4,000 Irish in revolt under James Fitzmaurice. It leapt up to 8,892 in 1580 at the height of the Desmond rebellion, but four years later was down to 2,000 again. During Tyrone's rebellion in Elizabeth's last years, when a powerful Spanish force had landed at Kinsale, it reached a maximum of 18,000. With the accession of James I, when the revolt had been suppressed and the Spanish menace was ended for ever, it fell to a mere police force of 1,100 in 1606.

Nor can it be said that the Elizabethan viceroys resigned

[1] *C.S.P. Ireland*, Vol. CXCIV, 38.

themselves to the limitation of English rule to the Pale. Periodically sections of the country in Ulster, Connaught, or Munster were closed to movement except in some armed strength; occasionally too it was considered temporarily impolitic, either on financial grounds or because trouble might be stirred up for which the authorities were not prepared, to enter a certain district. In general, however, viceroys, presidents of provinces, and their subordinates went where they would when they would, until Tyrone made Ulster temporarily impregnable.

Feats of arms as dazzling as any of those performed at sea in this great age of fighting mariners occurred again and again in Ireland. Perhaps the English and Welsh folk of those days knew of them— they must have heard of them from the demobilized or 'cassed' soldier, begging his bread from tavern to tavern, as was too often his fate. Yet there were few to put them on record and there have been few since to interest themselves in them.

CHAPTER III

THE ADMINISTRATIVE BACKGROUND

IN considering the demands of the Irish wars upon man-power, material, gold, and shipping, the reign of Elizabeth must be divided into two parts. During the first no other serious commitments engaged the military energy of the nation; during the second it was at war with the greatest power in the world. The strain of Tyrone's rebellion was far greater than that of the rebellions of Shane O'Neill and Desmond, not merely because Tyrone's rebellion was the most dangerous that occurred in Ireland, but also because in the second part England had to stand other and far greater strains. The first downright English challenge to Spain on land was the expedition to the Netherlands which resulted from the treaty of 1585. The force finally numbered some 7,400, for which the Queen contracted to pay £126,000 per annum, one-half of her ordinary receipts, and actually paid more. In 1587, 4,650 more men were sent, for the service of the States, and left for some time although the States refused to pay for them. There were also 1,800 troops in the pay of the States, whose pay also England often had to find.[1]

This was only the beginning. Within three years the country was involved in preparation for the coming of the Armada, which, besides meeting it at sea, entailed the muster of all available forces to oppose the army of 30,000 men intended to be landed under its cover, a strong, highly trained army under the ablest commander of the age. The defence force was inadequate in numbers and deficient in weapons. Its weakness furnishes proof that the barrel was scraped.

The defeat of the Armada did not end the efforts made against Spain or appreciably lessen the strain which they involved. In 1589 Sir Francis Drake as admiral and Sir John Norris as general led an expedition to Portugal, in support of the pretender to the throne, in which the troops alone probably numbered over 12,000. In the same year a force of between 3,000 and 4,000 went to France in aid of Henry IV. Both these forces suffered heavy losses, and the second almost disappeared. In 1591 a force of 2,700 went to Brittany, to be

---

[1] Neale, *E.H.R.*, Vol. XLV.

followed by contingents of about 6,000 in subsequent years, though not all these troops can be counted as new levies, a proportion being drawn from the Netherlands. In that same year 1591 another force of 2,700 landed in Normandy. In 1596 the great combined operation against Cadiz required about 6,000 soldiers, well over half of them raised at home for the occasion. In the mismanaged expedition of 1597 5,000 troops, four-fifths of them raised in England, were carried in the fleet.

In all these ventures casualties were high, from sickness when not also from the weapons of the enemy. In the Continental campaigns, apart from the brief amphibious expeditions, one student estimates that the losses were 50 per cent. of the troops sent out.[1] That is probably on the low side. It is unlikely that half the soldiers sent to Ireland ever saw their homes again.

Service in Ireland was the most unpopular of all, with the result that it was always most difficult to keep the ranks in Ireland full, because men would take any risk and use any subterfuge to avoid or get out of that theatre of war. Their absence was also more difficult to detect than on the Continent, because a fraudulent captain, on the occasion of the muster when the numbers with the colours were checked, could hire civilians to get into uniform and answer the names of missing men, for whom he would then draw pay.

The constitutional position with respect to military service was delicate. It was not altogether clear whether the Sovereign possessed the right to send the militia abroad, as was frequently done, or to levy troops for foreign service without the sanction of Parliament. However, this action, in later times to become a matter of controversy, was not so to any great extent under Elizabeth, any more than it had been under Mary. In affairs of this sort the Tudor monarchs got away with much that was not passed from their successors. Maitland's view is that the Act of 1557, which speaks of mustering and levying men to serve in the wars as a recognized legal practice, implicitly sanctioned impressment for foreign service.[2] It has also been suggested that there existed a current conception of a law of nature which empowered exceptional measures for self-defence, and a fortiori exceptional measures by the Sovereign for the safety of the realm. This would apply not only to conscription, but also to the forced loans.

[1] Cheyney, *History of England*, Vol. I, p. 304.
[2] Maitland, *Constitutional History*, p. 275.

The method of levying troops was to send a summons to each shire from which it was intended to draw them. The Queen herself addressed to the sheriff, and to the lord lieutenant when he became her instrument, a commission in general terms, giving the numbers and the purpose for which the men were required. This was accompanied or immediately followed by a more detailed message signed by the Lords of the Privy Council, stating the port from which the troops would sail, the date by which they would arrive there, and probably the manner in which they were to be equipped. The lord lieutenant was the Queen's agent. He might be absent from the county and delegate the task to deputies, sheriffs, and justices of the peace, but he remained responsible and was chided in the case of disobedience or slackness.

The county authorities might proceed to call for volunteers by beat of drum. These were the best type of soldiers, and the Crown was glad to get them. In 1566, during the rebellion of Shane O'Neill, writing to the Wardens of the Western and Middle Marches on the Scottish Border to raise fifty horse in each case, the Privy Council urged that every effort should be made to get volunteers, and certainly no district was likelier to provide them than these Marches.[1] As demands grew heavy, however, there became no likelihood of obtaining thus more than a small fraction of the numbers required, least of all for Ireland. The counties then resorted to what was in fact conscription, but haphazard and arbitrary conscription. Their job was to find the numbers called for, and they were not particular about the methods. They looked round first for those who could best be spared, which often came to mean those whom it was most desirable that the community should get rid of. Masterless men, rogues, and vagabonds, idlers generally, were picked up. If time allowed to await a local fair, it was an easy matter to surround the green or the field in which it was held and lay hands upon all the men of suitable age not following a useful and settled occupation.

The Privy Council did not object to this means of recruiting to begin with and even enjoined it on occasion. Gradually, however, the remonstrances of the military commanders against the type of man thus provided became so strong that they could not be disregarded. Then there followed a tussle between the Privy Council on the one hand and the lord lieutenants and their deputies on the other, the former emphasizing in message after message that the troops raised in former levies had been 'insufficient', 'loose', or

[1] A.P.C., Vol. VII, p. 313.

'lewd' persons and that the quality must be improved on this occasion. The Earl of Pembroke, for example, was reprimanded for the bad quality of fifty men from Radnor in 1598. 'The men', said the Privy Council, 'were taken out of the gaols and of rogues and vagrant persons, evil armed and sent forth so naked and bare, without hose or shoes, as they are not any way fit for service nor to appear amongst men, besides of that lewd behaviour as they had like to have mutinied and made an uproar in the town.' Clothing, it was added, had been provided by London contractors, and the deputy lieutenants would have to repay them the cost.[1] Bad weapons and armour were as often the subject of complaint as men of the wrong type. In the Desmond rebellion it was reported that calivers burst on discharge and injured the men who fired them.

We are apt to think, justly in some respects, of Queen Elizabeth as a very formidable monarch, whose subjects mingled fear with their affection for her. On the other hand, it is astonishing to discover how insubordinate and disobedient the Elizabethan people were as a whole. Shire after shire persisted in these forbidden courses, just as the military commanders persisted in still more flagrant abuses in the muster-rolls and in downright peculation, despite the threat of heavy penalties. The Crown, in fact, walked warily in these doubtful matters. The dislike of service was well understood and when the calls became heavy it was considered that some explanation was due to the Queen's subjects. In November 1598, in calling for a levy of 1,000 men, this was given in almost apologetic tone. It was well known, ran the message, how sparingly the Queen had always levied men except in emergency; this was an emergency. 'The state of Ireland being grown to a general defection, Her Majesty, both for the honour of her princely calling and of the realm, is to apply these speedy and effectual remedies that they may be able to cure so grievous a disease; for which respect Her Majesty is urged at this instant to make great levies of foot and horse and to lay a further burthen on the counties than otherwise Her Highness would do.'[2]

However, finding that once the contingent had reached the port of embarkation it was too late to amend its quality and that it had to be shipped as soon as the wind served, whatever it was like, the Privy Council took steps to have it inspected at the original muster. Experienced captains were sent to the counties concerned with orders not to pass the troops as fit for service until it had been

[1] *A.P.C.*, Vol. XXIX, p. 43.   [2] *A.P.C.*, Vol. XXIX, p. 312.

ascertained that their arms and clothing conformed with instructions and that they themselves were men of the right type. At the port there would be a second muster by the mayor, later by inspectors specially appointed, and probably by officers under whom the troops were to serve. These last were on occasion sent over from Ireland for the purpose. While abuses did not cease, an improvement in the type of men was gradually effected. Sometimes they and their equipment was so good that a message of gratitude was sent to the county which found them. In December 1598, Lord Norris, Lord Lieutenant of Oxfordshire and Berkshire, was specially commended for the speed of the recent levy in those counties and for the good quality of the recruits and of their equipment. Norris, however, had sons serving in high command in Ireland, so was more concerned than the average lord lieutenant of a county that the fighting material should be good.[1]

The better quality material was drawn from labourers, artisans—sometimes specially enlisted—sons of freeholders, shopmen, folk of all trades. They might have some militia training; they might have none, and in that case were unlikely to get much unless detained at the port by contrary winds. The objection to taking trained men was manifestly greatest when there existed a risk of a Spanish invasion, and it was at such times that the troops for the Irish service were likely to contain the largest proportion of untrained.

The method described applies particularly to the infantry. The raising of cavalrymen was individually much more expensive, but the total numbers were very much smaller. Although contingents of horse were included in the levies for which the lord lieutenants were directly responsible, the Privy Council commonly drew these from another source, the Church, not as odd a source as it seems at first sight because it was a great tenant of land. In this case it was the diocese, not the shire, which paid. Each bishop was assigned a number, perhaps a dozen, but even at that small figure the cost was substantial, because the assessed figure for providing and equipping a man and his horse was £25, and finally £30, since war raised prices then as now. Nominally, this levy was voluntary and a proof of the loyalty of the bishops; in fact they were left in no doubt of the disagreeable consequences of refusal.

It was not considered equitable that the Catholic recusants should escape the burden. In theory, the bishops paid to show their loyalty and the recusants to prove that they were not disloyal; but it may

[1] *A.P.C.*, Vol. XXIX, p. 398.

have been that the recusants were not trusted to serve themselves. Sometimes the two classes were incongruously lumped together, as in a warrant of 24 July 1598, authorizing a levy on clergy and recusants for twenty horses in the province of Canterbury, ten in that of York, and twenty-six from the recusants of the country.[1] In another case letters were sent to recusants directing them to provide half the cost of a light horseman apiece—that is, £15. They were addressed by name to recusants of Hampshire (ten), Somerset (one), Norfolk (seven), Sussex (two), Essex (two), Suffolk (one), Kent (two), Worcestershire (two), Leicestershire (two), Lincoln (two), Derbyshire (one), Lancashire (one), Cambridgeshire (one), Nottinghamshire (one), and Buckinghamshire (one). But six of them, for Yorkshire, Cumberland, and Durham, were left blank, to be filled in with the most suitable names by the Archbishop of York, he being in his capacity as a member of the Council in the North, and even more in that of President of the Northern Ecclesiastical Commission, more likely to be acquainted with the circumstances of those parts than the Privy Council.[2] In 1600 the lawyers were chosen to give proof of their affection by subscribing amounts averaging about £20 apiece and totalling over £2,000 for raising cavalry.[3]

The levies were provided, generally on the spot, with clothing and arms. The county paid some three-fourths of the expenses of clothing in 'coat money', the Crown the balance. The dress was uniform in the sense that the contingent from each shire wore coats of one colour, but the colour varied with the contingent. We hear of blue coats, of cassocks 'of motley or other sad green colour, or russet', which might be called a foretaste of camouflage.[4] An Irish observer speaks of a more conspicuous colour, but one which is a precursor of a great British tradition; an English company newly arrived in Munster during the Desmond rebellion was, he says, known as 'the redcoats'.[5] The cavalry were on occasion issued with red cloaks.

The fullest description of a private soldier's clothing dates from the time of Tyrone's rebellion. He wore in winter a cassock of broad Kentish cloth, lined with cotton (costing 17s. 6d.), a doublet of canvas with white linen lining (12s. 6d.), and a pair of Venetians or breeches of broad Kentish cloth, linen lined (13s. 4d.). He was provided with two shirts of holland with bands (8s.), three pairs of

[1] C.S.P. Ireland, Vol. CII (Pt. 2), 100.   [2] A.P.C., Vol. XXIX, p. 116.
[3] A.P.C., Vol. XXX, p. 29.   [4] Grose, Military Antiquities, Vol. I, p. 326.
[5] History of Catholic Ireland, p. 27.

ox-hide shoes (7s.), three pairs of kersey stockings (8s.), and a hat (7s.). In summer he wore no cassock; he was issued with only two pairs of shoes and one pair of stockings, and his hat cost only 3s. Shoes at 2s. 4d. appear cheap by comparison with stockings at 2s. 8d. a pair. The officer's winter cassock was trimmed with silk lace and his Venetians were adorned with silver lace, but his shoes and stockings were the same as those of the private and his shirts cost but little more.[1]

The strong Irish friezes were sometimes used to clothe troops already in Ireland, and the question of using them on a large scale was discussed. But in the main all came from England. It was necessarily so. The Elizabethan system and Elizabethan finance brought it about that when there was no great rebellion in progress the army in Ireland was reduced to a skeleton, so that the problem of clothing ceased to be of importance; when, on the other hand, there was a great rebellion and the army became numerous, the rebellion itself closed most of the normal sources of supply, the country was desolated, and dependence upon English exports of all kinds became absolute.

In general the sketch of the system of levying men for Ireland is a bare one: the Queen's commission for raising the troops, the report of the contingent's departure and arrival at the port, perhaps some comments upon its composition and standard of efficiency. In the case of Derbyshire, however, a glimpse is to be had behind the scenes, from the papers of the Earl of Shrewsbury, Lord Lieutenant of the County.[2]

On 7 March 1595, the Lords of the Council sent an order to Shrewbury to have in readiness 100 men for the Queen's service in Ireland. On the same day Burghley informed him that six 'dead pays' were warranted in this number. On the 9th Shrewsbury wrote to John Manners, Deputy Lieutenant, Sir Humphrey Ferrers, and John Harper, instructing them to muster ninety-four men. On the 14th he announced that Captain Merriman, Lieutenant Patrick Fleming, and Ensign Henry Pullen would be present at the inspection of the contingent, which they were to command. On the 14th also the Privy Council directed them to purchase the necessary arms from William Grosvenor. On 9 April Merriman, who was then at Chester, wrote to them commending Grosvenor's wares. On the 23rd Manners and the others certified that the troops had been handed over to Merriman.

[1] Harington, *Nugae Antiquae*, p. 17.   [2] *Rutland Papers*, Vol. I, pp. 326–81.

On 14 June came the order to levy three horsemen for Ireland, followed on the 24th by an order to the Bailiff of High Peak to collect sums for fitting them out. John Manners headed the list of eight names with £2 13s. 4d., the lowest sum being 6s. On 27 August 1596 Shrewsbury was ordered by the Queen to levy a further fifty foot, and on 10 September the Council stated that this body—reduced by 'dead pays' to forty-seven—would form one company with the same number from Staffordshire.

On 19 April 1597 Shrewsbury was directed to raise twenty-three more foot and to send them to Chester with a conductor who was to receive coat and conduct money there from a servant of Sir Henry Wallop, Treasurer at Wars in Ireland. On the 27th the conductor issued a certificate that, of these twenty-three, four had run away and that the arms of the rest were so bad that he had refused to take them, but would supply the defaults from armourers in Chester. Next day the Privy Council instructed Manners and Ferrers to imprison the runaways, who had returned to their homes.

On 18 July 1598 the Queen sent a commission to Shrewsbury to levy yet another 100 men, and on the 19th the Privy Council informed him that they would go to Bristol. On the 23rd, however, it changed its mind, owing to the long distance from Derbyshire to Bristol, and told him to send the men to Chester. Now came news of the disaster suffered in the battle of the Yellow Ford. On 28 August the Queen informed Shrewsbury that, 'in consequence of the late accident which happened to the Marshal', fifty men more were wanted. This commission was cancelled on 10 September, but not for long; on 17 February 1599, 'in consequence of the rebellion in Ireland, which increases daily', fifty men were to be raised. On the 24th, Sir Matthew Morgan, who was to take the force, made up to a company by men from Northamptonshire, wrote that he hoped they would be well armed; otherwise he would undertake to equip them himself, with arms and coats all uniform. Shrewsbury was himself never present during these levies, but he evidently took a keen interest in them. On 6 March he wrote to Manners that one Draycot Smith of Mickleover, who had been impressed, had only recently returned from service in Ireland and was the only stay of aged parents. It appeared to the Lord Lieutenant that ill-will rather than zeal for Her Majesty's service had led to his being called up, and he begged that he should be released.

The calls on Derbyshire continued. On 12 January 1600 the Queen commissioned Shrewsbury to raise another 100 men. This time, on the 14th, full details of their equipment were given. There were to be twenty pikes, ten halberds, twelve muskets with rests, twelve bastard muskets, forty calivers (the lightest of muskets) and six targets of wood with good swords. The pikemen and halberdiers were to be furnished with corselets, poldrons (or shoulder-pieces), and helmets; the musketeers with helmets. Each man was to have a canvas doublet, a pair of broadcloth Venetians, two shirts and bands, a pair of shoes, two pairs of brogues, a pair of kersey stockings or two of Irish frieze, a hat, and either a long, lined, broadcloth cassock or an Irish mantle. On the 26th Ferrers and Thomas Gresley suggested to Manners that £400 should be levied on the county for these expenses, £200 being sent to an outfitter, Alderman Sir John Harte, in London, for the clothing, £150 being reserved for the armour and weapons, and £50 for other charges. On 21 February Shrewsbury directed that £150 for the armour and weapons should be paid at the house of Mr. Rowe at Leicester and £200 for the clothing to Mr. Stamford, of the same city, who would pay it to the alderman.

This draft was not altogether satisfactory. On 10 March Browne, the conducting officer, furnished a list of nine men whom he had been compelled to change and three (including one of the replacements) who had fled. However, Mr. Browne, after marching the men to Chester, managed to deliver ninety-six of them, only two having run away on the road, while two more were rejected as 'insufficient'.

On 15 May there was word of a genuine volunteer. George Manners wrote to John Manners, his father, informing him that the bearer of the letter was a suitor to go to Ireland as a horseman. Actually in the following month Manners was personally ordered to provide one.

On 26 June Shrewsbury was directed to raise another fifty men, to be at Chester by 25 July. It will be observed that expedition was expected. Relays of post-boys would require at least four days to take the commission to the shire and the march to Chester would normally require five days. That leaves nineteen days for collecting the men and fitting them out. This party was to include carpenters, smiths, and bricklayers. No 'dead pays' were allowed for, because this was not a company or part of it, but a draft of reinforcements.

At the end of the year, on 6 December, fifteen musketeers were called for, to be sent straight to Lough Foyle. In their case there is an estimate of the total charge of getting them to Chester. No clothes were required except cassocks, at 16s. each; musket, helmet, bandoliers, and sword would cost 30s. a head; each man was to be given 10s. advance pay in his purse; conduct money for a three days' march would be 4s., making £3 per man or £45 for the levy. Five pounds added for the conductor brought the total to £50, but one suspects that this book-keeping was designed to present a nice round sum. Three days' marching would involve long and hard days on the road in mid-winter.

No new call came for over four months, till, on 28 April 1601, the Privy Council demanded another three horsemen. On 9 May a list was drawn up of the gentlemen who had to contribute towards this levy, and on the 13th came the first of the expostulations, from a man who had to pay 25s. On 28 June there is a welcome touch of humanitarian sentiment, the request for a return of money levied for the relief of maimed soldiers.[1]

On 23 July 1601 Shrewsbury was ordered to raise another fifty men, collecting £3 10s. per man in lieu of providing arms and apparel and forwarding the total sum to Sir Thomas Tasborough, the Teller of the Exchequer. On 29 September the Queen gave Shrewsbury the grave news that the Spanish fleet, bearing an army for Ireland, was at sea, and bade him raise another twenty-five men. On 6 October she ordered the number to be increased to sixty.

On 13 October the Lords of the Council pointed out to John Manners that 5,000 men had now been levied in various counties and that, in raising further horse, the Queen wished to do so without charge to the meaner sort of people. He was therefore ordered to send a horseman at his charge. There was to be a good horse, a saddle of Morocco or some other good leather. The man was to be sufficient and provided with a good cuirass and casque, a lance, and good long pistol, or else a sword and dagger, with a horseman's coat of good cloth. And, to close the list, on 16 October Manners, Ferrers, and Gresley certified to Shrewsbury that the last levy of sixty men had been despatched to Bristol.

The above is perhaps a tedious recital, but it has been inserted in the first instance because information of this sort is not often forthcoming, and in the second because it gives a notion of the heavy demands made on a thinly populated county in Tyrone's rebellion. Similar demands were falling upon every shire. When we read of

---

[1] This does not stand alone. Wiltshire, for example, provided a number of pensions of 50s. or more often £5 for maimed soldiers (Hist. MSS. Com., *Various Collections*, Vol. I, p. 70).

the continual prayers of the viceroys for more men and their complaints that they were being starved, we are apt to forget the serious efforts made by the Crown to see the Irish business through or what these efforts meant for a shire such as Derby, to which Ireland appeared a remote country and in which the inhabitants affected by the levies doubtless cursed its very name. It was unwilling men, torn from their homes for a cause which they scarcely comprehended, who finally subdued Tyrone and brought all Ireland into complete subjection at the end of the reign of Queen Elizabeth.

Suppose the contingent fitted out and ready to start, fifty or 100 men from Derbyshire, and Chester the port from which it was to sail. Another sum was now issued, called 'conduct money', in this case to be recovered presently from the Chancellor of the Exchequer, together with a sum for conducting officers' wages. Conduct money was calculated by the number of marching days required to reach the port from the shire—it would be normally, as stated, five days from Derbyshire—so that if the troops dallied they would go short. (One party of Londoners mutinied at Towcester because they were ordered to march further and wounded their officers; orders were sent to arrest them at Chester and carry them back to prison at Towcester.[1]) The payment was 8*d.* per day per man, so that the conduct money for our Derbyshire party of one hundred would be £16 13*s.* 4*d.*, plus £1 10*s.* for the conductor.

Meanwhile, the mayor of Chester would have had warning of the arrival of this and other levies converging upon his city and have been instructed to take up shipping to convey them to Ireland. When a great deal of shipping was plying to and fro, as it was during the periods of military activity, it was not difficult to assemble it, though it might be held up at Irish ports. The mayors of ports such as Chester and Bristol were responsible and at such times much-harassed men. What they must have dreaded above all was a long spell of contrary winds which left them with a mob of unruly soldiers slipping off at every opportunity. They had the aid of officers, but displeasure was apt to fall upon the mayors if there were many runaways and, into the bargain, they would very likely have to make up the numbers by forcibly enlisting fellow citizens. To make matters worse, there would perhaps come messages from the Privy Council forbidding a store of victuals destined to be transported with the troops to be broken into, in which case they would have also to find food locally, for issue at the port and on

[1] *A.P.C.*, Vol. XXIX, p. 214.

the voyage. But victuals at sea might be saved, thought the Privy Council philosophically, because the men would be sick all the time.[1]

As more and more troops were poured into Ireland during Tyrone's rebellion, the business became too big for a local official, however experienced, and special muster-masters were sent to the ports. And as the Privy Council gathered experience of these matters it issued instructions for very thorough inspections. When a contingent of 100 light horse was due to reach Chester, the Privy Council laid down the precise equipment: cuirass, vambrace or armour for the forearm, headpiece, petronel or large horse-pistol, sword, and dagger, for one half; and for the other half a 'horseman's staff' or light lance, small pistols in place of the petronel, and no dagger. Each horse was to be inspected, notes being made of its colour, height, special marks, and the state of saddle and bridle, after which the animal was to be ridden for soundness. A full return was then to be sent to the Privy Council.[2] Unless the muster-master was dishonest, and no man was less likely to be so, no room was left for error or fraud; but if a dozen men had dropped out on the road he could only report the matter.

The Derbyshire company would possess one advantage over the British troops of the present day, when military authority delights in putting Cockneys into kilts and men from Lancashire into the Duke of Cornwall's Light Infantry; the men raised in the shire would serve together as long as the company lasted, though it would be reinforced from the most convenient source. Unless they were involved in a rare disaster, companies decayed rather from sickness, especially dysentery and 'ague' or malaria, than from losses in battle, and when they were operating in bad weather their casualties from the former cause were very heavy. Companies becoming too weak would eventually be broken up and their remnants would go to others.

By 'pay' the Elizabethan understood a payment of wages up to date at long intervals, perhaps half a year. The word was not applied to the weekly advances, as subsistence allowance, which were known as 'lendings'.[3] But even lendings were often in arrears on campaign, and then, according to Maurice Kyffin, who was appointed to act as a sort of inspector-paymaster in Ireland, the troops helped themselves on the march, exacting from 3s. to 5s. a day for officers, 1s. for men, and 8d. for horseboys.[4] In 1576, when

[1] A.P.C., Vol. XXI, p. 17.   [2] A.P.C., Vol. XXIX, p. 32.
[3] Neale, E.H.R., Vol. XLV.   [4] C.S.P. Ireland, Vol. CCII (Pt. II), 108.

Sidney was Lord Deputy, the horseman received 9*d*. and the foot-man 8*d*. a day, the lieutenant 1*s*., and the captain 4*s*.[1] In 1582 the horseman's pay was raised to 1*s*.[2]

The expression 'dead pay' meant originally the pay of a man killed or discharged which was appropriated by the captain of his company. Then, with the contemporary genius for compromise, this abuse was legalized, and, as has been shown in the communications with the Earl of Shrewsbury, companies were enlisted with a deficiency of men of 5 or 6 per cent., the pay of the missing men being the legitimate perquisite of the captain. This system was copied by the Irish.[3] However, as might be expected, many captains were not satisfied with the legalized convention of the dead pay, but continued to draw pay for casualties. The captains also strenuously resisted attempts to decrease the proportion of legal dead pays.

From the beginning of Elizabeth's reign increasing efforts were made to check abuses of this kind. As early as 1563 instructions were issued that musters should take place on the same day, in order to prevent men being transferred from one company to another to answer their names in each.[4] The officer in command was informed only just before the muster took place. The staff of the muster-master was increased; and by 1600 he had twenty commissioners working under his orders.[5] Unfortunately, the captains who meant to be dishonest held a strong position, since soldiers were afraid to give them away, so that they either bluffed or corrupted the officers of the muster.[6] 'Only the common soldier shared the honour of being a mere victim with the Queen.'[7] And yet some improvement was effected, and there is no doubt that under the later viceroys the Crown at all events acquired a better knowledge of the forces actually available, even if it still had to pay for more men than were bearing arms in its service.

The big levies, which alone need be noticed, were naturally made in times of greatest danger and opposition. The year 1580 was such a time: Desmond was in rebellion in Munster; Baltinglas headed a brief revolt in Leinster; in Ulster Tirlagh Luineach O'Neill was hiring great numbers of Scottish mercenaries; there was some trouble in Connaught, and finally a Papal force landed at Smerwick. In June the Lord President of Wales was ordered to raise 800 men. Three hundred Londoners were despatched from Portsmouth,

[1] *Carew Cal.*, Vol. II, p. 44.   [2] *C.S.P. Ireland*, Vol. XCVI, 30.   [3] See p. 71.
[4] *Carew Cal.*, Vol. I, p. 355.   [5] *A.P.C.*, Vol. XXX, p. 159.
[6] Cruickshank, *Elizabeth's Army*, p. 90.   [7] Neale, *E.H.R.*, Vol. XLV.

staging in the Isle of Wight. In July orders were given for the largest levy yet made for Ireland, of 2,000 men, who were drawn as follows: 200 from Cornwall and 200 from Devonshire, shipped from Barnstaple; 200 each from Somerset, Gloucester, and Wiltshire, and 100 from Dorset, shipped from Bristol; 200 each from Shropshire, Hereford, Worcestershire, and Lancashire, and 100 each from Cheshire and Staffordshire, shipped from Chester. (It will be noted that the total given amounts in fact to 2,100.) In September the Lord Mayor of London was directed to raise another 500 shot, and to add a surgeon, two drummers, and a fifer to the force. Early in the following year another 1,000 were called up as reinforcements for weak companies: 300 from Wiltshire, Hereford, Monmouth and South Wales, sailing from Bristol; and 700 from Leicester, Derbyshire, Warwickshire, Shropshire, Lancashire, and North Wales, sailing from Chester.[1]

From 1598 onwards, in Tyrone's rebellion, was another period of strain, in which far larger numbers were sent. In August various counties were ordered to raise from fifty to 200 men each, the total being 1,700, with a warning that they must be good and not 'such refuse as the villages desire to be rid of for their lewd behaviour'. London was called upon for 400 men. For some reason the country levy was reduced to 1,000 and that of London postponed.[2] In October 2,000 more were raised for Munster, on this occasion from seven counties only, Devon and Somerset having to produce the unusually great number of 400 each. In November 1,000 men were demanded. In December 2,000 were raised for the Low Countries, to replace 2,000 veteran troops required for Ireland—a sensible procedure, since matters were quiet on the Continent. The Privy Council severely reproved the celebrated commander, Sir Francis Vere, in the Low Countries, because it learnt that he had sent weak companies of ill-armed men to Flushing, and he was directed to fill up the ranks from his best troops. In January 1599 the big levy of 3,000 was ordered, Yorkshire heading the list of the contributory counties with 400 men. Again the lord lieutenants were warned not to leave it to constables, who picked 'unapt and loose persons'. There were to be thirty pikes, thirty muskets, thirty calivers, and ten short weapons to each 100, no 'dead pays' being allowed because these men were needed to fill up the ranks. In February another 2,000 men were called for.[3]

[1] *A.P.C.*, Vol. XII, pp. 65, 79, 106, 209, 216, 360.   [2] *A.P.C.*, Vol. XXIX, p. 94.
[3] *A.P.C.*, Vol. XXIX, pp. 237, 312, 358, 388, 491, 540, 547, 572.

It may appear strange that in a country stocked with enormous herds of cattle, sheep, and pigs, and growing a considerable amount of corn, food should have had to be imported for the troops, but so it was all through. In 1568, when the force in Ireland numbered only about 1,700 men, the Crown entered into a contract with a purveyor named Thomas Mighte to victual the army. Though the country was then expected to provide the meat, Mighte was given permission to import 25,000 lb. of butter and 50,000 lb. of cheese annually, and licence to bring in wheat and malt in time of scarcity. He agreed to keep in hand a store of victuals for 800 men for eight months and oats for 200 horses for six months. There were to be sixteen 'flesh days' and twelve 'fish days' in the lunar month, cheese being also issued on the fish days. The daily meat issue was large, $1\frac{1}{2}$ lb. per head, and when troops were at sea they were to receive the generous beer ration of a gallon apiece per day, perhaps to drown the sorrows of seasickness.[1]

It would be wearisome and unprofitable to go through the list from beginning to end, but it is worth while to glance at the big contracts entered into in 1600, when a supreme attempt was being made to crush Tyrone's rebellion. Mighte had been a victualler, a quasi-official. John Jolles and William Cockain were substantial London merchants. Their contract provided for the victualling of 4,000 men for three lunar months; 2,500 in Leinster through the port of Dublin, and 1,500 in Connaught through the port of Galway. Payment was to amount to £5,950, half to be paid immediately and the other half three days after the receipt of certificates signed and sealed by the chief officers of the ports. The rations were to be on the following scale: bread, $1\frac{1}{2}$ lb. per man per diem, or 1 lb. biscuit; butter, $\frac{1}{2}$ lb. per man two days a week, $\frac{1}{4}$ lb. per man on two other days, issued on one day with porridge and on the other with pease; cheese 1 lb. per man two days a week; salt meat 2 lb. one day a week, or fresh meat $2\frac{1}{2}$ lb., or pork 1 lb., or bacon 1 lb. At the same time a second contract was entered into with John Wood of London to supply 3,250 men in Munster through the port of Cork on similar conditions.[2]

These contracts are given merely as examples. There had been others just before, and the system appears to have been satisfactory. On 20 May 1600 Sir Geoffrey Fenton wrote to Sir Robert Cecil that four supply ships had come in within the week. 'All that I have to say now', he added, 'is the great comfort that the army

[1] *Carew Cal.*, Vol. I, p. 379.   [2] *A.P.C.*, Vol. XXX, pp. 185 and 189.

findeth to be so seasonably supplied with victuals, giving them another manner of life to the service that ever I saw them to have.' And Mr. Secretary Fenton did not speak without experience.[1] The food contracts, together with those for clothing and equipment, suggest that many of the criticisms of Elizabethan military administration are unfair and superficial. At least it can be said that the Queen and her Privy Council learnt from past mistakes, and that they succeeded in effecting improvements even when their task was at its most difficult. They were struggling all the time against widespread disobedience, dishonesty, and, it may be added, westerly winds, which made the passage to Ireland difficult and were in particular often fatal to cargoes of victuals.

When on campaign, the army naturally took such cattle as it needed and could find, and if possible drove a herd along with it for immediate requirements. Its transport arrangements were generally primitive, but it made skilful use of the ports, estuaries, and navigable rivers, directing its marches upon them to meet shipping directed to them in advance. Many mishaps occurred, and half-starved troops would on occasion struggle in to the rendezvous to find that the supply ships had not arrived. When, however, there is taken into account how much ships sailing round the coast were at the mercy of wind and weather, it must be acknowledged that the staff work by which such expeditions were supplied was often of a high order. The men who organized these affairs were competent and understood the principles. And the system worked under the strong shield of sea power. That was overwhelming. The semi-piratical O'Malleys and O'Flaherties, the Scots in Cantyre and Antrim, did not venture to attack English supply ships.

In peace the English imitated in the Pale the Irish custom of the cess, for the supply of the troops and also that of the viceroy's large household and following. 'Cess', Sir Henry Sidney informed the Queen in 1577, 'is a quantity of victual and a prisage set upon the same necessary for such soldiers as here your Majesty is contented to be at charge with for their defence and so much as is thought competent for the expense of your Deputy's house. . . . The mass of this hath always been laid upon five English shires, and certain Irish countries adjoining, and the same distributed according to the number of the ploughlands into which the same shires are divided.'[2]

He was writing at a moment when strong objection was being taken to the imposition. The Lords of the Pale, advised by lawyers

[1] *C.S.P. Ireland*, Vol. CCVII (Pt. 3), 46.   [2] *Sidney Papers*, Vol. I, p. 180.

I SIDNEY SETTING OUT ON AN EXPEDITION

He hands a dispatch to a kerne; 'Donelle Obreane'. Behind the Lord Deputy stand light horse armed with lances. Facing him is the guard of the colours, armed with halberds; behind them a drummer and a fifer; behind them musketeers. Beyond are the pikes (*The Image of Ireland*).

who were their kinsmen, protested that the cess was unconstitutional, because it was not imposed by Parliament. Sidney retorted that it was customary and sanctioned by ancient usage. At the same time they complained of the exactions of the soldiers. 'When', said Sidney grimly, 'the soldier is appointed (through the wilfulness of the people, thereunto animated by the landlord) to assist the sheriff or other officer to levy that which is appointed for the soldiers it must be confessed that soldiers are no angels, nor yet among men the harmlest creatures. But this I dare avow, that there is not in Christendom a garrison, not remaining in a closed town, that doth less hurt to the country where they do remain than the soldiers of Ireland do to the good subjects of the same.' It all depended upon what the Lord Deputy meant by good subjects.

In this case Irish lawyers crossed to England, where they were roughly received by the Privy Council, but got some support from Ormonde, then at court—it was his usual policy, but it must be acknowledged that he came under the cess for lands in Carlow. After much heated discussion, in the course of which a number of the nobility of the Pale found themselves for a short time confined in the Castle, a composition was effected. The five shires of the Pale and the relatively peaceful neighbouring counties of Carlow, Wexford, and Kilkenny admitted that they were bound to supply officers and soldiers up to the number of 1,000, paying 1*d*. a day for each man of that number whether or not he were present in the county and deducting that sum in the case of all men whom they were required to victual fully. They were also prepared to furnish 9,000 pecks of oats to the horsemen of the Lord Deputy at 10*d*. sterling and sell at reasonable prices to him. Naturally, this arrangement depended on the power of the Crown to enforce it and of the Pale landlords to fulfil it. It could not be carried out unless the counties in question were reasonably quiet. It remains, however, an interesting example of adaptation of Irish customs to the uses of the English.[1]

The weaknesses of English military administration were many but the chief is to be found in the structure of English taxation and revenue. The Queen's personal parsimony contributed, and the dishonesty running right through the system resulted in waste. Acknowledging all this, it still remains the fact that great advances took place during the reign. The verdict of the historian Sir John

[1] *Carew Cal.*, Vol. II, p. 81. *Sidney Papers*, Vol. I, p. 194. Bagwell, *Ireland under the Tudors*, Vol. II, pp. 327-33.

Fortescue that no sovereign of England neglected and betrayed the soldiers 'more wantonly, wilfully, and scandalously than Elizabeth' is unjustified. English military administration under Elizabeth was in kind of its time, but rapidly improving. A study of the fitting out and maintenance of English expeditions to the Continent as compared with that of Spanish expeditions suffices by itself to prove this contention. Sound thinking and planning, within the limits of current conceptions of finance, conventions, and the civil administrative machinery, were applied to English military problems, and not least in Ireland. By the day of Mountjoy forces large by the standards of the time were competently and quickly raised, equipped, transported, and maintained. The critic who is always demanding more is thinking in terms of methods of much later times, some of which would have involved revolutionary and inconceivable changes in Tudor society.

CHAPTER IV

THE IRISH ARMIES

NO historian dealing with the better-known affairs of the reign of Queen Elizabeth permits himself to forget that it was a long reign which witnessed many fundamental changes. The military organization of the Irish is, however, not one of the better-known affairs. The evidence comes mainly from Englishmen, few of whom fully understood the subject, or has been interpreted by writers who were not always first-class Gaelic scholars, and few of whom had any experience in military history. Apart from mis-apprehensions, there has been a tendency to draw general pictures with details gathered from different periods, the composite result being true to no particular period. In fact, this military organization altered greatly in the course of the reign. The Irish force put into the field by Tyrone differed more markedly from that of Shane O'Neill than did the English force of Essex and Mountjoy, who opposed Tyrone, from that of Sussex and Sidney, who opposed Shane. Great as was the advance in efficiency on the English side, that of the Irish was greater still. Firearms, though handled on a different principle by the Irish, benefited them on balance more than the English. Shane may have been as able a man as his nephew Tyrone—some rank him even higher—but the task of Sidney was not as formidable as that of Mountjoy.

One of the few great Irish historians—that is, historians of the Irish—Professor Eoin MacNeill, holds that the Irish were not a people of warriors. In his introduction to the work of a distinguished disciple, he writes: 'Of war, in the ordinary sense, there is no instance in Irish history before Strongbow's campaign in Leinster. The word *bellum* is frequent in the older annals, but it always means a single battle.'[1] Irish forces did not remain in the field for more than a few weeks. Military service was the duty of one class only, the landed freemen, and their term of service was commonly brief. It was Shane O'Neill who changed all that. He armed his peasantry in general and was, by the testimony of Sir Henry Sidney, 'the first that ever did so of an Irishman'.

[1] Hayes-McCoy, *Scots Mercenary Forces in Ireland*, p. vii.

Yet if war in what Professor MacNeill calls 'the ordinary sense', was unknown before the Norman invasion and rare, apart from rebellions against the English, afterwards, there was plenty of fighting. The great chieftain who desired to have at his disposal troops of higher quality than his own people and to keep them longer in the field hired Scottish mercenaries, the *gallóglaigh* or gallowglasses, who settled in various parts of the country, and the itinerant 'Redshanks' who succeeded or augmented them. Next, he set about providing a better fighting element from his Irish subjects. This is first noticed in the fourteenth century, about a hundred years after the introduction of the gallowglasses.[1]

The new element was purely mercenary, composed of fighting men without other profession. They were maintained by a system known as *buannacht*, and were themselves known as *buannadha* (the system and the soldiers being given the conventional anglicization of 'bonaght' and 'bonaghts' in this narrative). It is convenient to confine these terms to the Irish mercenaries, thus distinguishing them from the Scots, who have their own suitable titles; but in fact the words apply to any mercenaries, including the Scots. If the Irish bonaghts were established long before the time of Tyrone's rebellion, it was he who first made them really formidable in arms. In the day of Shane, an Englishman, the famous Sir Francis Knollys, who was sent on a special mission to Ireland by Queen Elizabeth, stated that 300 Scots were 'harder to be vanquished than 600 Irishmen' in battle.[2] This was no longer true under Tyrone.

The manner in which the Irish bonaghts were maintained was known as coyne and livery. These words were somewhat vaguely differentiated, but the former may be taken to mean the billeting of the soldier and the latter the stabling and maintenance of his horse upon the inhabitant. 'By the word livery is meant horse-meat, like as by the word coigny is understood man's meat', says Spenser.[3] These men proved to be not only the most soldierly element in the forces of Tyrone's rebellion, but one of the most difficult problems of the Government of James I, after the pacification. They had learnt the trade of war, partly at the hands of Spaniards and of deserters from the royal forces, but no other trade. They would not work and continued to live by robbery. Lord Deputy Chichester, when trying to make Ulster safe for the Plantation, solved the problem in part by shipping these 'swordsmen' to the Continent,

---

[1] MacNeill, *Phases of Irish History*, p. 326.   S.P. Ireland, Vol. XVII (1566).
[3] Spenser, *View of the State of Ireland* (in Morley), p. 70.

to serve the Swedes.[1] Since the Irish lords habitually failed to control the excesses of their retainers, even when they tried to do so, it is not difficult to imagine how evil a system this was and how greatly it contributed to the misery of the people. It is not without significance that the word *buanna* came later to stand for bravo or bully.

Before the higher organization of the bonaghts by Tyrone, Irish forces were divided into three kinds, of which only the two first-named were of Irish origin. First came the cavalry, often largely made up of the lord's kinsmen and the gentlemen of his country. These troops were useful for reconnaissance and foraging, for pursuit of a broken enemy, but for little else. Since they rode without stirrups, they were not fitted for shock action and dared not face English horse except at the most favourable odds; for the English not only had stirrups, but also commonly rode much heavier horses. Coming from Continental warfare, Sir John Norris thought Irish cavalry fit only to catch cows. Spenser speaks of the Irishman riding on a 'pillion' without stirrups and holding his spear aloft above his head. Contemporary draughtsmen confirm both these points. The pillow-like saddle was divided into two humps by the tightening of the surcingle and thus provided some support for the buttocks of the man who bestrode it. The spear was used back-handed over the shoulder, instead of being held below the arm in the fashion of a lance. 'In joining with the enemy they bear not their staves or lances under arm, and so put it to the rest, but, taking it by the middle, bear it above arm, and so encounter.'[2] The shock of thrusting a lance against an opponent's armour when both horses were moving at a fair pace would certainly unhorse a man without stirrups. The Irish cavalrymen wore a steel cap and a shirt of mail, lighter than the Englishman's plate.

The second type was the kerne, the Irish light infantryman. He was unarmoured and carried either a bow—slightly shorter than the English long bow[3]—a sword or spear with a wooden target, or a handful of darts, as well as a skean or long dagger. On broken ground, in the mountains, amid the bogs, in the woodlands, he was like a gadfly. In a stand-up fight he was normally useless, and English horsemen could do what they liked with him—provided they could catch him. In one case, indeed, during the Desmond rebellion, when six horsemen charged a body of seventy kerne, 'so close they kept themselves as they would not break'; yet the fact that the

[1] Falls, *The Birth of Ulster*, p. 180.   [2] Dymmok, *A Treatice of Ireland*, p. 7.
[3] Joyce, *Social History*, Vol. I, p. 121.

cavalry took their chance against odds of over ten to one is proof of
the low estimation in which they held the kerne.[1]

It is not suggested that the kerne would not get to close quarters
if they saw an opportunity, if their enemy were exceptionally weak,
disordered, or short of powder. Then they came on in a torrent,
clashing their weapons together, 'in heaps without any order or
array', closing with an ear-splitting yell.[2] That yell has lived on,
with some other ancient customs. Officers of this century, training
Irish troops and striving to make them assault with a deep-throated
roar, found it hard to prevent the roar ending in a yell, though this
may be equally intimidating.

The kerne was a peasant, and there was no difference in his
apparel when fighting or herding cattle; nor in his appearance, since
he carried a weapon on both occasions. In war he had no protection
for his head, except his long lock of hair, known as a 'glibb', which
might serve to muffle the force of a blow. Spenser abominated the
glibb. When a man was 'on the run' he would either cut off the
glibb, which made him look a different person, or pull it over his
eyes, when it was 'very hard to discern his thievish countenance'.
Other evidence suggests that, when interrogated, the Irish would
pull forward their glibbs, so that their eyes should not betray them
if they lied. Anyhow, glibbs were obnoxious to the English, who
issued an ordinance for their abolition.

Kerne were well suited to the conditions of Irish warfare because
they could operate on ground where no other troops could move.
Their value was proved by the fact that the earlier English viceroys
habitually employed them. Sir John Perrott, when President of
Munster in 1571, wrote that they were indispensable. A hard-bitten
campaigner like Sir Francis Cosby, one of the most experienced
soldiers in Ireland, was employed as 'General of the Kerne' in 1564.[3]
If kerne ceased to be employed in the latter half of the reign, and
there is no mention of them as enrolled in the English service during
the rebellion of Tyrone, that was doubtless because it was no longer
safe to use them, though they fought in the English cause under
their own chiefs, especially in Ulster.

The third type was the gallowglass, the mercenary of Scottish
descent, the heavy infantry of Ireland. In the days of the rebellion
of Shane O'Neill and of Desmond the gallowglass wore a shirt of

[1] C.S.P. Ireland, Vol. LXXVI, 45.
[2] Spenser, View of the State of Ireland (in Morley), pp. 92, 96.
[3] S.P. Ireland, Vol. II, 60; Vol. XI, 52; Vol. XXIV, 4 (i).

mail and a helmet. His traditional weapon was the two-handed gallowglass axe, but he adopted other weapons as time went on. While the conventional differentiation is between Irish kerne and Scottish gallowglass, there were also certainly Scottish kerne and almost certainly Irish gallowglasses. The most patient of researchers has found no Irish name among the officers of the gallowglasses from the thirteenth century, when they appear, to the seventeenth, when they disappear; but this is not to say that there were no Irish in the rank and file.[1] The one distinction to which it is always safe to cling is that between light and heavy infantry. As English and Continental fashions invaded the Irish military world, the tendency, above all under Tyrone, was for the kerne to become a musketeer and the gallowglass a pikeman. Finally, in Ulster especially, but also in Connaught, there appeared from the time of Shane O'Neill onwards another wave of mercenaries from Scotland, who did not remain in Ireland, but returned home with their wages. These forces were frequently composed of all arms: horse, 'shot', bowmen, pikemen, halberdiers. The Elizabethans always carefully distinguish between the gallowglasses and these 'new Scots', but modern writers have tended to confound them.[2]

Here is the English estimate of the forces of an Ulster lord in 1575. At that time the English intelligence put the forces of all the Ulster leaders at the high figure of 8,356. Of this total Tirlagh Luineach O'Neill, the most powerful, had 2,000 men. They were made up of 200 horse, 400 gallowglasses, 1,000 kerne, and 400 Scots. The wage of the gallowglass and of the Scot was one 'beef' (bullock) per quarter as pay and two for food. The kerne got one heifer per quarter and his victuals. And it is amusing to find that the absurd convention of 'dead pays', in force in the English armies had also been adopted by the Irish. The captain of Scots or gallowglasses was allowed to reckon thirteen 'dead pays' in drawing wages for a band of one hundred; that is, his company numbered eighty-seven, he drew pay for 100, and pocketed pay for thirteen. He was also accorded six men's allowances for his own victuals.[3] That is a custom which has come down to the most modern times. In the First World War French generals received moderate pay, but drew a number of messing allowances which mounted with their rank.

[1] MacNeill, *Phases of Irish History*, p. 326.
[2] Including, unfortunately, the present writer in *The Birth of Ulster*, before he had learnt better.
[3] *Carew Cal.*, Vol. II, p. 9.

Through message after message sent by English soldiers to Dublin or to the Privy Council in England runs, like a refrain, a complaint that the Irish are becoming more and more efficient. It appears as early as 1575, when Burghley is told that they are learning the use of modern weapons.[1] In 1579 Sir William Stanley, the traitor who afterwards went over to the service of Parma in the Low Countries, but a fine fighting man, thought them as resolute as any troops in Europe. A year later he declared that the only remaining advantage of the English was their superior discipline. At the 'Ford of the Biscuits' in 1594 the Irish were aided by an ambuscade, but won the battle by fighting.[2] In 1595 Sir John Norris told Burghley that the northern rebels were far superior in strength, arms, and munitions to those of earlier days and that consequently the English could not operate without greater strength than heretofore. He said that 1,700 of the best foot and 300 horse did not even dare to march from Newry to Dundalk—only about ten miles as the crow flies—and that the foot would be moved by sea; the enemy then had some 10,000 men in the field. It will appear later that Norris was always a pessimist in Ireland, and that in fact the more vigorous Lord Deputy Russell did march up to the Blackwater later that summer; but the impression made on a famous English soldier on his contact with Ireland is worth noting.[3]

Even more significant is the verdict of Sir Henry Wallop, the Treasurer at Wars, who had almost unequalled experience as an observer and a great deal as a soldier. Tyrone's troops, he wrote to Sir Robert Cecil in 1596, could now affront the royal army in the open plain, instead of as formerly only in defiles and forests. They were well furnished with all the habiliments of war and well trained by experience.

Whence came this improved training? We may enumerate several factors: first, simply experience of war against the English; secondly, the genius of Tyrone himself; thirdly, the influence of senior officers like Tyrrell, who had served with the English; fourthly, a steady flow of deserters from the royal forces; fifthly, Spanish experience, occasionally available from Irishmen who had seen Continental service, but also from Spaniards themselves. The number of Spaniards in the country may have been exaggerated, but some there were. Sir Richard Bingham captured a few in Connaught in 1590. When Alonso Cobos, the Spanish emissary, visited

[1] S.P. Ireland, Vol. XLIII, 1.   [2] Four Masters, Vol. VI, p. 1,951.
[3] C.S.P. Ireland, Vol. CLXXX, 8, 9.

Ulster for the second time in 1596, he found half a dozen Spaniards who had been in the country since having been wrecked there at the time of the Armada. They begged to be taken home, but he told them they were useful where they were. They then signed a petition for money from Spain, which sounds as though O'Donnell or Tyrone, whichever it was that employed them, had not been over-generous. They said that they would be ready to act as guides and interpreters when a Spanish army landed.[1] About the same time the English learnt that Tyrone had a Spanish engineer. This man had apparently drawn up plans for turning Tyrone's castle at Dungannon into a fortress which would withstand the royal troops, but the Earl abandoned the project and demolished the place instead, in accordance with his policy of respect towards English artillery.[2] Tyrone did on occasion carry out some primitive field fortification. When Lord Deputy Burgh captured the fort on the Blackwater in 1597, he found trenches covering the ford and sharpened stakes driven into the bed of the river. And at the battle of the Yellow Ford Bagenal found his way impeded by a trench and by pits concealed under brushwood and sods. In 1600 Mountjoy found the Moyry Pass between Dundalk and Newry strongly and skilfully fortified, perhaps with the aid of the Spaniard mentioned.

Few recruits love a foreign drill serjeant, even when he is preparing them to wage a war of liberation. The Irish were no exception to the rule. During Tyrone's rebellion an observer at Drogheda reported that the people of his country said they loved the worst Englishman better than the best Spaniard. It would appear that their experience was chiefly of some hectoring and untiring monitor on the equivalent of the barrack square, striving to knock into their heads the principles of drill with the pike and the numerous movements appertaining to the priming and discharge of the musket.[3]

In general, the Spaniards confined themselves to sending gold, but this was extremely valuable to the northern rebels because it enabled them to purchase arms and munitions, above all muskets and powder, in Scotland. Apart from such stores as were captured or carried over to the Irish by deserters, Scotland was their main source of supply, and at one time Tyrone is said to have employed an agent in that country to negotiate the business. At the height of his rebellion, however, he could get powder all over Ireland, even from Dublin itself, said one observer. It was actually suspected that

[1] C.S.P. Spanish, Vol. IV, 654-5.   [2] See p. 189.
[3] C.S.P. Ireland, Vol. CXCVIII, 80, I.

he got it from England. On one occasion, the Privy Council wrote
to the Customs at Bristol that there was much powder in the city
which might go to the rebels; all munitions of war were to be
sequestrated.[1] There are fewer instances of the Spaniards sending
war material to Ireland direct, but on at least one occasion they
despatched a big consignment when Tyrone was in rebellion. In
April 1600 one of the Anglo-Irish Lords of the Pale, Lord Delvin,
had an agent at the Donegal port of Killybegs when two Spanish
ships arrived there. According to this man's report, they landed
2,000 calivers with 4 lb. of powder per piece, and matches and lead
in proportion, together with 2,000 pikes, a splendid aid to Tyrone
and O'Donnell.[2]

The best picture of a well-trained Irish force as seen through
English eyes—and from the Irish annalists one never obtains
practical details of this kind—comes from the scene of the parley
with Owney MacRory O'Moore near Kilkenny on 10 April 1600
at the end of which Ormonde was kidnapped by the rebels. Behind
Owney MacRory stood in formation a body of 300 bonaghts, well
drilled and well turned out. All the pikes were held at the trail, with
the left hand grasping the weapon in front of the right, ready for an
instant thrust. Sir George Carew and Lord Thomond were greatly
struck by the appearance of these troops, whom they described as
the best Irishmen they had ever seen. Such a force was indistinguishable in appearance from the English infantry at its best. Yet the
terms in which Carew and Thomond express their admiration are
in themselves proof that the spectacle was uncommon. There had
never been such Irish troops until Tyrone's organization of the
bonaghts, and even in 1600 the men whom the English had to meet
shaded off from this infantry of the highest standard to the wild
kerne of the type they had encountered from the earliest days.

It is to be noted too that, if Tyrone and his associates could not
have achieved the successes they did attain without the backing of
these trained troops, neither could they have done so without the
light and mobile irregulars. It is indeed possible that Tyrone went
too far in imitation of the English and Spaniards, just as T. E.
Lawrence thought the Arabs did, in their war against the Turks, in
imitation of the British. The main advantages of the Irish must in
the long run lie in their speed, ubiquity, endurance, and knowledge
of the country. Guerrilla warfare was their principal standby.

[1] *A.P.C.*, Vol. XXIX, p. 245 (29 October, 1598).
[2] *C S.P. Ireland*, Vol. CCVII Pt 2), 143.

From the English side the greatest dangers lay in ambushes and passages through difficult ground—bog, mountain, and forest. Amid all the successes of the Irish, not one, with the partial exception of the battle of the Yellow Ford, was gained in any other circumstances. Burgh wrote to Robert Cecil in 1597: 'For, as he [Tyrone] is the dishonestest rebel of the world, so is he the most cowardly, never making good any fight, but bogring with his shot and flying from bush to bush.' At night, said the Lord Deputy, 'he lodgeth dispersed in the thicks and holds no firm guards, but throws himself and all his into sundry groves, lurking scattered like wolves or foxes, fitter to hunt with dogs than to find with men; and so jealous and mistrustful is he, as he parts in the evening from his men, not suffering any to know his cabin save one or two to wait on him, and in the morning they meet upon some appointed place cut out in the woods'.[1]

When it was reported that Essex was coming to Ireland, a captain serving in the country took it upon him to write to Cecil a warning of what a new commander must expect, something different to the warfare he was used to. Tyrone's method, he said, 'will be skirmishes in passes, bogs, woods, fords, and in all places of advantage. And they hold it no dishonour to run away; for the best sconce and castle for their security is their feet'. These are memorable words, which contain the essence of Irish warfare.[2]

Such were the foes whom the English and their Irish auxiliaries had to meet, troops who could outmarch and nearly always evade them, who could hardly be brought to combat against their own desire, and who provided nothing in the way of an objective but a few strong places and their cattle. Under indifferent leadership the English would never have prevailed. As it was, under men such as Sidney, Ormonde, Carew, and Mountjoy, they succeeded in subduing the successive rebellions of Elizabeth's reign.

[1] *C.S.P. Ireland*, Vol. CC, 72.   [2] *C.S.P. Ireland*, Vol. CCIII, 7.

CHAPTER V

SCOTS GALLOWGLASSES AND REDSHANKS

FROM the Mull of Cantyre the coast of Antrim was always in sight except in thick weather. The island of Rathlin lay as a halfway house between the two. The people of the Western Isles of Scotland had in their veins a liberal admixture of Norse blood. They were hardy, predatory, and accustomed to the sea. The glens of Antrim were more fertile than their own country. It is thus no matter for astonishment that they should have crossed to Ireland, first to raid, then to settle; yet even so the manner in which their fighting men spread out and fixed themselves in the farthest limits of the country is curious.

It is in the thirteenth century that is found the first mention of the *gallóglaigh* or gallowglasses. *Gall* means foreign; *óglach* means a young fighting man. The gallowglasses were to the Irish foreign mercenaries, and one student of their history holds that they were foreign, not because they came from Scotland, but because of the Norse element in them.[1] The first gallowglass whose presence is recorded is a MacDonald, from Cantyre. The MacDonalds remained not only the most prominent of the gallowglasses, with the possible exception of the MacSweenys, but also in a rather different position to the rest because they were less cut off than others from their original homes in consequence of the coming and going between Cantyre and Antrim. Yet the MacDonalds, though they remained strongest in Ulster and became hereditary fighting men to the O'Neills, appeared in the other three provinces. One of their septs established itself firmly as gallowglasses to the O'Connors in Connaught.

The other great gallowglass family was that of MacSweeny (Gaelic, Mac Suibhne, anglicized as MacSweeny, MacSwiney, and otherwise). They also went predominantly to one district, Tyrconnell, where they became the gallowglasses of O'Donnell, but likewise spread out. In Tyrconnell they split into three septs, na Tuath, Fanad, and Baghuine. These sometimes weakened themselves by internecine strife, but they nevertheless became very powerful, ejecting local families from large territories and on occasion creating

[1] Hayes-McCoy, *Scots Mercenary Forces*, pp. 15–22.

trouble and anxiety for the O'Donnells themselves, their overlords. They appeared also in Connaught, where they served the O'Connors, the Burkes, and the O'Brians. They penetrated to the Desmond country in south-west Munster. When Sidney made his progress through Munster in 1575, five MacSweenys, all captains of gallowglasses, came to Cork to pay their respects to him, and he noted that, though they had no lands, they were as powerful and as much feared as any landowner. They served Ormonde in his country, and with the Butlers were for the most part employed on the side of the Crown.

Of other gallowglass families less is known. The MacSheehys were prominent in Munster, where they formed the backbone of the Desmond rebellion.[1] MacDowells, MacCabes, and MacRorys seem to have remained for the most part in Ulster, and the first two of these names are still widespread there; but MacDowells and MacRorys are also to be found in Connaught.

These gallowglasses sold their swords to the readiest buyers, but after a time a large proportion of them began to settle down, to such an extent that some of the families became extinct or nearly so in the Western Isles. Something has been said already of the system by which they were paid before this stage was reached.[2] In the sixteenth century they began to appear as leaseholders to their patrons, even on a large scale. 'Owen and Terlagh [MacSheehy] between them held in Co. Limerick nine quarter and twenty acres of land . . . in all 3,260 acres. And this Ballyhoa or Newtown sept was but one of the sections of the MacSheehys under the Earl of Desmond.'[3] Yet, if they changed their status, they did not change their occupation. Once a gallowglass, always a gallowglass; once a gallowglass family, always such. From father to son they carried on the tradition and trade of arms, until at last in the seventeenth century they merged in the population with which they had intermarried for centuries and ceased to be thought of as foreigners. What more typically Irish name than Sweeny exists to-day?

Finding a working system by which these warriors could be maintained upon the country, it is not surprising that the English Government made use of them. In 1568 Sir Thomas Cusack and John Chaloner, Secretary to the Lord Deputy's Council, were deputed to examine the captains of 'the three septs of the Queen Majesty's Gallowglasses'—we do not learn which these septs were—in order to find out what were the customary terms. The captains

---

[1] Bagwell, *Ireland under the Tudors*, Vol. II, p. 276.   [2] See p. 71.
[3] Hayes-McCoy, *Scots Mercenary Forces*, p. 67.

informed them that in Leinster, Munster, and Ulster, where the gallowglasses were engaged for a quarter, for every spear (that is, two men) they should be paid 5s. 8d. Irish, and, in addition, the country must provide them with their 'daily diets', half in money and half in kind: the money 1d. a day, with an allowance of corn for bread, and butter. In Connaught the gallowglass received only half as much in money and kind daily, but the wages for each spear for the quarter were higher, 7s. Irish.[1] The investigators then drew up a table showing the number of spears maintained at one time or another in the four provinces, together with the pay, ration money, and food, perhaps theoretical or historical rather than representing the current state of affairs.

A century or so after the first mention of the gallowglasses in Ireland one Margaret Bissett, accounted heiress of the Glens of Antrim and the island of Rathlin, brought these territories in dowry to a MacDonald, brother of the then Lord of the Isles.[2] A great influx of MacDonalds followed. A settlement was established which, despite fluctuating fortunes, was never to be ejected by English or Irish or both combined. Other Scots, who did not settle, engaged in trade. It is said that sometimes on a long summer's day, benefiting from a reaching wind for the passage out and home, a party would leave the Mull of Cantyre at dawn, hire horses on the Irish side to carry their wares to market, and be back in Scotland by night.[3] The distance across the North Channel is just over twenty miles between the nearest points. In the same way, when fighting on the Antrim coast and in want of reinforcements, the Scots could summon these by beacons in a matter of hours if the wind were favourable.

The Hebridean settlers intermarried with the Irish, and their principal name, that of MacDonald, gradually assumed the Irish form of Macdonnell. In the reign of Elizabeth one of their great figures, fierce in war and wily in council, the famous Sorley Boy (Somhairle Buidhe, fair-haired Charles), began to make Ireland rather than Scotland his habitual place of residence, and his sons, Randal and James MacSorley, did so to an even greater extent. After many vicissitudes, this paid Randal well; for in 1603, immediately upon succeeding to the throne of Ireland, James I and VI

[1] *The Rate of the Wages of the Galloglas*, p. 87.
[2] Gregory, *History of the Western Highlands*, p. 193. See also Hill, *Macdonells of Antrim*, Chaps. I and II, and Bagwell, *Ireland under the Tudors*, Vol. I, p. 271.
[3] Falls, *The Birth of Ulster*, p. 23.

granted him 'the Route' as well as 'the Glynns'—that is, the whole coast zone of Antrim, from just north of Larne to just short of the Bann.

What were the precise relations between MacDonald gallowglasses and MacDonald settlers in Antrim it is not easy to discover, but there can be no doubt that there existed a connexion between the settlers and the 'new Scots' of the sixteenth century. For them the Antrim coast furnished the doorway. During that century Clan Campbell, which, from its political links with Edinburgh, provided a sort of bridge between the royal power and the Western Highlanders, encroached upon the territory of the MacDonalds. The latter were weakening and were split into two halves, one in Cantyre, south Islay, and south Jura; the other on the mainland between Loughs Sunart and Hourn, in parts of Skye, in North and South Uist. Between them lay the Macleans, in North Islay and North Jura, on the mainland north of Lough Linnhe, in Mull, Coll, and Tiree, hostile, vigorous, and enterprising. At the back of the southern MacDonalds stood the thrustful Campbells. The Mac-Donalds, enervated by their own feuds and friction with their rivals, were no longer what they had been.

During this century, and especially from the days of Shane O'Neill, the old gallowglass families settled in Ireland proved inadequate to requirements in times when armed forces were tending to increase in size. A number of Irish lords then began to recruit more Scottish mercenaries. Of the clans which had provided the gallowglasses, the MacDonalds alone continued to supply mercenaries, the others having been blotted out or much diminished. But new clansmen took the place of the old, the foremost being Campbells and Macleans. MacLeods and MacKays also came over. It is not altogether easy to decide why these new mercenaries did not imitate their predecessors by settling down in Ireland. It may well be that Scotland had become a more desirable country and Ireland a less desirable. Perhaps too the Western Highlanders now felt themselves more foreign than the gallowglasses had been to the Irish and were so regarded by them. At all events the husbandmen were now kept at home and the mercenaries returned with their wages.

It has been suggested that the title of 'Redshanks' bestowed by the English upon these men was accorded to them in admiration of their hardihood in wading through rivers in winter, which made their legs red. One would rather have expected it to make them blue.

Red stockings or gaiters sound a more plausible explanation of the term. It was certainly not used in contempt. The English professed great respect for the 'Redshanks'. They proved invaluable to Shane O'Neill, to the O'Donnells, to Tirlagh Luineach O'Neill. Tyrone needed them less because, as already explained, he had for the first time created a drilled and disciplined Irish army—including the older gallowglasses as Irish—of his own. At the same time, for reasons to be given, he was unable to hire Redshanks as readily as his predecessors. English policy both towards the settlers in Antrim and the mercenaries who came across the water was vague and fluctuating. They were manifestly a danger and a nuisance, and when that aspect was in the foreground of the English view, as it often was, the desire was that they should be driven out of Ireland. Yet sometimes it appeared that they might be most useful in taming a rebel chief or confederacy, and when that impression prevailed all sorts of projects were mooted for their employment on the side of the Government.

Throughout the reign of Elizabeth Sorley Boy MacDonald and his kinsmen created one of the chief problems. He was already well over fifty when the Queen succeeded, but he had in front of him nearly thirty years of full energy and over thirty years of life. Elizabeth's first instructions to her Lord Deputy, the Earl of Sussex, bade him accept the submission of 'Sorle', the chief captain of the Scots, who, she was told, desired to become her true liegeman.[1]

He made overtures to the Government for a league against Shane O'Neill and sought letters of denization (or naturalization) from it. However, English policy soon changed. Peace with Shane followed in 1563, and now he was urged to attack the Scots and applauded when he did so successfully. His defeat of the brothers James and Sorley Boy near Ballycastle gave him the opportunity virtually to extirpate their settlement. Sorley Boy remained a prisoner in Shane's hands for two years.

This was the true principle of *divide et impera,* since Shane and the Scots were now mortal foes, and it was the Scots, as will soon be related, who struck the final blow against the Ulster prince. Sorley Boy next devoted himself for some years to the tumultuous affairs of the Western Isles and Highlands, largely to fighting the Macleans, but reappeared in Ireland in 1571. After a period of warfare with the English he came to a composition, but, the Essex plantation scheme affecting his interests, he found himself again in

[1] *Carew Cal.,* Vol. I, p. 288.

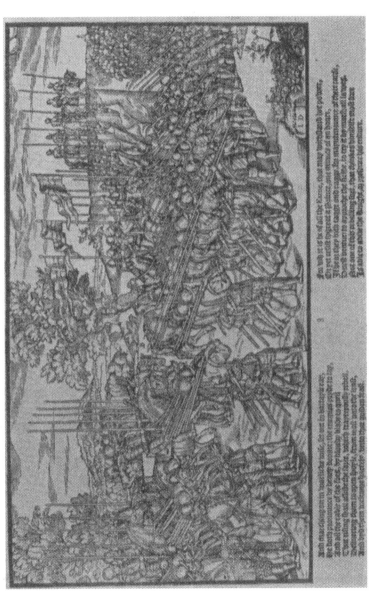

2 SIDNEY ON THE MARCH

A party of horsemen in the van; musketeers in two 'wings' in front of the pikemen; cavalry in rear, with more musketeers on their flanks (*The Image of Ireland*).

opposition and was defeated near Toome, where the Bann flows out of Lough Neagh. Essex followed up his success by a deed accounted black even by the standards of the Irish wars, the slaughter of the whole Scottish population of Rathlin: men, women, and children. Yet this savagery seems to have had no ill effect upon the settlement in Antrim; for Sidney afterwards found 'the Glynns' full of corn and cattle.

In August 1584 Lord Deputy Perrott and his Secretary, Sir Geoffrey Fenton, reported that there were 4,000 Scots in Ulster, and that 200 of the musketeers were 'inland' (or Lowland) trained soldiers who had served in the Low Countries. This was a most unusual component of a Scots mercenary force and one which could scarcely have been despatched to Ireland without connivance on the part of the Scottish Government.[1]

Only three or four hundred of these Scots were with Sorley Boy, but in that year he again returned to Scotland and brought back with him about January 1585 a force estimated to number 2,000. He arrived in time to stave off the complete defeat which was threatening his nephew at the hands of Sir William Stanley, but once more suffered a reverse. He opened fresh negotiations with the Lord Deputy, declaring that he wanted to be a true subject, and in the summer of 1586 made a humble submission, acknowledging past faults and follies, including that of having held the chief Scottish fortress in Antrim, Dunluce Castle, for King James VI. The coast belt was then divided between him and MacQuillan, the local Irish chief. From that time forward there was less trouble with the Scottish settlement, though the Redshanks who came over for a season's fighting continued to cause anxiety.

The hiring of the 'new Scots' was often a family affair. Shane O'Neill was allied by marriage to the Macleans and the Campbells, and this alliance facilitated his importation of mercenaries. Tirlagh Luineach O'Neill married Lady Agnes MacDonald, widow of James MacDonald of the Isles and daughter of the Campbell Earl of Argyll. This unromantic match between an elderly Irish chieftain who drank like a fish and a middle-aged Scots widow was from the bridegroom's point of view a method of obtaining mercenaries and from that of the bride's relations an insurance policy for the Antrim settlement. Lady Agnes, a vigorous and intelligent woman, got Tirlagh as many mercenaries as he could take, and more than he could afford, thus enabling him to maintain his position as the chief

[1] C.S.P. Ireland, Vol. CXI, 67 and 70.

power in Ulster. She afterwards proved a restraining influence which kept him on reasonable terms with the Government, but perhaps proved a good bargain in the marriage market in that way also.

Then we find Tyrone losing his power to hire Macleans and Campbells through his ill-treatment of Shane's sons, the MacShanes, and his execution or murder—which must depend upon the point of view—of one of them. He later put himself into the bad books of another great clan, the MacDonalds, by repudiating and sending home a daughter of Sorley Boy's brother, Angus, who appears to have been kept as his mistress until he had got a previous wife off his hands.[1] It thus befell that when his real testing time came, at the end of 1601, he was left virtually to his own resources by the Scots and only a few hundred men of the MacDonalds served with him at the battle of Kinsale, under his son-in-law, Randal.

Another great Ulster chieftain, Hugh Manus O'Donnell, married a MacDonald, Finola, known as 'Ineen Dubh' or 'the dark daughter'. She was the daughter of James MacDonald of the Isles and of the Lady Agnes just mentioned. She also supplies an instance of an enterprising Scots wife dominating a sluggish Irish husband, but she exhibited a savagery of which no trace can be found in the record of her mother. She too was the channel by which great numbers of Scots mercenaries came to Ireland, in this case to serve with her son, Hugh Roe O'Donnell. In his upbringing and the hatred of the English which she inspired in a member of a family recently loyal, she exercised a great influence on the fate of Ireland.

On several occasions negotiations between the courts of England and Scotland on the subject of the mercenaries took place. In 1583 Elizabeth requested the Ambassadors of James VI to ensure that the people of the Isles and the 'north parts' of Scotland should not be allowed to pass over to Ireland and serve the rebels there.[2] The execution of Mary Queen of Scots, if it did not greatly distress her son, James VI, offended his people, and it was some time before amicable discussion of matters such as the hiring of Redshanks was resumed. The Scots continued to come over. In 1594 Tyrone admitted that 3,000 of them had landed in the Route, but protested that they had not been brought over by the inhabitants of Ulster. In the earlier stages of his rebellion they were employed in great numbers, though more by O'Donnell than by him. They gained one success by themselves when they defeated and killed Sir John

---

[1] See p. 172 for Tyrone's marriage to Mabel Bagenal.
[2] *Cal. Scottish Papers,* Vol. VI, p. 455.

Chichester near Carrickfergus in November 1597, and they played a part in Tyrone's great victory of the Yellow Ford. The Scottish Government was well enough pleased to embarrass the English in Ireland without committing itself, but as Elizabeth's life drew towards its close and the question of his succession to the English throne came into the foreground James became more circumspect. When English power in Ireland was at its lowest and another big wave of mercenaries might have destroyed it, he responded graciously to the appeals of the Irish Council, to whom he sent a direct message, giving the lie to Tyrone's boast that he had expressed his sympathy with the Irish cause.

'Whereas we are credibly informed', he wrote, 'that there is a report spread in those parts of a favourable letter which is said to have been sent from us to Tyrone to the encouragement of the rebel . . . we are content freely to profess that such hath been our love to our dearest sister and great respect to all her good subjects that we have carefully avoided the least means of any just offence that might be offered to them.' He would, he said, take steps to prevent the Cantyre men from going to Ireland.[1] The Council sent a letter of gratitude, but added briefly and drily that a Scottish vessel had just brought powder and ball into Lough Foyle. Scots did serve thereafter with the rebels, but never on the old scale, though, as has already been stated, there were reasons other than the King's love to his dearest sister of England why Tyrone found it hard to obtain their services.

Queen Elizabeth did not stop at opposing the Scots when they landed in Ireland or at providing naval patrols in the North Channel to keep them out. She also established direct touch with the Western Highlanders and strove to set up a party favourable to her own interests, not without some success. She got into communication with Maclean of Duart and with Argyll himself.[2] In 1595, a critical time in Ireland when Tyrone was perhaps only half in rebellion, her friends managed to delay the passage of a great mercenary force and to keep at home some who might have joined it. In the end, after a little naval engagement in which the Scots suffered loss, having seven of their galleys sunk, Lord Deputy Russell was informed by the naval commander, Captain George Thornton, that Tyrone was unlikely to get any more Redshanks.[3] And it was the resentment of

[1] *C.S.P. Ireland*, Vol. CCII (Pt. 3), 143 (i).
[2] *Cal. Scottish Papers*, Vol. XI, pp. 250, 465, 495, 676.
[3] *C.S.P. Ireland*, Vol. CLXXXII, 10 (i), CLXXXIII, 17 (i).

Argyll and Maclean against Tyrone for the death of Shane's son, their kinsman, rather than the naval victory, that he gave as the reason.

While, however, the English had in the earlier years of Elizabeth's reign often enough employed bodies of gallowglasses as such, they never took a force of Redshanks into their service on a large scale or for more than one expedition. Proposals that they should do so were debated. Russell was an advocate of their enlistment, and in December 1596 towards the end of his viceroyalty, the Privy Council informed him that the matter was under consideration. But it was manifestly a risky project. As Sir Geoffrey Fenton, Secretary to the Irish Council, put it to Burghly, it had ever been 'a rule of policy in this government to keep the Scots out of Ireland, as a people that have wild pretences to Ulster and have long time footed in some parts thereof, and yet the Crown of England cannot expel them'.[1] Why then invite them in? Who could guarantee that those brought over to serve the Crown would not transfer their swords to the rebels? They had been kept out with difficulty only a short time before, and now it was actually proposed to facilitate their passage. Even if Campbells and Macleans were safer than MacDonalds and MacLeods, all mercenaries were apt to change sides, and it would be impossible to control Highland mercenaries in Ulster.

These arguments prevailed. It is, indeed, not certain whether the Queen was ever enthusiastic about the project of introducing Scots to serve against the rebels. If she could have got the definite backing of the Scottish Crown, as might have happened had she lived and the rebellion lasted longer, she might have become so. As it was, nothing was done, though in November 1600 Sir Henry Docwra, the English commander on Lough Foyle, was informed by the Privy Council that they had entertained an overture from a gentleman at feud with Tyrone—who must have been either Sir Lachlan Maclean of Duart or his secretary, George Achinross—to recruit a Scottish force for service in that station, certainly the most suitable in which to employ these troops. Men were actually enlisted, but none ever reached Ireland, unless it were to serve on the other side; for even after this a small body of Scots joined Tyrone.[2] The Queen and her ministers were certainly undecided in the matter, but it cannot be doubted that they came to the correct decision in the end.

[1] C.S.P. Ireland, Vol. CXCVI, 27, 67.
[2] C.S.P. Ireland, Vol. CCVII (Pt. 6), 16. Cal. Scottish Papers (Thorpe), Vol. II, 789, 796.

It would have been madness to invite more Scots to put a finger in the pie.

In fact, the last of the great Elizabethan rebellions ended without either the itinerant Redshanks or the Antrim settlers playing any notable part in the final stages. On the other hand, Kinsale was the last battle in which the gallowglasses served in large numbers. They lost heavily on that field, and little more is heard of them as professional fighting men. And, though Randal MacSorley was to flourish in Antrim, the growth of the settlement was to take a strange turn. Dour and pushing Lowlanders from Ayr, Renfrew, and Dumbarton were to intrude into this Gaelic heritage, and to-day it is this type which is most characteristic of the Glens of Antrim. The Queen may have been fortunate in that when the Irish most needed aid the Western Highlanders were least disposed to give it, either because they were quarrelling among themselves or were incensed against the chief Irish leader. Nevertheless, the great power exerted from Scotland on the Irish side is one more tribute to the courage and pertinacity of Elizabeth and her servants, down to the humblest, in Ireland. She and they had to face not only Irish rebels, but also their tough Scottish allies all the time, with occasional intervention from Spain.

CHAPTER VI

THE REBELLION OF SHANE O'NEILL

JUST before the death of Queen Mary on 17 November 1558 the Lord Deputy of Ireland, Thomas Radcliffe, Earl of Sussex, had been given leave to visit England to report. He arrived to pay his court to Queen Elizabeth, her successor.[1] Ireland passed into the temporary charge of the Lord Deputy's young kinsman, Sir Henry Sidney, who was sworn Lord Justice. The country was quiet at the moment, but unrest was to be expected from the succession of a Protestant to a Roman Catholic queen.

There were prospects of trouble in Ulster which had little to do with this change. The old Con Bacagh O'Neill, Earl of Tyrone, was dying, and his inheritance was in dispute. When Con had been ennobled by Henry VIII, his earldom had been conferred upon him for life with remainder to Matthew, or Ferdoragh, O'Neill, who was created Baron Dungannon. Matthew may or may not have been the Earl's son, but he was certainly not legitimate; and at the time of his birth his mother was the wife of a blacksmith. Moreover, the Earl had a son, Shane, who was legitimate and an able and ambitious man into the bargain. Shane had murdered Dungannon shortly before Mary's death. He then proceeded to rob and bully his tottering father, who fled from him into the Pale, where he died early in 1559. Shane O'Neill, accepted as chieftain by the people, claimed the title as well as the Celtic sovereignty, but the English would not go back upon the patent, absurd though it was. Shane had disregarded a provision of Brehon law whereby a father could legitimize a bastard, but the English lawyers had not distinguished themselves in the matter.[2]

Sussex returned to Ireland as Elizabeth's Lord Deputy in the summer of 1559. The policy laid down for him was prudent. Though it was desirable that all the country should be brought into subjection, the financial burdens were so heavy that nothing more was expected of him than to keep things reasonably quiet.[3] Sussex

[1] *Cal. Patent Rolls, Philip and Mary*, Vol. IV, p. 457.
[2] Maine, *Early History of Institutions*, p. 53.
[3] *Carew Cal.*, Vol. I, p. 285.

had little to do but hold the Queen's first Parliament, in January 1560, after which he went once more to England, this time leaving as Lord Justice another young man whose connexion with Ireland was to be as notable as that of Sidney, Sir William Fitzwilliam. The signs of trouble increased, and evidence was produced that Shane O'Neill was plotting with the great Geraldine Earls of Kildare and Desmond. Shane was hiring Scottish mercenaries, as was his rival, Calvagh O'Donnell of Tyrconnell, who deeply resented his claim to paramount authority in Ulster.

Much against the grain, Sussex returned once more in May 1560, now highly honoured by the title of Lord Lieutenant. This time his instructions were stiffer. Shane was to be brought to obedience by force if other means failed. The settlement of Leix and Offaly, ordered by Mary, was to be proceeded with. Irish lords who desired to hold their lands from the Crown were to be encouraged to come under the system of Surrender and Regrant.[1]

However, for the time being no move was made against the Ulster chief, and in May 1561 he scored a success thoroughly typical of his methods. When Shane met a foe in the field it happened more than once that he was defeated and ran away, and he had suffered one such disaster at the hands of Calvagh O'Donnell some years before. He now got his opportunity for revenge through the treachery of Calvagh's wife Catherine, a Maclean and widow of the fourth Earl of Argyll, a civilized woman who had yet come under the spell of the savage Shane. He seized husband and wife, kept the former for years in chains, made the latter his mistress, and soon caused her to repent for her wickedness by his vile treatment.

What was more serious from the English point of view was that this act placed him in effective control of Tyrconnell. His pretensions and his insolence were becoming insupportable. Sussex issued a proclamation to reveal to the people of Ireland how easily the Queen had treated Shane 'and how small effect her gentle, favourable and merciful dealing with him hath wrought in his cankered and traitorous stomach'.[2] The Lord Lieutenant then marched north and occupied Armagh. Yet the expedition was a failure. The problem which was to vex Elizabethan viceroys and commanders until the end, that of bringing an Ulster chieftain in revolt to a trial of arms in the open field and the lack of objectives, never approached solution on this occasion. Shane withdrew into the fastnesses of Tyrone,

[1] *Carew Cal.*, Vol. I, p. 291.
[2] S.P. Ireland, Vol. IV, 13 (i) (23 June 1561).

and Sussex had not the resources or the supplies to follow him.

By comparison with his nephew—supposing him to have been in truth his nephew—Hugh O'Neill, second Earl of Tyrone, Shane was a barbarian, yet he was in some respects the stronger character. Where Tyrone was to fawn, even in rebellion, Shane bragged and threatened. He would confess that the Queen was his sovereign lady, but boasted that he never made peace with her but by her seeking; Ulster had been the realm of his ancestors and he would keep it with his sword, against English, against the O'Donnells, or anyone else. Haughty and outspoken, there was no compromise for him. Extremely ambitious, he was not content to be the greatest Irish chief—though his people revered the chieftaincy far more than any English honour—but hoped to become Earl of Ulster, a great title now merged in the Crown. His intelligence was acute, and he imposed his will upon his own people. His organization for war was more thorough than that of any of his predecessors. On the other hand, his personal courage was open to doubt, and he was cruel, treacherous, and vindictive. He was also a drunkard, even by contemporary Ulster standards.

He now gained a secondary and partial success, none the less damaging to English prestige. Sir George Stanley, Marshal of the Army, led a force of some 1,200 men, including gallowglasses and hired Scots, with a following of Irish kerne, to raid cattle on the borders of Monaghan. As it withdrew, Shane, also employing Scots and gallowglasses, surprised the rear guard under Jacques Wingfield, Master of the Ordnance, killed some fifty men, and threw the remainder into confusion. Stanley, on hearing what had happened, turned and drove off the enemy in a combat wherein Fitzwilliam distinguished himself. But the cattle were not brought in, and Wingfield had some trouble to free himself from the imputation of cowardice, though he did so finally to the Queen's satisfaction. This was not a satisfactory incident.[1] It has been well said that the forces of a settled government get no credit for small successes over rebels, because they are expected to gain them, whereas rebels acquire prestige for the slightest successes at the expense of governments. On 31 July Sussex retired to Newry to collect fresh supplies.

Fruitless negotiations followed, Shane taking a higher tone than ever. In September Sussex tried again, and this time carried out one of the most remarkable expeditions of that period. There is no

[1] S.P. Ireland, Vol. IV, 22, 25. Four Masters, Vol. V, p. 1587.

record of his strength, but it cannot have amounted to more than 600 or 700 in English troops, the rest being Scots mercenaries, gallowglasses, and kerne provided by the hosting in the Pale. Passing over Slieve Gullion, the Lord Lieutenant marched to Omagh and from there to Lough Foyle, sweeping in 4,000 cattle as well as the O'Neill's precious brood mares. Unwilling, however, to encumber his column with this vast herd, he had to slaughter the greater proportion of the beasts. And when he reached the Foyle ill fortune awaited him. The supply ships which would have enabled him to prolong his operations had not arrived. He therefore returned to Newry. Shane retorted by burning four villages in the Pale, but Sussex considered that the credit of the army had been restored. The historian Bagwell, always hostile to Sussex, mocks at these pretensions, but if Shane had not fought it was because he feared to, and it was a considerable feat to march through a hostile Ulster to Lough Foyle, as later viceroys were to find. The expedition at all events exercised a remarkable effect upon Shane.[1]

Negotiations were resumed, and finally Shane agreed to go to court under a safe conduct. Accompanied by the Earls of Kildare and Ormonde, whom he regarded as guarantors of his safety, he came up to Dublin, paid his respects to the Lord Lieutenant, who gave him a civil welcome which hardly concealed his hatred, and took ship to England. Sussex himself soon followed, leaving Fitzwilliam to act as Lord Justice.

Shane appears to have reached London on 3 January 1562. He brought with him an escort of gallowglasses, bare-headed, with hair flowing on to their shoulders, their linen vests dyed with saffron, *vel humana urina infectis*, as Camden pleasantly remarks, with flowing sleeves, short tunics, and shaggy cloaks.[2] He repeated his version of the illegitimacy of the murdered Dungannon, but confessed his rebellion with howls after the Irish fashion, did homage on his knees, and signed a submission on 6 January. Elizabeth kept him hanging about, undecided what to do or how to reconcile his claims with the rights of Dungannon's elder son, Brian O'Neill. On 13 March she wrote to Fitzwilliam, directing that the youth should be sent over to her, doubtless because, apart from the legal rights of the case, she desired to see for herself what promise there was in him. That she was not to know. On 12 April, probably on

[1] *C.S.P. Ireland,* Vol IV, 52, 54, 55, 56. Bagwell, *Ireland under the Tudors,* Vol. II, p. 30.
[2] Camden, *Annales,* Vol. I, p. 94.

his way to take ship, Brian was waylaid and killed by Tirlagh Luineach O'Neill between Newry and Carlingford.[1]

This new murder—though no such name would have been given to it in Ulster—brings on the scene another O'Neill who was to occupy an important position for a long time to come. Tirlagh was a cousin of Shane's and his tanist or designated successor, and the removal of a possible rival from the path of a tanist was a normal Irish proceedure. He was less fierce and cruel than Shane, but at the same time less ambitious and determined. Indeed, Tirlagh was marked by a geniality which in his cups degenerated into buffoonery, and in later life he became besotted with drink. Irish historians have poured scorn upon his weakness, but we who have learnt to appreciate the value of compromise may feel rather that there was a gleam of statesmanship in his nature, in the light of which he could see the boundaries between the possible and the impossible. He wanted to die a chief, and he did, whereas Shane died a hunted wolf and Tyrone died a miserable old exile living on Italian charity.

It was impossible to prove that the young man's death was directly connected with Shane, and the Queen could hardly detain him any longer. On 30 April a list of articles was drawn up. Shane, having taken the oath of a subject and offered to reduce Ulster outside Tyrone to peace—a delicate way of saying that Elizabeth hoped to use him to tame the Antrim Scots—was to be not only lord of Tyrone, but also to have the rule of O'Cahan's country, east of Lough Foyle, and the greater part of Antrim, though not to take bonaght or levy tribute outside Tyrone. He was to submit to the Queen's principal Minister and Council controversies arising between himself and others, to give service whenever a hosting was made in Ulster. The issue with O'Donnell was to be decided by half a dozen arbitrators, of whom the Earls of Kildare and Ormonde were to be two. These were pretty good terms for a chief whom the Queen had recently ordered her viceroy to subjugate, and of whom she had published such a bitter condemnation.[2]

He showed no sign of having become a reformed character on his return; in fact, before the summer of 1562 was over, Sussex reported to his mistress that the articles were not being carried out, that robbery and burning were going on again, and that Shane had taken many thousands of cattle from the lands of the O'Donnells. At first no effort was made to punish him. The English Government was playing a deep game, hoping for a clash between the Irish chief

[1] S.P. Ireland, Vol. V, 44, 82.　　　　[2] S.P. Ireland, Vol. V, 99.

and the Antrim Scots and feeling that, whatever the outcome, it could not fail to be serviceable. Sussex, who now had seven years' experience of Ireland under Mary and Elizabeth, did not think the policy would pay, and was at odds with the Queen about the treatment of Shane. The only sound course, he reported, was to expel him from Tyrone, where he was usurping the rights of the Crown and the Earldom of Ulster. An English President of the province should be established in Armagh, where a strong town should be built. All the havens should be secured. The town of Carrickfergus should be fortified and Newry should be made into a fortress. A new town should be established on Lough Foyle and likewise fortified. Until these matters could be settled the Queen should not only tolerate the MacDonalds on the Antrim coast, 'but should also gratify them in their requests and by all the means that may be retain them in her service'.

He went on to advise that Presidents with Councils should be set up in Connaught and Munster, the former living at Galway and Athlone, and the latter at Limerick, Cork, or Waterford. As regards Munster, the essential was that the nobility should be made to live within the law. The principal governor should continue to reside in the Pale, whence aid could be sent to whatever district was in need of it, but should make annual visitations to the other provinces. Sussex may not have been a great soldier, but he was a statesman and he knew his Ireland. No President of Ulster was ever installed, but his other suggestions were sooner or later adopted. They were not, however, backed by adequate force until matters grew desperate, with the consequence that it was not until the Queen lay on her deathbed, forty years later, that the issue was decided.[1]

Early in 1563 the Government resolved upon another expedition against Shane, who had ventured to raid as far as Armagh and was dominating the loyal O'Donnells. Sussex collected victuals to support the army for two months and directed that they should be put into Dundalk by 3 April. This time he sought the aid of the Scots and requested Sorley Boy MacDonald to hold the line of the Bann and to send troops to Armagh for the Queen's service. Something was hoped for also from Tirlagh Luineach O'Neill, who was inclined to abandon Shane's service and side with the English. Again, however, expectations were not fulfilled. Sussex complained that the officials failed him with the victuals and that the Irish kerne who should have accompanied him did not arrive. Owing to these

---

[1] *Carew Cal.*, Vol. I, p. 330.

defaults, he was unable to effect a meeting with Tirlagh and had to cut short his raid. But he got as far as Clogher, in south Tyrone, had some successful skirmishing with the Irish, and again took a large number of cattle, though most of them were driven into Fermanagh, which Shane controlled. Once more Shane came to terms and on 11 September made his submission. He was accorded the jurisdiction enjoyed by his predecessors, and again the comfortable formula was reached that all outstanding disputes should be referred to arbitration. Previous indentures with the Queen—that is, those made on his visit to England—were no longer to remain in force. Worst of all, the 'concord' established between O'Neill and the O'Donnells —in fact, their abject submission—was recognized. The policy of sacrificing weak friends to strong foes in Ireland was not invented by the English statesmen of the nineteenth and twentieth centuries.[1]

Yet neither Sussex, nor Fitzwilliam, whom he left in charge during his frequent visits to England, could seriously be blamed. They had not the strength to enforce a creditable settlement. The regular forces of the Government consisted of 275 horse, 600 harquebusiers, archers, and pikemen, and ninety-six foot in forts.[2] For an expedition the force had to be made up from four sources: the tenantry of the Pale, no great warriors outside their own shires and in large degree required to stay at home and protect them; hired gallowglasses, only moderately reliable; hired Scots, hard to obtain and always inclined to bargain about how much they would do and how far they would go; and the Government's own kerne, good for reconnaissance, for burning houses, and for cutting throats, but of no value for serious fighting against the Irish. The remarkable thing is that the early viceroys were able to do as much with their motley armies as they did and that they penetrated much deeper into hostile country than successors commanding forces more numerous, more homogeneous, and better equipped and supplied; but, as has already been pointed out, the latter had to meet a more formidable opposition.

Further agreements were made with Shane, not to his disadvantage. In 1564 he made up his mind to attack the Scots in Antrim. His object was to acquire their lands for himself, but he was not averse to acquiring also some merit in the eyes of the Crown, and he let the Irish Government know what he was about to do. It fully approved. To let the two sides weaken each other suited its book,

[1] *Carew Cal.*, Vol. I, pp. 349–54. *C.S.P. Ireland,* Vol. VIII, 34, 39, 45, 47.
[2] S.P. Ireland, Vol. VIII, 40.

and to embroil Shane fatally with the Scots appeared desirable. Sir Nicholas Arnold, then Lord Justice, wrote to Shane in August congratulating him on his intention.[1] The first encounter was not conclusive, but a decisive stroke was dealt in the spring of 1565, when the Scots colony was unusually weak. Shane marched swiftly into Antrim, and on 2 May fell upon the Scots on the Glenshesk river which runs into Ballycastle Bay. He enjoyed a superiority of two to one and utterly defeated the Scots. Of his prisoners he saved from death only a few of note, including the two leaders, the brothers James and Sorley Boy MacDonald, and two Maclean chieftains. He wrote jubilantly to Fitzwilliam to announce the capture of these valuable prizes and boasted that he had killed 700 Scots. The aid which, now as on many occasions, the Scots sent over arrived too late. A third MacDonald brother, Alexander Oge, put to sea with several hundred men and landed on Rathlin island. There, however, he learnt of the rout and slaughter of the clansmen and returned to Scotland.[2] The colony had been virtually exterminated, and its strong places, including the almost impregnable castle of Dunluce, fell into the hands of Shane. The great O'Neill, now at the summit of his power, cannot have foreseen that his triumph was to be his death warrant.

Some of the Irish officials expressed themselves as pleased with the course of events, but the Queen—and doubtless her astute adviser, William Cecil—had changed her mind again. Shane had made himself virtually the sovereign of Ulster, and she was no longer to be deceived by the pretence that he was acting in her cause. She determined to send Sir Henry Sidney to Ireland as viceroy to take a strong line against the O'Neill. In other words, she adopted the policy advocated by Sussex, but put its execution into new hands. And from her point of view she did well.

Sidney had been acting as Lord President of Wales, and was permitted to retain the emoluments of that office as the cheapest way of providing him with funds sufficient for his task. This was a piece of typical early Elizabethan finance. Otherwise, he obtained less than he had demanded. He was expected to overcome Shane and keep the whole of the turbulent country in order with less than 1,000 English soldiers and a few hundred kerne. He had asked that eight 'dead pays' should be allowed in a company of 100 men, in the hope of keeping the captains honest, but was allowed only six.[3]

[1] *C.S.P. Ireland*, Vol. XI, 8. [2] S.P. Ireland, Vol. XIII, 38.
[3] S.P. Ireland, Vol. XIII, 82.

He was not appointed Lord Lieutenant, but Lord Deputy, though it had been the original intention to accord him the higher honour. There were always some reservations in Elizabeth's admiration for the most masterful of all her Irish viceroys. He was certainly one of the ablest, if not the greatest of them all.

His instructions were issued to him in several drafts in the latter part of 1565. Privately, he was told that he might make one more effort to reach an accommodation with Shane, but that if this failed war was to be the only alternative. The O'Donnell power, the best balance to that of the O'Neill, was to be restored in Tyrconnell. An interesting light on the Government's view of the state of Ireland appears from the order that, in addition to the shires of the Pale, Cork and Kerry (under Desmond's influence), Kilkenny and Tipperary (under Ormonde's influence), Wexford, Waterford, Limerick and Carlow were to be considered as coming within the scope of English law, and sheriffs were to be maintained within these counties.

Sidney was held up by storms and contrary winds in Cheshire and Wales for two months, and was not sworn in until 20 January 1566. What he saw filled him with gloom. A few weeks after his installation he wrote to Leicester that Shane was the only rich and strong man in Ireland; he could muster 1,000 horse and 4,000 foot; he could burn up to the gates of Dublin and return unfought. Kilkenny and most of Munster had been spoiled by internal quarrels and outrages, and one could ride thirty miles without seeing a habitation, whereas these districts had once been as well populated as many English counties. The troops he found 'beggar-like and insolent', sometimes allied with the Irish.[1] He began by getting rid of a number of Irish soldiers who had been enlisted in the companies, and soon had in his hands an instrument capable of great achievements.

From Westminster he received a measure of support, certainly not very large by comparison with the magnitude of his task, but better than had appeared probable when he left the court. Perhaps Leicester was his intercessor. First, the Queen decided to obtain a clear picture of the state of Ireland from a man more disinterested than Sussex, who had returned to court and was not on good terms with Sidney. She therefore sent over her Vice-Chamberlain, Sir Francis Knollys, on a special mission. He was to confer with the Lord Deputy and bring back information on a great number of

[1] S.P. Ireland, Vol. XVI, 35.

points. Could Shane be reformed except by war? If not, what was the force deemed necessary? How strong was the garrison? How many reinforcements were required? What was the situation as regards arms, victuals, and money? What was the most suitable season for a campaign—could it be set on foot by July? What was the best method of keeping out the Scots? What was the value of hostings in the Pale and the gallowglasses of the loyal nobility? Sidney was bidden to keep down costs—that was inevitable—but the Queen committed herself to the promise to 'omit no reasonable charge'.[1]

Knollys found that Sidney had already achieved good work in organization, but that he would need more regular funds and must have reinforcements. There was no question now of temporizing; Shane had gone so far as to address a letter to Charles IX of France, begging for troops for the expulsion of the English. It was proposed that brigantines should be stationed off the coast to keep out the Scots.[2] The Vice-Chamberlain backed the Lord Deputy's proposal for an autumn campaign, when it would be possible to destroy a large proportion of the harvest, and the horses of the royal forces, having been kept out during the summer, would be fitter to stand exposure.

The Queen, on Cecil's persuasion, overcame her habitual parsimony to a certain extent. She gave Sidney leave to raise 200 horse and 200 foot in Ireland. She herself raised 1,000 men at home, including 300 trained soldiers from Berwick, and placed in command of them a well-tried soldier, Colonel Edward Randolph. The majority were to come from the west and to sail from Bristol. And, since arms and equipment provided by the counties had in the past been unsatisfactory and not uniform, she decided that on this occasion she would provide or buy the material herself—but make the counties pay for it. Instructions were sent to the Lord Lieutenant of each county in the following form:

'Whereas we have ordained that [here there is a blank to be filled in with the number of men] shall come to Bristol and that the counties from whence they shall be sent shall not arm them but shall provide such sums of money as may serve to buy armour and weapons for them according to a form prescribed and sent to the Justices of the Shires for which purpose we have ordered that a quantity of armour weapons and munitions shall be sent out of our store to Bristol our will is that you shall at Bristol see the said men armed and weaponed as hath been determined and shall levy and receive to our use the money due for the same.'

[1] S.P. Ireland, Vol. XVII, 20 (18 April 1566).   [2] S.P. Ireland, Vol. XVII, 67.

Shane's good intelligence service doubtless brought him word of what was afoot, and he anticipated the invasion by raiding the Pale in force. Sidney was not far enough advanced in his preparations to permit him to keep the field, but John Fitzwilliam repulsed an attack on Dundalk with loss. Shane burnt a few villages and the church of Armagh. He also drove out Shane Maguire from Fermanagh, who hastened to Dublin and, with Calvagh O'Donnell, accompanied the Lord Deputy on his march to the north.

This expedition was designed to put a permanent bridle upon Ulster by establishing a force on Lough Foyle. Its next most important objects were to set up the O'Donnell in Tyrconnell and the Maguire in Fermanagh. Sidney understood the principle of Irish warfare which was afterwards realized by Mountjoy and Carew, but had been neglected by Sussex and was to be neglected even more notoriously and disastrously by Essex. It was waste of time to base a campaign on bringing a rebel force to a decisive action. If the Irish wanted to keep out of the way, they could probably do so, and then there would be nothing to show, except perhaps some cattle, for the expenditure, the fatigue, and in all likelihood the losses from sickness, of the army. There must be tangible, attainable, and fruitful objects in every big expedition.

Sidney set out from Drogheda on 17 September 1566 on learning that Randolph had landed in Lough Foyle. He marched to Armagh and thence into Tyrone, burning and preying. In desperation, Shane was appealing to John Fitzgerald ('John of Desmond'), uncle of the Earl of Desmond, and to the MacDonalds whom he had mortally affronted and estranged; but got no aid from either. As they approached Fermanagh Shane Maguire died, thus missing by a few weeks at most his restoration to power in his own country. Near Lifford Randolph was met, and, as he declared Derry to be suitable for a garrison in the Foyle, was left with 600 foot and fifty horse to hold the place. Sidney then crossed into Tyrconnell and marched to the castle of Donegal. All this time there had hardly been a sight of Shane or his army and only one slight skirmish. Donegal and then Ballyshannon were handed over to Calvagh O'Donnell. Belleek castle was hurriedly abandoned by Shane's people and also restored to O'Donnell hands. Sidney then marched to Sligo, where Donogh O'Connor Sligo surrendered his strong castle and was permitted to hold it for the Queen.[1]

The viceroy then moved south, through the Curlieu hills, and

1 S.P. Ireland, Vol. XIX, 7, 11, 12, 43.

from Boyle to Athlone, where he crossed the Shannon, swimming his horses over and losing a few. He went on into Munster, but that part of his expedition has nothing to do with the O'Neill. He told the Queen proudly that on the whole march only three men died of sickness and that the rest were in good health. The horses too were fitter than they would have been had the expedition been undertaken earlier in the year. The solid results lay in the restitution of O'Donnell, but in general the march had made the Irish venerate the Queen's name and inclined to appeal to her justice. He was justified in lauding his achievement.

Randolph found Derry an unpleasant spot. He could not buy provisions for love or money, and his troops suffered from sickness. Old Calvagh O'Donnell, who might have organized a supply service for him, died as the result of a riding accident, 'a man', say the annalists, 'so celebrated for his goodness that any good deed of his, be it ever so great, was never a matter of wonder or surprise'. Immediately afterwards Shane struck at Randolph, but that veteran of many wars was not asleep. The fight was at enormous odds, though Sidney's statement that Shane employed 5,700 men seems exaggerated. He may have had that number at his disposal, but they were not all engaged on the Foyle. He was thoroughly repulsed and fell back, leaving 300 dead behind him. The English lost only a single man, and yet this loss was damaging; for it was the Colonel. The famous Humphrey Gilbert, then a young captain at Derry, was sent home with the Lord Deputy's despatch to the Queen.[1]

The end of the Derry garrison was disastrous. On 21 April 1567, a windy day, sparks from the forge set fire to the powder which was stored in the ruined church of St. Columba. A number of men were killed by the explosion, and all the wooden buildings of the camp were burnt out. The troops, who might have held out had Randolph been alive, embarked on such vessels as were in the Foyle and sailed to Carrickfergus. The boats did not suffice to carry the horses, and the cavalry, only forty strong, rode through Ulster and made their way to safety. Thus ended the most promising attempt to secure the future tranquillity of Ulster which was to be made in that generation. It is remarkable, and not to the credit of the English and Irish Governments, that, though the strategic value of Lough Foyle was thoroughly understood, English soldiers did not again encamp at Derry until 1600, though Essex visited it in 1574. The Irish believed that the explosion and fire were the revenge of St. Columba for the

[1] *C.S.P. Ireland*, Vol. XIX, 29, 44. Four Masters, Vol. V, p. 1,607.

desecration of his church. He assumed the form of a gigantic wolf with bristling hair, which came out of a wood, galloped to the church, and spued into a powder barrel sparks which caused the explosion. 'I will not take upon myself to vouch for the truth of this story', says the historian of Catholic Ireland cautiously. 'Upon fame and long-standing tradition let it rest.'[1]

Yet the other object of Sidney's expedition to the north had been achieved. The power of the O'Donnells had been re-established in Tyrconnell, and it sufficed to settle the account of Shane, who was already going fast downhill. He decided that the English withdrawal from Derry afforded him an opportunity to subdue their protégé, and acted at once, crossing the Swilly by a ford near Letterkenny in May with a force of several thousand men. Hugh O'Donnell concluded that death was preferable to the long torment endured by Calvagh and inspired the men he had at hand, only about 400 in number, to dare all rather than witness a renewal of the oppression and degradation of Tyrconnell. Throwing prudence to the winds, they marched straight upon the invader. The Tyrone gallowglasses were drinking and keeping no watch when the Tyrconnell men fell upon them. What followed was not so much a battle as a killing. In the end the survivors of Shane's army fled back to the ford, but the tide had now risen to bar their way. The butchery continued on the left bank, and many who took to the water were drowned. Thus Shane's great force, so long organized, so carefully husbanded, was cut to pieces in a day by a handful of foes. What his losses in killed were is matter for guess-work—the infuriating annalists of Lough Cé tell us that it is 'not possible to reckon or tell all that were drowned there'. At all events, the army disappeared.[2]

The O'Neill was powerless. Should he throw himself on the mercy of the Lord Deputy? He decided against that move. Hearing that Alexander Oge MacDonald had landed at Cushendun with a strong force, he now adopted the desperate expedient of making an appeal to the Scots; if they would provide him with the time, he might raise another army, and together they would conquer Ulster. He cannot have known that Alexander Oge was in correspondence with Sidney, who had approved of his landing. The MacDonalds did not refuse to receive Shane, and he rode into Antrim with a miserable remnant of fifty horse. James MacDonald, captured on

[1] S.P. Ireland, Vol. XX, 77, 83. *History of Catholic Ireland*, p. 4.
[2] S.P. Ireland, Vol. XX, 97. Four Masters, Vol. V, p. 1,611. *Annals of Lough Cé*, Vol, II, p. 395.

the Glenshesk in 1565, had died of a wound received in that battle, but Shane brought with him his widow, Lady Agnes, and his brother, Sorley Boy, whom he had ever since kept a prisoner.

The MacDonalds took pride in lavish hospitality, and they had prepared a feast for Shane. Whiskey and sack drunk in combination lead to excitement, but it may well be that what followed had been planned in advance. Certainly Sorley Boy, again at liberty among his fellow countrymen, could have prevented it by the raising of a finger. After all, there was bad blood enough between Shane and the MacDonalds. A quarrel broke out, and Shane was hacked and stabbed to death. The Constable of Carrickfergus managed to secure his head, which he despatched, 'pickled in a pipkin', to Dublin, where it was stuck up over the Castle gate.[1]

Shane O'Neill must be accounted a great man after his fashion by reason of his personality, his boldness, and an intelligence overcoming the disabilities of lack of education and of knowledge of the world, which in his case hardly extended outside Ulster, except perhaps to some degree to the Western Isles. His defenders assert that his savagery was not exceptional in the age and even that he displayed on occasion a sort of uncouth chivalry. It is hard to say where this appeared. Poor old Calvagh O'Donnell, who was brave enough to defy him even in captivity, was kept chained so that he could not stand upright. Yet at court Shane had struck observers as a man of mark. His statesmanship amounted to skill in the endeavour to make himself overlord of Ulster and little more, but the same may be said of the Earl of Tyrone, his nephew, and of Hugh Roe O'Donnell, who was to become chieftain of Tyrconnell. Patriotism in the modern sense was experienced to a greater extent by the Munster rebels, Fitzmaurice and Desmond, than by these Ulster chiefs. After Shane's death, though there was plenty of trouble in Ulster, no major revolt took place in the province for upwards of thirty years.

[1] *C.S.P. Ireland*, Vol. XXI, 8. Hill, *The Macdonells of Antrim*, p. 141.

CHAPTER VII

THE FITZMAURICE REBELLION

NEITHER the Earl of Sussex nor Sir Henry Sidney had been able to devote all their energy and attention to subduing Shane O'Neill. The worst distraction had been the hostility between the great Earls of Ormonde and Desmond in the south. The Butlers and Geraldines had long been rivals, and the near relation between these two men created by Desmond's marriage to Ormonde's widowed mother did little to bring them together. Desmond, who succeeded to the title in 1558, was proud, turbulent, and intractable, but scarcely a man of ability; indeed, in later life he gave evidence of feebleness of mind as well as of body. He suffered both from palsy and from the effects of an early wound.

Of his opponent there is much more to be said. At the accession of Elizabeth, Thomas Butler, tenth Earl of Ormonde, known as 'Black Thomas' from his dark hair and complexion, was only twenty-six years of age, but had already, during the reign of Mary, shown not only that he was going to be a great figure, but that he had enough originality to plan for himself a remarkable line of conduct. He was brought up a Protestant, the first of his house, though under Mary he conformed to Roman Catholicism like others; he was an intense and almost fanatical loyalist; but he would also be a mediator between the English and the Irish. Although he had been about the court in England and dressed as a great and wealthy English nobleman, he was welcomed with delight in Tipperary and Kilkenny when he first appeared in 1554.

There were to be a number of viceroys in Ireland during Elizabeth's reign, some of them remarkable figures, but Ormonde, except for brief periods in the wings, was in the front of the Irish stage until the year 1600. The individual enterprises of others may on occasion have exceeded his, but he was the most notable personality in Irish public life if the reign be taken as a whole. Ormonde must be accounted a great man, even granting that his position and prestige made it possible for him to accomplish what would have been almost impossible for others. In a generation of dishonesty and intrigue he kept his hands clean, though certainly not neglecting his own interests. Stern and merciless in civil war, he yet sought opportunities to avoid it and to bring it to an end as early as possible, after which he would beseech the Queen to show her clemency by granting pardons to those who had not committed themselves irremediably. If the viceroys had adopted his policy, Ireland would have been happier and much English blood and treasure would have been spared. The northern lords, the uncouth Shane O'Neill as well as the courtly Earl of Tyrone, treated him with profound respect even when they were in the full course of rebellion. They never had a hard word for him, however bitter their mood, and neither had other Irishmen, always excepting Desmond and his followers.

Unfortunately, however, Ormonde became involved in English political strife and in the hostility between the Sussex and Leicester factions. He was the intimate friend of Sussex, whom he accompanied on all his northern expeditions in the reigns of both Mary and Elizabeth, fighting on foot in every battle and skirmish.[1] His friendship with Sussex brought upon him the dislike of Leicester; and Sidney, though brother-in-law to Sussex, was Leicester's man. So when Sussex or his adherent Fitzwilliam held the viceregal sword Ormonde was in high favour; when it was Sidney or Essex, he was out of favour. Cross-currents sometimes appeared, since Ormonde was a friend of Perrott, who was on indifferent terms with Fitzwilliam, but broadly speaking Ormonde stood for the Sussex party. In consequence, the Leicester faction was inclined to back Desmond against him, and, when Desmond had been branded a traitor and could no longer be backed, to question Ormonde's ability to put an end to the rebellion and even his sincerity. His steadiest and most constant friend was the Queen, and after her William Cecil, later Lord Burghley. 'I must say, "Butler-aboo!" against all that cry, as I hear, in a new language, "Pope-aboo!" ' Cecil wrote to him in 1580, during the Desmond rebellion.[2]

A double dispute about possession of certain manors, including that of Clonmel, on the Suir, and over prize wines brought into Youghal and Kinsale, caused the first serious difference between the two earls. It was settled in 1560 without bloodshed, in Desmond's favour.[3] Raids by Desmond's vassals on Ormonde's lands, however, followed. In 1562 the rivals appeared at court, after long delays on the part of Desmond in obeying the summons. Desmond showed himself disrespectful and defiant, much more so indeed than Shane

[1] Cox, *Hibernia Anglicana*, p. 395.   [2] *C.S.P. Ireland*, Vol. LXI, 26.
[3] *C.S.P. Ireland*, Vol. II, 32.

O'Neill had been earlier that year. Finally, the Queen and Council lost patience with him and committed him to a mild form of custody. He was permitted to return to Ireland in 1564. In the following year his wife died, disastrously for him, since her death removed the last restraining influence to which he would harken and the last link between him and Ormonde.

That very year indeed they came to blows and there occurred an extraordinary event, the last private battle—that is, a battle fought without a royal commission on either side—on the soil of the British Isles between two noblemen. It was at the ford of Affane on the Blackwater. Desmond was defeated, wounded, and captured. Now indeed the Queen was infuriated, as well she might be; for these two were lords educated in the English fashion and they had reverted to a practice horrifying in English eyes, especially in royal eyes. Once more she summoned both of them to England, and administered to them the gravest reproof. They entered into recognisances to keep the peace and abide by whatever judgment might be given.[1] The affair became a party issue, Sussex coming forward to testify that Desmond had no right to be in the Decies, where he had been caught, that he had maintained traitors, that he had never served the Queen, whereas Ormonde always had. The opposite party, chiefly represented by Sidney, took Desmond's side—that is Leicester's.[2]

Desmond returned to Ireland, but Ormonde stayed—too long in fact for his honour and the interests of his family under the rule of an unfriendly viceroy. Lovers of scandal declared he had become Leicester's rival in the affections of the Queen. One Spanish Ambassador reported that he was every day in higher favour and that the Archbishop of York had reproved the Queen for her conduct; three years later another declared that she held him back when he was about to start for Ireland.[3] The insinuations may be disregarded, but there existed a sentimental link between the two stronger than that which might be expected to bind a Queen and a great and faithful subject of about her own years and exceptional personal charm. Long afterwards she wrote to him of a private understanding which, she said, could not be committed to paper to be carried across the sea. And when in 1600 Ormonde was released after having been kidnapped and held prisoner by the rebels, he, then a man of

[1] Four Masters, Vol. V, p. 1,603.
[2] C.S.P. Ireland, Vol. XIV, 39 (8 August 1565). Bagwell, Ireland under the Tudors, Vol. II, p. 92.
[3] C.S.P. Spanish, Vol. I, pp. 549, 553; Vol. II, p. 180.

sixty-eight, writing in fervid loyalty to his 'most gracious and dread sovereign', ended by saying that he could give her no more than what she had always possessed, 'being your old servant Lucas his faithful heart and true service, which shall continue until the last hour of his life'. She in her reply kept up the old jest of their youth embodied in the name, bidding Lucas comfort himself and believe that he could never desire more happiness than she wished him and his.[1]

One result of his absence was that his brothers, Edmond, Piers, and Edward, got out of hand. Sir Warham St. Leger, his enemy, was appointed President of Munster. The Queen reproved Sidney, alleging that the appointment showed a bias against Ormonde, but it must be confessed that she herself was now showing the opposite bias. On the other hand, Ormonde's rival, Desmond, was arrested by Sidney and again sent to England with his brother John, and both were shortly afterwards imprisoned in the Tower. During Desmond's restraint, but while he was still in Ireland, a royal commission appointed to decide between them found overwhelmingly in Ormonde's favour.[2]

The disaffection of the Butlers was in part due to the arrival in Ireland of a striking figure, Sir Peter Carew, veteran of many wars. Study of ancient records had convinced him that he was the rightful heir to immense possessions in Ireland, mostly in Munster, granted by Henry II to his ancestor, Robert Fitz-Stephen. He embarked upon a long campaign in support of these claims. In 1568 he gained an initial success. Lord Deputy Sidney and his Council recognized his right to the Barony of Idrone, in Carlow, and he established himself in a castle at Leighlinbridge. A few miles away lay Clogrenan Castle, the property of Sir Edmond Butler, who was naturally alarmed and unsettled by the proximity of this formidable land-hunter. When Sir Edmond began to show signs of disloyalty, Carew stormed his castle. Thereby he incurred reproof from the Queen, who considered that he had contributed to the pushing of the Butlers from the straight path. To anticipate a little, Carew continued to prosecute his greater claims in Munster. Finally he appeared to stand upon the brink of triumph. Several great landowners, including the Barrys in Cork, professed themselves willing to become his tenants. At this point, however, he died, in 1575. His much younger cousins, Peter and George, served during the Desmond and Baltinglas

---

[1] *C.S.P Ireland*, Vol. CCVII (Pt. 3), 110, (Pt. 4) 36.
[2] S.P. Ireland, Vol. XXI, 10.

rebellions. Peter was killed at Glenmalure, George surviving to become one of the great figures of the Irish wars.

Shortly after the death of Shane O'Neill Sidney visited England, leaving Lord Chancellor Weston and Sir William Fitzwilliam to act as Lord Justices.[1] It became clear that the passing of Shane did not of itself suffice to bring tranquillity to Ulster. Tirlagh Luineach O'Neill was on good terms with the Scots and hiring Redshank mercenaries from among them. To make his weight felt and punish chiefs who had disobeyed him, he suddenly burnt a dozen or more of what were called by courtesy 'towns'—otherwise small collections of hovels of wattle and daub—some within the Pale.[2] He raided up to the outskirts of Newry. In 1569 it was reported that he had 3,000 Scots and as many Irish as had ever served Shane. He became so threatening that a large proportion of the scanty forces in Ireland had to be moved up towards the Ulster border, thus leaving the south unprotected. Fitzwilliam found himself in an awkward fix when the relatively minor disorders of Fitzgerald raids and 'the Butlers' wars' suddenly changed into an open rebellion in the south.

James Fitzmaurice Fitzgerald[3] was a more formidable character than his cousin, Gerald, Earl of Desmond. His father, Maurice Fitzjohn Fitzgerald, had borne the sinister and well-merited Irish sobriquet of *à totane* ('of the burnings' or 'the incendiary'), and the son, if more civilized, was equally unruly. He became Captain of Desmond when Desmond was incarcerated, and his ambition seems to have been to start with to seize his kinsman's lands and perhaps possess himself of the earldom. He had the religious and nationalist fervour and the powers of leadership that Desmond lacked.[4] It was he who seduced Ormonde's brethren from their allegiance, and he was probably responsible for the treason of the McCarthy More, head of the second chiefry in the south after that of Desmond, and newly created Earl of Clancarty or Clanclare. Fitzmaurice made an indifferent start in his revolt, being soundly trounced by a kinsman,

---

[1] Sidney is sometimes described as having been thrice viceroy. He was actually in England on this occasion about ten months. His return cannot be described as another viceroyalty.

[2] S.P. Ireland, Vol. XXV, 79.

[3] Described hereafter as 'Fitzmaurice'. Irish surnames were coined in this way: a Tirlagh O'Neill, son of Henry O'Neill, would be known as Tirlagh MacHenry O'Neill. Presently 'O'Neill' would be dropped and the surname established as 'MacHenry'. Hence the great numbers bearing the names of Fitz-Thomas, MacShane, McHugh, etc.

[4] Mathew, *The Celtic Peoples and Renaissance Europe*, p. 159.

the Lord of Lixnaw, whose lands he invaded in July 1568, nominally to distrain for rent. But the country was drifting into confusion, and in Munster famine seemed likely, owing to the burning of stored food. On the return of Sidney from England, little as he loved Ormonde, he wrote that only his presence would quiet the country. Bold man that he was, and unfair to the young Butlers as he showed himself, Sidney did not venture to push matters to extremes against them while their elder brother was sitting at the Queen's feet. However, about Christmas, as Ormonde still dallied, Sidney felt constrained to go south himself and hang a number of Edward Butler's followers at Kilkenny and Waterford.[1]

The next exploit of Fitzmaurice was more serious. In June 1569, accompanied by his ally Lord Clancarty, who now 'disdained the title of earl', he stormed the abbey-castle of Tracton, west of Cork Harbour, and slaughtered or hanged every man of the little garrison. A little later the sovereign, or mayor, of Waterford reported that Fitzmaurice was encamped close to the town walls with 1,400 gallowglasses, 400 pikemen in mail, 400 musketeers, and 1,500 kerne. The country was devastated; English settlers near Cork were killed; others, who escaped that fate, were stripped naked and sent into Waterford, and this indignity was actually inflicted upon 'the honest housewives of the country'; and the rebels boasted that they could take Cork when they chose. They demanded as its ransom that Mrs. Grenville, the wife of the famous Richard Grenville, the Sheriff of Cork, who had sailed that week for England, and Lady St. Leger should be handed over to them; but, scared as the citizens were, they did not lend themselves to such an infamy.[2] Relations between Spain and England were at this time passing through a bad phase owing to the detention in English ports of Spanish ships carrying specie to the Duke of Alva in the Netherlands, and the Spanish Ambassador, Don Guerau de Spes, wrote that there was now a favourable opportunity to overthrow English rule in Ireland by sending aid to Fitzmaurice.[3] The Lord Deputy had gone towards Connaught, which had been in a disturbed state, with the intention of establishing a President in the province—a task which he had to postpone for a short time—and no part of the country was entirely free from turmoil and revolt except the Pale. It has to be acknowledged, where the south is in question, that Sidney had contributed

[1] *C.S.P. Ireland*, Vol. XXVI, 18, 59.
[2] *C.S.P. Ireland*, Vol. XXVIII, 37, 38, 43; Vol. XXIX, 5.
[3] *C.S.P. Spanish*, Vol. II, 103.

to his own troubles by lending himself to the party warfare waged
by Leicester in England and by throwing Ormonde's brothers into
the arms of Fitzmaurice. When the house of Butler was found on
the side of the rebels it was indeed time for its head to appear.

Ormonde at last came over, in August 1569, landing at Rosslare,
in Wexford. He was delayed by the difficulty of getting through to
his own country, in which Sidney refused to give him any aid.
Before he reached Kilkenny, by way of Waterford, English troops
had been engaged against Sir Edmond Butler. On Ormonde's
arrival, however, his brothers at once came in to him. They vowed
that they had never meant to revolt and complained bitterly of
Sidney's treatment. They had been told that the Queen was about
to marry Ormonde's foe, Leicester. They now awaited the Lord
Deputy's pleasure.[1] Edmond afterwards broke away and was on the
run for a time, but came in again eventually.

Without the aid of the Butlers, Fitzmaurice proved less formidable than hitherto. In September Humphrey Gilbert, now a colonel
and stationed at Cork, inflicted a heavy defeat upon him and Lord
Clancarty. Exploiting his success, Gilbert relieved Kilmallock and
captured or received the surrender of twenty-three castles held by
the rebels, slaughtering all who resisted and not sparing their
women and children. On 4 December Clancarty, Fitzmaurice's
chief adherent, came in and acknowledged his treason.[2] The rebellion was to some extent in hand, though it was far from being over.
Gilbert was knighted by the Lord Deputy for his services. Ormonde,
however, still felt dissatisfaction with the Lord Deputy's attitude to
himself and his house. To Cecil he described Sidney as 'bent to do
me any disgrace or discredit he can hear'. More significant still of
relations in Ireland, he made Fitzwilliam the bearer of his letter to
England, obviously also informing him of its contents and providing
him with material to state the case more fully.[3]

After labouring much with the Queen, Cecil had persuaded her
to appoint presidents of the provinces of Munster and Connaught,
each with a Council, a much-needed measure of decentralization.
There was no definite prospect of extending it to Ulster, which did
not possess a town worthy of the name and in which there could be
no pretence that the Queen's writ ran. Sir John Pollard was appointed President of Munster and Sir Edward Fitton of Connaught.
Some delay followed, and Pollard was unable to go. Cecil worked

[1] *C.S.P. Ireland*, Vol. XXIX, 60, 70.   [2] S.P. Ireland, Vol. XXIX, 64, 67, 68, 83.
[3] S.P. Ireland, Vol. XXIX, 75.

out the rates of the emoluments, which were higher than those first decreed, and was then met by the Queen's refusal to allow the increase. Elizabeth did not care for spending money, even when she had it. Eventually, however, Sir Warham St. Leger, son of a former viceroy, was appointed to Munster—against the Butler interest, as has been mentioned—and Fitton was established in Connaught by Sidney in person. The unfortunate man found that he had entered a wasps' nest, which he was ill advised enough to stir with a stick, beginning by burning what he was pleased to call 'idols' in the churches. The Earl of Thomond, who doubled the parts of a peer and the chieftain of the O'Brians' country of the same name, later known as Clare, came out in revolt. He was followed by the O'Rourke in Leitrim and by some of the Burkes in central Connaught. A distinction must, however, be made, as so often, between the man who held a title from the Crown and those who did not. Thomond's motive was hatred and fear of the Queen's servants in Ireland. He was far from being an extreme nationalist and was ready, if hard enough pressed, to proclaim his complete loyalty. This made his subjection less difficult.[1]

Sidney gave the task to Ormonde, after they had met, settled their differences, and vowed to renew their former friendship. Ormonde raised a force from his own palatinate and estates, Sidney giving him only 300 kerne. He was, however, provided with a generous commission: he could proclaim rebels, take submissions, and prosecute as he chose. It was a campaign of pure prestige, with no opposition to speak of. Terror of his frightful severity in war on the one hand, hope based on his benevolence and clemency to the repentant on the other, did his work for him. Thomond surrendered on the understanding that Ormonde, his cousin on his mother's side, should have the custody of his country. The rebel went to France instead of to the Queen's presence, as he had promised, but afterwards changed his mind and received a free pardon. The other rebels of the country came in, and all its castles were occupied. A handful were executed, but Ormonde's traditional policy was shown in his words addressed to Sidney: 'The Queen hath many good subjects here, if they were but cherished and not over-pressed.' The condemnation of Fitton's methods could hardly have been plainer.[2]

The pacification of Thomond was helpful to Fitton, at the time

[1] S.P. Ireland, Vol. XXX, 4, 15.

[2] *C.S.P. Ireland*, Vol. XXX, 50. *Carew Cal.*, Vol. I, p. 401. Four Masters, Vol. V, p. 1,639.

almost a prisoner in Galway, but it did not extend to the rest of Connaught. The Lord President was relieved by a force sent by Sidney and joined hands with the Earl of Clanrickarde to face the rebels. He was attacking a party of them in Shrule, on the borders of Mayo and Galway east of Lough Corrib, when MacWilliam, hereditary chief of the Mayo Burkes, came to its rescue. A battle then occurred which must be accounted one of the most curious of Elizabeth's Irish wars. On both sides the main strength lay in gallowglasses. With Fitton and Clanrickarde were many chiefs of Upper (southern) Connaught and their followers, a body of MacDonald gallowglasses of a Leinster sept, five 'battles' of Mac-Sweeny gallowglasses, one of MacDowell, and 300 English cavalry. The MacWilliam, Shane MacOliver, led the Burkes of his own county of Mayo, a force of MacDonald gallowglasses, and O'Flaherties, who dwelt on the north shore of Galway Bay and were better known as boatmen than as land warriors, and such Scots mercenaries as he had been able to hire. It will thus appear that the different septs of the MacDonalds fought on opposing sides.

The rebels, advancing on foot, found the presidential forces drawn up to meet them. Harquebusiers and bowmen took heavy toll of them, but they charged home and drove the royalists back. Fitton had, however, kept his force of English cavalry in reserve. Just when it appeared that the victory would rest with the MacWilliam, the cavalry rode into his flank, scattered his men, and restored the fortunes of the day. It was Fitton who bivouacked on the battle-field. The victory was not fully decisive, since it was not followed up, but the Mayo rebels dispersed to their homes.[1]

All this time James Fitzmaurice had been almost impotent, attended only by a handful of men. When, in the winter of 1570, Ormonde marched into Kerry on rumours of a French landing, and demolished Dunloe Castle, near Killarney, he met with scarcely any opposition, and the Irish annalists say that this was because, while Desmond was in prison, Fitzmaurice had no real following in the country.[2] Yet Fitzmaurice was by no means done with. In March 1571, he appeared suddenly at Kilmallock, in southern Limerick, with a body of MacShechy and MacSweeny gallowglasses, broke into it, burnt it, and of course looted it thoroughly. The account of

[1] C.S.P. Ireland, Vol. XXX, 5 (24 June 1570). Four Masters, Vol. V, p. 1,641. The units are misleadingly described as 'battalions'. In fact a 'battle' of gallow-glasses numbered from sixty to eighty, not counting armour-bearers.
[2] Four Masters, Vol. V, p. 1,649.

its wealth in jewels and plate given by the annalists is probably exaggerated, but one sentence may be recorded for its significance. The raiders, they declare, took away to their woodland haunts treasures which 'the father would not have acknowledged to his heir, or the mother to her daughter, the day before'. That is surely an illustration of the mistrust created in the very bosom of the family by the confusion and violence of the period. Ormonde's brother Edward, doubtless eager to display loyalty after his pardon, pursued the rebels hotly and recovered a large proportion of the cattle carried off. Ormonde himself considered that there had been gross negligence, if not treachery, in Kilmallock.[1]

St. Leger's presidency of Connaught had been revoked, and after a considerable period his successor arrived, about the date of the burning of Kilmallock. This was another remarkable Elizabethan figure, Sir John Perrott, reputed to be the son of Henry VIII. As gallant as he was energetic, Perrott's character was marred by a childish rashness and in the years of his subsequent viceroyalty by a violent temper which brought about unseemly wrangles in his own Council. Having seen him established, Sidney quitted Ireland on 7 April 1571, leaving Fitzwilliam to act as Lord Justice.

If parts of Munster and most of Connaught were still disturbed, Leinster was placid and Ulster surprisingly quiet. Tirlagh Luineach O'Neill could have made matters very unpleasant if he had chosen to do so, and he did cause great anxiety. But Tirlagh was not the man to march on Dublin or to head a revolt of all Ireland, and the fact that there was revolt in Munster and Connaught meant little to him, provided his own situation were secure. Though well provided with mercenaries, Tirlagh did not raise the standard of revolt. He used them chiefly as a threat to extend his power over his neighbours, the O'Donnells, Maguires, and MacMahons. Why should he go the way of Shane when he was left uncontrolled to reign as a prince over virtually a whole province? After his one great raid towards Newry he remained quiet for some time. His inactivity was in any case compulsory for a while, since, while supping with his new spouse, Lady Agnes MacDonald, he was accidentally shot by his jester at what must have been a lively party. Moreover, it was one thing to hire mercenaries and another to pay them. Tirlagh was finding his establishment costly. He was, Sidney wrote, 'eaten out', and the Scots grew weary of him. In January 1571 a treaty was concluded with him, and it was signed and sealed by

[1] C.S.P. Ireland, Vol. XXXI, 21, 27. Four Masters, Vol. V, p. 1,653.

Sidney on 3 March, just before his departure. Most of the mercenaries went home for lack of pay.[1]

In the south the improvement was scarcely maintained. Fitzmaurice, whatever the extremities to which he was reduced, always seemed to be able to hire enough 'naughty idle' MacSweeny and MacSheehy gallowglasses to seize any opportunity that offered itself. The country was left without a viceroy for nine months, till in December 1571 Fitzwilliam was appointed Lord Deputy. The Queen praised his ability and fidelity, but sent him very little money. Though a capable man, he had no military background like Sidney, but under the presidential system the special task of the viceroy was Ulster and Leinster, while the Presidents conducted affairs in the other two provinces. The garrison numbered only 2,031 men, at a cost of £32,442 10s. 0¼d. per annum. Perrott in Munster had but 500 English troops and 200 Irish, but he set out from Cork to Kilmallock and persuaded the people to return and begin its reconstruction. In a circular march during the spring of 1571, with Limerick as its furthest point, he took a number of castles and killed a number of rebels, but wore out his troops by marches through woods and bogs on the trail of men whom he could not hope to catch. Later on he failed to take Castlemaine, in Kerry, for lack of powder, and Fitzmaurice seized the opportunity of his being engaged in the siege to make new raids.[2]

A little later that year Perrott challenged Fitzmaurice to a duel, which it was agreed should be fought twenty-four a side. Ormonde made every effort to stop this lunacy, but Perrott actually went to the rendezvous. Fitzmaurice did not turn up, perhaps fearful of treachery; for both sides were very suspicious in these wars, and not without cause.[3] In 1572, however, Perrott partially redeemed his previous failure when Castlemaine, after a three months' siege, surrendered to him, having run out of provisions; but once again a calamity occurred when his back was turned. Fitzmaurice went into Connaught, at first in hope of getting a force to relieve the castle. There he was joined by the Earl of Clanrickarde's sons, wild young men, who gathered together a band of Scots mercenaries and MacSweeny and MacDonald gallowglasses. This horde swept over half Connaught, penetrated into peaceful Leinster to fire Mullingar, turned back and burnt Athenry, and slaughtered those who had

supported the President in earlier fighting. What were the sentiments of Clanrickarde about the revolt of his graceless sons is
unknown, but there is no reason to suppose him to have been other
than a loyalist at any time. To put pressure on the youths, he was,
however, locked up in Dublin Castle and then, inconsistently,
released to induce them to submit, which he succeeded in doing.[1]
But Fitton was driven out of his province and the presidency of
Connaught lapsed.

Affairs looked ill, but were better than they seemed. As so often
happens with mercenaries, the Scots did not want to go further
afield or to serve for longer than their contracts. The heavy hand of
the Lord President had diminished the enthusiasm of Munstermen
for service with Fitzmaurice, and his force was reduced to 600 men.
With these he was ill advised enough to camp near Kilkenny.
What the presidential force had been unable to do, the Butler
gallowglasses accomplished. A body of 300 of them, with sixty
horse, led by Sir Edmond Butler, fell upon him by surprise in
November 1572, killed over 100 of his men, and scattered the rest
in flight. He held out a little longer, but the hounds were pressing
hard upon him. Learning that mercy would be accorded to him,
he came in, and on 23 February 1573 made humble submission to
the Lord President.[2] That phase of the Fitzmaurice rebellion was
over; Connaught was quiet; and in the astonishing and hardly
accountable fashion in which such things occurred in Ireland, as
if a black cloud had been blown off the sun, peace came suddenly.

The lessons of the fighting in Munster during the years of Fitzmaurice's first revolt are simple enough. If the English forces, or
for that matter the levies of the Butlers, strengthened by a little
equipment from the Government's stores, could close with a rebel
body even at disadvantageous numerical odds, they could generally
count on victory. But there was great difficulty in doing so. The
Irish could always outmarch the English. Ormonde and his brothers
had accomplished more in pacifying Munster and Clare than so fine
a soldier as Sidney or so determined and tireless a leader as Perrott.
If more money had been advanced for the purpose, Perrott could
have employed more gallowglasses and kerne, as he desired. There
never was money enough to pay even the English troops. Some of
Fitton's men left him in the lurch in Connaught for want of victuals

---

[1] C.S.P. Ireland, Vol. XXVII, 11 (i, ii, iii), 12. Four Masters, Vol. V., p.
1,661.

[2] C.S.P. Ireland, Vol. XXXVIII, 42; Vol. XXXIX, 40 (i).

in 1571, when they had had no pay for two years. In the following
year Perrott was halted by a mutiny for the same reason.[1]

Having settled with James Fitzmaurice, the Government at once
determined to give Desmond a chance; the Geraldines were popular
in their great domain, and it seemed desirable to fill the void left
by the absence of the head of the Munster branch. The Earl signed
articles pledging himself to abandon the Irish customs of coyne and
livery on his estates and to keep no gallowglasses. On arrival in
Dublin he proved far from pliant. It was thought wiser to detain
him there for a time, while his more discreet brother, Sir John, was
allowed to go on into Munster. Perrott regretted that Desmond had
some and feared that he would create fresh confusion in Munster,
which was now remarkably peaceful, with the plough everywhere at
work. Perrott himself had to go to England on sick leave and his
toil was to a large extent undone when, in November 1573, Desmond
escaped from Dublin, made his way to Munster, and 'took to the
fern'.[2]

Yet he did not go into revolt, though he was known to be in
communication with Fitzmaurice. He committed one act which
came near to treason, though so cleverly carried out that it left him
with some defence against the charge. On Christmas Eve a band of
Irish were admitted by the treachery of the porter to the much-
disputed keep of Castlemaine and took possession of it. On Christmas Day Desmond came upon the scene, ordered them out, and
when they obeyed put in his own warders. The wandering kerne
who seized the castle had almost certainly acted in collusion with
him, but he could claim to be acting as the champion of law and
order, while at the same time refusing to hand over Castlemaine.
However, nothing serious came of his adventure, and in September
1574 he once more surrendered. Some further confusion had been
caused in Munster, but for the next five years the province was to
be fairly quiet.[3]

[1] S.P. Ireland, Vol. XXXII, 37; Vol. XXXIV, 4 (i).
[2] C.S.P. Ireland, Vol. XL, 52; Vol. XLII, 88.
[3] S.P. Ireland, Vol. XLIII, 26. C.S.P. Ireland, Vol. XLVI, 47.

CHAPTER VIII

SIDNEY'S SECOND VICEROYALTY

WHILE Fitzmaurice was in revolt in Munster the Queen and her Council had given their approval to a curious colonization scheme in Ulster, the object of which was to extend English influence beyond the two points of Newry and Carrickfergus at which alone it was then established. This project may be called the ancestor of the Ulster Plantation carried out by Sir Arthur Chichester under the auspices of James I nearly forty years later, but it was undertaken in a lighter-hearted spirit and without the careful planning which distinguished the work of the greatest of all Irish viceroys.

The ground was not ill chosen. It was the peninsula of the Ards in Down, between the sea and Strangford Lough, which 'might easily be defended by garrisons placed in a strait neck of land by which it was jointed to the rest of the island'. It was also the only district in Ulster where there still dwelt a few of the old Norman families, much reduced and largely hibernicized though they were. The man who undertook the task was Sir Thomas Smith, legal scholar, astrologer, former Vice-Chancellor of the University of Cambridge, Provost of Eton, and Ambassador to France, and at this time Secretary of State.[1] The agent was his illegitimate son, also named Thomas, who proposed to carry out the colonization with 600 men and was probably the author of a flowery pamphlet setting forth the scheme.[2]

This pamphlet naturally alarmed the head of the Clandeboye sept of the O'Neill family, Sir Brian MacPhelim O'Neill, whose chieftaincy covered the Ards and who professed to have given good service to former viceroys, and he protested vigorously. Fitzwilliam, recently appointed Lord Deputy, wrote in March 1572, that 'Mr. Smith's grant' was likely to cause a revolt in Ulster.[3] Even if Brian MacPhelim could be squared or subjugated, there was Tirlagh Luineach O'Neill in the background—and Sorley Boy MacDonald and his Scots.

[1] Strype, *The Life of Sir Thomas Smith*, p. 177.
[2] Bagwell, *Ireland under the Tudors*, Vol. II, Chapter XXIX.
[3] C.S.P. Ireland, Vol. XXXV, 32, 44, 45.

The younger Smith did not appear until October, and then his enterprise proved a fiasco. What resources he possessed is not known, but in cash they do not appear to have been great, to judge by a receipt to Burghley, for the sum of £333 6s. 8d. for 'the maintaining of soldiers'.[1] He brought only 100 men. Brian MacPhelim marched into the Ards, burnt goods, raided cattle, and killed Henry Savage, the head of a Norman family who favoured Smith's project. Smith fled to shelter behind the walls of Carrickfergus and appealed to the Lord Deputy for help. Since Fitzmaurice was still unsubdued and trouble had broken out in the Pale itself, it is not surprising that Fitzwilliam made no response. Besides, he thought the whole business crazy.[2] Smith was finally killed.

Before Smith's scheme—or young Smith himself—was dead Elizabeth countenanced one much more ambitious, sponsored by a greater figure. Walter Devereux, Earl of Essex, was an attractive, gallant, and determined, but not very intelligent person, high in the Queen's favour. In May 1573 he put forward a proposal that he should have in fee not only the Ards, but also Clandeboye, the Route and the Glynns (the whole of Antrim), together with the fisheries of the Bann and Lough Neagh, and a seven years' licence to transport men, money, food, and munitions from England. He demanded also the authority of martial law, power to 'annoy' Scotch and Irish malefactors, and the right to parley with rebels and to administer oaths of fidelity to Her Majesty. The Queen accepted the proposal, and a contract was signed by which he was to go to Ulster that autumn with 200 horse and 400 foot raised at his charges, while she would send equal numbers at hers. Every adventurer who joined the expedition was to receive, for each horseman maintained, 400 acres, and for each footman, 200 acres, in fee simple at a rent of 2d. English per acre. No part of the territory was to be assigned to any Scots Irish or mere Irish. For seven years Essex was to be the Queen's Captain-General in Ulster. It was an undertaking which may be considered the forerunner of those of the modern chartered companies.[3]

It must be confessed that if the Smith scheme was reckless the Essex scheme appears ridiculous. It was open to all the objections of its predecessor and added others of its own. The projected colony could be in no way self-contained, like a plantation of the Ards

---

[1] *Salisbury Papers*, Pt. II, p. 55. [2] *C.S.P. Ireland*, Vol. XXXVIII, 25, 31, 38.
[3] *Carew Cal.*, Vol. I, pp. 439–44. Corbett, *Drake and the Tudor Navy*, Vol. I, p. 199.

alone. It was sure to raise far more bitter opposition. The full enmity
of the Scots was likely to be incurred by extension of colonization to
Antrim, and to this would be joined that of the MacQuillans, the
Irish family who disputed possession of the Route with them.

Having borrowed £10,000 from the Queen on the security of his
lands, Essex embarked at Liverpool in August 1573. His fleet was
scattered by a gale, and only a part of his company reached Carrickfergus. Brian MacPhelim received him with cautious respect, but
soon began to show hostility. Essex seized some of his cattle and
made such preparations as he could for the winter by salting the
carcasses. He put a large garrison into Belfast Castle, including Irish
kerne procured for him by a young man who had recently appeared
in Ireland, the Baron of Dungannon, grandson of the first Earl of
Tyrone and son of the Dungannon murdered by Shane. The
English-speaking and English-educated newcomer was destined, as
second Earl of Tyrone, to be the most formidable of all England's
enemies and notably of Robert Devereux, Essex's son; but meanwhile he appeared to Essex 'very forward in the service, and is the
only man of Ulster that is, in my opinion, meet to be trusted and
used'.[1]

It is often asserted that Fitzwilliam thwarted Essex, but no proof
of this is forthcoming. The viceroy was naturally a pessimist, and
in this case his judgement was sound. Eventually 600 foot, 200 horse,
and 200 kerne, with 100 labourers, were brought together at
Carrickfergus. But, as usual, the foe melted into air when approached. Once Essex, with Dungannon in his company, got a
weak blow home against Brian MacPhelim, killing a few kerne and
taking a few hundred kine, but this was no great exploit. The
adventurers forsook him and the troops grumbled and in some cases
deserted. The Irish shrewdly asserted that the war was not the
Queen's—that was the disadvantage of a private adventurer, however good his patent, unsupported by the official forces of the
Crown.[2]

There was some talk of making Essex viceroy, which would have
withdrawn him from his present position without loss of face to the
Queen and to himself; but Elizabeth would not have it. In the
summer of 1574 he was employed by Fitzwilliam, in company with
the Earl of Kildare, in negotiations with Desmond, who was given
a safe-conduct for the purpose. This meeting helped to bring about

[1] Devereux, *Lives and Letters of the Devereux*, Vol. I, pp. 33–42.
[2] *C.S.P. Ireland*, Vol. XLII, 34, 55, 64.

the surrender of Desmond already recorded, so that Essex had accomplished at least one piece of service. In September 1574 he was instructed to parley with Tirlagh Luineach, who was in one of his more adventurous moods. Essex, with such of his own troops as he could spare, 120 gallowglasses, 600 kerne, and the 'rising out' of Magennis of South Down and MacMahon of Monaghan, moved to the Blackwater. Tirlagh lost his nerve and would not venture to meet him at the appointed place. Essex therefore crossed the river into Tyrone. The harvest had been good, and he found great ricks of corn in the fields, which he burnt, after the custom of Irish warfare. Tirlagh attempted to surprise the camp near Clogher, but was driven off. Essex went as far as Lifford, on which very few Englishmen had ever set eyes, and then to Lough Foyle, where ships from Carrickfergus brought him supplies. Hugh O'Donnell, who had been inclined to return to the O'Neill camp, reaffirmed his allegiance to the Crown and was given the custody of Lifford Castle. The expedition was not brilliant, but as successful as most made into Ulster.[1]

Technically, Essex knew his business as a soldier. He cut wide rides in the woodlands on the borders of Tyrone so as to facilitate invasion when required. In June 1575 he fought an action with Tirlagh Luineach, after which the O'Neill came to terms, largely, it would appear, because he feared interference from the O'Donnells in his rear. In July Essex successfully engaged Sorley Boy's Scots, though he had to withdraw afterwards for want of supplies. He then committed an atrocity which has blackened his name, though only because we regard him as a more knightly figure than most of his contemporaries. He sent an expedition in three frigates commanded by Captain Francis Drake, one of his associates in the colonization scheme, with troops under Captain John Norris, to Rathlin, where they slaughtered everyone, women and children included, though there were relatively few fighting men on the island.[2] Petty and brutal as was this 'combined operation', it possesses interest because it brought together, when they were junior and obscure, two great men who were later to co-operate on a far greater scale. In August Essex resigned his grant in return for the barony of Farney in Monaghan and the sinecure of Earl Marshal of Ireland. He died of dysentery in Dublin on 21 September 1576,

[1] Devereux, *Lives and Letters of the Devereux*, Vol. I, pp. 75–90.
[2] Corbett, *Drake and the Tudor Navy*, Vol. I, p. 208. S.P. Ireland, Vol. XLV, 11. *C.S.P. Ireland*, Vol. L, 4; Vol. LII, 44, 77.

aged thirty-six, having utterly failed in his ambitious enterprise. Sorley Boy, stung to passion, advanced on Carrickfergus and burnt the wretched town. The garrison of the castle sallied out to meet him, but the troops broke before the fury of the Highland charge, and the survivors were glad enough to regain the shelter of the strong walls.[1]

In Leinster there had been some unrest, particularly in Queen's County, or Leix. Here the chief of the O'Moores, Rory Oge, gave trouble in 1572, trouble which increased when the soldier who generally kept him in order and the universal mediator, Ormonde, paid a visit to England. In Wexford the O'Byrnes of Wicklow murdered an Englishman, for which Captain Francis Agarde, Seneschal of their country, took heavy revenge. Such broils were, however, unavoidable and not to be regarded too seriously. Much more menacing was the fact that, though Desmond remained inactive, James Fitzmaurice slipped off to France, sending a message to Ormonde that he had gone for the sake of his health. Moreover, the head of the other branch of the Geraldines, Gerald Fitzgerald, ninth Earl of Kildare, fell under suspicion of plotting to obtain the viceroyalty. He had previously been in high favour and, after Ormonde, most often employed in efforts to bring back to the fold those who had strayed from loyalty. Now, in May 1575, he was himself apprehended. He was sent to London and held there temporarily under a mild form of arrest, in the custody of the Lord Keeper, Sir Nicholas Bacon.[2]

Fitzwilliam, fairly successful as a viceroy, had been pleading for recall, protesting that he was sick, that his wife had to sell stock at Milton to pay his expenses, even that his marriageable daughters were losing the chance of finding suitable husbands. It was not easy to find a man for the job. Essex was rejected, and it had been decided that the office of Lord Deputy should not be held by an Anglo-Irish lord. This barred Ormonde, otherwise an obvious choice and the grandson of one of the viceroys of Henry VIII. Speculation about the might-have-been in Elizabethan Irish history is unprofitable, and it is possible that Ormonde would have failed through the jealousy and hostility of English officials; but it is reasonable to surmise that such prospects as existed of a tranquil and loyal Ireland would have been brightest in his hands, splendid achievement as was to be the viceroyalty which now followed.

[1] *C.S.P. Dom.*, 1547–80, p. 531. *C.S.P. Ireland*, Vol. LIII, 22.
[2] *C.S.P. Ireland*, Vol. XXXVI, 16; Vol. XXXVII, 11, 13.

At last Sidney was persuaded to go once more. He received the sword on 27 September 1575 and went with his predecessor to Drogheda, whither as many Dubliners as could afford to had removed to avoid the plague raging in the capital.[1]

The new Lord Deputy, active and enterprising as ever, at once resolved to take advantage of the partial success of Essex against the Scots and Tirlagh Luineach O'Neill. He went north to Carrickfergus with 400 foot and 200 horse, finding the town virtually destroyed and the force in the castle in poor case. Moving up along the Antrim coast, he found it rich in corn—the hot summer which had brought on the plague had favoured the harvest—and full of cattle. Sorley Boy, who had gone almost crazy over the tragedy of Rathlin, was nevertheless confident in his own strength and proud of his victory at Carrickfergus. Sidney concluded an armistice with him and was prepared to leave him in possession of the Glynns, though there was another strong claimant. Lady Agnes O'Neill wanted the Glynns for her MacDonald son, and promised that he would defend it in the English interest against his uncle, Sorley Boy; but this typical Campbell policy did not attract Sidney. The Route Sidney considered should be restored to its Irish owners, the MacQuillans.

Northern Armagh, which had been assigned to the young Lord Dungannon, was desolate, and Armagh Cathedral had been burnt. Tirlagh Luineach, who had so lately refused to parley with Essex, came to see Sidney without demanding a protection. Sidney recommended that he should be created a peer and given a grant from the Crown for his lands. Lady Agnes, who had once been looked upon as a disturbing influence in Ulster, now desired 'to have her husband live like a good subject and to have him nobilitated'. It was a mistake on the Queen's part that she did not follow her viceroy's advice. Perhaps she was influenced by Sidney's belief that wounds, ill-health, and hard drinking would soon carry Tirlagh off; this was a gross miscalculation, and Tirlagh was to prove, as a number of his countrymen have proved, that Irish whiskey and sherry are not always preventives to longevity. He had nearly another twenty years to go.[2]

Leaving Ulster quiet, Sidney passed down into the Pale. His Ulster despatch was sent on 15 November 1575; his next was from Waterford on 16 December. In the interval he marched through

[1] C.S.P. Ireland, Vol. VIII, 26, 30. Four Masters, Vol. V, p. 1,681.
[2] Sidney Papers, Vol. I, pp. 75-80.

Meath, Kildare, King's County, Queen's County, Carlow, Wexford, and Kilkenny. At Kilkenny Castle he was nobly entertained by Ormonde, who then rode on with him to Waterford. Everywhere he conferred with the principal gentry, Irish and English. There was little unrest reported to him, except on the Dublin borders, where Feagh MacHugh O'Byrne was conducting night raids and occasional 'daylight bodraggs' from his Wicklow glens; but there was evidence enough of past incendiarism. One of the great firebrands, the determined and perhaps evilly used Rory Oge O'Moore of Queen's County, came in to Kilkenny on protection from Ormonde and in the Cathedral confessed his faults and promised to live better. 'Worse than he hath been he cannot be', commented the viceroy drily.

Sidney next moved to Cork. Halting at Dungarvan Castle in the Decies, he was visited by Desmond, who humbly offered Her Majesty any service that she desired of him. Youghal was not visited because it had been too thoroughly despoiled by Fitzmaurice to be capable of housing the viceroy and his train. At Cork all was merry as a marriage bell, the townsmen courteous and hospitable, the English troops and gallowglasses well lodged, Sidney's dwelling thronged with the local nobility—Fitzgeralds, Butlers, MacCarthys, Barrys, Powers, O'Brians, O'Sullivans, O'Carrolls, O'Callaghans, O'Mahons—and some representatives of the ruined ancient English families of the province—Arundels, Rochforts, Barretts, Flemings, Lombards, 'now all in misery, either banished from their own or oppressed upon their own'. Then towards Limerick, passing by Kilmallock, now miraculously restored after its burning, to meet an assembly of friendly notables, as at Cork, though on a smaller scale.

On 27 February 1576 he entered Thomond, and through it passed on to Galway, where again he was honourably received and entertained. Here the story was not pretty. He found 'plenty of murder, rape, burning, and sacrilege', though it seemed to him that the victims exaggerated their cases. He set up a provost marshal with a small force of twelve horsemen and twenty-four footmen, clear proof that he was thinking in terms of petty crime rather than of revolt. He also formally shired the province, creating the counties of Sligo, Mayo, Galway, and Roscommon. With MacWilliam Iochtar, supreme chief of the Mayo Burkes, he accomplished a remarkable piece of diplomacy. MacWilliam spoke no English, but could converse with the Lord Deputy in Latin and professed himself anxious to live quietly, hold his lands from the Queen, and expel the itinerant Scots. Sidney arranged that his MacDonald gallowglasses, without whom MacWilliam was helpless, should hold bonaght from the Queen, as they were glad to do.

Sidney returned by way of Athenry, a woeful spectacle, burnt out by Clanrickarde's crazy sons, and Athlone, where sessions were held. On 13 April he reached Dublin, after the most remarkable and successful progress made by any Elizabethan Irish viceroy.[1]

The journey has been but sketched in outline. It must be added that Sidney's talents as soldier and strength of mind as a governor were equalled by his administrative abilities and capacity for quick and sound decisions. These qualities had been exhibited at every stage. In summing up, he put first among the dangers the weakness of the Protestant Church. He thought that Ireland would never remain peaceful without an English army, but did not consider that this need be large. He told the Privy Council sharply enough that he was not being fairly supported because no new President had arrived in Munster since Perrott's departure and the office had been allowed to lapse in Connaught since Fitton had been driven out, though now the province was tranquil. An experienced soldier, Sir William Drury, became President of Munster in the summer of 1576. None was appointed in Connaught, but a tough and formidable man, Colonel Nicholas Malby, became military governor.

Ireland had seldom been more peaceful then when Sidney returned to Dublin. There was a minor anti-climax when, some two months later, the wretched young Burkes symbolically divested themselves of their English clothes, crossed the Shannon in breach of their oaths, and smashed restored buildings in Athenry. It was maddening for Sidney, because they had been freed on parole by his kindness of heart, as the Irish annalists remark. It is clear also that they feel no sympathy for these 'beggarly bastard boys', as the Lord Deputy called them. He went at once to Connaught, where he seized Clanrickarde's castles. That done, he found time to hurry off to Limerick to install Drury as President of Munster, but by September this indefatigable man was back in Connaught, bringing with him Malby, the new Governor, and a force of Butler gallowglasses under Edward Butler. This time he was accompanied by his celebrated son, Philip, who was paying him a brief visit, but was soon recalled to Dublin by the fatal illness of his dear friend, the Earl of Essex. Sidney could not catch the Burkes, but he chased

[1] *Sidney Papers*, Vol. I, pp. 81–109.

their Scottish followers over the border into Ulster. 'The wilds, the recesses, the rugged and rough-topped mountains, the hilly and intricate woods of their native territory, were the only parts of it possessed by the sons of the Earl at this time.' In other words, they were on the run, and there was no real revolt.[1] The unfortunate peasantry, the 'churls', suffered bitterly through the English system of leniency to the sons of great men, and the English failed to gain the support of the churls because these expected the aristocratic criminals to be reprieved and restored, with opportunity to take vengeance.

In Munster Desmond's conduct was disquieting, and once he disappeared into the fastnesses of Kerry and raised a little army, but nothing came of this and he promised to dismiss his men. Rory Oge O'Moore, again in revolt, was, after some successes and many burnings, routed and slain by Barnaby Fitzpatrick, Baron of Upper Ossory, in 1578. He had been 'the head of the plunderers and insurgents of the men of Ireland in his time; and for a long time after his death', say the annalists, 'no one was desirous to discharge one shot against the Crown'. Connaught was reduced to awe by the terrible punishment inflicted upon followers and tenantry of the young Burkes by Nicholas Malby. He was savage in his wrath, but at the same time an Englishman whom Irish soldiers would follow through any trials, against any odds, and against their own cousins, 'a man learned in the languages and tongues of the islands of the west of Europe, a brave and victorious man in battles throughout Ireland, Scotland, and France in the service of his Sovereign'.[2]

If his methods were often hard and those of his subordinates, Malby, Drury, and others, harsher still, Sidney had been a great success and his second viceroyalty had been a brilliant one. But he was costing a lot of money at a time when the Queen was being hard pressed to aid the Dutch and had already promised them a considerable loan on certain conditions.[3] Sidney had also rubbed relatively loyal nobility and gentry of the Pale the wrong way by his treatment of the question of quartering troops on the country. Whether it was the penury of the Queen, or the influence of Ormonde—who considered him to be at once too severe and pro-Geraldine—or the matter of the cess in the Pale, it is not easy to

[1] Four Masters, Vol. V, p. 1,689. *C.S.P. Ireland*, Vol. LVI, 26. Bagwell, *Ireland under the Tudors*, Vol. II, p. 323.
[2] Four Masters, Vol. V., pp. 1,707, 1,845.
[3] Read, *Mr. Secretary Walsingham*, Vol. I, p. 341.

determine. The historian Birch believed that his recall was due to the third factor and to the offence which he gave to the magnates of the Pale. If so, as often happened, there were two sides to the question. These men were hard landlords, who kept idle bravos to do their bidding and allowed them to make their living out of the peasantry, and the peasantry suffered more at the hands of the retainers than at those of the relatively few troops quartered in the Pale. The newly arrived Lord Chancellor, William Gerard, successor to the worthy Weston, was no friend of Sidney's, but he put the case thus in a letter to the Privy Council: 'These gentlemen who now complain should take some taste of the pain which the poor perforce abideth. For, Mr. Secretary, say what they list, I find it by their own confession the gentlemen never lived so civilly and able in diet, clothing, and household as at this day; marry, the poor churl never so beggarly.'[1]

At all events, Sidney was recalled at the height of his power and success. He left Ireland in September 1578, having appointed Sir William Drury to act as Lord Justice. He took the luckless Clan-rickarde with him.

It is not pretended that Sidney fully understood the Irish problem, even from the English point of view, still less that his methods would have solved it over a long period of time. Yet none had achieved greater temporary success. There was no period during the reign of Elizabeth when English rule was accorded so broad an acceptance. And every act, every movement, every letter of the man is stamped with grandeur. Noble-minded, gracious, honour-able, brave, and energetic, he is not only one of the great figures of the great Elizabethan age, but at the same time one of the most attractive. His second viceroyalty was far more felicitous than his first, and he was expanding in wisdom and in mental stature. It is idle to predict what would have happened had he been left in office. It may be that he would have been able to prevent Desmond from entering into his terrible rebellion, since Desmond was a weakling and was dragged in by stronger men when there was no one in Ireland as capable of restraining him as Sidney would have been. That, however, is but speculation. What is certain is that one of the ablest representatives of England in all the time of the rule of the English Crown was leaving Ireland at the moment when that country stood upon the brink of calamity.

[1] Birch, *Memoirs of the Reign of Queen Elizabeth*, Vol. I, p. 9. *Carew Cal.*, Vol. II, p. 72. For details of the cess, see p. 64.

CHAPTER IX

THE DESMOND REBELLION: FIRST PHASE

IRISH wars and disturbances were brought about by the ambitions of Irish or Anglo-Irish magnates, by their dislike of rival magnates or of the royal officers, by nationalist sentiment, by religious sentiment, or it might be by a combination of these influences. The strongest factor was religious sentiment, encouraged by the agents of the Papacy and sometimes working up from the masses until it impelled half-reluctant lords to action. In the period up to the second viceroyalty of Sidney the most notable of these agents was Father David Wolf, S.J., who even during a confinement of several years in Dublin Castle exercised great influence all over the country. Finally, he escaped to Spain, probably liberated by sympathizers within the walls who had previously carried his messages.

Irish intrigues on the Continent were nothing new, but the first Irish layman to play with skill on the politico-religious strings was James Fitzmaurice. In 1569 he sent to Spain an ecclesiastic of ability, like himself a Geraldine, Maurice Reagh Fitzgibbon, titular Archbishop of Cashel. Fitzgibbon made fervent appeals to Philip II and to the Pope, declaring that the Irish would accept as king any prince of His Catholic Majesty's blood who might be appointed. At that time His Catholic Majesty showed no great enthusiasm in the matter. He was engaged in delicate negotiations about the seizure by the English of Spanish ships carrying valuable cargoes and money to the Netherlands, which lasted several years, and he decided to keep the Archbishop waiting without a definite answer while he observed how Queen Elizabeth behaved.[1]

The delay brought down upon the head of the Archbishop the anger of Fitzmaurice, then still in revolt in Ireland. On 4 May 1570 he and his council or 'parliament' addressed to Fitzgibbon a letter full of bitter reproaches for his alleged weakness. They said that unless King Philip afforded them speedy aid they would be forced to make peace with the English—as Fitzmaurice in fact did in 1573. They stated that in their company were 'two of the leaders of those who rose in revolt against the Queen in England', and that these

[1] *C.S.P. Spanish*, Vol. II, p. 210.

men had made them various proposals on which they were suspending judgement until they knew the King's intentions about Ireland. This revolt was, of course, the rising of Northumberland and Westmorland, which had broken out in 1569 and was put down by the former Lord Lieutenant of Ireland, the Earl of Sussex. A number of the chief rebels had fled across the border into Scotland; but this statement, unlikely to have been invented, that two of them had reached Ireland, is of great interest.

Equally so is an assertion that some members of the English Privy Council, who favoured the Irish rebels in secret, had told them that the Queen was considering how she might come to terms with the King of Spain. Whether or not the message really came from members of the English Privy Council—and it is much more likely that the Irish is meant—the information was true. The Irishmen bade the Archbishop warn the King that Elizabeth's object was the ruin of all Catholics whom she could reach. They instructed him to invite Philip to send his brother, Don John of Austria, to be their king; if he would, they would engage themselves to become Philip's faithful vassals. They expressed confidence that as soon as Don John set foot in the country he would win the allegiance of all Ireland and that 'other foreign provinces' would afterwards be subjected to his rule. It was the lack of a king, they remarked with some point, that weakened and divided them and allowed the English to set brother against brother. They candidly admitted that, unless they received outside aid, they could not maintain control over their own people, who would join the English and fight as their allies. Again they spoke the truth. They used terms of astonishing force, seeing that they were addressing an archbishop, telling Fitzgibbon that if he were remiss in carrying out the duties of his mission the divine wrath would descend upon him.[1]

During the same year there arrived in Spain from Ireland a clever, flashy, and disreputable adventurer, an Englishman and a Catholic, with piracy in his past. Thomas Stukely was for a time

[1] The importance and interest of this hitherto unpublished document found at Simancas (L.8336, folio 27) are so great, in view of the statement that fugitives from Northumberland's rebellion were in Ireland, of the allegation that members of the Privy Council had dealings with the Irish rebels, and of the invitation to Don John to become King of Ireland, that it is printed in full at the end of this chapter. It is here translated from archaic Castilian into which it had been translated from the original Latin by a Spanish secretary. No signatures are appended to the Castilian copy, but it can be accepted that the letter came from Fitzmaurice and his associates. It was despatched from Tralee.

in favour with the Spaniards, more so than Fitzgibbon, who disliked and distrusted him. Stukely was, indeed, not an ornament to a national or religious cause. At the beginning of 1572 the disappointed Fitzgibbon appeared in Paris and had the nerve to call on Walsingham, then negotiating, as English Ambassador, for a marriage between the Queen and the Duke of Alençon. He told Walsingham that he had put a spoke in Stukely's wheel in Spain and had now come to France in the hope of being allowed to return. Walsingham did not quite know what to make of him, but there seems no doubt that he was intriguing for aid from the faction of the Guises in an invasion of Ireland.[1]

Stukely lived for a while in luxury at the cost of the Spaniards. He caused a certain anxiety in England, since it was from time to time reported that the King would put at his disposal a powerful force to be sent to Ireland. Outliving his welcome, he went off to the wars in 1571 and is said to have fought at Lepanto. He certainly afterwards attracted the attention of Don John of Austria.[2]

It was the Pope rather than the Catholic King who in the end provided such aid as was forthcoming. After two years in France, from which no help was to be had, James Fitzmaurice went to Rome, where he received a warm welcome. Stukely, who had outlived his welcome in Spain, turned up too, looking for resources to invade Ireland. To do him justice, he was always all for fighting. According to the story told—it is true, over a generation later—by an Irish writer in touch with clerical circles, a force of about 1,000 men was raised by a curious expedient. Bands of robbers and highwaymen skulking in the Apennines were induced to enlist in return for pardon. And since worldly pardon was deemed insufficient, as well it might be, they were accorded also spiritual indulgences, to be gained by contemplation of crucifixes with which Stukely was supplied. He also obtained a number of professional officers for his bravos, and ships to carry his force. He reached Cadiz in the spring of 1578, where he issued some magnificent passports to Irishmen returning home, describing himself as 'Marquess of Leinster [a title bestowed on him by the Pope] and General of our Most Holy Father Gregory XIII, Pontifico Maximo'.[3] He next sailed to Lisbon, and there the odd adventure took a still odder turn. Sebastian, King

[1] Digges, *The Compleat Ambassador*, pp. 36, 60, 74.

[2] Mathew, *The Celtic Peoples and Renaissance Europe*, pp. 139–41.

[3] *Sidney Papers*, Vol. I, p. 263. Mathew, *The Celtic Peoples and Renaissance Europe*, p. 145.

of Portugal, was fitting out an expedition against the Moors. Stukely suggested that he should accompany him to Ireland, but instead he induced, or it may be compelled, Stukely to sail with him to Morocco. In the battle of the Alcazar the King and nearly everyone else were killed. It is said that Stukely died bravely, and this is credible. He was all for fighting.[1]

Fitzmaurice did not sail with Stukely. He was not, however, deterred from going to Ireland by the fact that the main force had deserted him, though he had once put forward an appreciation that 6,000 men with vast quantities of arms were required even for the first landing. Perhaps he had been driven desperate by the coldness of the Continental Catholics. Sir William Drury, the Lord Justice, was not a little perturbed when he learnt that invasion might be expected, since the Queen's ships on the Irish station were under repair; he was destitute of money, victuals, and munitions; and Tirlagh Luineach O'Neill was in one of his more dangerous moods and had refused to visit Drury when he went to Newry. The Lord Justice hired a ship to look for Fitzmaurice, but it did not find him. He sailed into Dingle Bay on 17 July 1579.[2]

The venture appeared on the face of it to be crazy, and yet it fulfilled its purpose in lighting the spark of rebellion, though this was largely accidental. The total number of men brought ashore by Fitzmaurice at Smerwick is variously given, but seems to have been less than 100, Spaniards, French, Irish, and English. Few Irish recruits joined him. He began the construction of a fort, perhaps to protect the arms he had brought until he could distribute them. The most notable member of his expedition was the Jesuit Dr. Nicholas Sanders, an Englishman notorious for a bitter attack upon the Queen and now employed to issue proclamations and write letters to possible adherents. Two printed proclamations, in English and Latin, stated that the Pope had deprived Elizabeth of her unjust possession of her kingdoms and had appointed Fitzmaurice his captain. He was not fighting against a lawful sceptre, but 'against a tyrant which refuseth to hear Christ speaking by his Vicar'.[3]

There were at the time only 1,211 royal troops in the country.

[1] *History of Catholic Ireland*, p. 20. Bagwell, *Ireland under the Tudors*, Vol. III.

[2] *C.S.P. Ireland*, Vol. LXV, 36; Vol. LXVI, 2, 12; Vol. LXVII, 40.

[3] *Carew Cal.*, Vol. II, p. 409 (wrongly entered under the year 1569, before Fitzmaurice's flight from Ireland). *C.S.P. Ireland*, Vol. LXVII, 40 (ii). *History of Catholic Ireland*, p. 20.

Orders were at once issued to embark a reinforcement of 600 men at Barnstaple, but for the time being, on reports of Fitzmaurice's weakness and that he had at most 300 men with him, preparations in England were stopped. The Lord Chancellor and Council ordered the mustering of all able-bodied men in the Pale and directed that all leaders of blind folk, harpers, bards, rhymers, and loose and idle people with no master should be executed by martial law. It sounds a curious method of providing against revolt, but those who inspired it knew their Ireland. These wanderers on the road were the regular agents and firebrands of rebellion, and there was on the statute book an act authorizing proceedings against them. Help was available from Connaught; for the able and confident Sir Nicholas Malby considered his province so safe that he turned his back upon it and led 600 English and Irish troops down to Cork.[1]

Desmond at first appeared likely to remain loyal and attack Fitzmaurice, for whom he had no love; and if he had done so there would have been little need to remember the other's landing. Drury despatched to Desmond Sir Henry Davells, who, after reconnoitring the fort, begged him to put at his disposal a company of his gallow-glasses and sixty musketeers. With this force he was confident of taking the place, with the aid of an English privateer in the harbour commanded by Captain Thomas Courtenay, which had just cut out and captured such of the Spanish ships as had not sailed for Spain. Desmond replied that his troops were not good enough. He always found it difficult to make up his mind and was now wavering on the brink of revolt. That night Davells and Arthur Carter, Provost Marshal of Munster, were murdered in their beds at an inn by John of Desmond in person, by agreement with James Fitzmaurice and probably with the object of committing Desmond.[2]

The force in the fort now broke up. Fitzmaurice himself made for Connaught, with only a small bodyguard, possibly meaning to go through to Ulster, where Tirlagh Luineach O'Neill had thousands of men under arms and was taking a truculent tone with the Government. Passing across the lands of a sept of the Burkes, Fitzmaurice commandeered some horses from the plough. This roused the countryside against him; a body of gallowglasses overtook him; and in the combat that followed he was shot dead. For the nationalist cause the loss was heavy, since the finger of James Fitzmaurice was

---

[1] *C.S.P. Ireland*, Vol. LXVII, 71; Vol. LXVIII, 8, 13, 23, 45. *Cal. Patent Rolls, Philip and Mary*, Vol. IV, p. 76.

[2] Hooker (in Holinshed), Vol. VI, p. 410. Four Masters, Vol. V, p. 1,715.

worth the arms of the other Geraldine chiefs of his time. Though
John of Desmond announced that he would continue the struggle,
it looked as though all might be nearly over.[1]

Drury now arrived in Cork with some 500 men. He afterwards
moved to Kilmallock, where he was visited by Desmond. It was
still doubtful what the Earl would do, and Drury was clearly at a
loss how to deal with him. He was actually arrested, but almost
immediately released, and accompanied the Lord Justice on an
expedition. At Springfield the English suffered a reverse, which they
laid to the account of Malby's Connaught kerne. The Connaughtmen took to their heels, but it would be hard to say whether this
was through cowardice or dislike of opposing the Geraldines.
Another blow followed. The tried and trusted Drury, who had long
been ailing, had to leave the field and retire to Waterford. On the
way, Lady Desmond—a Butler by birth like the Earl's first wife—
came to him and handed over her only son. But Drury died shortly
after reaching Waterford.[2]

Time after time delays occurred in the despatch of a new viceroy
after the recall of his predecessor. These were due on occasion to
discussion of monetary terms and sometimes to the raising of fresh
forces, so that the new man should make a fair start; but it is to be
feared that they were more than once the Queen's own fault. She
had many great qualities, but speed in making up her mind was not
one of them. Now there was no Lord Deputy, and his substitute
had been removed by death. Another stopgap, and a pretty good
one, was found in Sir William Pelham, who had recently arrived in
Dublin as an expert in fortification, to improve the defences of the
Pale. Ormonde, who had spent three years in England, had now
returned and had been appointed the Queen's General in Munster.
Before, however, either of them reached the scene, Malby, who took
over the Munster command temporarily, gained a welcome success
at Monasternenagh, in Limerick, on 3 October 1579. Reinforcements from England had raised his strength to about 1,000 men, but
he estimated the force under John of Desmond to be twice as strong,
and more than half of them were well-appointed MacSheehy
gallowglasses. It was a tough struggle. Sir William Stanley, later to
become one of the most notable of Elizabethan traitors, but then
in good odour as a determined soldier, despite known sympathies
with the old faith, told Walsingham that the rebels behaved as

[1] Four Masters, Vol. V, p. 1,717.
[2] *C.S.P. Ireland*, Vol. LXIX, 17. Hooker (in Holinshed), Vol. VI, p. 414.

3 THE DEFEAT OF THE IRISH

Irish saddles without stirrups, and breeching instead of cruppers; snaffle bridles. The Irish bagpiper lies dead, his pipes beside him. The Irish horsemen use their spears back-handed (*The Image of Ireland*).

resolutely as the best soldiers in Europe. They first advanced, displaying 'the Pope's banner', but then drew up behind a ditch to await Malby's onslaught. They stood two assaults, but in the third the English set upon them so fiercely that they broke, whereupon Sir John of Desmond put spurs to his horse and fled. Pressed Devon and Cornwall ploughmen showed themselves superior to the professional gallowglasses, as generally happened when the fight was in the open, partly because the former were rather the better armed. Stanley stated that Desmond had aided his brother with troops, though not himself present during the fighting.[1]

Still, he had not finally committed himself. He argued that he had served against James Fitzmaurice and his own brethren, whereas Malby had wantonly attacked his men. He took credit for the handing over of his son, though this seems to have been done by his Countess without his knowledge. He had an interview with Ormonde, who urged him to make his submission. The terms were that he should come in to the Lord Justice, surrender one of his castles, Askeaton or Carrigafoyle, hand over Dr. Sanders, and carry on the war against his brothers John and James. Ormonde disliked Desmond, but now as ever strove for pacification rather than war, so much so as to incur English suspicions that his heart was not in the business. It was never in the business of war against his countrymen, and especially against noblemen—for there he shared the preconceptions of the English—while a chance of peace on reasonable terms remained. Yet his terrible dealings with the Desmond country were to show that he did not hesitate when that chance disappeared, whatever his English critics might say of him. For a time Desmond's attitude was so uncertain that the Spanish Ambassador, who naturally hoped for trouble, informed Philip II that he had gone over again to the side of the Queen.[2]

Desmond was given one last chance, to come in to the Lord Justice by 8 a.m. on 2 November, when he would be permitted to go to England and state his case. He did not come and was on that same day proclaimed a traitor. He was accused of practising with foreign powers to invade the country by the agency of Fitzmaurice, of conniving in the murder of Davells and Carter, of letting Fitzmaurice escape from the fort at Smerwick, of handing over some guns from Dingle to the rebels, and of sending his gallowglasses to fight under his brothers. It was announced that any of his adherents

---

[1] *C.S.P. Ireland*, Vol. LXIX, 53. Hooker (in Holinshed), Vol. VI, p. 416.
[2] *C.S.P. Ireland*, Vol. LXX, 4 and 8. *C.S.P. Spanish*, Vol. II, p. 606.

who presented themselves to Pelham or Ormonde would be received as liege subjects.[1]

It was not unusual for Irish notables who had been proclaimed traitors to be received to mercy on easy terms, and this might have occurred on the case of Desmond. He now committed an act which made such a prospect remote. He approached the walled town of Youghal, opened negotiations with it for the delivery of some wine, on 15 November seized it by a *coup de main*, killed all those who had resisted his entry, then sacked and burnt the place. The mayor and corporation were criminally negligent, if not worse, and some of the citizens set up ladders against the walls to assist the rebels. Much plunder was taken, so that 'many a poor, indigent person became rich and affluent by the spoils of this town'.[2]

Ormonde had at his disposal a force of the nominal strength of 950 men, much smaller when the sick were deducted, but a reinforcement of 300 was on its way to him. He took the field early in December. He had no cannon to batter Desmond's major castles, such as Askeaton, and Pelham, who had returned to Dublin, could send him none. But he swept into Connello, in Limerick, whence Desmond drew supplies and in which he had quartered his troops. He burnt the villages and carried off the herds. Then he made for Cork, capturing 1,400 cattle and driving them into the city. In an expedition of twenty days, he had supplies of bread for only five, waded across seven swollen rivers or streams in the course of a single day, and slept without shelter. 'It is easier to talk at home of Irish wars than to be in them', said the newly arrived Sir Henry Wallop. Leaving some of his troops to rest after their exertions, Ormonde then marched to Youghal. On the way he laid hands upon the mayor, tried him for treachery, and hanged him in front of his door. He found the place deserted and the walls thrown down. It is said that the only living being within the town was a friar, whom he spared because he had given Christian burial to Davells.[3]

Ormonde now left a garrison of 300 men in the ruins of Youghal, with orders to draw in the people from round about and repair the town. Before leaving Limerick, he had left a garrison in Adare, from which a raiding party ran into trouble and got back only with difficulty. Desmond tried to lure the troops out again by leaving a herd of cattle within sight of the walls, and when that failed, 'sent

[1] *Carew Cal.*, Vol. II, p. 162.

[2] *C.S.P. Ireland*, Vol. LXX, 32 (ii), 64. Four Masters, Vol. V, p. 1,723.

[3] *C.S.P. Ireland*, Vol. LXX, 64, 70. Hooker (in Holinshed), Vol. VI, p. 425.

a fair young harlot as a present to the constable, by whose means he hoped to get the house; but the constable, learning from whence she came, threw her (as it is reported to me) with a stone about her neck into the river (Maigue).'[1]

The Queen had shown displeasure with Pelham about the proclamation of Desmond as a traitor, not from any sympathy with him or sentiment that the Lord Justice had acted unfairly, but because she knew all too well that the campaign would cost a lot of money. Desmond was always expensive, and even when he visited London in disgrace had contrived to borrow from her. She insisted upon the disbandment of some 400 troops. Pelham was deeply hurt by her treatment, but was consoled by Burghley, who told him not to be discouraged and that there were those about the court who would stand by him; the Queen was now realizing, he said, that economy would not pay in the long run, and victuals for 2,000 men for three months had been ordered. The Lord Justice himself reached Waterford on 24 January 1580 and, with his eyes on Askeaton, made arrangements to have a ship with cannon and munitions sent round into the Shannon.[2]

The levying of reinforcements in England can be summed up as order, counter-order, disorder. On receipt of news of the landing of James Fitzmaurice in July 1579, preparations had been set afoot on a big scale. The Lord President of Wales (Sir Henry Sidney, former Lord Deputy of Ireland) was directed to raise 1,000 men; Dorset, Somerset, Devonshire, and Cornwall were to muster 1,000 more; the President of the Council of the North was instructed to raise 200 light horse; and a force of 300 trained troops from the garrison of Berwick was also to be sent. Sir John Perrott, with a commission as Admiral of the Queen's Ships, was ordered to cruise off the west coast of Ireland, convoying on his passage there a ship loaded with munitions, which was to make for Waterford or Cork. His fleet was to consist of the *Revenge, Dreadnought, Swiftsure, Foresight,* and *Achates.* When, however, word reached London of the death of Fitzmaurice the preparations were partly cancelled. The northern horsemen were held up. Next orders were sent to Bristol and Chester to send the Welshmen home except for 100 men. Then it was decreed that the horse should go after all, because the bulk of the cavalry in the country was Irish and inferior in

---

[1] *Carew Cal.*, Vol. II, p. 205. Hooker (in Holinshed), Vol. VI, p. 426.
[2] *C.S.P. Ireland*, Vol. LXX, 72; Vol. LXXI, 21. *Carew Cal.*, Vol. II, pp. 186, 188, 204.

quality to the northerners. Meanwhile, however, 600 men had sailed from Bristol before the cancellation was received. As will appear, the outbreak of Desmond made a fresh levy necessary, but the rebellion might have been nipped in the bud if adequate forces had been sent in good time.[1] This was hardly to be expected of Queen Elizabeth.

In the middle of February 1580 Pelham marched out from Waterford on his way to Limerick. Owing to the impossibility of moving carriages in the winter, he took no tents and carried such supplies as were necessary on the backs of porters. The total forces under his orders and those of Ormonde in Munster at this time were 2,828; but, though the number which they led into the field is not exactly recorded, it may be assumed that it did not exceed half this figure. The rest were required in garrisons of towns and castles, and in any case supply was a matter of extreme difficulty. Pelham told the Privy Council that, whereas it had been alleged that the soldier stationed at Berwick lived a harder life than the man stationed in Ireland, 'if I have any judgment, all the soldiers of Christendom must give place in that to the soldier of Ireland'. There was, he said, as wide a gap between the comfort of the Irish and the Berwick soldier as between that of the Berwick soldier and of an alderman of London.[2]

He found little in the way of victuals at Limerick, all the country having been burnt, though some food was expected by sea. Having billeted his troops, he ordered each householder to provide ten days' bread for his lodger. At Limerick he waited for Malby, who was to bring a company from Connaught, and for the new Treasurer at Wars, Sir Henry Wallop, who arrived from Dublin on 7 March 1580, with £4,000. Then, hearing that Ormonde had left Cork, he moved out and met him at Rathkeale, sixteen miles to the south-west, on the 10th. Separating slightly, but moving parallel, they marched westward, burning anything that would take fire and killing all whom they met. Some food having arrived at Glin, on the lower Shannon, and word having come in that ships with more and with cannon, powder, and lead were lying at Dingle, they crossed the mountains into Kerry. Tralee was found burnt out, but they garrisoned the abbey. Then they marched on to Dingle, but learnt that the ships had left for the Shannon. Overwhelmed by a snowstorm, they struggled back to Tralee. The wet had now made the mountains impassable, so that they could not return by the way they had come. Instead, they crossed the swollen Feale, in which some men and horses were drowned, and arrived back on the Shannon, where the ships now awaited them. It had been one of the most remarkable winter marches of the Irish wars, and though Desmond had not been seen, some notables had surrendered. As to the methods employed, the evidence of the Four Masters is as follows: 'It was not wonderful that they should kill men fit for action, but they killed blind and feeble men, women, boys, and girls, sick persons, idiots, and old people. They carried their cattle and other property away to the Lord Justice's camp.'[1]

Having got his ships and the guns in them, Pelham could deal with Desmond's strong castles on the Shannon, a business which he thoroughly understood. He started with Carrigafoyle, held by sixteen Spaniards who had come with James Fitzmaurice and fifty Irish, commanded by an Italian. After two days' battering with guns skilfully placed so that the ruined walls should fall into the moat, the place was stormed, and all not killed on the spot were afterwards hanged. Askeaton was to come next, but its garrison and that of Balliloghan fled for fear of the fate which had overtaken the defenders of Carrigafoyle. It was a shrewd blow for Desmond, whose revolt seemed to be on its last legs. He still had 600 men with him, and in mid-April fought a stiff combat with an English force of about half that strength which made a sortie from Adare. This time it came to push of pike, which was becoming rarer now that the musketeers so often decided the issue. The Irish were forced to retreat, but without heavy loss.[2]

In June Pelham and Ormonde entered the miserable county of Kerry once again. Pelham surprised Desmond, nearly caught him and Dr. Sanders, and took 2,000 of this cattle. He then made for Dingle, while Ormonde passed through Killarney, an Englishman with his force lamenting that so lovely a land should have to be despoiled. At Dingle the Lord Justice found the English squadron under Admiral Sir William Winter. Ormonde marched through Iveragh and reached Valentia Island, his path marked by great fires which could be seen from Pelham's camp fifteen miles away across the waters of Dingle Bay. After a visit to Cork, the Lord Justice

[1] *C.S.P. Ireland*, Vol. LXXII, 12. *Carew Cal.*, Vol, II, pp. 225, 236. Four Masters, Vol. V, p. 1,733.
[2] *Carew Cal.*, Vol. II, pp. 243, 248.

withdrew to Limerick, where he gave his exhausted troops some rest.[1]

Pelham's strategy had been, first, to clear the rebels out of Limerick and keep them in poor and mountainous Kerry; secondly, to blockade the Kerry coast so that they should not be revictualled by O'Flaherties, O'Malleys, or other Connaught shipowners; thirdly, to devastate the country so that they should find no provisions in it; and, finally, to drive Desmond into a corner and finish with him. The last aim had not yet been reached, but Desmond was in sore trouble and the countrymen were cursing him for the horrors he had brought upon them. The unfortunate man answered their reproaches by saying that if foreign aid did not come soon he would go abroad. Now, however, a series of events were to occur which gave the rebellion a new lease. Malby was keeping Connaught quiet with a handful of men. Ulster looked threatening, since 1,500 Scots had recently landed and Tirlagh Luineach O'Neill was making arrogant speeches when well warmed with whiskey, but the Ulsterman stayed in his own province. It was in the Pale itself that the next diversion was to take place, and the chief actor was a young Anglo-Irish peer.

James Eustace, third Viscount Baltinglas, had recently visited Rome, had returned burning with zeal for the old Church, and was led into revolt by religious motives. Ormonde strove to restrain him, but without avail. By himself he was not very formidable, but it was another matter when his near neighbours, the O'Byrnes of Wicklow, under Feagh MacHugh, a master of partisan warfare, allied themselves with him. And in August, just about the time when Baltinglas entered into open rebellion, the new Lord Deputy arrived and a less prudent and experienced hand than that of Pelham went to the stiff Irish helm. Arthur, Lord Grey de Wilton, arriving in Dublin on the 12th, could nevertheless not take the oath because Pelham had the sword with him in Munster, and did not do so for the better part of a month, in the course of which he suffered a serious setback. Apart from that, it was a tragedy, not least from the point of view of the Geraldines themselves, that the change should have come at such a moment, since the horrors that followed might have been avoided had Pelham been able to pursue his policy only a little longer. Among his last acts was the detention of a number of Munster lords at Limerick and the quartering of gallowglasses on their lands. Desmond was in despair and talking of surrender; in

[1] *C.S.P. Ireland*, Vol. LXXIV, 56.

fact, Lady Desmond came to seek terms from Pelham in August. John of Desmond, after some private negotiations on his own behalf, decided to fight it out. With Dr. Sanders and a little party of horse, he escaped through a hole in the English net and joined Baltinglas on the Wicklow border. His brother James, raiding Muskerry from Kerry, was attacked by the Irish Sheriff of Cork, Sir Cormac MacCarthy—who himself had only recently made submission to Pelham—with 150 English soldiers, was wounded, and captured. He was later hanged, drawn, and quartered.[1]

Desmond actually approached Sir William Winter and demanded a passage to England. It was probably the report about the change in government which prevented his surrender. A new viceroy sometimes brought a new policy, and he may well have hoped to get better terms from Grey than from Pelham. So the unfortunate rebel made off once more into the woods and glens of Kerry, followed by a hundred or two gallowglasses, and the opportunity of ending the tragedy was missed. The Privy Council hoped that Pelham would stay and put his military skill at the disposal of the new Lord Deputy, but he was sick and perhaps unwilling to serve under Grey. He therefore returned to England. So passed from the Irish scene, after a brief appearance upon it, a man who might have scotched the Desmond rebellion. The annalists say of him, to the anger of their modern translator, that, in proportion to the length of his stay, no Englishman had been more successful or 'more nobly triumphant'.[2]

Lord Grey showed great energy in Ireland, if it was not always well directed. His viceroyalty acquires a particular interest from the fact that among his followers were Edmund Spenser, who came over as his secretary, and Walter Raleigh, one of the captains of the companies raised for his service.

It has already been recorded that when James Fitzmaurice raised the standard of revolt large musters of reinforcements for Ireland had been ordered, but that these had been in great part cancelled. Considerable reinforcements had, however, reached the country, so that Pelham left behind him over 3,000 troops in Munster. In June 1580 the Lord President of Wales was directed to levy 800 men, those from the northern part of the principality embarking at Chester, those from the southern at Bristol. In early July London

[1] *Carew Cal.*, Vol. II, pp. 292–3. *C.S.P. Ireland*, Vol. LXXV, 40; Vol. LXXVI, 19.
[2] Four Masters, Vol. V, p. 1,737.

was directed to send 300 men to the Isle of Wight, to save 'pestering' the shipping by making part of the journey to Ireland overland. On 16 July a great levy was called for to accompany the new Lord Deputy, 2,100 strong. In September came a second levy from London of 500, and, to anticipate a little, in March 1581 another levy of 1,000 men.[1] The Desmond rebellion proved expensive enough, but the Queen could never realize that delay involved heavier calls in the long run.

Although he had not received the sword in August, Grey judged it necessary to move at once against Baltinglas and the O'Byrnes, impelled in part by his fury that rebels should assemble within twenty-five miles of Dublin, in part because he distrusted Kildare, to whom the southern defence of the Pale had been confided. What force he took with him is not revealed, but it consisted chiefly of newly arrived recruits. Moreover, this fact was well known to the rebels, since one of Kildare's captains, Gerald Fitzmaurice, had gone over to them and taken his company with him. On the approach of Grey, they withdrew from the open ground into the gorge of Glenmalure. It was as ugly a place as could be well imagined, very deep, underfoot 'boggy and soft, and full of great stones and slippery rocks, very hard and evil to pass through; the sides are full of great and mighty trees upon the sides of the hills and full of bushments and underwoods'.[2]

Grey light-heartedly thought he would use his infantry as spaniels to flush the hares inside for his cavalry to ride down, but what the infantry encountered resembled wild cats rather than hares. The seventy-year-old Cosby, General of the Queen's Kerne, who had come to Ireland to serve her sister Mary and knew something about the Wicklow glens and their O'Byrne inhabitants, warned his insensate superior of the danger, and then, when his words were disregarded, went in quietly to his death. The commander of the detachment was a veteran from Berwick, Colonel George Moore, a 'corpulent man', whose weight proved his undoing. He too was slain, as was Peter Carew. His brother George, destined for so much fame, was kept out by his uncle, Jacques Wingfield, and remained with Grey and Kildare. Sir William Stanley, commanding the rear guard, covered the retreat which amounted to a flight, and Grey himself, pushing forward his cavalry, checked the pursuit and forced the rebels back into the glen. It was reported that not more than

---

[1] Details of these levies are given on p. 61.
[2] Hooker (in Holinshed), Vol. VI, p. 435.

thirty Englishmen were slain—though Elizabethan soldiers tended to minimize casualties, and no one bothered to count the heavier losses of the Irish kerne—but the moral effects were unfortunate. It was by incurring such accidents that a rash commander might undo years of toil and care by the sleepless experts of Irish warfare.[1]

Malby, who was on a visit from Connaught to Leinster and saw the affair, declared that the clothing of the new companies in red or blue coats was a grave mistake, but it is doubtful whether his objection to them was mainly because they served as good targets, as a modern historian would lead us to suppose. It was rather because they distinguished the recruits from the old soldiers and led the rebels to concentrate upon them. Like others before and after him, he considered that the coat-money might best be expended in purchasing in Ireland jerkins and hose of frieze, with mantles in which the soldiers might sleep.[2]

As was to be expected, though no universal conflagration occurred, flames of revolt began to lick the countryside in various districts as news of the reverse spread. In Ulster Tirlagh Luineach O'Neill broke off negotiations in progress, and invaded and despoiled the lands of Hugh Magennis in South Down. He proclaimed that he was henceforth supreme in Ulster as Shane had been, that the other chiefs must acknowledge themselves to be his vassals. The Baron of Dungannon, still a pillar of loyalty in the north, was deserted by his kinsmen, who drove his creaghts over to Tirlagh, and he himself had to take to the woods. In Connaught Brian O'Rourke rose again in arms. In Leinster John of Desmond and the O'Byrnes, issuing from the glens of Wicklow, besieged Maryborough. Only in Munster were matters still relatively favourable. There Colonel Sir George Bourchier, left in command of the troops under the general orders of Ormonde, had the situation in hand. Yet it was from Munster that the next serious threat was to come.[3]

The safety of Ireland from invasion depended upon command of the sea. The conquest of the island, if the invaders were strong enough and adequately supported by Irish rebels, was just possible even in face of English sea power, because a considerable fleet might get through, as was to be proved at Kinsale in 1601; but it was

---

[1] C.S.P. Ireland, Vol. LXXV, 83. Camden, Queen Elizabeth, p. 241. Four Masters, Vol. V, p. 1,737.

[2] Bagwell, Ireland under the Tudors, Vol. III, p. 62.

[3] C.S.P. Ireland, Vol. LXXV, 74, 75, 77; Vol. LXXVI, 6, 15, 32.

improbable unless the invasion could be fed and supported by what modern military slang calls a 'follow-up', by reinforcements and supplies. If the English fleet were well placed this was not likely to be the case, even if the first expeditionary force eluded it and got ashore. In 1580, however, the naval commander, Sir William Winter, left his post without orders, to refit in England. He had been trying to get away for some time, on the plea of shortage of provisions, and had been restrained only by positive orders to remain and by the stern warning of Pelham that an invasion was expected. Directly Pelham's eye was off him he sailed, and immediately afterwards, on 12 September, a foreign fleet appeared in the harbour of Smerwick. It was not a distinguished performance judged by the high standards of the Elizabethan Navy. Winter was doubtless in difficulties, but Pelham was aware of these and yet thought that the Admiral might have remained. The supply ships were actually encountered by one of his captains, Richard Bingham, whose ship, the *Swiftsure*, had become separated from the rest of the squadron.[1]

The invaders were a force raised by the Papacy. It has sometimes been described as Spanish, but was in fact nearly all Italian, though Philip II provided financial aid. The disturbance following the English setback in Glenmalure might seem to have afforded it a favourable opportunity, but the prospects of the expedition were in fact negligible. It would hardly be remembered to-day but for the bloody incident which has rendered it famous.

LETTER FROM IRISH CHIEFS TO THE ARCHBISHOP OF CASHEL

Note on the Cover

Translated from the Latin, 4 May 1570. Desire for Don John of Austria as King. Copy of the letter of the Catholic Chiefs of Ireland to the Archbishop of Cashel, of IIII of May, 1570.

They complain bitterly of the weakness which he has displayed in carrying out his mission and demand that he shall urgently solicit vigorous aid from His Catholic Majesty; otherwise they will find themselves reduced to making peace with the English. They request him to speak to the King about proclaiming his brother, Don John of Austria, King of Ireland, as one of the surest means of securing his ends.

[1] *Carew Cal.*, Vol. II, pp. 272, 274, 278, 314. *C.S.P. Ireland*, Vol. LXXVI, 49.

Text

No words can express our astonishment that in all this time Your Grace has received no decision from His Majesty about the business for which you were sent. We have suffered greatly through this long delay. While waiting in hope that these negotiations would be carried through, we might, with God's help, have won many important victories over our enemies.

As regards neither property nor person can we readily trust the English, even though they firmly engage themselves to peace with us, because among the bitterest foes (which the English are to us) no pledge, however solemn, can be considered binding, so that none can believe or trust such foes. We find ourselves in perplexity because, if we are driven to make peace with them, it is clear what will follow, since nothing would be more to their taste than to attack and invade our people in time of peace, as you know they have done in the case of many nobles and chiefs in the past. If, on the other hand, we do not make peace, they are so powerful in their own kingdom as well as in ours that we shall be quite unable to resist them unless God should afford us exceptional aid, since our own people will join them and they will wage war together as allies. Hoping that by the favour of His Catholic Majesty our safety would be assured, we have so far preserved ourselves and all our possessions, though during this year we have been in great danger through not having received a response from His Majesty or news of how far we have been admitted to his favour, and we have greatly missed your intervention.

We trust that if you have been negligent in carrying out this business retribution will fall upon you and that you will not escape the divine wrath. At the time of writing we are so enraged with you that we have contemplated addressing a letter to His Majesty and in it blaming you for gross delays, because even if we needed nothing of you you were not in this serving your country. We beg of you therefore, in view of our needs and dangers, not to delay further but for your own good and that of the country diligently to importune His Majesty for aid. We shall maintain as high a spirit as ever. If God permits the contrary to happen and no hope is left to us but that of suing for peace, then, as we have said, this will bring many evils in its train.

We must also inform you that there are now with us two of the leaders of those who rose in revolt against the Queen in England

and that they are seeking our friendship for themselves and for their allies and making many proposals which it would take too long to set out here. We do not intend to consider them until Your Grace has advised us of His Majesty's will with regard to our affairs, because our firm and foremost intention is to serve His Majesty faithfully with all our strength. By your last letter we understood that His Eminence the Cardinal and the King's Secretary had intervened favourably in these negotiations to your satisfaction. We wrote to them recently, as you will be aware from our other letters if they have reached your hands, and expressed to them our thanks for the many favours we have received. If occasion serves, we shall recompense them from these lands as far as lies in our power; if not, we trust that God will be their paymaster, since he rewards each one of us according to his deserts. It is he who has redeemed us with his precious blood, and he will confer upon them a reward beyond price. If by chance the many preoccupations of His Majesty draw him deeply into other affairs and wars against the enemies of the orthodox faith, he will also succour us in our necessity in response to our supplications.

According to certain Englishmen of the Council of England, who have favoured us, albeit clandestinely, it is the intention of the Queen to seek peace with His Majesty in order that he may not be moved by his wonted benevolence to realize our danger and to assist us. His Majesty ought to reflect that such a proposal by the English would not be to his advantage but is in fact put forward simply in order the more effectively to ruin us and all Catholics. Having considered among ourselves and with our council this most difficult and important matter, it appears to us that Your Grace should approach His Majesty with a request that his most honourable brother, Don John of Austria, should be proclaimed our King. We would engage ourselves to be His Majesty's most faithful subjects and vassals, as we have promised in our letters. Concerning all this we have written to the said Don John a letter which Your Grace will hand to him. You will discuss not only with His Majesty but also with the said Don John these intricate affairs so that he may send us his reply to our petition. If it be granted, we trust to God that as soon as Don John sets foot in Ireland all our people will give him their allegiance and will make him not only King of Ireland but also of other foreign provinces which we will subject to his rule. For if we had a King like other nations none would venture to attack us, on account of the spirit of our people in war, the stoutness of their hearts, and the fertility of their soil. Because we have not a King and are divided among ourselves the English attack and rob us daily, and we suffer grievously as a result. Your Grace well knows how they sow enmity between two brothers in order to destroy them individually and seize their possessions.

So, as we have constantly insisted, if His Majesty with God's help does not assist us we shall have before us two alternatives, neither of which it would be wise to choose: either to abandon ourselves to complete destruction or to content ourselves with only a fraction of our estates, coming to a composition and making peace with them, which they will respect as little as they usually do. We therefore beg of you once more that, unless you have ceased to be interested in these negotiations, you will bring them urgently to His Majesty's attention, so that he may realize the sufferings we endure day and night and the cruel war which the English are waging against us, and so that he may defend and preserve us. This would be easier than to liberate us after all had been lost.

Vale. From Tralee, May 4th, 1570.[1]

[1] Arch. Gen. de Simancas, L.8336, folio 27.

CHAPTER X

THE DESMOND REBELLION: LAST PHASE

THREE weeks after the Italians had reached Smerwick, Grey in Dublin told the Queen, on 5 October 1580, that he disbelieved the report of their landing. She had let him down easily after the accident of Glenmalure and he was now taking matters lightly enough. He said he would temporize with Tirlagh Luineach and send him a butt or two of sack. However, he judged it wise to set out for Munster, leaving the Pale in charge of Kildare, who showed signs of standing firm after all.

Ormonde, who was nearer to the scene of action, marched with several hundred men to Smerwick Harbour, Desmond not venturing to stand in his path. He encountered some of the invaders in the open, captured prisoners, and was informed by them that the whole landing party was not more than 700 strong, though more were said to be expected, but that they had arms for 5,000. They were engaged in strengthening the earth fort built by James Fitzmaurice and mounting guns in it. After a close reconnaissance, he decided that, while there was no great strength in the fort, he could not attack it without artillery, of which he had none. Unimpressed by the enemy's attempt to bring him under the guns of the fort by skirmishing, he drew off, dropped a force in observation, and himself rode back towards Kilkenny to raise cattle for the needs of the Deputy's forces. Cattle were not plentiful in Kilkenny, which had been raided since the revolt of Baltinglas by the O'Moores of Queen's County, and unless he were on the spot the royal troops would go short. As there is no mention of his having been present at the events which followed in Kerry, it is to be assumed that he remained to keep an eye on Baltinglas and the rebels of the Pale and to guard his own lands against them.[1]

A proportion of Ormonde's force had, however, joined Grey, who himself led 600 foot and 200 horse, all English, from Dublin. In mid-October the army in Ireland numbered 6,437 men, with 1,344 on the way. Not all these reached Ireland. Some of the men from Lancashire, always a stronghold of Roman Catholicism, waiting for a ship at Chester, declared that they would not fight against their

[1] *C.S.P. Ireland*, Vol. LXXVII, 12. Hooker (in Holinshed), Vol. VI, p. 437.

co-religionists in Ireland and were sent home. This was a very rare if not a unique occurrence in the Irish wars, and did not take place until after the extinction of the Italians in their fort. And, whatever the Lord Deputy thought, others, especially Lord Chancellor Gerard, were anxious about the attitude of Kildare. Gerard told Burghley of his suspicion that there were 'bees in our bosoms', and his astute correspondent would know very well to whom he referred. The bees were in the plural because another magnate of the Pale, Christopher Nugent, Baron of Delvin, Kildare's son-in-law, was with him in the field and deep in his plans.[1]

Grey marched to Dingle, and there camped to await Admiral Winter, who returned after revictualling in England and entered Smerwick Harbour on 5 November. He landed eight guns, without which no assault would have been practicable, and also provided some victuals. On 7 November Grey pitched his camp before the fort, and that evening mounted his culverins, with which he opened fire next day. Two of the enemy's guns on the side attacked were put out of action, so that he could reply only with musketry. That night the besiegers advanced their trench to within 100 yards of the enemy's ditch and on the night of the 9th checked a sortie designed to drive the labourers from their work. Next day, the 10th, the enemy's fire was hot, while that of the English had little effect. Then Grey noticed that the most dangerous volleys were coming from a timber penthouse and left the trench to order the guns to fire on it. Sir William Winter himself laid and fired, and at the second shot the shelter was demolished. After two more rounds a man leapt on to the bank, holding out a white sheet and craving a parley, which was granted.

An Italian camp-master came out and begged that the fort might be delivered and the garrison allowed to depart. Grey replied that, since there were Spaniards in the garrison, a representative of that nation must come out also, whereupon a Spanish captain appeared. The Lord Deputy sternly demanded who had sent these troops; he presumed it was not the King of Spain, who was in amity with the Queen. They admitted that the King had not sent them, and the Italian stated that they had been sent by the Pope for the defence of the Catholic faith. To this Grey retorted that he would not have been greatly astonished if men under the orders of an absolute prince, such as Philip II, should sometimes take in hand wrong actions, but that their fault was aggravated 'by the vileness of their

[1] C.S.P. Ireland, Vol. LXXVI, 65; Vol. LXXVII, 25, 43; Vol. LXXIX, 6.

commander'. He added, according to his own version, that they could expect no conditions from him, except that they should surrender the fort and yield themselves to his will for life or death. Some further discussion followed, but, Grey avers, no promise was given that any lives should be spared.

On the morning of the 11th the commander and about a dozen officers came out, trailing their rolled ensigns. Grey then ordered weapons and armour to be laid down and sent in companies, 'who straight fell to execution'. About 600 were slaughtered. Many more terrible acts have been committed in war, but the cold horror of this has continued to leave its mark upon the pages of history after over three centuries and a half.[1]

Grey's statement that he gave the wretched creatures in the fort no promise of mercy is more probably true than false, though there can be no final judgement on the point. Grey's word is supported by Edmund Spenser, who was present; but he is a somewhat prejudiced witness, as the Lord Deputy's secretary and admirer. It must be noted too that he gives a rather different version of what the envoys said. According to him, they told Grey that they had not been sent either by the Pope or by the King of Spain but were adventurers come to serve the Irish for hire. This is unlikely. It was a common enough practice to refuse mercy to foreigners taken in arms without commission, and these men, even though they could not produce one, would surely have pretended that they had some authority, since otherwise their doom was almost inevitable. Against Grey stands a strong Irish tradition that they were promised mercy, and, since Irish tradition is often near the truth, this may be worth more than the similar version of the unreliable O'Sullivan Bere. The annalists of Lough Cé make no suggestion of treachery. The luckless foreigners, whose understanding of what Grey said may well have been incomplete, probably believed they had been promised their lives. The story is ghastly, whether or not Grey broke his word. The Queen made no comment on that aspect of it, though she did say that she wished a few officers had been sent to her 'to have extended either justice or mercy'. She bade the Lord Deputy express her thanks to her troops. They at least merited her approval; for they had endured exposure to mid-winter storms, so that there were many sick and not a few deaths.[2]

[1] C.S.P. Ireland, 1574–85, Preface, p. lxix.
[2] C.S.P. Ireland, Vol. LXIX, 13. History of Catholic Ireland, p. 20. Annals of Lough Cé, p. 437.

4 SIDNEY RETURNS IN TRIUMPH TO DUBLIN. In front ride trumpeters, yeomen, herald, and mace-bearer. He is greeted by the Lord Mayor and Aldermen. Beside him is borne the sword of state (*The Image of Ireland*).

The Spaniards took the matter lightly enough, and indeed it scarcely concerned them, except that they had provided money and port facilities and allowed a few volunteers to join the force. Bernardino de Mendoza, the Ambassador in England, reported to Philip that there had been no real resistance, and that he considered it a cowardly affair, but thought that the surrender had been made on condition that the lives of the besieged should be spared. The King replied three months later—evidence of how long an official message might take to reach Madrid from London—that he was grieved at the loss of the soldiers of His Holiness, but especially by their bad behaviour. He bade the Ambassador keep on watching Ireland and reporting. Mendoza informed him, again just three months later, that he had never entered into communication with the insurgents because he had no instructions to do so. His attitude was diplomatically correct. He carefully reported English preparations and provides the interesting information, which must have given him malicious pleasure to impart, that when the City of London was ordered to levy 500 men this was done without beat of drum in order that people should not realize the magnitude of the effort.[1]

Desmond had done nothing to aid the Italians. Baltinglas and Sir John of Desmond had tried to do something, but moved too late, as was the Irish habit. Yet John of Desmond again marched across southern Ireland and re-entered Kerry unmolested just after the Lord Deputy had quitted Munster. Grey hastened back to Dublin, which he reached about 8 December, on account of anxiety about the behaviour of Kildare in the Pale. Lord Chancellor Gerard and other officials had drawn up a long list of charges against Kildare, which were accepted by Grey at their face value. Kildare and Delvin were arrested and shortly afterwards sent to London. It is possible that Kildare was a victim of the suspicion of the officials. This is not to say that he was innocent; he was playing for power. But the boundary between the policy of Ormonde, who also played for power, but was accounted by the Queen a good subject while bitterly criticized by her officials, and that of a man like Kildare, has to be carefully drawn. An Irish emissary sent by Baltinglas afterwards stated under examination that Kildare had addressed a treasonable letter to the Pope, and if this be true then Gerard is justified; but Kildare's guilt was assuredly of a nature very different to that of Desmond.[2] He was afterwards liberated and allowed to return.

[1] C.S.P. Spanish, Vol. III, pp. 53, 69, 88, 121
[2] C.S.P. Ireland, Vol. LXXIX, 24, 25, 26, 27, 31; Vol. CIV, 38 (i).

A danger had been removed by the annihilation of the Italian landing party and the capture of the arms which it had brought with it, but the Desmond rebellion was not over. In fact, John of Desmond was causing anxiety in Kerry, where the companies at Dingle were gravely reduced by death and sickness. Ormonde was directed to finish the affair, but remained for some time in Dublin, and when he returned was accused by the English in Munster of not being vigorous enough and of being unpopular with the troops. There was still no President, perhaps because he would have cost more money than Ormonde as Lord General. Six hundred troops were dismissed, but the new arrivals were dying so fast that the numbers available were proving insufficient. After much discussion, Ormonde's commission was revoked by Grey in June 1581. According to the Lord Deputy, he took his dismissal well, and this version may be accepted before that of the bitter comment of Sir Henry Wallop, representing the hostile officials. The Queen and Privy Council had decided to try appeasement and in April had offered an amnesty, excepting Desmond, his brother John, and Baltinglas, with certain others, whose names were added by Grey. The Lord Deputy did not like the new policy and begged to be recalled. Nor did it prove effective; for by 17 July few of the rebels had availed themselves of the opportunity of pardon.[1]

The Government had, in fact, allowed its grip to slip. Yet, though it was unknown to the English for some two months, death had, about the beginning of April, removed an enemy who was none the less formidable because his arms were spiritual. Dr. Sanders, a fugitive in the woods throughout the winter, died of dysentery and was buried in secret. Few English Roman Catholics, however sympathetic to Irish grievances, have exercised strong influence in Ireland, but he was an exception. 'Sanders had been three years in Ireland. He had brought upon the country only bloodshed, famine, and confiscation, and yet among the starving people none could be found to earn a reward by betraying him.'[2]

Some secondary material successes were gained. Baltinglas fled to Ulster and thence to Scotland, afterwards sailing to Spain. One of his brothers was captured in a combat in which the Irish charged with the pike, an unusual occurrence. In Connaught the vigorous Malby chased back into Ulster a well-equipped force of 600 Scottish

---

[1] C.S.P. Ireland, Vol. LXXXII, 41, 42; Vol. LXXXIII, 43, 45, 48; Vol. LXXXIV, 24. Bagwell, Ireland under the Tudors, Vol. III, p. 91.
[2] Bagwell, Ireland under the Tudors, Vol. III, p. 90.

mercenaries who had come in with the connivance of Clanrickarde's restless sons. In June 1581 Colonel John Zouch made a surprise attack on Desmond's camp, killed a number of his men, but missed their leader. And though Tirlagh Luineach O'Neill in Ulster fell upon and defeated the O'Donnells, temporarily good subjects, and stood at the head of a great force of 700 horse, 2,500 Scots, 1,500 gallowglasses, and 'an infinity of kerne', a peace was patched up with him again after Grey had marched up to the Blackwater. The veteran threw up his hat for joy. Tirlagh never wanted war if he thought he could be left in power undisturbed.[1]

A more important success achieved had in it an element of luck. In early January 1582 Sir John of Desmond walked into an ambush laid by Zouch for another man and was killed. His turquoise set in gold was sent to Elizabeth, his *agnus dei* to the Earl of Bedford, and his head as a new-year gift to Grey. John Fitzgerald was a more vigorous man than his brother Desmond, who was now a cripple, and his death represented a loss to the rebels.[2]

However, the first effects were unfortunate for the Government because the Queen hastened the disbandment of the forces in Ireland. She at once ordered another 700 men to be dismissed, and in the three months of November and December 1581 and January 1582, 3,296 were discharged. Grey wrote despairingly to Walsingham that he had postponed the 'thrusting out' of the last 700 to save them from starvation, since he had no money to pay them. Several 'unfortunate incidents' occurred almost immediately, including the destruction of one of Zouch's companies commanded by Captain Apsley in west Cork.[3]

Everybody, including himself, was now anxious that Grey should go. For once there was no division of opinion. The Queen complained of expense and lack of results; officials and soldiers considered him inefficient; the Irish hated him. It was not merely on account of his severity; they were used to nothing else and their own methods of war were ferocious. Sidney, whom the English wanted back and for whom it was said the very children in the Dublin streets were crying, had been a hard man. Fitzwilliam, who was proposed and would have been welcome to the soldiers though not himself a

[1] C.S.P. Ireland, Vol. LXXX, 76 (i); Vol. LXXXI, 42 (i); Vol. LXXXII, 45; Vol. LXXXIII, 58, 59; Vol. LXXXIV, 8, 11, 44; Vol. LXXXV, 5, 13; Vol. LXXXVI, 77.

[2] C.S.P. Ireland, Vol. LXXXVIII, 10 (i), 14 (i), 15.

[3] C.S.P. Ireland, Vol. LXXXVIII, 36, 40; LXXXIX, 9; Vol. XC, 29.

soldier, was heavy-handed. No, it was the terrible waste without result, the appalling famine in Munster without a victory, which had aroused the loathing of the Irish—that and perhaps the killing of the Italians in Smerwick Harbour. The Queen recognized the honesty and energy of Grey and got at least as far as to draft a letter telling him so. But from Nonsuch, on 10 July 1582, she sent his letter of recall. Six weeks later he delivered the sword to Sir Henry Wallop and Adam Loftus, Archbishop of Dublin, the latter of whom had recently become Lord Chancellor on the death of Gerard.[1]

It still remained to decide who was to put an end to the Munster revolt. Walter Ralcigh, by no means his friend, told the Privy Council that Ormonde was the best man for the task, and his advice was finally taken. The announcement of Ormonde's appointment as Governor of Munster was made on 3 December 1582 when he was in England; but he did not reach Waterford until 21 January 1583. He found the situation much deteriorated. County Waterford and his own palatinate of Tipperary, far from the main scene of action, had been despoiled. Youghal had recently almost fallen again, the rebels actually getting a footing within the town. Outside Munster things were fairly quiet. As usual, the doings of Malby in Connaught were the bright spot. He had pacified the Clanrickarde Burkes and further north MacWilliam, with his wife Grace O'Malley, famous in history and legend, had quietly submitted to him.[2]

Ormonde had the fullest powers and 1,000 mobile troops under his direct orders. He had, however, to face the hostility of most of the English officials. Wallop, one of the Lord Justices, was alarmed by the report that he might be made Lord Deputy, as Burghley would have wished, and declared that he was already too great for Ireland and that he was grossly overpaid, an argument likely to appeal to the Queen. Most bitter of all was Sir Warham St. Leger in Cork. This man, whose own conduct of affairs had been far from brilliant, constantly asserted that the Irish earl would fail ignominiously. His dislike of Ormonde was warmly returned by the latter, who declared that his only occupation was drinking and sending false reports to England.

The Governor took up his headquarters at Clonmel, on the southern boundary of his own county of Tipperary. His first aim

---

[1] *C.S.P. Ireland*, Vol. LXXXVIII, 29; Vol. XCII, 11; Vol. XCIV, 17.
[2] *C.S.P. Ireland*, Vol. XCVIII, 8; Vol. XCIX, 26, 34, 37.

was to clear the rebels out of it and that of Waterford, so as to localize the struggle. Eventually he intended to pen Desmond into Kerry. Kerry had the reputation of being a stronghold, but it was also practicable to make of it a trap, and even an Irish force, if driven into one of its peninsulas, would find it hard to break out.

The moving story comes to us in a series of despatches from Ormonde to the Queen, to the Privy Council, to Burghley, with for antiphon complaints, criticism, and forebodings from the English officials. The Lord Justices Loftus and Wallop are relatively moderate, and Chief Secretary Fenton is not extravagant, but the roared abuse and accusations of Sir Warham St. Leger become indecent. Since he was a stout soldier, he probably meant what he said in demanding to be sent to face the cannon anywhere distant from Ormonde, who, he had decided, would never love him. As Ormonde knew what he was writing, from Burghley himself, it was unlikely that he ever would. He felt some anxiety lest his work should be undone, as it had been before, by unfavourable reports, perhaps especially when his dear friend and champion at the Council Board, Lord Sussex, died. But Burghley meant him to see the business through this time.

The first stage of his campaign was carried out with great speed and extraordinary success. In September 1582 Desmond had stood at the head of 2,000 foot and 200 horse. In the following month Fenton had reported that he was stronger than ever he had been, while the English companies were in disorder and most of the captains on leave in England. Slackness and over-confidence had spoiled the results of previous efforts and prolonged the tragedy. This state of affairs was transformed by Ormonde. By 28 February 1583, after having carried out several night raids to break up bodies of the enemy, he was able to report to the Privy Council that Desmond had fled to the mountains of Slieve Logher, in Kerry, some eight miles east of Tralee. Ormonde's design was to keep him in that county and then advance with the sword in one hand and pardon in the other. He had power to extend mercy to everyone, up to the highest, save Desmond himself, and he used it fully.[1]

On the date given above he could announce that thirty-nine gentlemen had been killed and 339 received to mercy. By 5 April another thirty-three had been killed and 335 had surrendered, including one of the most important, the Geraldine Baron of Lixnaw. On 28 May another 134 had been killed and 247 had

[1] *C.S.P. Ireland,* Vol. XCIX, 76.

submitted. By this time Ormonde had cut Desmond off from all relief, disposed companies so that he should not break back, and put his principal followers to the sword. The rebel who had led over 2,000 men the previous autumn had now with him not above eighty. Lady Desmond herself had surrendered. On 11 June the last of Desmond's prominent adherents, John FitzEdmond Fitzgerald, Seneschal of Imokilly, submitted. With a touch of compassion, Ormonde reported that the 'unhappy wretch', the Earl, was wandering about, forsaken of all men, while the poor Countess lamented his folly. His band of adherents had shrunk still further. Ormonde had his own difficulties, including shortages of supplies and of cavalry, though he had ample foot; above all, he was hampered by the practices of Sir Warham St. Leger, which he denounced as unhonest and 'very lewd'. St. Leger thought that even now Desmond might be induced to submit—naturally through the instrumentality of St. Leger. Some negotiations between Desmond and Ormonde did actually take place, but the rebel's proposals were such as would have left him almost as strong as ever, and the Lord General refused to entertain them.[1]

Towards the end of June Ormonde marched into Kerry, visited Dingle, and passed through west Cork to Cork city. His object was to see that no aid to Desmond was coming in by sea and ascertain how the reclaimed rebels were behaving. He found them repentant. He was himself, he told Burghley, wearied out by bloodshed. He was cutting down his troops, since all fighting was at an end. The country was going under the plough again.[2] Desmond, however, still remained at large, and the last phase was hanging fire. The end came about suddenly and dramatically.

Desmond, with the coming of winter, returned to an earlier hiding-place, the wooded Glenageenty below the flank of Slieve Logher. On 9 November 1583 he sent out a raiding party who drove off cattle and horses belonging to Maurice O'Moriarty, chief of a small sept on the southern side of Tralee Bay. These desperate outlaws also stripped naked O'Moriarty's wife and children. The Irishmen were so humbly submissive that, before they pursued, they asked leave to do so of the commander of the company at Dingle. Next day, with about twenty-five kerne and six soldiers from the keep of Castlemaine, they tracked the cattle towards Desmond's retreat. That night they caught sight of the glow of a fire in a hut

---

[1] *C.S.P. Ireland*, Vol. XCIX, 77 (i); Vol. CI, 10; Vol. CII, 48, 84, 88.
[2] *C.S.P. Ireland*, Vol. CIII, 15; Vol. CIV, 68.

on the flank of the glen. They surrounded it and closed upon it at first light.

Desmond had with him in the cabin but a single attendant, who fled. The Earl himself, half crippled—it has been surmised from the effects of the wound received at the ford of Affane, eighteen years before—was wounded by the sword of one of the Castlemaine soldiers, Daniel O'Kelly. The unfortunate man cried out: 'I am the Earl of Desmond! Save my life!' Owen O'Moriarty, the brother-in-law of Maurice and in command of the party, is said to have replied: 'Thou hast killed thyself long ago, and now thou shalt be prisoner to the Queen's Majesty and the Earl of Ormonde, Lord General of Munster.' Since Desmond could not walk, they began to carry him. Then, it is said, seeing some of his kerne and fearing a rescue, Owen O'Moriarty ordered O'Kelly to cut off his head. O'Kelly did so. Is the tale a true one? We who, in a world to which savagery worse than that of the sixteenth-century Irish wars has returned, have too often heard with scepticism of men 'shot while attempting to escape', may not be sure about this, but there was no particular object in killing Desmond if he could be brought back alive.

The head was sent to Ormonde and by him to the Queen, who had it set up on London Bridge. Sickened as he was by the whole affair, the Lord General did not conceal his satisfaction that his traducers had been silenced. 'So now', he wrote to Burghley, 'is this traitor come to the end I have long looked for, appointed by God to die by the sword to end his rebellion, in despite of such malicious fools as have divers times untruly informed of the service and state of Munster.' He went on to thank Burghley for joying with him in the birth of his son and heir. The child, born two months before, was not destined to succeed his father.

Speaking of Desmond's last struggles, the Irish annalists sum up thus: 'His people, however, were so much in dread and awe of the law and the Sovereign of England that they began to separate from him, even his own married wife, children and friends, so that he had but few persons to accompany him from one cavern of a rock or hollow of a tree to another. . . . God thought it time to suppress, close, and finish this war of the Geraldines.'[1]

In viewing events in an age in which lineage and position are

[1] Four Masters, Vol. V, p. 1,793. *C.S.P. Ireland,* Vol. CV, 67. Bagwell: *Ireland under the Tudors,* Vol. III, p. 113. (Here evidence from some other sources is assembled.)

highly regarded, the tragedy overwhelming a great house in the person of a great nobleman is not to be measured by his private virtues and accomplishments. It becomes a tragedy of the first order because it has been felt to be that in so many breasts. Better men, with higher gifts and nobler personalities than Desmond himself, died for Desmond. They are forgotten and he is remembered, without injustice. If he was deserted by all at the end, he was never betrayed for the reward upon his head. The cynic may retort that this was because the would-be betrayer knew that he would be denied absolution if he ventured to succumb to the lure of the reward; but there is no doubt that honour was a powerful motive with the poorest. Desmond lives on in tradition and in legend. The great Anglo-Irish historian, visiting the scenes of his revolt at a time within the memory of men who are still alive, was told by countrymen near Holycross, in Limerick, that the ghost of the Earl, mounted on a ghostly horse shod with silver, sometimes rose by night from the neighbouring waters of Lough Gur. And when in winter a gale from the Atlantic swept up the valleys, the folk of Kerry still called upon the traveller to listen to the famous and intimidating howl of the Desmond gallowglasses borne down the wind.

CHAPTER XI

THE SPANISH ARMADA

FROM the death of Gerald Fitzgerald, Earl of Desmond, to the rebellion of Hugh O'Neill, Earl of Tyrone, no major revolt occurred in Ireland. There was a great deal of unrest, first of all in Connaught, later on also in Ulster, and the incidents which possess significance from the military point of view must be recorded. By far the most important event bearing upon the power of the Crown in Ireland is the return along its coasts of ships of the Spanish Armada, a number of which put into its harbours. Otherwise the period will be passed in more rapid review than in the case of those which precede and follow it.

The horrors and sufferings which accompanied the Desmond rebellion are notorious. The pen of one of the greatest of English writers, Edmund Spenser, has left a terrible picture of half-human creatures, whose legs would not bear them, crawling on all fours out of thickets to feed on carrion. St. Leger, no sentimentalist, lamented that as many as seventy people a day sometimes died of starvation in the then little town of Cork. Yet the first faint signs of recovery appeared before the end of the revolt—that is, after Ormonde had reduced Desmond to impotence. Ireland lived by the land, and so long as there remained seed and breeding cattle recovery would come sooner or later, far sooner than after modern wars in a civilization based upon urban life and production.

The country was left without a viceroy for just two years, Grey having departed at the end of August 1582, and his successor not arriving until 9 June 1584 or receiving the sword until 21 June. Sir John Perrott had been chosen for his experience of Ireland and especially for his knowledge of Munster, where the settlement of the escheated Desmond lands would be his primary task. This energetic man had not improved in character since his last appearance upon the Irish scene. His temper had always been hot; now it showed itself explosive. Within his first fortnight he found himself at odds with Treasurer Wallop, who had been the virtual governor since Grey had handed over the sword; but Wallop, taking Walsingham's prudent advice, restrained himself and excused the Lord Deputy's 'passionate disposition'.[1]

A President of Munster had also been chosen, John Norris, one of a famous band of brothers and the best known of Elizabethan soldiers. He was already experienced in the Irish wars and had, under the orders of Essex, carried out the slaughter of the Scots in Rathlin. No President of Connaught was yet to be appointed, but Malby, who had died, was to be replaced as Governor by Sir Richard Bingham, who was distinguished as both sailor and soldier and who had displayed energy and seamanship in aid of the operations in Kerry. He had served with the Spaniards when England and Spain were allies, had probably fought at Lepanto and had certainly been present at St. Quentin. This choice appeared excellent, but was to prove less successful than might have been expected. Malby had been severe enough, but, whereas he had been relatively popular with the Connaught Irish—and Conyers Clifford, later in the reign, was to be even more so—Bingham's excessive harshness brought detestation upon his head.

Perrott's first duty was to install these new Governors. He went first to Athlone with Bingham. The unhappy Earl of Clanrickarde, who had suffered so much from the behaviour of his sons, had been sent back to Ireland, but had died in 1582 and had been succeeded by his son, Ulick. Another new holder of a western peerage was young Donogh O'Brien, fourth Earl of Thomond, known later as 'the Great Earl'. They and others came to pay their respects to the Lord Deputy. Perrott then went south, but, hearing of a landing of Scots in Ulster, stopped at Limerick and returned to Dublin. He had appointed Wallop to survey the Desmond lands, and after a preliminary study of the question the Treasurer reported to Burghley that they were so wasted and the province was so empty and starved that it would take long to repeople. A messenger from Tirlagh Luineach O'Neill, with some project for a new southern rising with his aid, had been apprehended; but it was all vague and the Munster lords had no intention of engaging in another revolt while Perrott and Ormonde were on the scene.[2]

Perrott marched into Ulster on 25 August 1584 with 2,000 troops and some Irish auxiliaries. Many of the Munster gentry accompanied him, one of the rare occasions when this occurred. The Scots did not await his coming, but fled from Lough Foyle before he

---

[1] *C.S.P. Ireland*, Vol. CX, 69; Vol. CXI, 1, 13.
[2] *C.S.P. Ireland*, Vol. CXI, 43, 90.

reached Newry. The ships which he had sent to intercept them missed their galleys by about an hour. He pushed on into Antrim and besieged their chief stronghold, Dunluce Castle, which he described as very strong, on a rock overhanging the sea and divided from the mainland by a deep, natural ditch. The fortress was commanded by a Scot, 'who, when I sent to summon them to yield, refused talk, and proudly answered (speaking very good English) that they were appointed and would keep it to the last man for the King of Scots use'. However, he did not fulfil his threat, and Perrott quickly got possession of the place. He had already settled with Tirlagh, who had come to meet him without safe-conduct. Ormonde, who accompanied the Lord Deputy, wasted the wooded district of Glenconkeine, then part of Tyrone, now in Londonderry, sweeping out of it great numbers of cattle, in order to deprive the Scots of food if they should come again. How complacently the Irish bards regarded war waged by their own chiefs—and Ormonde, though an Anglo-Irish nobleman and a Protestant, would count as such with an adherent of the Butlers—is illustrated by the verse dedicated by a eulogist to this exploit. Ormonde was indeed wealthy, kinder-hearted than most of his time, provident, and bountiful; yet these epithets have an odd ring in the poet's context:

> He took from Raghlin, in the land of Alba,
> After hard-fought combats, a prey of cattle;
> Thrice he set Glen-Concadhain on fire,
> This wealthy and tender-hearted chieftain.
> He left no herds around Loughneagh,
> The seer so provident and bountiful.

Rathlin was accounted part of Scotland (Alba). The tender-hearted chieftain's visit and his previous burnings of Glenconkeine must have been in the reign of Mary.[1]

The quietude of the country was again interrupted in November, when fresh parties of Scots appeared. Sir Henry Bagenal advanced to meet them, but was hampered by the failure of his shipping to reach him near Cushendall, in Red Bay, found some difficulty in holding off their attack on his camp, and had to retreat to Carrick-fergus. Sir William Stanley, summoned from Munster, marched with two companies to Ballycastle, where a troop of cavalry was already stationed in Bunamargey Abbey, the burial place of the MacDonalds.

---

[1] *C.S.P. Ireland,* Vol. CXI, 88. Four Masters, Vol. V, p. 1,821. Hill, *The Macdonnells of Antrim,* p. 161. Cox, *Hibernia Anglicana,* Pt. I, p. 307.

He also was attacked in camp, alongside the abbey, on 1 January 1585. It was a complete surprise. At the head of the Scots foot were half a dozen horsemen, 'who had upon their staves wads lighted, wherewith they suddenly set the roof of the church, being thatched, on fire'. Stanley himself, fighting in his shirt for want of time to don armour, was wounded thrice, in the back (and, as this needed explanation, he recorded that it happened when he turned to urge his men forward), in the arm and side, and in the thigh. The enemy was driven off, but the horses could not be got out of the burning abbey in time to pursue, and some were burnt inside it. To fill Stanley's cup of bitterness, twenty-four oared galleys of Scots passed across Ballycastle Bay, but the calm was so flat that his ships could not pursue. However, the Scots, finding there were more blows than booty to be got in Ulster, for the most part returned to their own country within the next three months. Sorley Boy MacDonald, after attempting negotiations to establish himself at the expense of his own kinsmen, finally fled.[1]

The Irish Parliament met on 26 April 1585. The House of Commons was made up of three elements: the old Anglo-Irish, who predominated; native Irish; and English officials, soldiers, and settlers. Perrott looked magnificent in his robes and deeply impressed by his dignity all the visitors to Dublin. These included a number of Irish chiefs who did not sit in Parliament, but whose presence bore tribute to the Lord Deputy's prestige. As the annalists remark, 'the greater part of the people of Ireland were at this time obedient to their sovereign'. Among the greatest of these chiefs was Tirlagh Luineach O'Neill (uncomfortable in English clothes and suggesting that his chaplain should be put into trousers, so 'that the boys will laugh at him as well as at me'), Hugh O'Donnell, Cuconnaught Maguire, and Ross MacMahon, from Ulster; Brian O'Rourke, O'Connor Don, and O'Connor Sligo, from Connaught; O'Sullivan More and O'Sullivan Bere from Munster; and there were a large number of lesser men.

If, however, Perrott was popular with them, he was not so with his own officials, who were infuriated by his overbearing temper, and the strong parliamentary contingent from the Pale opposed his measures. His double attack on Poyning's Act—which in effect diminished the power of the Deputy—by direct repeal and by an act to authorize certain statutes and ordinances 'notwithstanding

[1] *C.S.P. Ireland*, 1574-1585, Preface, p. ccxxiii; Vol. CXII, 90 (1); Vol. CXIV, 67; Vol. CXV, 36.

Poyning's Act', was defeated. Parliament was twice prorogued, first for a few days, and on 25 May for eleven months. The chief fruit of the earlier sessions was an act for the attainder of Baltinglas and his brothers. In the last session the main feature was the Desmond attainder. Desmond himself, his brothers John and James, and James Fitzmaurice (all four of whom were dead) were named, and their lands were vested in the Crown, without prejudice to innocent parties upon them. Parliament was dissolved on 14 May 1586. The Queen's view of the proceedings may be guessed from the fact that she summoned no other for the rest of her reign.[1]

In Ulster Perrott had been so far the most successful of the Elizabethan viceroys. He had established garrisons in Dunluce, Ballycastle Bay, and Coleraine. It seemed that he had tamed the Scots. Tirlagh O'Neill was on better terms with the English than he had ever been. Hugh O'Neill, Baron of Dungannon, who had rendered good service in the province during the Desmond rebellion, appeared a model of loyalty, and had sat in the House of Lords and established his right to the title of Earl of Tyrone. In August 1585, during the long prorogation, Perrott had gone to Dungannon and confirmed an agreement made between him and Tirlagh whereby Tyrone was put in possession of all the O'Neill country south and east of the Mullaghcarne mountains at a rent of 1,000 marks a year, for seven years, during which he would acknowledge Tirlagh's paramountcy or 'captainry'. Before the end of this period Tirlagh was likely to be dead and the whole would revert to Tyrone. Since Tirlagh had already appointed Tyrone his tanist after the Irish fashion, the latter had good prospects of a peaceful succession. Though it was beginning to appear that Tyrone was ambitious, Perrott could not have foreseen how much trouble was being stored up by these arrangements.[2]

The tireless Scots, however, appeared yet again. In August 1585 Francis Stafford, colonel of the forces at Carrickfergus, with 170 men, fought a sharp but indecisive action with 1,200 Scots and Irish, in which pikes were couched forty times. And in October, Dunluce Castle, by which Perrott set great store, was surprised and retaken, the garrison being killed.

The English Government was now at last determined to come to terms with Sorley Boy, an action which it might have taken years

---

[1] Routledge, *E.H.R.*, Vol. XXIX. Four Masters, Vol. V, p. 1,827. Bagwell, *Ireland under the Tudors*, Vol. III, pp. 140–50.

[2] *C.S.P. Ireland*, Vol. CVIII, 56; Vol. CXVIII, 59, 62.

before. In June 1586 the old man came to Dublin, where he saw the head of his son Alastair, recently killed in a skirmish, spiked above the Castle, and said proudly that he had other sons. He made humble submission, prostrated himself in front of a portrait of Elizabeth—though perhaps with his tongue in his cheek—admitted the folly of past deeds, and declared himself a subject of the Queen. He was granted a patent of denization and the lands between the parallel rivers Bann and Boys (to-day the Bush) with other territory further east, the remainder of the Route being settled upon Theodore MacQuillan. This land was to be held by Sorley and his heirs male upon knight's service for a rent of sixty beeves, and a pledge to support the royal forces in war. A month earlier his nephew, Angus of Dunnyveg, had on 16 May obtained two-thirds of the Glynns on similar terms, though it seems to have been thought that Sorley Boy would acquire most of this from him by negotiation. It was expressly laid down that neither he nor his heirs should retain more than thirty Scots, except those who had become natives of Ireland, without licence from the Government. The MacDonalds had obtained secure possession of the Antrim lands for which they had so long fought and intrigued.[1]

The most serious trial of arms during Perrott's administration took place in Connaught. In Mayo the Burkes came out with some hundreds of men, and word reached Bingham that they were expecting a body of Scots mercenaries. On 12 July 1586 he marched against them. They suggested a parley, but nothing came of this because they flatly refused to recognize the Queen's rule or to admit sheriffs. Bingham thereupon proclaimed them traitors and executed their hostages in his hands. Driving away thousands of cattle, killing right and left, chasing the remnant from bush to bush, he soon reduced them to such a state that they would be unable to afford any aid to the Scots.[2]

The Scots duly arrived, landing in Lough Foyle and moving down to the Erne at Belleek, apparently waiting to find out if any life remained among the Burkes. It was reported that they numbered between 1,400 and 1,500, besides Irish musketeers and kerne. Bingham, expecting them to enter Roscommon, hurried into that county to intercept them, then, hearing that they were still on the Erne, moved by forced marches to Sligo, which he reached on

---

[1] *C.S.P. Ireland*, Vol. CXV, 54 (i); Vol. CXXI, 4; Vol. CXXIV, 29, 76, 83, 85. Hill, *The Macdonnells of Antrim*, p. 181.

[2] *C.S.P. Ireland*, Vol. CXXV, 47. Docwra, *Relation*.

28 August. He had with him 400 foot, of whom 300 were Irish, lately enrolled, sixty horse, and Irish 'risings' of 100 horse and 200 kerne. The Scots had in the meantime received further Irish reinforcements, and he considered them too strong to attack unless he could draw them into a 'champagne', or open country. A fortnight later they tricked him. On a dark and tempestuous night they rushed the bridge over the Owenmore river at Collooney, where the guard of Irish horse fled. Four hundred got over there before his infantry reached the scene, the rest crossing by a ford of which he knew nothing. They were loose in Connaught, and he did not know which way they were going.[1]

Having had enough of the Irish 'risings', he sent them home, but picked up a force of nominally 200 foot and 40 horse sent by the Lord Deputy, and at Castlemore, in east Mayo, a few more reinforcements. He still had not much more than 500 foot and eighty horse. At this point he realized that the enemy had gone west towards Ballina instead of south towards Roscommon, as he had at first supposed. He turned and marched after them, through Aclare, and was then guided by Irishmen through the night across the Slieve Gamph mountains to their position at Ardnaree, opposite Ballina on the Moy, which here forms the boundary between Sligo and Mayo. On Thursday, 22 September, he launched a surprise assault. The Scots were aroused from sleep by the shouts of their camp followers. They contrived, according to evidence from both sides, to set themselves in some sort of battle array, but it was none the less a remarkable feat on the part of Bingham to catch these wily Redshanks so far unawares. He exploited his advantage in a manner typical of his energetic and ruthless character.

First his horse, supported by 'loose shot' or musketeers in skirmishing order, drove what he calls their vanguard, perhaps the camp followers thrown out as a screen, back into their main body. Another charge broke them completely. The Governor, said one of his captains, Thomas Woodhouse, charged 'like a brave gentleman' with his handful of horse before the foot could join in. Men of his rank were always well mounted, and all Woodhouse claimed for himself was that 'I was as near him as I could'. With the Moy river at their backs the Scots, once their array was broken, were helpless, and the affair became a massacre. Their two leaders, Donald Gorme and Alexander Carragh MacDonald, sons of James MacDonald of the Isles and nephews of Sorley Boy, were both killed. 'I was never,

[1] *C.S.P. Ireland*, Vol. CXXVI, 31 (i).

since I was a man of war', Woodhouse wrote to Fenton, 'so weary of killing men; for I protest to God, for as fast as I could I did but hough them and paunch them, sometimes on horseback, because they did run as we did break them, and sometimes on foot.' Every man, woman, and child, but for about eighty who stripped and swam the Moy, to escape naked into Mayo, were killed with the sword or drowned in the river. About 1,400 fighting men perished, together with nearly as many more camp-followers, women, and children. Bingham lost only the merest handful. Bingham's limitations in warfare on a larger scale against the better-trained Irish levies of the Tyrone rebellion were yet to be revealed, but in this type of campaign he was unsurpassed, and the marching powers of his troops were extraordinary. Whatever may be thought of his conduct from the moral point of view, he had here read a lesson which was as effective as it was terrible and which was to be long remembered.[1]

Perrott himself had set out for the west, but all was over by the time he reached Mullingar. The officials, who believed him to be actuated by jealousy of Bingham, were delighted that he failed to add to his credit. He was on bad terms with all of them, and a disgraceful scene occurred in the Council Chamber itself, when he struck the aged Marshal, Sir Nicholas Bagenal, who fell to the floor, and each accused the other of being drunk. He had fought with Loftus, who successfully opposed his scheme to use the revenues of St. Patrick's to found a university. He was also at loggerheads with Bingham and supported his opponents when charges were levelled against his administration of Connaught. Bingham was acquitted of these charges, but since relations between him and the Lord Deputy had become a matter of scandal, the Queen and Privy Council decided to send him to Holland, where it was proposed that he should act as Leicester's successor. If he had assumed the command in the Low Countries he might have found himself opposed to his old companion in arms, Sir William Stanley, who had raised an Irish regiment for service there, had betrayed Deventer on the Ijssel, and espoused the Spanish cause with his troops. Bingham was, however, reinstated in his government, though he did not return for some time, and the news was the last straw for Perrott. He wanted to be relieved, and his wish was granted. His successor was the former viceroy, Fitzwilliam.

[1] *C.S.P. Ireland,* Vol. CXXVI. Four Masters, Vol. V, pp. 1,849–52. Docwra, *Relation.*

For all his faults, Perrott had been one of the most successful of viceroys, if success is to be measured by the quietude of the country when he quitted it and by the regard in which he was held by the Irish chiefs. He had been unable to settle the escheated Desmond lands, but had at least advanced well into the stage of planning and survey. Beyond a few wood-kerne and robbers, there was not a rebel in Ireland at his departure. The poor of Dublin and the Pale lamented his going. Old Tirlagh Luineach O'Neill stood on the quay watching his ship until she disappeared below the horizon and then burst into tears.

A few words must be spared for the tragic fate of so great a figure upon the Irish scene, though his end has little to do with the history of Ireland. Not long after his return he had to face a number of charges, many of them, if true, evidence only of bad temper and crudely vigorous expressions lacking in reverence to the Queen. He had used 'evil words' about her in respect of her verdict about St. Patrick's; he had expressed contempt for her letters; he had called her sword of state 'a paltry sword'; and a good deal much coarser. On the political side, he was said to have shown favour to Papist traitors. Far more serious was a letter, a copy of which was forwarded by Fitzwilliam in February 1590, said to be in his hand and bearing his ostensible signature, in which he was made to convey an offer to Philip II of Spain to assist him to secure the kingdoms of England and Ireland. It was believed at the time and has been accepted since that this letter was a forgery, and probably the work of a rogue named Charles Trevor, who afterwards fled to Scotland. However, a year later Perrott was sent to the Tower, and in 1592 was tried for treason. The trial has always been considered a scandal. He was found guilty, but the Queen, evidently shocked, infuriated though she had been by reports of his sayings, refused to sign his death-warrant. It was expected that she would pardon him, but he died that year, still in the Tower, having protested his innocence to the last. He was at least spared one of the worst penalties inflicted upon traitors; for his son was permitted to inherit.[1]

Perrott may have been in later years an evil-tempered and on occasion a foul-mouthed man, but he was not a traitor. And the agony of the stone, an evil which he shared with both Fitzwilliam and Sidney, may excuse a great deal. Fitzwilliam comes none too well out of the affair, since, without showing obvious animus, he

[1] *C.S.P. Ireland*, Vol. CLXI, 19. *C.S.P. Dom.*, Vol. CCXXXI, 73. Bagwell, *Ireland under the Tudors*, Vol. III, p. 229.

accepted trumpery pieces of evidence at their face value; but he cannot of course be blamed as strongly as the learned and capable judges, who did the same thing, with so much more serious a responsibility.

Sir William Fitzwilliam was now sixty-two. He had been Governor of Fotheringay at the time of the execution of Mary Queen of Scots and had treated her with sympathetic respect. He lacked the energy and activity of Perrott and was a confirmed pessimist, always grumbling and bewailing his lot in tearful tones; but he knew Ireland well; his judgement was sound; and he had all his wits about him. He needed them; for it was certain that the Spanish Armada would arrive while he was Lord Deputy in Ireland. His appointment was announced in February 1588 but he did not receive the sword until July 1st.[1] On the 19th the Armada was sighted from the Lizard.

It had always been considered possible that the Spaniards might attempt to land a force in Ireland. In April 1587 a Dublin mariner, Miles Brewitt, reported that he had been taken before the Spanish Admiral, the Marquess de Santa Cruz, at Lisbon, who had asked for news of Perrott, an old acquaintance—'but he is a great Lutheran, which is a great pity'. The Spaniard wished he had one of Perrott's horses and one of his hawks, which were apparently celebrated. He next asked about the state of Ireland, and Brewitt replied that it had never been quieter. 'I hear so', said the Admiral. Brewitt claimed to have told him that the fortifications were strong. The Irish sailor also met James Fitzmaurice's son, who boasted that the King had promised 5,000 men for Ireland next year. He professed himself certain that all Ireland, but for Dublin, Waterford, Cork, and Drogheda, would declare for Philip II. From other sources, however, Brewitt heard that King and people were weary of the importunities of the many Irish refugees in their midst and spoke of them as Irish beggars. In point of fact, Ireland was at this time a secondary Spanish objective. The intention of Santa Cruz was to lie in the Thames estuary until the success of the landing force under Parma from the Low Countries was assured. He would then sail to Ireland before returning to Spain. All the Spanish troops would be left with Parma in England, but the fleet would carry to Ireland enough Italians and Germans from Parma's army to assure the conquest of that country.[2]

[1] C.S.P. Ireland, Vol. CXXXV, 96.
[2] C.S.P. Ireland, Vol. CXXIX, 32. C.S.P. Spanish, Vol. IV, p. 193.

It would not have been a difficult task. At the time of Brewitt's interview with Santa Cruz there were only 1,761 English troops in the Irish list and the material was in a wretched state: guns rusty and carriages rotting for want of men to maintain them, supplies of powder and arms deficient. In any case, it may be said that the invasion of Ireland would have had little significance if the Spaniards had first firmly established themselves in England, since Ireland would then have become indefensible. Even after the attempted invasion of England had failed, however, large-scale landings in Ireland would have been highly dangerous, despite the exhaustion of the Spaniards who reached the Irish coasts after passing north of Scotland.

Fitzwilliam was promised that the English fleet would land 10,000 men in Ireland in case of need. He published a statement to this effect to allay excitement, but he would rather have had 3,000 or 4,000 men on the spot to daunt 'the pride of the traitorous sort within the realm' and to meet the invaders at their first landing. On news of the arrival of Spanish ships on the Irish coast the Queen issued orders for reinforcements to be sent to Waterford, but when such vessels as could do so sailed again and he began to hear of the miserable state of the survivors of those which were wrecked, the Lord Deputy wrote that the reinforcements might be held up. His policy was simple: to kill every Spaniard who came ashore and upon whom he could lay hands.

Curiously enough, if Ireland was the last place where the English wanted to see the Spaniards, it was also the last place to which the Spaniards wanted to go. The Captain-General, when he set his course for the north, had no thought of the possible advantages of landing several thousand troops in Ireland; he wanted to get back to Spain and dreaded the dangerous Irish west coast. Nothing could be plainer than the course which he ordered to be held. The English translation is contemporary:

'*The course that shall be held in the return of this army into Spain.*'

'The course that is first to be held is to the North-north-east, until you be found under 61 degrees and a half [north of the Shetlands]; and then to take great heed lest you fall upon the island of Ireland, for fear of the harm that may happen unto you upon that coast. Then, parting from those islands, and doubling the Cape in 61 degrees and a half, you shall run West-south-west until you be found under 58 degrees [west of the island of Lewis]; and from thence to the South-west to the height of 53 degrees [roughly west of Galway Bay]; and then to the South-south-west, making to the Cape Finisterre, and so to procure your entrance into the Groyne [Coruña] or to Ferrol, or to any other port of coast of Galicia.'[1]

Moreover, Medina Sidonia did in fact lead the greater part of his surviving fleet well to the west of Ireland, and it was ships which lost touch with him that reached the Irish coast and were in many instances lost there. Three of these followed Juan Martinez de Recalde, Captain-General of the Biscay Squadron. Recalde himself anchored inside the Blasquets, off the Kerry coast, but the natives were either unwilling or too scared to give him aid and he had to use force to obtain water. He made sail again and reached Coruña with many dying men aboard, to die himself of exhaustion shortly afterwards. He was accounted one of the best of the Spanish admirals and had distinguished himself in the fighting in the Channel. A small vessel entered Tralee Bay, a little further north, and the twenty-four survivors of the crew were captured by Lady Denny, whose house was nearby, and hanged either by her or by her husband when he arrived. At least seven ships lay in the Shannon for some days—the mayor of Limerick reported that eleven originally entered the estuary—of which one was burnt by her crew as unseaworthy and one went ashore. The rest sailed again with the first wind. Two more were seen in the Arran Islands. One anchored close inshore, but found it impossible to make a landing in two boats in the hard weather, perhaps because the crew were so exhausted.[2]

The Governor of Connaught, Sir Richard Bingham, in letters to Walsingham and to the Queen, gives the most precise account of the Spanish losses of any to be found on the English side, though only for his own province. 'They were', he writes, 'by contrary weather driven upon the several parts of this province, and wrecked as it were by even portions, 3 ships in every of the 4 several counties bordering upon the sea coasts, viz., in Sligo, Mayo, Galway, and Thomond. So that 12 ships perished that all we know of on the rocks and sands by the shore side, and some 3 or 4 besides to seaboard of the out isles, which presently sunk, both men and ships, in the night time. . . . Other great wrecks they had both in Munster and in Ulster, which being out of my charge I have not so good notice of,

---

[1] *The Defeat of the Spanish Armada* (Navy Records Soc.), Vol. II, p. 240.

[2] *C.S.P. Ireland*, Vol. CXXXVI, 24, 29, 30 (i), 34, 38 (ii), 43. *C.S.P. Spanish*, Vol. IV, p. 415 (Medina Sidonia to the King). *The Defeat of the Spanish Armada* (Navy Records Soc.), Vol. II, p. 383.

but the same (I doubt not) is fully made known unto your Honour.'[1]

In Ulster three ships entered Killybegs, all severely damaged and only one, the *Girona*, a big galleass of Naples, sound enough to be repaired. This was done with the aid of the MacSweenys, the gallowglass clansmen of the neighbourhood. Meanwhile, the greatest, most inspiring, and popular figure of the Armada arrived on the scene. Don Alonzo de Leyva was in command of the troops and carried in his pocket a secret commission to succeed Medina Sidonia in command of the whole Armada in case of the death or incapacitation of the latter. Driven into Blacksod Bay, on the Mayo coast, his ship, *La Rata Santa Maria Encoronada*, broke up. The company was, however, saved, and crowded into a transport, the *Duquesa Santa Ana*. She in her turn was driven into Loughros Bay, in Donegal, and went on the rocks, but again all were saved. The sailors and troops then made their way to Killybegs over the hills, carrying de Leyva, who had been hurt by the capstan of the transport and was unable to walk or even to ride. While the Spaniards waited for the completion of repairs to the *Girona*, MacSweeny Banagh fed them, first on beef and mutton, but later on horseflesh, for which they had to pay. There was no hope of reaching Spain in the patched-up galleass, so de Leyva decided to make for Scotland. Fortune had aided him twice, but she did not for a third time bestow her favours upon him. The overcrowded and unseaworthy *Girona* was wrecked on a rock near Dunluce Castle, and virtually every soul in her perished.[2]

One of the great ships, *La Trinidad Valencera*, of the Levant Squadron, with many more than her complement aboard, was wrecked in O'Dogherty's country of Inishowen. Some 460 landed in a state of starvation and surrendered on promise of life to an officer named John Kelly. The Spanish officers were then separated from the men and the latter to a large extent butchered with lance and bullet. Some 150 escaped and were kindly treated by a 'savage gentleman' named O'Cahan, the lord of the country east of the Foyle, now northern Londonderry, and a vassal of the O'Neills. They were passed on to the MacDonalds in Antrim, who shipped them to Scotland. They reached Edinburgh, where they were well

---

[1] *The Defeat of the Spanish Armada* (Navy Records Soc.), Vol. II, p. 261. It must be recalled that Thomond, or Clare, then formed part of Connaught, though it was shortly afterwards transferred to Munster.

[2] *C.S.P. Spanish*, Vol. IV, p. 502. *The Defeat of the Spanish Armada* (Navy Records Soc.), pp. 300, 387. Bagwell, *Ireland under the Tudors*, Vol. III, p. 178.

treated and were among the number eventually repatriated by the Scots. The killers of the Spaniards in this case were two brothers, Richard and Henry Ovenden, henchmen of Tyrone's and commanding Irish companies in English pay, Kelly being an ensign in their force. Those most likely to pay ransoms were sent to Drogheda, and were, except for two noble prisoners saved by Bingham in Connaught, the only Spaniards who landed in Ireland, fell into English hands, and were granted their lives. If therefore the action of the Ovendens appears savage, it was no worse than that of the English.[1]

There exists little evidence in support of the common belief that the shipwrecked Spaniards were slaughtered in large numbers by the Irish, except in this case of the Ovendens. Nearly all the killing must be laid to the account of the English, and above all to that of Sir Richard Bingham and his superior, Sir William Fitzwilliam. There is a story which may be accepted that on one beach a gallowglass slew a large number of helpless men with his axe, and on several occasions the Irish looted Spaniards of all they had, down to their clothes. But they rarely killed them, and they must have had a hand in assisting the 400 or more who, according to Fitzwilliam, escaped to Scotland. Bingham was the chief executioner. He told the Queen that he had put to the sword at least 1,100 in his province; he had in the first instance spared fifty gentlemen, doubtless for ransom, but the Lord Deputy, who marched through Connaught towards the north in November, ordered these also to be killed and actually directed him to hang half a dozen young Dutchmen, whom he had spared as being pressed men. These actions must be accounted harsh, even by the standards of the age. A generation ago they would have been regarded as unspeakably horrible, but the world to-day has reverted to savagery to such an extent that it cannot launch so heavy a reproach.[2]

The motive was fear. There were few troops to guard or convoy prisoners, and it was apparently expected that much larger numbers would be taken. If the Spaniards, after resting and being fed, had broken out of captivity or been rescued by Irish sympathizers, they would have become a deadly menace to English power. In October, before it was known how many Spaniards had sailed again and when the last report put the number in Tyrconnell alone at 2,400, the

---

[1] C.S.P. Spanish, Vol. IV, p. 502. C.S.P. Ireland, Vol. CXXXVI, 36 (iii), 43 (xii). The Defeat of the Spanish Armada (Navy Records Soc.), Vol. II, p. 271.
[2] C.S.P. Ireland, Vol. CXXXIX, 2, 25.

Privy Council warned Fitzwilliam not to attack them except at an advantage and never to risk a defeat. He was to be reinforced as soon as possible by 2,000 men from Wales, to be raised by Sir John Perrott; but these troops were not required. A piece of deplorable vulgarity attributed to Perrott when put on trial shows, if it can be accepted as true, that in his view at least nerves at court were not quite as steady as patriotic chroniclers and historians have told us. Perrott had been out of favour, but, he said, "now the Queen is ready to bepiss herself for fear of the Spaniard, I am become her white boy again'.

The total strength of the Armada, including all supply ships, was approximately 130 ships. Of these sixty-three were lost, the fate of thirty-five of them being unknown. Only two were sunk in battle, two abandoned to the English, and five lost on the French and Dutch coasts. There are definite accounts of the loss of seventeen in Ireland, but this is a minimum figure and the total is probably over twenty. Ireland in that case accounted for a third of the losses in ships. And during the whole terrible episode not a man stirred throughout the country.

CHAPTER XII

TYRONE MOVES TOWARD REBELLION

ALL such ships of the Armada as had not been wrecked had sailed home. There was still talk of another Spanish expedition, this time against Ireland, and Lord Deputy Fitzwilliam suggested it might be headed by the traitor, Sir William Stanley, who had not sailed with the Armada, but had continued to serve with the Spaniards in the Low Countries. This was only a plea for insurance, as at this moment there was no evidence of danger. The Irish garrison in January 1589 numbered 4,110 foot and 710 horse.[1]

With the settlement of the Desmond territory already on his hands, Fitzwilliam now found himself involved in the problems of the 'country' of another great though lesser chieftain. This affair of Monaghan is of interest because it was to such an extent definitive that Lord Deputy Chichester did little more than restore it when he carried out the Ulster Plantation in the reign of James I, but even more so because it illustrates the clash between the English systems of feudal grants and primogeniture and the Irish system of tanistry.

In 1589 Sir Ross MacMahon died without leaving a legitimate son. He was the feudal grantee of Monaghan, except for the Barony of Farney granted to Essex, and was considered a 'good subject'. He was also regarded by his people as the MacMahon, supreme chief after the Irish fashion. By English law his successor was his brother, Hugh Roe MacMahon; on the Irish side a kinsman, Brian MacHugh Oge MacMahon, came forward as tanist. Fitzwilliam was anxious to break up these great chiefries if opportunity offered, and he thought that the best solution would be to partition the county between three, the third being Ever MacCooley MacMahon, chief of the Barony of Cremorne. The MacMahons would not agree to any such division of the county, so Fitzwilliam, as he was bound to in such circumstances, acknowledged the claim of Hugh Roe. He also lent him troops, since the tanist, as usual, had taken into his pay many swordsmen. Unfortunately, Hugh Roe, though installed by the English as a grantee in a position which he would not have been accorded under the Irish system, proceeded to behave as if he had

[1] *C.S.P. Ireland,* Vol. CXL, 51.

been an Irish chieftain pure and simple and one of the olden kind. With the very troops obtained from the Deputy, he invaded Cremorne to distrain for rent, burnt a part of the country, raided cattle in Farney, and rescued men arrested by the Sheriff as traitors. The Queen was inclined to accept all this as a matter of course, but Fitzwilliam took another view. In the autumn of 1590 he himself entered the county, brought Hugh Roe to trial at Monaghan Sessions, and hanged him.[1]

He then divided the county, still excepting Farney—which, to his regret, the young Earl of Essex would not give up—among eight chief lords, who were awarded large demesnes as personal property and other holdings on which were planted 280 freeholders, paying 7s. 6d. to the Queen and 12s. 6d. to their lord for each tate, nearly 100 English acres. The Church lands were leased to private individuals. It was as fair a settlement as could well have been devised by an Englishman in such a case, but the taint of corruption has clung to it, and it has been alleged that Fitzwilliam took bribes in connection with it. No evidence has ever been produced to justify this assertion, and the Lord Deputy himself denied it, 'in the presence of God, by whom I hope to be saved'.[2]

The settlement of the Desmond estates was fated to be overthrown in the Tyrone rebellion. Its weakness was one which applied also to that of King's and Queen's Counties and which special care was taken to avoid in the Ulster Plantation of James I. Leaving the moral issue out of account, it is apparent that, if English settlers were to be established upon lands forfeited by Irish lords for rebellion and treason, they must be furnished with local protection beyond the scanty garrisons of royal troops likely to be maintained in time of peace. The only reliable protection was a high proportion of English tenants, trained in the bearing of arms, and they would have to be offered benefits substantial enough to induce them to quit their farms or their occupations in England. It is true that attempts to bring this about were made in the Munster settlement and that the tenants in chief themselves put forward proposals to that effect. Yet the scheme was never sound in this respect. A number of tenants appear to have returned to England on finding that Munster was not the land of promise. In October and November 1592 it was reported that there was a 'reasonable show' of tenants on most of the Desmond lands and that the estate was quiet, 'without any stir

[1] C.S.P. Ireland, Vol. CLI, 2; Vol. CLIV, 22; Vol. CLV, 8, 19.
[2] C.S.P. Ireland, Vol. CLX, 43. Falls, The Birth of Ulster, p. 103.

or known troubles in any part thereof'.[1] But it had no solid foundation on which to withstand adversity.

Among the chief tenants were Sir Christopher Hatton, Sir Walter Raleigh, Sir Edward Fitton, and Sir William Trenchard. Edmund Spenser received the castle of Kilcolman, near Doneraile, with over 3,000 acres. One result of the extinction of the Desmond name and power which had scarcely been foreseen was the increased importance of the MacCarthys in Cork and in lesser degree of the O'Sullivans in the south-western limits of Cork and Kerry. The chiefs of these countries were to play an important part in the Munster phase of the Tyrone rebellion.

The only serious troubles in Ireland during the period immediately after the passing of the Armada occurred in Connaught. In March 1589 a band of the Mayo Burkes came out and were joined by Sir Morrogh ne Doe O'Flaherty and the Joyces with some 600 men from Galway. The pretext of the revolt was the harshness of Bingham's administration, and the method to burn the villages and raid 3,000 cattle from those who did not join the rebels. Lieutenant Francis Bingham marched at top speed against them and came up with them at a place described as 'Castle Annaclare'. They stood to meet him behind a hedge, but he broke their ranks, killed over 100 of them, and scattered the rest.[2]

This period was marked by an enquiry into the conduct of Bingham, accused by the Irish of unlawfully executing a gallowglass captain, and of other offences. He was on no better terms with Fitzwilliam than he had been with Perrott, and many of the officials considered him unduly severe; but he was strongly supported by Walsingham. The Irish view of his actions is illustrated by the statements of the Lough Cé annalists. Bingham, they say, 'made a bare, polished garment of the province of Connaught'. When the 'Justiciary of Erinn [Fitzwilliam]' heard of the evil, he marched in anger to Galway, and ClanWilliam came in and left hostages in the town. 'There never came into Connaught such wicked people as were in that army.' However, no charge was brought home to Bingham either in Galway or at a subsequent inquiry in Dublin, and he remained in his appointment.[3]

[1] C.S.P. Ireland, Vol. CLXVII, 8, 21.
[2] C.S.P. Ireland, Vol. CXLIII, 12 (vi, vii). I cannot identify the place, but it was in the Barony of Kilmaine, in southern Mayo.
[3] Annals of Lough Cé, pp. 493, 499. Bagwell, Ireland under the Tudors, Vol. III, p. 210.

He soon had more work to do. Sir Brian O'Rourke, supreme chief of Leitrim, one of the most powerful men in Ireland below the first three or four, had aided the Spaniards, and still had fourteen of them, who were training his kerne. Though formerly a loyalist, his present political views may be judged from the story that he had made a wooden effigy on which was written the words 'Queen Elizabeth', urged his retainers to hack it with axes, and, tying it to his horse's tail, dragged it through the mire. It was actually one of the charges made against Perrott at his trial that he had not arrested O'Rourke on hearing of this incident. He now came out into rebellion, and the Mayo Burkes, probably encouraged by the charges against Bingham and by his absence in Dublin to confront them, made fresh trouble. Bingham, after giving them a period of grace and receiving no submission, set about them in his accustomed style, with the aid of the great Connaught lords, Clanrickarde and Thomond. In March 1590 he wrote grimly to Fitzwilliam that they and their Clandonnell gallowglasses had all submitted; now the time had come to deal with O'Rourke.[1]

The reckoning was swift. Being sick himself, the Governor sent his brother, Sir George. After some stiff fighting, O'Rourke fled from his county, eventually passed into Scotland, was handed over by James VI to the English, and was tried and executed at Tyburn. He died proudly, as he had lived.

The worst feature of Elizabethan military administration concerned the pay of the troops. The Privy Council generally, though not always, provided as much money as appeared on paper sufficient to meet expenses, but frequently not enough to meet charges which it was difficult to assess in advance. When this happened the Irish Government fell into debt. On the other hand, the English authorities believed, often enough with reason, that some of the funds found their way into the wrong pockets and would have gone very much farther had the accounts been honestly kept. Again, when a sum was consigned to Ireland insufficient to meet both past debts and current expenditure, there was a tendency to disregard the former, even when they included arrears of pay and allowances. And, when an advance in pay was wrung from the English Exchequer, it was occasionally bestowed only on newly-formed companies, leaving veterans long in Ireland on the old standard.

The Lord Deputy himself became involved in an ugly incident brought about by the chaotic state of Irish finance. Sir John Norris,

[1] *C.S.P. Ireland*, Vol. CLI, 32 (ii, iii); Vol. CLXI, 19.

President of Munster, had gone to Flanders after the dissolution of Perrott's Parliament, leaving his brother, Sir Thomas, acting as Vice-President in his place. Sir Thomas's own company of foot had been sent north of the Shannon. In May 1590 it marched to Dublin in a mutinous state to demand arrears of pay, and assembled on the bridge in front of the Castle gate. Fitzwilliam was in these later years often accused of lack of energy, but he showed plenty of nerve on this occasion. He rode out on to the bridge with Sir George Carew, bearing the sword of state. The troops opened out to let him pass, addressing prayers to him; but one man caught at his bridle, whereupon he snatched his weapon from him and drew his rapier, striking several men with it. Carew was ready to draw the Queen's sword, but it never came to that. When Fitzwilliam shouted to the horseman and servants about him to disarm the troops, they laid down their arms. They were in no vicious mood and spoke of their grievances with the greatest respect. Carew and other observers were struck by the Lord Deputy's courage and restraint. Doubtless he was sorry for the unfortunate men. A couple of years later he wrote to Burghley that he wished the Lord Treasurer could hear as he did the pitiful complaints of the poor unclothed soldiers.[1]

In the general quietude following the defeat of the Armada neither the men on the spot nor the English Government could guess that a volcano was going to erupt in Ulster; but it is not difficult for the historian to note the growing heat of its fires. The situation, especially in Tyrone, was such that, if there had been no rebellion, even if the English had made of Ulster an independent state, there would probably have been a bloody civil war. In the years that had passed since his return to Ireland when the elder Essex was Governor of Ulster, the Earl of Tyrone had established himself. He had overcome the suspicion with which the North at first regarded him when he came back to it half-anglicized. He still professed loyalty to the Queen, and there had been little in his conduct to which exception could be taken, but he clearly resented the settlement of Monaghan, and already some signs of his swelling ambitions were visible.

He did not need to abandon English clothes in order to ensure the fidelity of his followers, as had been the case with some other Irish chiefs. He even ventured upon an English marriage. Mabel Bagenal, daughter of the old Marshal who had been struck by Perrott in the Council Chamber, must have been some sixty years younger than her father when she attracted the attention of Tyrone, who was

[1] *Carew Cal.*, Vol. III, p. 31. *C.S.P. Ireland*, Vol. CLVII, 51; Vol. CLXVI, 34.

probably forty-five or forty-six and had already had two wives, if not three. He had divorced the first, who came of the eastern branch of the O'Neills, and the second, an O'Donnell, had died. He had also gone through a ceremony of betrothal with a daughter of Tirlagh Luineach, but evidence that he ever married her is doubtful. However, he had so winning a way with him that in August 1591 Mabel Bagenal eloped from the house of her sister, Lady Barnewall, wife of a prominent Anglo-Irish gentleman of the Pale, and was married to the Earl by the Thomas Jones, Bishop of Meath and future Archbishop of Dublin, who explained his extraordinary performance by the plea that he had acted as he did for the sake of the lady's honour. A historian has called the new Countess of Tyrone 'the Helen of the Elizabethan wars'. She did not bring about a war, but she created in the bosom of her brother, Sir Henry Bagenal, furious that his blood should be mingled 'with so traitorous a stock and kindred', bitter resentment against her husband, which contributed to its outbreak. Like all Tyrone's wives—and there was another to come—Mabel's fate was unhappy. Eventually, not choosing to share his favours with his mistresses, she went to her brother at Newry, where she died in 1596.[1]

There may be said to have been at this time three strong rival parties in the O'Neill country, supporting different branches of the family. The foremost was that of Tyrone himself, which owed much of its strength to English support. Then came that of Tirlagh Luineach, who had long maintained himself by means of a certain prudence and caution which might almost be called statesmanship, but who was now old, ailing, and fighting a losing battle with Tyrone. The third party was that of the MacShanes, the sons of Shane, shadowy personages, none of whom would seem to have inherited their father's energy and ability, though they possessed a fair following. One of them, Hugh Gavelach, who fell into Tyrone's hands in 1589 or 1590, was hanged by him, a doubtful piece of policy, because it offended his mother's clan, the Macleans.[2]

The lease by Tirlagh Luineach to the Earl of the south-east part of County Tyrone had given rise to disputes between the two. But it ought to have been clear to Fitzwilliam that, as soon as Tirlagh died—and though he recovered again and again from sickness and

---

[1] *C.S.P. Ireland*, Vol. CLIX, 38, 39. Falls, *The Birth of Ulster*, p. 42. Bagwell, *Ireland under the Tudors*, Vol. III, p. 223. *The Dictionary of National Biography* gives the date of Tyrone's birth as '1540?'. He was probably born about 1545.

[2] *C.S.P. Ireland*, Vol. CLI, 71.

drinking bouts, so that he seemed to be eternal, he could not last much longer—Tyrone would lay his hands upon the whole chiefry and would prove to be a subject of a very different type. In May 1593 Tirlagh Luineach thought well to make over his Irish chiefry to his kinsman, who then began to style himself the O'Neill. He was anxious to keep the peace for the time being; but his headstrong young son-in-law, or son-in-law to be, Hugh Maguire, the new chieftain of Fermanagh, was prepared neither to remain loyal to the Crown nor to submit to the authority of Tyrone, and into the bargain was opposed by a half-brother in his succession.

In Tyrconnell also there was ample promise of trouble. It has been recorded that its chief, Sir Hugh MacManus O'Donnell, had married Ineen Dubh MacDonald, stepdaughter of Tirlagh Luineach O'Neill. The aim of this fierce and capable Scots virago became henceforth to secure for her beloved eldest son, Hugh Roe, the chieftaincy of the country, and she would stop at nothing to do so. Perrott, realizing her ambition, had decided to lay hands upon the boy and keep him as a pledge for the quietude of Tyrconnell, and in 1587 had kidnapped him by means of the bait of a ship laden with wine which had put into Lough Swilly, and had lodged him in the Castle. After one abortive attempt to escape, young O'Donnell broke out in 1592 and with the aid of Tyrone made his way back to his own country, where he was received with enthusiasm. An illegitimate half-brother, who had aspired to seize the chiefry, had been put out of the way by the masterful Ineen Dubh. And it was doubtless at her instigation that Hugh's father decided to abdicate and have him installed as the O'Donnell with full ceremony. One of his first acts was to drive out a company, commanded by Captain Willis, Sheriff of Fermanagh, which was quartered in the monastery of Donegal and is reported from Irish sources to have behaved disgracefully. Whatever the conduct of Willis had been, his presence would have been unwelcome. 'It suited neither O'Neills nor O'Donnells to have sheriffs and gibbets so near them.'[1]

The bad treatment he had received at English hands, combined with the influence of his mother, set Hugh O'Donnell, then aged about nineteen, upon the path of rebellion. In the spring of 1593 he entrusted to the Catholic Archbishop of Tuam a letter to the Irish lords in the service of Philip II of Spain. He told them of his escape from the Castle, of the hardships he had suffered in reaching

[1] *C.S.P.Ireland*, Vol. CLXV, 3. Bagwell, *Ireland under the Tudors*, Vol. III, p. 226.

his own country, and of his expulsion of Willis. He and his friends were, he said, only waiting to raise the standard of revolt against the English Crown. The Irish lords in Spain were to facilitate the Archbishop's mission, which was to obtain Spanish aid. He pledged himself to fight to the death. It cannot be said that he ever deviated from this resolve, as Tyrone did, though he temporized on occasion.[1]

Fitzwilliam marched up to Dundalk in the summer of 1592, but Tyrone, still anxious to gain credit for loyalty, which would be useful to him in his differences with Tirlagh Luineach, acted as mediator. He brought Hugh Roe—who like a number of other Ulster magnates had become his son-in-law—to meet the Lord Deputy, and the young chief made humble submission in Dundalk church, vowing that he would be as loyal as his father had been.[2]

Even if he had fulfilled his pledge, which, as we have seen, he did not intend to do, there would have been stirring times in Tyrconnell. Though he was intensely popular with the great majority of the people, his succession to the chiefry was not undisputed. The most formidable claimant was Neill Garve ('the Rough') grandson of Hugh Roe's uncle, the good old Calvagh who had been Sidney's firm friend and ally. Neill Garve married Hugh Roe's sister Nuala, and appeared at first to be prepared to accept his paramountcy; but in fact he cherished boundless ambitions.

So Tyrone—and with Tyrone went Armagh—Monaghan, Fermanagh, and Tyrconnell were all in a highly combustible state. Moreover, the significance of Ulster was heightened by the personalities of three of the chieftains of its countries. The Earl of Tyrone, middle-aged, crafty, patient, but inspiring complete obedience, with the talents of a commander of the Fabian school and a genius for organizing successfully an unpromising material, represented its brains and skill. The power to arouse enthusiasm, devotion, and fanaticism among the peasantry was represented by Hugh Roe O'Donnell and Hugh Maguire, handsome, attractive, and brilliant creatures, of whom the O'Donnell was perhaps the more talented and the Maguire the sounder, though both came to such early ends as to leave judgements of this sort doubtful. As a fighting man pure and simple, Neill Garve O'Donnell excelled them all, but his arms were to be employed mainly in the English cause, and he had no conception of the broader issues of the conflict.

The first serious trouble occurred in 1593. In May of that year Hugh Maguire raided Sligo and Roscommon, at the head of about

[1] Arch. Gen. de Simancas, E.838.   [2] C.S.P. Ireland, Vol. CLXVI, 44.

1,000 men from Fermanagh, but accompanied also, according to the confession of an Irish eyewitness, by 100 of Tyrone's men under his henchman, O'Hagan. The Lord Deputy, not altogether to the Queen's liking, gave Tyrone a commission to receive his submission and bring him in. According to Tyrone's story—but all his stories are suspect, since his subtlety developed into something like inability to avoid disguising the truth—Maguire agreed to come to Fitzwilliam in Tyrone's company, if sent a protection for three months. Fitzwilliam thanked Tyrone and sent the protection, but Maguire did not appear. Instead came a message from Tyrone to say that 'the traitor Maguire' had now raided Monaghan, showing how little regard he paid to the Queen's clemency. Fitzwilliam hesitated no longer. He ordered the Marshal, Sir Henry Bagenal, to move against Maguire and called upon Tyrone to prove his loyalty by aiding him.[1]

Bagenal, who had been engaged in some petty police operations in Monaghan after Maguire's departure, concentrated at Omagh, in Tyrone. His force numbered only about 400 strong, but he was joined by the Earl of Tyrone with 200 horse and 600 foot. It was to be the first trial, on a small scale, of the O'Neill forces organized and led by their new chief. This feature lends interest to the affair and causes the magniloquently named 'battle of the Erne Fords', which might otherwise be considered but a skirmish, to assume a certain importance.

Maguire's strength was estimated to be 1,200 men, of whom between 400 and 500 musketeers, archers, and gallowglasses were encountered on 10 October holding a position on the south side of the river Erne, near Belleek, covering two fords. It was by no means certain that a much stronger hostile force would not have to be met; for Hugh Roe O'Donnell was near at hand, at Ballyshannon, and reported to be searching his tender conscience about the propriety of leaving Maguire unsupported. He did not actually move on this occasion.

Maguire had occupied in strength a big salient created by a bend of the river, always a feature favourable to a force which seeks to force a passage. Bagenal and Tyrone took full advantage of it, posting musketeers on either flank to sweep it with fire. Meanwhile, a party of English foot was drawn up for a frontal attack across a ford which led on to it. Just as this assault was about to be launched, Tyrone's quick eye noted that the ford was wide enough to take

[1] *C.S.P. Ireland*, Vol. CLXX, 5 (ii), 24 (iv); Vol. CLXXI, 3, 33.

5 THE PASSAGE OF THE ERNE AT BELLEEK, 1593

The Anglo–Irish Allies force the ford under cover of flanking fire (*Cottonian MSS*).

horse on the flanks of the foot. He then brought up his Irish horse so that it and the infantry crossed simultaneously. The flanking fire had done its work, and resistance was slight. The enemy fled before Maguire could bring up his reserves. He was hotly pursued, and there was heavy killing in the flight. He lost some 300 men, whereas on the loyalist side the casualties numbered only three killed and a score of wounded. Among the latter were the joint leaders, Bagenal being bruised by a blow from a gallowglass axe, which fortunately for him fell flat, and Tyrone having an Irish lance or javelin driven into his thigh. A ludicrous feature of the affair was that they agreed to praise each other's exploits in their reports. Tyrone fulfilled his promise, writing that Bagenal had killed several men with his own hands, though there was, he said afterwards, no evidence of the Marshal having killed any man. Bagenal omitted this tribute to Tyrone. The relations between the brothers-in-law had been bad, and their common victory brought about no improvement.[1]

Maguire's revolt was scotched, and he himself was a fugitive. Tyrone ended his message to Fitzwilliam with the words, 'hoping before I die to do Her Majesty many more days' service', whereas in fact he was never to do her another. He now had the excuse of his wound to retire to Dungannon and keep away from affairs in which he had taken part in some doubt and for his services in which he considered that little gratitude had been shown. Bagenal also quitted the scene, but he left 300 men with Connor Roe Maguire, Hugh's half-brother and rival, known as 'the Queen's Maguire'. One of their tasks was, with the aid of Bingham, to secure Maguire's castle at Enniskillen. This proved to be a tough nut and was not taken until 2 February 1594. The island of Enniskillen was then divided from the mainland on all sides by wider stretches of the Erne than is the case to-day. The English under Captain Dowdall displayed skill and energy in the operations. Two boats were launched in the lough, the larger, an 18-tonner, being first used to carry food and munitions to the camp. The light falcons and falconets employed did not break down the walls, and it was decided to transport a culverin to the scene, but this does not appear to have arrived. In the morning Dowdall put 100 men into his big boat, protecting them from missiles by hurdles covered with hides. One Connor O'Cassidy, a member of a sept subject to the Maguires,

[1] *C.S.P. Ireland*, Vol. CLXXII, 2, 4, 7, 8, 19. *Carew Cal.*, Vol. III, p. 88. *History of Catholic Ireland*, p. 71.

steered the boat under the wall of the barbican, in which the crew made a breech with pickaxes and other instruments. On entering the barbican, they threatened to blow up the whole place, whereupon the garrison, thirty-six fighting men, with about the same number of women and children, surrendered.[1]

Meanwhile, the conduct of both Tyrone and O'Donnell was becoming more and more suspicious, and they were obviously making no attempt to restrain adherents from riotous actions. In March, Fitzwilliam being too ill to leave Dublin, Lord Chancellor Loftus, Sir Robert Gardiner, Chief Justice of the King's Bench, and Sir Anthony St. Leger, Master of the Rolls, were sent to Dundalk to conduct negotiations. Tyrone played a curious game of hide and seek. He professed to be afraid that his enemy, Bagenal, would lay hands upon him. He made an appointment for dinner at a house called Castleton, a mile from Dundalk, but did not keep it. Then he promised to come there next day with O'Donnell, but Gardiner had to ride out half a mile to meet him and then found him alone. He wept on speaking of the Queen's favours—tears always came easily to him—but complained bitterly that recent services had not been requited. Gardiner retorted that he had not come to talk about the past. Eventually Tyrone rode away and brought O'Donnell, then withdrawing and leaving him alone with Gardiner. O'Donnell understood English, but scarcely spoke it, so Sir Henry Duke, an old soldier, acted as interpreter. O'Donnell professed his loyalty, but said that he went in fear of his life, obviously hinting at Bagenal's hostility. After some further talk, Gardiner decided that O'Donnell was no more than a creature of Tyrone's and would do as he was bidden by him. Again meeting the Earl, Gardiner told him he was dining at Castleton and enjoined him to come with O'Donnell. Again he did not turn up, but when the Chief Justice was at table a message was brought to him that he was at the gate with a large company.

Then ensued an extraordinary and perhaps symbolical scene. Gardiner came out to find a number of the nobility of Ulster assembled on horseback. Besides Tyrone and O'Donnell, he noticed the former's brother Cormac, his half-brother, Tirlagh MacHenry, a son-in-law, a son of Tirlagh Luineach's, and John O'Dogherty, chieftain of Inishowen. The party began to move towards Dundalk. First Tyrone protested his loyalty. Then followers snatched at his bridle to draw him away. With tears in his eyes, he said to Gardiner:

[1] *C.S.P. Ireland*, Vol. CLXXII, 25; Vol. CLXXIII, 19.

'I pray you let me not lose you, that hath been my dear friend.'
Gardiner answered that the Earl need not lose him unless he first
lost himself. On further urging from the company, Tyrone turned
his horse's head, but in doing so plucked Gardiner's sleeve and said:
'I pray you send Tom Lee with me.' So Thomas Lee, a gallant
but unscrupulous adventurer who had distinguished himself on the
Erne and was to die as a traitor after the outbreak of the younger
Essex, and Sir Edward Moore, an Anglo-Irish magnate of County
Louth, neither of them desirable influences, rode away with him,
and Gardiner proceeded towards Dundalk. Soon, however, Lee
and Moore rode back, to say that some of the party had pointed
weapons at their breasts, whereupon Tyrone had advised them to
leave him.[1]

It is easy for the historian to describe a scene of this sort, but when
the evidence, though it bears upon it the stamp of meticulous
accuracy and of having been compiled by an orderly legal intellect,
comes from one side only, it is difficult to assess its significance. Was
that masterly dissembler Tyrone merely play-acting? It might be
concluded that he was were not his conduct on this occasion so
closely in accord with all that is known of his hesitant disposition,
the difficulty that he found in making up his mind in time of crisis,
his doubts about English intentions, the conflicting pulls between
genuine friendships such as that with Gardiner and his interests as
an Irish chief, and perhaps most of all the steady, persistent influence
of kinsmen and 'urriaghts'. In war Tyrone was predominant; all
would do his will. Yet he was in the grip of the system. 'You do
not know the North', he said later, after he had gone into rebellion,
in objection to a proposal that his sons should be educated in
England. 'The North' was a power which he could use for his own
ends, but which encompassed him. Now, it would seem, he was
hanging in the balance, and that evening's ride was an occasion
when 'the North' pressed down the scales in favour of war.

The affair was not yet over. Tyrone sent another message, that if
he were accorded a formal protection he would return to state his
grievances. He arrived at Dundalk that same night, and the whole
of the following day was spent in drawing up the document. On
Thursday 14 March he handed it in. The commissioners refused
to accept certain passages and induced him to make alterations. Then
he bade them farewel'.

Tyrone's 'griefs' mingled serious things with petty. He complained

[1] *C.S.P. Ireland*, Vol. CLXXIII, 89 (i).

of false accusations engineered by Fitzwilliam and Bagenal. He asserted that in Upper Clandeboye, south of Belfast Lough, his followers had been removed and 'base men' of the Marshal's faction put in in their place; and generally that those who bore him affection had been discredited and others preferred. He declared that Thomas Henshaw, Seneschal of Monaghan, and the vice-constable of the fort were hated by all the tenants. He brought up the old grievance that his foster-brothers, the Ovendens, had compelled the surrender of 500 Spaniards in Tyrconnell, but had received no recompense or share of the ransom. He himself had got no reward for his service with the Marshal in Fermanagh, but had been called a traitor; and on one occasion the Marshal had raised a false alarm in hope of finding him unready. He considered that the Lord Deputy and the Marshal were leagued against him, while, since the death of Leicester, Hatton, and Walsingham, he was destitute of friends. His friend Hugh Roe MacMahon had been executed for distraining for rent, as was within his right. Finally, he had never received the sum of £1,000 which had been left to his wife, Mabel Bagenal, by her father.[1]

Making their report to the Privy Council a few days later, Loftus, Gardiner, and St. Leger recommended that a pardon should be offered to Maguire and that the commissions of Bagenal and Henshaw should be revoked. They would appear to have believed that personalities had played a prominent part in the troubles and that the conduct of these men had been provocative. What was described as 'a kind of truce' with Tyrone was now observed, pending further instructions from the Queen.

It was a question not merely of new instructions but also of a new instrument to carry them out. Lord Deputy Fitzwilliam's health had broken down. Earnestly demanding release at the beginning of the year, he had written to Sir Robert Cecil: 'It is God's good blessing that this state is reduced to that staidness of quiet that the infirmities of the Governor, old, weak in body, sick in stomach, racked with the stone, bedrid with the gout, and disgraced with restraints, do not make it stagger. It is not good to let things hang long upon a feeble stay.'[2]

It would have been well had the Queen acted at once on the advice of her old servant. She realized that the situation was serious and, probably in March, drafted a warrant for the appointment of Gardiner and Sir Richard Bingham to act as Lord Justices in the

[1] *Carew Cal.*, Vol. III, p. 87.   [2] *C.S.P. Ireland*, Vol. CLXXIII, 10.

event of the death of the Lord Deputy or of his becoming completely incapacitated by sickness. It did not go as far as that. Fitzwilliam remained in possession of his faculties and judgement, though he had to lie up in Dublin. On 3 May 1594 Elizabeth drew up instructions for his successor, Sir William Russell, son of the Earl of Bedford. They were remarkably favourable to Tyrone, who was to be informed that one of his foes, Fitzwilliam, was being withdrawn and that the other, Bagenal, would be forbidden to take any action against him. These instructions were not, however, delivered to Russell until 25 May and then, as so often happened, he was held up by contrary winds. He reached the Head of Howth on 31 July, but did not receive the sword until 11 August, having refused to do so until a full report of the state of the country had been compiled for him. And in the interval the forces of the Government had suffered a defeat which history must thus inscribe upon the record of Fitzwilliam's viceroyalty, and which brought the general revolt very much closer.[1]

Hugh Roe O'Donnell had thrown off the mask and joined Hugh Maguire in investing Enniskillen in June. Fitzwilliam had prepared and elaborately equipped a relief force under Sir Henry Duke and Sir Edward Herbert, in strength forty-six horse and 600 foot, with a train of carts and pack-horses carrying provisions to revictual the castle. O'Donnell already had at his disposal great strength in Scots mercenaries, some 3,000 of whom landed in Antrim in July; but he sent a message to Tyrone calling for aid. Once again Tyrone hung in the wind. O'Donnell's action appeared to him rash. At the last moment his brother Cormac joined the rebels with 100 horse and 300 musketeers. Even the Irish are not prepared to say whether or not he was acting with Tyrone's assent, but he had taken a step toward committing him.

O'Donnell remained in front of the castle, while Maguire and Cormac O'Neill pushed a few miles southward with about 1,000 men, a large proportion of them Scots, to intercept the relief force. They laid an ambush for it at the ford of Drumane over the Arney stream, a little above the point where it enters the Erne river between Upper and Lower Lough Erne. Many actions of these wars are difficult to reconstruct precisely, especially as regards the sites, but there can be no doubt in this instance, since it may be assumed from examination of the ground both that the ford is traversed by the modern bridge and that the old track, after crossing it, followed

[1] *Carew Cal.*, Vol. III, p. 90. *C.S.P. Ireland*, Vol. CLXXV, 23, 35, 43.

the course of the modern road from Cavan to Enniskillen. This road, north of the bridge, makes a sharp bend to the right to avoid a hill, round the flank of which it passes and by which it is dominated. To-day there are only hedgerow trees on the hill, but it seems to have been thickly wooded in those times. On 7 August the advancing English horse failed to discover the Irish lying hidden on and about the hill, and the infantry, covering the provision train, bumped straight into them.

'The ambuscade was successful', say the annalists, 'for they came on without noticing anything until they fell in with Maguire's people at the mouth of a certain ford. A fierce and vehement conflict and a spirited and hard-contested battle was fought between the two parties, till at length Maguire and his forces routed the others by dint of fighting. . . . Many steeds, weapons, and other spoils were left behind in that place, besides the steeds and horses that were loaded with provisions on their way to Enniskillen. . . . The name of the ford at which this great victory was gained was changed to Bel-atha-na-in-Briosgadh (Mouth of the Ford of the Biscuits), from the number of biscuits and small cakes left there to the victors on that day.'[1]

The Irish exaggerate the English numbers, but it may be noted that the latter would not count the horseboys and 'churls' in their company. The losses, which again would be fighting men only, were fifty-six officers and men killed and sixty-nine wounded, nearly one-fourth of the force's strength. If these numbers appear trifling, the stage of rebellion in which considerable forces fought on the side of the Government had not yet been reached, and the combat has always been ranked as important in Irish history. Duke and Herbert, writing from Cavan, did not conceal the severity of the repulse and reported that they had been glad enough to draw off any of the force to safety.[2]

A week after this reverse, which made so unfortunate an ending to his viceroyalty, though from the moral rather than the material point of view, Fitzwilliam took his weary body aboard ship and sailed for home. He was worn out, though he lived until 1599. Beside Sidney and Mountjoy he is a heavy, lethargic, and unattractive figure, though, like most of the viceroys of the reign and so many other Elizabethans, he endears himself to posterity as a vivid correspondent. Not a great man, he had been all his life a steady

---

[1] Four Masters, Vol. VI, p. 1951. *History of Catholic Ireland*, p. 79.
[2] *C.S.P. Ireland*, Vol. LXXV, 47.

public servant. He was trusted by the Queen and Council, as could not be better shown than by the fact that he was sent to Ireland for his second viceroyalty on the very eve of the coming of the Armada. He did not profess to be a trained soldier, and was never accorded strong military support, but he made the most of what he had and suffered no disasters, unless this last affair of the Arney be accounted such. Like others, including his successor Russell, he was accused of accepting bribes, but the Queen and Burghley took no notice of these allegations. There was little nicety in such matters in those days, and the Lord Deputy may have taken presents of cattle—the principal Irish currency—from time to time, but even that is uncertain. He made no serious mistakes, except that, like others in England and Ireland, he supported Tyrone against his rivals to a degree which proved to have been imprudent and was deluded into the belief that he would make 'a good subject'. And even in that respect his eyes were opened before those of his staff. Measured by the magnitude of his task and the slenderness of his resources in the long years in which, whether as Lord Justice or as Lord Deputy, he governed Ireland, Fitzwilliam must be accounted a capable and conscientious ruler.

CHAPTER XIII

REVOLT AND TRUCE IN ULSTER

WHILE Fitzwilliam was on the point of sailing, the astonishing news arrived that Tyrone was on his way to Dublin without a protection. Fitzwilliam refused to defer his passage. Thus, when Tyrone rode in on 15 August 1594 he had not to confront the only man whose charges against him would have carried great weight. He assuredly showed no want of nerve on this occasion, doubtless counting on the inexperience of the new Lord Deputy, who would hardly care to precipitate a crisis at the start of his viceroyalty, and on well-wishers in the Council. He made humble submission to Russell and promised to restore peace, get rid of the Scots, pay a composition, and send in his eldest son, with the understanding that he should be educated at Oxford or Cambridge and meanwhile, of course, serve as a hostage for his father's good behaviour. Tyrone's most bitter enemy, Bagenal, had some charges ready. Among them was the grave one that Tyrone's kinsmen and followers, without losing his favour, had been associated with the Papal Archbishop MacGauran, titular Primate of all Ireland, who had come to Ireland with missions from the Pope and the King of Spain and had been killed during Maguire's raid into Connaught. However, Bagenal had not got his evidence at hand, and the Lord Deputy decided to defer consideration of the charges and let Tyrone go.[1]

The Queen afterwards expressed her serious disapproval of this failure to detain the Earl when he was without a protection; she described it, in fact, as 'a foul oversight'. She reproached the Council, rather than the Lord Deputy, since he was a new man and therefore particularly in need of sound advice. It was a Tudor instinct to lay hands upon troublesome and suspect persons unless they had rigidly protected themselves by documentary safe-conduct. Tyrone found reasons to avoid the performance of any of the promises made in Dublin.[2]

No fault could be found with Russell's energy. A week after

[1] C.S.P. Ireland, Vol. CLXXV, 52, 56. Carew Cal., Vol. III, pp. 95-9, 221.
[2] Carew Cal., Vol. III, p. 100.

receiving the sword, on 18 August 1594, he set out to relieve Ennis-killen with all the force he could muster, about 1,000 foot and 200 horse. He moved west into Roscommon, crossed the Curlieu hills, and then passed through Counties Sligo and Leitrim, making this roundabout march in order to pick up some further companies. He met with no opposition worthy of the name, but all the scouts and spies sent out were captured or deserted, so that he came within a mile of the castle without knowing whether it still held out. It was in fact resisting, but he arrived, on 30 August, only just in time. The warders were 'reduced to that extremity as they lived upon horse-flesh, dogs, cats, rats, and salt hides, and at our entry into the castle had but one horse left alive, which the day after was to be slaugh-tered'. He reduced their strength from forty to thirty and put in six months' supplies, including live cattle. He returned to Dublin by way of Cavan, where he left 200 foot. He complained that there were too many Irish in the old garrison companies, 'these garrison bands being in effect the strength of the realm, so long as they were continued English'.[1]

That winter fresh trouble broke out in Wicklow, where the looting of the famous partisan, Feagh MacHugh O'Byrne, reached such a scale that the Lord Deputy's intervention was sought by the local Irish. On 16 January 1595 Russell paid a flying visit to the district and nearly caught the O'Byrne chieftain in his house at Ballinacor. Feagh MacHugh just managed to escape, and fled into the tangled glens. Russell himself had to return to Dublin immedi-ately, but left a garrison at Ballinacor. He had, however, made no deep impression on the rebels; for on the night of the 30th they appeared in force close to the walls of Dublin and burnt the village of Crumlin. Russell came out into St. Thomas's Street, ordered the gates to be opened, and sent out a force of cavalry; but cavalry could not catch O'Byrnes in the dark.

This was insolence not to be borne. Russell set out again on 1 February. A number of Feagh MacHugh's followers submitted; others were taken and executed. It was not, however, until after Russell had returned to Dublin—he marched back on 23 February— that a notable success was gained. Feagh MacHugh's outstanding subordinate, one Walter Reagh Fitzgerald, a bastard of the house of Kildare, who had been wounded and was now hiding in a cave, was caught, brought to Dublin, and on 10 March hanged in chains. The country of the O'Byrnes was a little quieter thereafter, and though

[1] *C.S.P. Ireland*, Vol. CLXXVI, 11. *Carew Cal.*, Vol. III, p. 222.

Russell visited it again in April, he could now afford to spend some of his time hunting and fishing.[1]

In early February 1595, Tyrone's old friend, Sir Edward Moore, was directed to negotiate with him and his adherents. On the 16th, however, a body of Tyrone's men, led by his bastard brother, Art MacBaron, appeared on the Blackwater, with their matches alight and bullets in their mouths, and assaulted a stone fort established to cover the ford over the river. They were driven off with loss, but then attacked a wooden work, which was surrendered to them. The constable of the stone fort then also tamely surrendered. So the technique of the Ford of the Biscuits was repeated: Tyrone himself remained in the background, but a brother led his troops against the forces of the Government. Whether his brothers were dragging him on—perhaps the more probable explanation—or he was using them as his tools, is no longer a question of the first importance. A few days later one of his bands, with which he may have actually been present, carried out an incendiary raid into Cavan and penetrated into Louth.[2]

Both sides were preparing for a trial of strength. Tyrone had enormously increased his forces and was believed to be maintaining 1,000 pikemen, 4,000 musketeers, and 1,000 cavalry, while outside the provinces of Munster and Connaught the Lord Deputy had for the moment only 1,100 men. The English Government was, however, alive to the danger and had decided to withdraw 2,000 troops from Brittany, though only 1,616 by the poll were actually shipped at Paimpol, sick and 'dead pays' doubtless accounting for the deficiency. At the same time orders were issued to raise 1,000 men in England, 100 of them being that levy on Derbyshire which has already been described.[3]

Russell had asked for a good senior commander, since it was never practicable to employ Ormonde in the north for long, and he may have had some doubt about the capacity of Bagenal. What the Government did was to send him Sir John Norris, with a special patent which made him independent in Ulster. This was an inconvenient arrangement for the Lord Deputy, besides putting a personal slight upon him, since he was an experienced soldier, who had distinguished himself against the Spaniards and had been Governor of Flushing. Norris, still nominally holding the appointment of Lord

[1] *Carew Cal.*, Vol. III, pp. 225–30. Four Masters, Vol. VI, p. 1,955.
[2] *C.S.P. Ireland*, Vol. CLXXVIII, 39, 53 (ii), 55.
[3] See p. 55. *C.S.P. Ireland*, Vol. CLXVIII, 53, 63, 71, 78.

President of Munster, a function carried out by his brother, Sir Thomas, had fought brilliantly since passing over to the Continent, notably in the capture of Crozon. He was now, however, in indifferent health and appeared out of his element in Irish warfare, so small in scale by comparison with that to which he was accustomed yet so much more difficult to a commander unused to irregular fighting. He made a lesser effort than Russell to accommodate himself to the relations established between them, and the intermittent friction between the two hampered their joint efforts. A third brother, Sir Henry, came over with the troops from Brittany. None of these three gallant brethren was destined to survive the Irish wars.

The Brittany contingent under Henry Norris reached Waterford on 19 March 1595, and he reported that the captains were unwilling to march to Wicklow because the men had been accustomed only to short marches in France and were weak in the legs after the voyage. John Norris arrived at the same port on 4 May, on the eve of a spell of misfortune. O'Donnell, Maguire, and Cormac O'Neill had recently raided Longford and driven off a vast herd of cattle. Then the rebels recovered Enniskillen. Russell's information was that the garrison had surrendered on promise of quarter, but had been killed. He cannot fairly be blamed. There was at the time no possibility of driving the Irish away from the castle. All that a relief force could have done would have been to put in fresh supplies, and the Lord Deputy's intelligence was that Enniskillen was adequately supplied. On the other hand, little forts with garrisons of twenty-five and upwards held out for long periods on many occasions, provided they had food and ammunition, since the Irish did not possess artillery and were not at their best as storming parties.[1]

Next Tyrone and his associates invested Monaghan Castle. On this occasion, however, aid was nearer at hand. On 25 May Bagenal marched out from Newry with some 1,500 men, made up in part of companies from Brittany, in part of old companies containing some veterans, but brought up to strength by recruits from England. He had very sharp fighting on the road, though the Irish did not come to push of pike. He revictualled Monaghan, but could not leave as much powder and lead as he would have desired owing to the amount expended in reaching the castle and the needs of the return march. And it was found that he had retained none too much in his hands.

[1] *C.S.P. Ireland*, Vol. CLXXVIII, 102, 119.

On 27 May he set out again for Newry. Tyrone, now strongly reinforced, with certainly 4,000 horse and foot and perhaps 1,000 more, met him about the scene of the previous day's combat, in the neighbourhood of Clontibret. For the first time the O'Neill tactics were displayed in their deadliest form, the musketeers galling the column with continuous fire from the flanks. The pace was reduced to a crawl, and it got slower and slower as more and more wounded had to be picked up and carried along. The column was compelled to halt that night short of Newry, with little powder or ball left. If Tyrone had been a bolder man he would have launched a night assault, but he remained inactive. Next morning a small reinforcement appeared from Newry, and late in the day the whole force got back to its shelter, very weary and not a little shaken. The losses reported, thirty-one killed and 109 wounded, were high enough for warfare of this nature, but even then may have been below the real figures. There was material here for serious consideration on the future of the war in Ulster.[1]

This, so far as it went, was a limited success, though it might have been a disaster. It was followed at the beginning of June by another setback. Sir Richard Bingham's cousin, Captain George Bingham, Governor of Sligo, was murdered by the ensign of his Irish troops, Ulick Burke, who then betrayed the place to O'Donnell. Sir Richard did not consider that he had the means to recover it. Sligo and Enniskillen were strategic points of high importance. Sligo was the one strong place in north Connaught. Enniskillen commanded an easy passage between Ulster and Connaught. Moreover, the equally important point of Ballyshannon, on the lower Erne river, was accessible from Sligo, and it had been the intention of the English to occupy it shortly. That prospect had now receded, and Ballyshannon was not to come into English hands for another seven years.[2]

Sir John Norris having arrived, the Lord Deputy and he set out for Armagh with the substantial force of 2,882 men, marching by way of Dundalk and Newry. At both these places Tyrone was proclaimed a traitor. Armagh was reached on 30 June 1595, and the Cathedral was fortified. The army then camped on the Blackwater, Tyrone lying on the far bank. There was little object in crossing the river until there was a harvest to burn. It was at this time that Tyrone,

---

[1] *C.S.P. Ireland*, Vol. CLXXIX, 95. Hayes-McCoy, *Ir. Hist. Studies*, June 1949.
[2] *C.S.P. Ireland*, Vol. CLXXX, 16, 31. *History of Catholic Ireland*, p. 87. Four Masters, Vol. VI, p. 1,973.

hearing of the arrival of artillery at Newry, abandoned his scheme of making his castle at Dungannon into a great fortress and dismantled it. The enemy's cavalry attempted to interfere with the return march in the Moyry Pass, between Newry and Dundalk, but was driven off by a charge of the royal horse, whereupon a supporting party of footmen fled into a bog, throwing away its weapons. The expedition had been fairly satisfactory, in that Armagh and the Blackwater ford had been made secure. The worst feature was the ill-will and pessimism of the new Lord General. Norris sulked because Russell had taken the field, protested that the Lord Deputy was jealous of him, asserted that he was ill, and begged to be recalled.[1]

By September Armagh had to be victualled once more, and this time Russell left the task to Norris. He was given a commission as General of Her Majesty's Forces in Ulster to suppress the revolt and with power to promise pardon and protection to such of the rebels as would make submission. More troops had now arrived in Ireland and the companies had been ordered to take twenty Irishmen apiece, though it was admitted that this was a risky experiment. Norris marched on 1 September, and had no difficulty in reaching Armagh.[2]

Owing to lack of draught horses, Norris had to make two trips, and on his return was attacked about midway between Armagh and Newry, which would be near the present site of Markethill. It was an affair of small numbers only, but the cavalry fighting was brisk. Norris was wounded in the arm, and his brother, Sir Thomas, who had come up from Munster to serve with him, in the thigh. The Irish were driven off, but it was taken as a portent that they had ventured to attack in such easy country. Their horse, said Sir Geoffrey Fenton, who was acting as an administrative staff officer to Norris, were more enterprising than the English. As for the English foot, Norris, voicing an old complaint, stated that the last two companies were nearly all 'poor old ploughmen and rogues'.[3]

Summing up the lessons of the expedition, Sir Henry Wallop, the Treasurer at Wars, indulged in some plain speaking to Burghley. The nominal strength of the forces had risen to 7,000, and 4,000 would have to be fed by the Queen that winter. He could find beef and malt in Ireland; but meal, biscuit, wheat, and some cheese

[1] *C.S.P. Ireland*, Vol. CLXXI, 42, 43.
[2] *C.S.P. Ireland*, Vol. CLXXXIII, 8. *Carew Cal.*, Vol. III, p. 118.
[3] *C.S.P. Ireland*, Vol. CLXXXIII, 9, 19, 21.

should be sent from England. He also wanted money to provide salt meat and herring for the garrisons of Armagh and Monaghan, so that they would need to be revictualled less often, a very important point, since most of the available forces were required to convoy the transport on each occasion. Then, the scandalous shortage of draught horses must be remedied; he required some good ones from home and money to buy such as were available in the country, 400 to 500 in all. At present the troops could carry victuals for only about a week, continually harassed by the enemy, so that they marched but slowly; this left them no time to perform useful service. He wanted another £1,500 for fortifications, brewhouses, bakeries, and stores. Burghley, he said, wrote to tell him how unpleasant 'your motions for money are unto Her Majesty and how much she misliketh the excessive greatness of her charge'; but there was no avoiding heavy charges now, and the cheapest policy would be to equip the army so as to put it in good heart and enable it to finish the war quickly. In any case it was his view that the war must be conducted defensively rather than offensively until the spring. This was a masterly document.[1]

Tirlagh Luineach O'Neill had tried to impress upon the English what trouble they were laying up for themselves by patronizing Tyrone. He lived just long enough to see his prophecy on the road to fulfilment, dying at Strabane that September. The veteran had lost a great share of his importance since his resignation of the title of the O'Neill to his kinsman, but while there remained life in his body he had not ceased to count in Ulster politics. It was only after his death that Tyrone went to the traditional site of Tullahogue and had himself formally elected chief. His actual power may not have been greatly increased, but his prestige became still higher. Tirlagh may have been irresolute, and in later life lethargic, but it is not unreasonable to suggest that he possessed a large fund of common sense, and that this was not an unlimited commodity in the Ireland of his day.

For the present it suited the Government to mark time, but it so chanced that Tyrone, despite his accession of strength by the death of Tirlagh, had also reasons for desiring to wait. It was learnt in Scotland that the Campbells and Macleans were incensed against him because he had hanged Hugh Gavelach O'Neill, and that he was finding difficulty in obtaining Scots mercenaries, though he was getting powder from Glasgow. He was now definitely seeking

[1] *C.S.P. Ireland*, Vol. CLXXXIII, 57.

Spanish aid, as the English were aware. They had laid hands upon a priest, Piers O'Cullen of Clogher, who had returned to Ireland after three years in Spain and had been ordered by Tyrone to write to the King of Spain. The only hope of re-establishing the Catholic religion, ran a letter signed by both Tyrone and O'Donnell, rested upon the assistance of Spain; now or never the Church must be succoured. They beseeched the King to despatch a force of from 2,000 to 3,000 with money and arms for their own followers. 'We hope', they said, 'to restore the faith of the Church and so secure you a kingdom.'[1]

Though the Government had this evidence in its hand and Tyrone could not deny it, negotiations for a truce were allowed to proceed. Norris's emissaries got into touch with the Earl, and on 18 October 1595 he and O'Donnell both confessed to having forgotten their duty and promised to have no communications with foreign princes. Tyrone stated that he had not sought aid from Spain before 20 August, which was most improbable, since in the letter quoted above, written on 19 September, he complained that he had received no answer to previous appeals. He said that he had taken the title of the O'Neill in case some rival assumed it, and that he now renounced it. The truce was to continue until 1 January 1596, and one month longer if the Lord Deputy desired. On Tyrone's part this was playing for time; on that of Elizabeth shrinking from the losses and expenses of a major war in Ireland.[2]

Of the two Irish lords Tyrone at least made the more pretence of restraint. O'Donnell had been extending his sway in Connaught, a great part of which he now openly dominated, after laying scores of villages in ashes. In July Bingham had failed to retake Sligo Castle. Tearing down the *Crannchaingel*, or lattice-work between chancel and nave of the abbey church, covering it with hides, and putting wheels under it, the English pushed this engine under the walls of the castle, with the intention of using it as a 'sow' or shelter beneath which a breach could be made; but the defenders smashed it with rocks and the survivors of those who had been sheltering beneath it fled. Bingham retreated across the Curlieus into Roscommon. In October eight companies of the Connaught garrison, sent to relieve a fort on the Moy near Ballina, suffered another reverse. Finding that the castle had already fallen, the force began to

[1] *C.S.P. Ireland*, Vol. CLXXXII, 63; Vol. CLXXVIII, 71 (viii), 77 (i). *Carew Cal.*, Vol. III, p. 122.
[2] *Carew Cal.*, Vol. III, pp. 122, 125.

retreat, but was caught by a strong body of Connaughtmen, with 200 Scots. The enemy skirmished until the royal musketeers had run out of bullets and were reduced to discharging buttons and stones. The newly arrived English companies, of which Bingham had received several, were so clumsy in the handling of their arms that the officers took their powder and ball from them and gave them to the Irish musketeers, who did good service. The rebels claimed to have inflicted a heavy reverse upon the detachment, and Bingham himself admitted that his men were thrown into partial confusion. The days were gone when he could scatter the Irish like chaff. In November Russell himself marched to Galway. The rebellious Burkes were willing to come in and make submission, but O'Donnell prevented them from doing so. Altogether affairs were bad in the province, where nothing could be done except to cling to the fortresses. In Ulster one was lost, Monaghan being delivered to the MacMahons without resistance just before Christmas.[1]

Nevertheless, the truce was renewed until 1 May 1596. This time Sir Henry Wallop and Sir Robert Gardiner represented the Government. Tyrone and O'Donnell displayed extreme suspicion. They refused to come into Dundalk, but met the Englishmen in open country on 20 January. They insisted that the five persons on either side should wear no arms but swords and that two officers of each side should stand between those engaged in the parley and the troops of the other. The commissioners found Tyrone outwardly submissive, but O'Donnell haughty and arrogant; in fact, but for their knowledge that accommodation was earnestly desired by the Government, they would have broken off negotiations in view of his insolence. Yet, if Tyrone's words were gently spoken, their sense was defiant. He would not accept a President of Ulster; he protested against the stationing of a garrison at Armagh; he refused to set free the MacShanes; he would not send in his son. The commissioners were constrained to grant 'liberty of conscience' to Tyrone's and O'Donnell's countries, but refused to accord it to all men in Ireland.[2]

The Queen disliked these proceedings, yet ordered them to continue. She did not want the truce to lapse while the weight of the Cadiz expedition lay on her shoulders. In April Tyrone proved a degree more reasonable. He promised not to interfere with the garrison at Armagh, though still objecting to its presence, and dis-

[1] C.S.P. Ireland, Vol. CLXXXIII, 84 (i); Vol. CLXXXV, 3, 10 (i); Vol. CLXXXVI 12 (ii). Four Masters, Vol. VI, p. 1,983.
[2] Carew Cal., Vol. III, pp. 149–65. C.S.P. Ireland, Vol. CLXXXVI, 22 (vi).

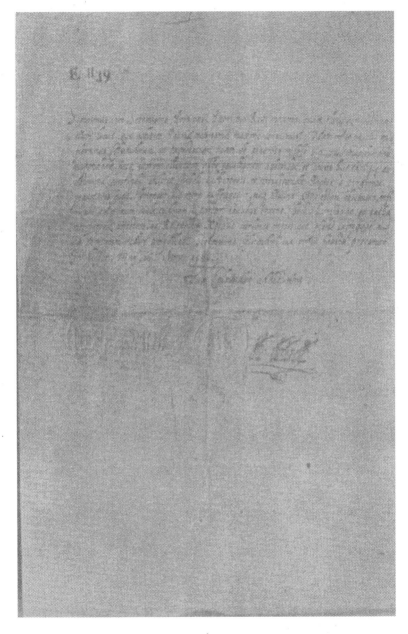

6 LETTER FROM TYRONE AND HUGH O'DONNELL TO THE PRINCE OF ASTURIAS
Signed and sealed by both. Tyrone uses the forbidden title, 'O'Neill'. His seal
bears the famous Red Hand of Ulster (*Archivo Gen. de Simancas*).

claimed authority east of the Bann. After much discussion, he was granted a pardon, though he put off receiving it until after midsummer. The secondary chiefs, including the heads of the MacMahons of Monaghan and the O'Reillys of Cavan, made humble submission in the market-place of Dundalk on 23 April. There was no sincerity on the Irish side in these dealings and at best a vague hope that something favourable would turn up on the English.[1]

Meanwhile, on 6 March Bingham arrived at Boyle to revictual Ballymote Castle in Sligo. He found an Irish force holding the Curlieu hills and failed in his effort to persuade the leaders that he had a right to pass in time of cessation. But he fought his way through and accomplished his mission. Almost simultaneously a band from Connaught with Scots mercenaries crossed the Shannon into King's County, evidently intending to link with the O'Byrnes. This brought Russell out post-haste from Dublin. Picking up a levy of Palesmen on his march, he fell upon the intruders and drove them back over the river with heavy loss. One party took refuge in Cloghan Castle and refused to surrender. A soldier managed to set fire to the thatched roof by tossing a torch up on to it, and the defenders were then quickly accounted for by fire or the sword, two women and a boy being saved by Russell's intervention.[2]

The Government continued to send troops to Ireland, but they continued to melt away by sickness and desertion. On 25 February 1596 warrants were issued for the enrolment of 1,493 foot and 300 horse, all the horse and 285 of the foot to be raised by the Archbishop of Canterbury. On 10 April it was reported that 1,269 foot had been shipped at Chester, but 221 had been left behind, whereof some had not yet reached the port, some were sick, some mad, some in prison, and some had run away. By the 18th the number of foot safely aboard had been raised to 1,418, and 150 horse had also been embarked. In September there was another levy of 1,000, from eighteen counties, Northumberland and Lincolnshire finding 100 each, and Cheshire and Lancashire, Buckinghamshire and Bedfordshire, Shropshire and Worcestershire, Cambridge and Huntingdon, Berkshire and Oxford, Warwickshire and Leicestershire, Nottinghamshire and Staffordshire, Derbyshire and Hereford being linked together in pairs to provide in each case a company of 100. In October the call came to Devonshire for 300, to the Council in the North for 400, and to the Lord President of Wales for 300. In

[1] *C.S.P. Ireland*, Vol. CLXXXVIII, 53, 54, 55, 67 (i).
[2] *C.S.P. Ireland*, Vol. CLXXXVII, 34. *Carew Cal.*, Vol. III, p. 243.

December, however, there was a cancellation, the Queen deciding that troops awaiting a wind at Bristol should be sent home, the mayor discharging the shipping and storing the armour, weapons, and coats. In this case the lieutenants were paid 3s. a day, with 8d. a man, for the return to their respective counties. And in this same month the total muster in Ireland had risen only to 617 horse and 5,732 foot, as against 657 horse and 4,040 foot in October 1595.[1]

Immediately after the death of his English wife, born Mabel Bagenal, Tyrone married Catherine Magennis, daughter of the Lord of Iveagh, sending back to her kinsfolk a girl of the Mac-Donalds who had been, so to speak, on approval in his country. This caused a further estrangement with the Scots. However, he could put such considerations out of his mind while he spent his honeymoon at Castle Roe, he and his 'young lady' salmon-fishing in the Bann. He was disturbed by a message that a Spanish ship had entered Killybegs. He went off to Lifford to meet the Spaniards, but since he knew that the English were aware of the arrival of the ship, thought well to inform Norris on 6 May that a Spanish gentleman had brought him a message, but that he had refused to accept foreign aid.[2]

Tyrone's dealings with the English and Spaniards constituted a masterpiece of diplomatic skill and duplicity. Having put himself right, so far as he could in the circumstances, with the Government, he proceeded to extract from the Spanish representative a formal acknowledgement that he had refrained from making an advantageous settlement with the Queen in the hope of Spanish aid. If this aid were not forthcoming, his reliance upon it would have ruined him. He thus appealed to Spanish chivalry and honour as well as to Spanish interest.

'I, Captain Alonso Cobos', wrote the Spaniard, 'hereby certify that I arrived in this realm of Ireland at the time when the Irish chiefs had almost concluded peace with the Queen on terms satisfactory to themselves, and that, solely on conscientious grounds and out of affection for His Majesty, they desisted from finally making peace, taking up arms against the Queen of England and sincerely turning their hearts to God and the King, in whose service as faithful vassals they remain during His Majesty's pleasure. As I know this to

---

[1] C.S.P. Ireland, Vol. CLXXXVI, 82; Vol. CLXXXVIII, 25, 51 (ii); Vol. CXCVI, 38. Carew Cal., Vol. III, p. 127. Salisbury Papers, Pt. VI, p. 558. C.S.P. Dom., 1595–1597, pp. 292–3. Cal. Treas. Papers, Vol. I, p. 2.
[2] C.S.P. Ireland, Vol. CLXXXIX, 2, 13, 27.

be the truth, I give this solemn testimony at the request of the chiefs, under my hand and seal. Lifford, 15 May 1596.'[1]

As a further insurance with the English, Tyrone sent to Dublin the brief and formal letter of encouragement from Philip II which Cobos had brought to him, having exacted a pledge from the bearer that it should either be destroyed or returned, without a copy being taken. This pledge Russell, to his discredit, refused to acknowledge, and kept the letter. Tyrone, O'Donnell, Maguire, and MacWilliam Burke addressed letters to the King begging for armed force to restore the Catholic faith and that the Archduke Albert should be sent as their prince. They asserted that they had received most favourable offers from the Lord Deputy, full freedom and liberty of conscience for Catholics, and that if aid were not sent to them they might after all be forced to make peace with the heretics. Tyrone and O'Donnell thought it worth while to write to the young Prince of Asturias, requesting him to use his influence with his father in their cause. The following is a translation from the Latin used by their scribe:

'We have already written, most Serene Prince, to the Great King your father, as fully as our haste allowed, what we thought to be most necessary for ourselves and for the country. We implore Your Highness in this regard that Your Highness will respond graciously to the expectation which we have conceived of his generous spirit and will enrol us specially upon the register of his clients, and, as is his wont, will aid in his clemency this most excellent and just cause, that of asserting Catholic liberty and of freeing the country from the rod of tyrannical evil, and that, with the help of the Divine Majesty, he may win for Christ an infinite number of souls, snatching them from the jaws of hell, and may wholly destroy or compel to return to reason the ministers of satanic fury and the impious disturbers of the Christian state. We pray that all good may befall your most Serene Highness.

'At Leffer, May 16th, 1596.
'Your Highness's most devoted
'O'Neill, H.   Aodh O Domhnaill.'[2]

---

[1] *C.S.P. Spanish*, Vol. IV, p. 619. The date is N.S., so that it was immediately afterwards that Tyrone wrote to Norris.

[2] 'Leffer' stands for Lifford. Tyrone signs with the princely title of O'Neill, but using English script, whereas O'Donnell uses a Celtic script. The seals are stamped on the paper, without the use of wax or ink, in a manner which surprises by its modern air (Arch. Gen. de Simancas, E.839).

Two other Spanish officers, Luis de Cisneros and de Medinilla, also interviewed Tyrone. They had brought a full questionnaire drawn up with the object of finding out his precise needs. The officers formed the opinion that the Irish were sincere in their defence of their faith. Their strength was estimated to be 6,000 foot and 1,200 horse, and they asked for arms for 10,000 men. Unfortunately, from the Spanish point of view, it did not appear possible to supply them with artillery from any port which the Spanish fleet was likely to be able to use. The officers had instructions to send their pilots to Sligo, Donegal, and other harbours, and to engage Irish pilots who would return with them to Spain. These Spaniards were not lacking in prescience; it was in the slowness of their actions that their worst fault lay.[1]

The Spaniards gave the Irish lords their promise that aid would be sent that year, and they had every reason to believe that it would. An expedition was indeed fitting out. England, however, struck first. An Anglo-Dutch fleet commanded by Lord Howard of Effingham, carrying an army of 6,000 men under the command of the Earl of Essex, reached Cadiz on 20 June. There were only between fifteen and twenty Spanish galleys in the harbour, with over forty merchantmen. After a fierce struggle in the Puntal Channel, the naval resistance was overcome, and that of the forts did not prove serious. The city capitulated after hard street fighting, paid a ransom for the lives of its inhabitants, and was looted. Bad management permitted the merchant captains to discharge the most valuable part of their cargoes, and most of the galleys escaped. The rich treasure fleet was also missed by a couple of days. Nevertheless, it was a heavy blow for Spain, a terrible humiliation to begin with and involving great loss in shipping and stores.[2]

Even then Philip II tried to keep his promise, though his main motive was desire for revenge. With remarkable speed, an expedition was prepared at Lisbon and Vigo. Troops were withdrawn from Brittany and the Mediterranean to take part in it. Large numbers of Irish noblemen, gentlemen, and priests joined it. But, rapid as had been the organization, it had taken too much time, and the 'Second Armada' sailed dangerously late, on 13 October 1597. Four days later it ran into a great gale, was dispersed, and suffered heavy losses. Essex was at that time at sea, returning from his expedition to the

---

[1] *C.S.P. Spanish*, Vol. IV, pp. 620–7.
[2] Cheyney, *History of England*, 1558–1603, Vol. II, Chap. XXVII. Corbett, *The Successors of Drake*, pp. 59–101.

Azores, but was luckier than the Spaniards in that his ships were blown towards their own harbours.

So Tyrone's hopes were dashed. If a Spanish force of several thousand men had landed at this time in Ireland it would have given a great deal of trouble, but, as ever in such circumstances, no final success would have attended it without the backing of command of the sea.

About the beginning of July 1596 Sir John Norris and Sir Geoffrey Fenton set out for Connaught in the hope of coming to terms with its principal rebels. Both of them reached the conclusion that the troubles in the province were due to two causes: the influence of O'Donnell and the severity of Bingham. If they could not remedy the former evil, they could do away with the latter. So strong was their feeling against Bingham—which was naturally fostered in every possible way by the Burkes, transported with delight at finding a breach in the English ranks—that Russell, somewhat doubtfully, suspended the Governor while negotiations were in progress. Losing his patience and his temper, Bingham left Ireland without permission in September, and was promptly committed to the Fleet Prison. The Connaught rebels submitted nominally, which meant that they would remain quiet until O'Donnell again stirred them up.[1]

In September the Government learnt that another Spanish ship had arrived on the Donegal coast. What it did not know was that this ship bore the emissary who had visited Tyrone in the spring, Alonso Cobos. He entered the same harbour, Killybegs, on 26 September (N.S.), after a passage of only ten days from Coruña, and met the northern chiefs at the monastery of Donegal on Sunday, 6 October (N.S.). He delivered to them copies of a letter from Philip II, and they vowed that they were prepared to die in his service. Once again the Spaniard told them that the longed-for aid would arrive in the near future, and once again, as we have seen, he was justified in saying so, though it did not appear. They considered that Galway would be the most suitable port for a Spanish fleet and that the town would surrender on its arrival. Cobos, a man of character who had served at Lepanto, in Tunisia, Portugal, and ten years in the Low Countries, discovering that Tyrone had sent Norris the letter brought from the King of Spain in May, reproved him. Tyrone's excuse was that Norris knew of the arrival of the ship and he had concluded that the best means of deceiving him was to

[1] *C.S.P. Ireland*, Vol. CXCI, 6, 9, 23, 25; Vol. CXCII, 2; Vol. XCIII, 12, 28.

send the letter and pretend that he had told the King he wanted no aid. Cobos firmly warned him to keep his promises better in future. He took back with him fervid messages from the chiefs to the King. It was on this occasion that he found the party of survivors from the Armada serving in the ranks of the Irish.[1]

Little prospect of an improvement in the state of Ireland existed while the Lord Deputy and his military commander were not only personally on bad terms with one another, but divided on policy. Norris frequently complained of Russell's jealousy. Russell asserted that Norris was slow and too well affected to Tyrone. Writing to Essex in December 1596, Russell said that he had left the pacification of Ulster to Norris in view of the 'very large patent for it' which he had been given by direction from England and which he had proclaimed with a flourish at Drogheda. Now, said the Lord Deputy, he pretended to be sick, lay up in Athlone, and was 'trying to thrust me into those actions so to lay to my charge any failure or fresh outbreaks'. Russell had a good deal to complain of, but there was no pretence about the ill health of Norris.[2]

The divergence of their political views was, however, still more unfortunate. Norris was all for appeasement. He professed to believe, even after the visit of the Spaniards, that Tyrone had not in the past intended to rebel and did not now. He urged that he should be treated gently. Russell, on the other hand, had come round to the view that appeasement had failed, that O'Donnell and the Connaught rebels in particular were trifling with the Government, and that it was time to abandon the series of truces which were giving Tyrone opportunity to organize his forces and favouring the prospect of Spanish aid.[3] The solution of the problem which was beginning to appeal to the Queen and Burghley was to revoke the appointments of both men, recalling Russell and sending Norris back to Munster. This certainly implied dissatisfaction with Russell, since there would have been no great difficulty in recalling Norris and leaving the Lord Deputy in office. As usual, a delay occurred, and Russell remained until the spring of 1597.[4]

One last task fell to his lot, and, as it was well executed, enabled him to leave the country with some remnant of credit. In November

---

[1] See p. 73. Arch. Gen de Simancas, E.839, folio 150. C.S.P. Spanish, Vol. IV, pp. 637–42.

[2] Birch, Memoirs of the Reign of Queen Elizabeth, Vol. I, p. 277.

[3] C.S.P. Ireland, Vol. CXCI, 45; Vol. CXCII, 30.

[4] C.S.P. Ireland, Vol. CXCVI, 27.

1595 Feagh MacHugh O'Byrne, impressed by Russell's forcible dealings with his country, had come in and surrendered. His pretensions, however, remained high, and there was a long debate about his pardon and future status. Just after this question had been decided favourably for him, he promised Tyrone to annoy the English. In September 1596 he recovered Ballinacor. That ended the prospect of pardon. Russell always had a taste for conducting in person operations in Wicklow, not, to do him justice, because they were easy, but because he could at any time return to Dublin, to the Council board, and to the general supervision of affairs, in one day's ride. He now at once marched to Rathdrum, in the heart of the rebel's country, and began to build a fort near Ballinacor. He did not remain in Wicklow himself, but efforts to end with Feagh MacHugh continued throughout the winter. The hovels of the O'Byrnes were burnt and their cattle were driven off, but none could lay a hand upon Feagh MacHugh.[1]

On 7 May 1597 Russell left Dublin to join the forces operating in Wicklow. Marching with great speed, he reached the central glens early next morning. Three columns entered that fastness by separate routes. Feagh MacHugh was surprised by one company, and as he fled ran straight into another, commanded by Captain Thomas Lee. He was caught in a cave, but was spared the grisly fate that awaited him in Dublin. 'The fury of our soldiers was so great as he could not be brought away alive', says the scribe who compiled Russell's journal. Sergeant Milborne, commanding the party which had cornered him, cut off his head and brought it to Russell. After one of the quickest campaigns on record in Ireland, the Lord Deputy rode back to Dublin on the 9th. 'All the way the people of the country met him with great joy and gladness, and, as their manner is, bestowed many blessings upon him for performing so good a deed and delivering them from their long oppressions.' There is no evidence from the English side about the intelligence upon which Russell had acted, but it is virtually certain that he had been informed where Feagh MacHugh was lying. The Irish annalists declare that O'Byrne was betrayed by his relatives.[2]

Feagh MacHugh O'Byrne was, by comparison with Tyrone, a simple-minded savage, but the English had a high opinion of his natural ability. In his own wild country he was a formidable

[1] *C.S.P. Ireland*, Vol. XCIII, 9, 10, 32.
[2] *Carew Cal.*, Vol. III, p. 258. *C.S.P. Ireland*, Vol. CXCIX, 28. Four Masters, Vol. VI, p. 2,016.

opponent, and he had lately leagued himself with the Ulster lords. Whenever there was serious trouble in Ireland there was likely to be an O'Byrne who could take advantage of it, but it must have seemed unlikely that the glens of Wicklow would immediately bring forth another Feagh MacHugh. In point of fact, they did so within two years.

In January O'Donnell had once again entered Connaught with a great force, burning and preying. The new Governor, Sir Conyers Clifford, a soldier who had distinguished himself in the expedition to Cadiz, was worried about the small proportion of Englishmen in his companies. Clifford was an energetic man, and within a very short time had received the submission of several Connaught lords who had given their allegiance to O'Donnell. In March he did what Bingham had failed to accomplish—recovered Sligo Castle, with the aid of its lawful proprietor, Donogh O'Connor Sligo.[1]

While Russell was engaged in Wicklow his successor, Thomas Lord Burgh, was on his way. He reached Ireland on 15 May 1597, and received the sword on the 22nd. He found English rule and authority non-existent in the north. There had as yet been no definite breach with Tyrone, but there was small hope of avoiding one. He had received his pardon in July 1596 with apparent pleasure, saluting the event with a volley from his camp, but had then drifted away once more. The inevitable broils between outpost troops had contributed to ill-feeling, and he was surrounded by 'damnable counsellors', who urged him to march into Connaught in aid of the rebels in that province. At the end of November his men made a surprise attack on Armagh, but failed to take the fort on the Blackwater, and it was reported that he was further recruiting his forces on hearing that a relief force was being prepared. Yet when Norris marched north in January 1597, he was met at Dundalk on the 18th by loyal messages and a promise that Tyrone would either allow Armagh to be revictualled by the royal forces or actually put in food himself. No hostile action occurred, though the Irish forces numbered about 3,000, as against 2,000 under the command of Norris. A meeting took place, but led to nothing tangible, and a letter from Tyrone to O'Donnell, signed 'O'Neill', was immediately afterwards intercepted, describing his conversations with the commissioners and urging his ally to keep Connaught well occupied. In April he coolly cancelled a second meeting and went off to greet another party of Spaniards who had come to Killybegs in two ships,

[1] *C.S.P. Ireland,* Vol. CXCVIII, 3, 23.

one carrying war material and the other wines. On the 26th Norris found at Dundalk messengers stating that the Earl was prepared for further negotiations, but by this time the Lord General's fellow commissioners had gone back to Dublin in disgust. Such was the state of political affairs when Lord Burgh took office.[1]

Russell would appear to have been no disciplinarian or organizer, and the army was in a wretched state, though this was in large part due to the fact that pay and supplies had not kept pace with reinforcements. Burghley had despatched to Ireland a downright, capable, and courageous official named Maurice Kyffin to check the musters, and he had found them in chaos. On the northern frontier he discovered a number of 'suborned *passe-volants*' in the ranks, answering to the names of dead or absentees. In the Pale he could not make up his mind which was the more grievous, the outcries of the soldiers for want of pay, or of the country people, whom they robbed and pillaged. Whole districts were left without habitation or tillage. 'Between the rebels on the one side and our own soldiers (being for the most part Irish and living altogether on the spoil) all is devoured and destroyed.' Another report, probably also his, stated that the cavalry was spread out over the whole of the Pale for subsistence, and that while each trooper had one boy and two horses, some of the officers had as many as three boys. Companies of foot would also sweep the country for thirty miles in a day, accompanied by boys and women, and if they were not satisfied with the food and money they could wring from the inhabitants they would maltreat them. However, Kyffin warmly praised the work of Sir Conyers Clifford in Connaught, and in June 1597 was able to report that the checks on the musters had been useful and that the twentyone bands of horse and seventy-eight companies of foot stationed in Ireland were now stronger.[2]

Russell had not been a weakling, but he had been in general a failure. The new Lord Deputy came to a confused and decayed inheritance.

[1] *C.S.P. Ireland*, Vol. CXCI, 34; Vol. CXCII, 26; Vol. CXCV, 49; Vol. CXCVI, 31 (vii); Vol. CXCVII, 42, 46, 59 (i); Vol. CXCVIII, 32 (iii), 67, 69 (ii).

[2] *C.S.P. Ireland*, Vol. XCVII, 89, 91; Vol. XCIX, 39, 98. *Carew Cal.*, Vol. III, p. 271. Kyffin's use of a French word for substitutes at the musters conveys a hint of the prevalence of the abuse. '*Passe-volant*' is defined by Larousse as '*faux soldat que l'on faisait figurer dans une revue pour grossir l'effectif de la compagnie et justifier les états de solde majorés*'.

CHAPTER XIV

TYRONE IN REBELLION

THE viceroyalty of Lord Burgh was the briefest of the reign of Queen Elizabeth. It is not easy to assess the capacity of the man for his post, and speculation about how he would have fared had he been accorded time for a reasonable trial of his abilities is scarcely worth while. Clearly, no Elizabethan viceroy, with the exception of his two successors, Essex and Mountjoy, had to face a more difficult task. He arrived at a moment when the situation demanded a soldier even more than a statesman, and, though not without military experience, he was by training a diplomatist rather than a commander. Yet he did not fail in the field. The impression made by his correspondence is favourable. It gives evidence of a quick and intelligent mind. A lively, original, and agreeable light gleams forth from his messages to the Queen and Privy Council. An unusual and graphic turn of phrase suggests a character out of the ordinary. His energy was undeniable. Unfortunately, even at the moment of his assumption of office, his health was bad. He had been compelled to submit to his blood being sucked by 'loathsome worms'—that is, leeches. The health of Elizabeth's Irish viceroys would make an interesting study. Three of them—Sidney, Perrott, and Fitzwilliam —suffered from the stone. One, Essex, was handicapped by persistent dysentery. Mountjoy was delicate and compelled to take particular care of himself.

At almost the moment in which Burgh received the sword Tyrone's men were repulsed in front of Carrickfergus and Newry, but the Lord Deputy at once decided that he must go to the north that summer. Despite the poverty and devastation of the Pale, he ordered a general hosting to take place on 1 July 1597. He would act as commander-in-chief in Ulster. Sir John Norris, his commission having been revoked, met Burgh in Dublin, took leave of him with apparent goodwill, and returned to his Presidency of Munster. By June he was inspecting fortifications, in view of the possibility of a Spanish landing. He was, however, suffering from an old wound, which carried him off at the beginning of September. He had gained little success in Ireland, but his character and record won him respect. His death was naturally pleasing to the disaffected. We learn from the historian of Catholic Ireland that it was accomplished by the Evil One, who had contracted to support him on the usual terms and now came to Mallow to claim his bargain. When the scared servants forced the door of the room in which the two were together, the Devil had gone, but Sir John's body was so twisted that his head and the upper part of his chest faced backwards. He died at midnight. The moral is that Tyrone must have been an exceptional soldier to have discomfited a foe aided by the Devil; but then, of course, he himself was aided by the Good God.[1]

Burgh found that a great part of the kingdom was reasonably quiet. The whole trouble proceeded from the 'two arch rebels', Tyrone in the north and O'Donnell in the north-west, who drew others into confederacies and undid the work of reclaiming them. 'Branches will sprout as long as the root is untouched', Burgh wrote to Sir Robert Cecil, who was gradually taking over supervision of Irish affairs from the hands of his ailing father. 'Bring the axe thither, and they do wither; lop them, others spring; cut that [the root], all decays.' His determination was to maintain constant contact with Tyrone. 'I will encamp by him, force him, follow him, omit no opportunity by night or day to prove his quarters. . . . I will, God willing, stick to him and if need be lie on the ground and drink water ten weeks.'[2]

Having assembled 500 horse and 3,000 foot, Burgh set out for Newry on 5 July. He took with him several members of his Council, leaving with the remainder in Dublin a commission for government under the broad seal and directing them to consult with Ormonde about the defence of Leinster in his absence. He halted at Dundalk to meet the rising out, but the days were gone by when forces of this kind were of any value for an expedition into Ulster. He therefore took with him only the draught horses and cattle which the Palesmen had brought and dismissed them to guard the borders. After camping near Newry, he reached the Blackwater on the 13th. Tyrone had in June withdrawn his advanced guard, which had been blocking Armagh, across the river after being beaten in a combat with Captain Turner and losing his hat in his flight. Now, however, Tyrone's whole force had to be faced, and it considerably outnumbered that of the Lord Deputy. The Blackwater ford was, moreover, covered by fortifications on the far bank; stakes driven

---

[1] C.S.P. Ireland, Vol. CXCIX, 66, 95. History of Catholic Ireland, p. 97.
[2] C.S.P. Ireland, Vol. CC, 5, 8.

into the bank rendered the passage more difficult; and it was commanded by flanking parties of musketeers.[1]

On 14 July the ford was assaulted. The shaky, half-trained troops
wavered, but the Lord Deputy, going forward in the midst of a
little band of gentlemen volunteers, drew them on by force of
example. Wading in above his waist, he was himself the second man
across. The defences were carried with a rush, and Tyrone's main
body made no effort to support the defenders; but there was a high
proportion of casualties among the volunteers, Burgh's brother-in-
law, Sir Francis Vaughan, and Captain Turner being killed. Next
day a surprise attack by the Irish was beaten off, though not before
it had effected some confusion and loss. Burgh then demolished
Tyrone's works and himself dug on the near bank of the river an
earth fort—simply a circular ditch with the soil which had been
extracted piled up to make a wall. What had been achieved was
largely due to the Lord Deputy's own courage and personality, with
what he called 'the rawest army that ever prince so long paid'.[2]

So far Burgh had done well, but his next decision may have
contributed to the difficulties of his lieutenant, the Governor of
Connaught. Sir Conyers Clifford had gone far towards restoring
the situation in his province, and his achievements, particularly
the recovery of Sligo, had compelled O'Donnell to withdraw across
the Erne. Burgh had instructed Clifford to capture Ballyshannon
at the same time as he himself appeared on the Blackwater. It was
then his intention that the two forces should unite on Lough Foyle
in accordance with the long-conceived scheme for bridling Ulster.
After his success, however, Burgh changed his mind. The usual
shortage of supplies was one reason, and it was said that he had only
biscuits and good words for the army; but he had also got wind of
a rebel plan to march past his flank through Cavan and raid the
Pale as soon as he advanced. He therefore decided to halt for the
time being and build fortifications at various points along the
Ulster border.

Clifford, for his part, was delayed by the fatigue of reinforcements which had marched from Dublin to join him and again by
the difficulty of collecting supplies. He reached the Erne on 29 July
to find the fords strongly held by O'Donnell. A skilful manœuvre
gained him a passage next day. Keeping his main body facing
Ballyshannon, as though he meant to force his way across at that

---

[1] *C.S.P. Ireland*, Vol. CXCIX, 101, 102.
[2] *C.S.P. Ireland*, Vol. CC, 24, 25, 27.

point, he sent his second-in-command, one of the few first-class
soldiers then in Ireland, Sir Calisthenes Brooke, by night to a ford
near Belleek, higher up the river. This ford was held, but not
strongly, and Brooke overcame the opposition, though losing in the
process a lord whom the English could ill spare, Inchiquin, one of
the most powerful loyalists of the west, killed by a bullet entering
his armpit, where he was unprotected by armour.[1]

At dawn Clifford marched after Brooke, and the whole force
crossed. He then advanced, driving back skirmishers, to the abbey
of Asheroe, three miles from Ballyshannon, where he camped and
remained the following day to rest his troops. Supplies sent by sea
arrived and two small field pieces. The castle was strongly defended,
the garrison including a number of Spaniards. Next day Clifford
closed upon the castle, and the day after drove off an attempted
relief force, but his light guns made small impression on the walls.
That night came black news. A harper told Clifford that he had
seen a letter to him from Burgh, which the Irish had intercepted,
informing him that the Lord Deputy was falling back from the
Blackwater to Newry, and that Tyrone's brother Cormac was
about to join O'Donnell with another 1,000 men. Both these
pieces of information were in fact correct. To make matters worse,
Maguire and Brian O'Rourke had crossed the Erne to cut him off
from his base.

Clifford now realized that he and his force were doomed unless
they could get out. He had under 1,200 with him, a large proportion
of them Irish, though some were Continental veterans. His powder
was down to one barrel and his lead was short. He assembled the
troops and made them a brief speech of encouragement, whereupon
'the poor men with great comfort swore to follow whatsoever I
would appoint'. There was little hope of reaching any ford other
than that beside which he now stood at Ballyshannon, and it was a
bad and dangerous one, just above the famous Salmon Leap. Nor
could there be any hope of concealment. With drums beating and
colours flying, the force moved over the ford, Brooke marching
behind the baggage animals with the rear guard. According to the
Irish version, a number of soldiers and pack-horses, slipping on the
slabs of rock on the river bottom, were carried to their death over
the rapids.

Before the passage was complete the enemy attacked on both
banks. He was driven off, and Clifford was enabled to form up again

[1] Four Masters, Vol. VI, p. 2,023.

on the left bank. Then he marched. For six hours, during which he covered but eight miles, he was constantly attacked by 1,000 foot and 300 horse, while behind he could see two more battles of foot, in all 2,000 strong, and another regiment of horse. Time after time the enemy charged, and time after time was driven off with loss.

Now, however, the powder had come to an end. It would have gone ill with Clifford but that a drenching shower fell, putting out the matches of the Irish, so that their calivers were of no more use than his own. The Irish continued to attack, but were beaten off with the pike. Presently their foot abandoned the pursuit, leaving the horse to follow Clifford's men for some miles further. Then the horse also drew off. It was a wonderful achievement to have saved the force from destruction, but the affair was none the less a reverse, and Ballyshannon was as far off as ever. The Irish had named the Arney ford in derision the Ford of the Biscuits; now, in generous spirit, they called that by which Clifford had crossed the Erne the Ford of the Heroes (Casan-na-gCuradh).[1]

Having completed the fort on the Blackwater by 1 August, Burgh decided to draw back the field army to Newry in order to collect further supplies. He sent Sir Geoffrey Fenton back to purchase 600 or 700 beeves in the Pale, a task which Fenton expected would prove difficult, in view of the present poverty of the country. On the 11th the Council in Dublin reported that it had procured 300, at the high price of 30s. a head, double the usual rate paid by the Government, and for ready money, which had to be borrowed. After a fruitless exchange of messages with Tyrone, the Lord Deputy marched into Cavan in mid-August, and having made that shire safe, returned to Dublin at the beginning of September. He had established a chain of garrisons which he thought would prevent Tyrone from carrying out any scheme such as that of advancing into the Pale while the main English Army was advancing towards Lough Foyle. Burgh still intended to place a force there, and looked forward to a winter of great activity. He was confident of success if the Queen would only keep him well supplied and if the King of Scots could be persuaded to put a stop to the export of powder to the rebels. He thought that the financial strain was telling on Tyrone and that he could not much longer maintain his full force of bonaghts.[2]

Whatever happened, Burgh had to revictual the Blackwater fort

[1] Four Masters, Vol. VI, p. 2,033. *C.S.P. Ireland*, CC, 83 (i).
[2] *C.S.P. Ireland*, Vol. CCI (Pt. 1), 7. Four Masters, Vol. VI, p. 2,035.

by 10 October, and Tyrone was well aware of the fact. He was gathering troops to prevent him from doing so and was reported to have called O'Donnell to him. Then he determined to take the fort by a *coup de main* before the relief force should arrive. On 2 October the assault was launched. The storming party had, it was later learnt, received the sacrament before attempting their enterprise and sworn individually not to abandon it. The stout-hearted and well-tried Welsh commander of the garrison, Captain Thomas Williams, was ready. Tyrone's attack was bloodily repulsed and his thirty scaling-ladders fell into the hands of the defenders. It is with pleasure that one finds an old maimed soldier who had served with Williams being assured of a house in 1617.[1]

Immediately afterwards Burgh appeared. He brushed aside such opposition as was attempted, reached the Blackwater, revictualled the fort, and strengthened the garrison. It was his apparent intention to advance into Tyrone, a prospect which caused the Council some anxiety, since his strength scarcely sufficed to place an adequate garrison on Lough Foyle and Clifford was no longer in a position to co-operate. Burgh was, however, taken ill with 'an Irish ague' even before he reached the Blackwater. Rapidly growing worse, he had to be carried back in a litter through Armagh to Newry. There he died on 13 October. By his will, which he did not succeed in signing, he left his best Garter and George to the Queen. The Marshal, Sir Henry Bagenal, deeply moved and consumed by anxiety, wrote that night to Elizabeth: 'It hath pleased God to take to his mercy my most honourable Lord your Deputy: a gentleman who, for his forwardness and valour in your service, was as zealous in his prosecution thereof as any whatsoever his predecessors in my time and did with as great honour to Your Majesty, during his short continuance, acquit himself in all his actions.'[2] It was indeed a grievous loss to the State, though how great neither Bagenal nor the Queen could as yet conceive.

When the bad news reached London there was some talk of sending Russell, who had little desire to go a second time, or Sir Robert Sidney, younger son of the former viceroy. But, amid the anxiety about the 'Second Armada', which sailed on the day of Burgh's death, it was certain that no immediate appointment would be made. It was, indeed, as usual deferred far too long. Sir Thomas

---

[1] *C.S.P. Ireland*, Vol. CCI (Pt. 1), 7. Four Masters, Vol. VI, p. 2,035. Hist. MSS. Com., *Various Collections*, Vol. I, p. 296.
[2] *C.S.P. Ireland*, Vol. CCI (Pt. 2), 12, 14 (i).

Norris was appointed sole Lord Justice, with Ormonde as Lieuten-
ant-General, but on 15 November Elizabeth ordered Norris back
to Munster and directed the Council to appoint in his place two
Lord Justices, Adam Loftus, Lord Chancellor and Archbishop of
Dublin, and Sir Robert Gardiner, Chief Justice of the Common
Pleas. Ormonde was retained as military commander.[1]

In Ulster the Government suffered a secondary reverse owing to
the impetuosity of the commander on the spot. Sir John Chichester,
Governor of Carrickfergus, had been generally successful since his
recent appointment to that post. He had recovered Belfast Castle
from the O'Neills of Clandeboye and taken that of Edenduffcarrick
on Lough Neagh. He had had some trouble with the Scots in
Antrim, and had arranged a parley with James MacSorley Mac-
Donald over a question of raids and counter-raids. On 4 November
James approached Carrickfergus in astonishing and unjustified
strength—according to the English version, 1,300 men, including
500 well-appointed Scots musketeers. Chichester came out with the
majority of the garrison, five companies of foot and one of horse.
After marching four miles he found himself face to face with the
Scots, and halted to allow his main body to close up on the advanced
guard. A discussion now took place, one experienced officer urging
that, despite the insolence of the Scots, the parley should be proceeded with, if for no other reason than because the troops were
fatigued by an expedition from which they had but just returned.
On the main body coming up, Chichester turned to its commander,
Captain Merriman, and said to him jocularly: 'Now, captain,
yonder be your old friends. What say you? Shall we charge them?'
Merriman and others, notably Moses Hill, in command of the
cavalry, were only too ready.

At first the Scots gave ground, falling back from one hillock to
the next. Then, noting that when Chichester attempted to charge
he was followed by only a handful, the rest of the horse shirking,
they charged in their turn. The royal troops broke. Chichester,
trying to stop the rot, was shot through the head, and a disaster
followed. A reinforcement, including sick, sallied out from Carrickfergus and checked the Scots, saving the foot from complete
destruction. Nevertheless, about 180 were killed and from thirty
to forty were wounded, out of a force which cannot much have
exceeded 350 men. The whole affair was absurd, because the Scots

[1] *De Lisle and Dudley Papers*, p. 299. *Sidney Papers*, pp. 71, 73. *C.S.P. Ireland*,
Vol. CCI (Pt. 2), 23, 38, 50, 72.

had not meant to fight and were not in altogether unfriendly mood. As James MacSorley wrote in answer to reproaches: 'My comminge from hance was to hawe parlitt vithe the governor concerninge stealthes that was committit be capten mansells hoers in absence of Shir Jhonne Chichester, and that to hawe gotten restitutionne of the sameing stealthes, and as is vell knowen, he used & followed capten merimanne & mayster hilles counsel, & followed me & did dryve me from hill to hill to hawe effectit his bad intentioun and as the gentill men that is heir in handis vithe us knowes, it besemeth the gentill men that vas vithe us to do for them selfes or die.'[1]

The other incident was equally stupid on the English side. Ormonde had demanded of Tyrone, pending negotiations about to take place, that he should recall a body of Ulstermen who had been stirring up trouble in the O'Byrne country in Wicklow. They had withdrawn to King's County, and perhaps intended to make their way northward. Their commander, Richard Tyrrell, a former officer of the Queen's army, was one of the ablest men ever to appear in the rebel ranks. On 7 December a company of the garrison of Philipstown made an unprovoked attack upon him and was overwhelmed, only twenty escaping.

Meanwhile, Tyrone's messages had borne a submissive air, and the Queen had decided to tread once more the old, weary road of appeasement. This time she directed that Ormonde should act as envoy, a good choice since he was held in deep respect by Tyrone. The terms drawn up were on their face severe. Tyrone was to make submission on his knees in public; he must denounce his alliance with other rebels, who would have to treat separately; he must renounce the title and style of O'Neill, which was treasonable by statute; he must disperse his forces and dismiss foreigners, take no action against Her Majesty's 'urriaghts', deliver up the MacShanes, help to build up the Blackwater fort—which was becoming ruinous —to its former strength, give full information about his dealings with the Spaniards, admit a sheriff, send in his eldest son as a pledge, pay a fine. Commissioners would order restitution on both sides for outrages committed. However, the strength of the Government's attitude was much diminished by the private instruction to Ormonde that Tyrone might be admitted to pardon on pledging himself to the most necessary engagements in this list.[2]

---

[1] Hayes-McCoy, *Scots Mercenary Forces*, p. 288. 'The gentill men . . . heir in handis' were prisoners. *C.S.P. Ireland*, Vol. CCI (Pt. 2), 63 (i), 96 (i).

[2] *C.S.P. Ireland*, Vol. CCI (Pt. 2), 95 (i).

Ormonde first met Tyrone near Dundalk on 10 December and heard the usual professions of loyalty and the usual complaints against Bagenal. After further discussions Tyrone made submission and gave an undertaking covering the majority of the demands of the Government. Yet his complaints were still arrogant in tone. Thomas Jones, Bishop of Meath, reasoned with him over the proposal that he should send in his sons. He pointed out—we may suppose in all sincerity, since it was a view current in Dublin—that if Tyrone were to die his half-brother Cormac might grab his lands and steal his eldest son's inheritance, whereas if they were with the English this would never be permitted. Tyrone refused flatly. 'You are deceived,' he said. 'You know not the North as well as I do. My country will never esteem them if they be absent.' He was probably right.[1]

One favourable result of the truce was that Ormonde was enabled to revictual the Blackwater fort, Tyrone himself actually sending in some cattle. Ormonde's report on it was, however, unfavourable. The walls continued to crumble and required constant exertions on the part of the garrison to keep them in tolerable repair. The garrison was short of clothing, of spades, and other necessities, and much in need of malt 'after so long drinking of the Blackwater river'.[2]

In March 1598 further negotiations took place. In April O'Donnell was induced to come to a meeting. These chiefs preserved a certain solidarity, and one of the strongest obstacles to a settlement at this time was their support in Connaught of a MacWilliam whom the English did not consider to deserve that title. It was indeed a strange development that the Government, which misliked these old princely titles and positively forbade a peer like Tyrone to use one, should now become a purist regarding their validity and should declare for a true MacWilliam against a pretender. The truce was renewed for six weeks from 16 April. In May the Lord Justices and Ormonde agreed to extend it for another ten days, so that, unless again renewed, it would end on 7 June. There seemed good reason to suppose that it would be renewed.[3]

Further reinforcements arrived. In March 612 veterans who had been serving in Picardy reached Waterford. This contingent, however, furnished an astounding example of how troops might

[1] *Carew Cal.*, Vol. III, p. 276. *C.S.P. Ireland*, Vol. CCI (Pt. 2), 99, 122.
[2] *C.S.P. Ireland*, Vol. CCI (Pt. 2), 115.
[3] *C.S.P. Ireland*, Vol. CCI (Pt. 2), 89; Vol. CCII (Pt. 1), 9.

melt away when under orders for Ireland. It was reported that 1,110 had originally been mustered, and Ormonde had been told to expect 900. Doubtless the residue either deserted in the country or managed to get aboard supply ships instead of transports and bribed the captains to take them home. Ormonde now had under his command a great number of companies, most of them containing very few men. He therefore broke up several and distributed the troops among others.[1]

On the expiration of the truce Tyrone acted. There is no apparent reason why he should have chosen this moment rather than another; it may be that he could no longer withstand the pressure from his followers. The occasion does not seem particularly favourable and, the Spanish fleet having been driven back in the previous autumn, the chances of Spanish aid on a large scale were not rosy. However, he waited no longer. His forces were so powerful that he could afford to split them up. One section marched to the Blackwater and blockaded the fort. Tyrone himself went into Cavan to attack the castle, vowing that he would not leave it while he could get a cow out of the Pale to feed his men. A third body moved down into Leinster, where there existed ready tinder for their flame among the O'Moores, Kavanaghs, and O'Byrnes. The Lieutenant-General decided to deal with this trouble himself and on 10 July fell upon the rebels in Leix and inflicted heavy loss upon them, but had to lament the death of his nephew, James Butler, who had been well known as his page at court.[2]

The Queen was in no doubt about the danger now. On 18 and 19 July a large force of 1,472 men landed at Dublin, and of this only 129 were missing. However, this contingent misbehaved itself in the capital, 'brabbling with one another, selling their clothes and arms, and running away'. Over half of it was sent to Kells to keep it out of mischief. In early August Sir Samuel Bagenal, the Marshal's brother, was ordered to embark 600 men at Chester, and to sail to the rendezvous of Olderfleet, near Carrickfergus; and Captain Charles Egerton was to embark 1,350 men at Plymouth. The final destination of both these forces and of a squadron of 100 horse embarking at Chester was to be Lough Foyle, the importance of which was realized by Ormonde as clearly as by Sidney and others. Special instructions were issued that the supplies destined for their use when in garrison were not to be broken into. Buckets, platters

---

[1] *C.S.P. Ireland*, Vol. CCII (Pt. 1), 88; (Pt. 2), 47.
[2] *C.S.P. Ireland*, Vol. CCII (Pt. 2), 62, 110.

and dishes, taps, tap-borers, and funnels were included in the stores. Biscuit or meal was provided for 2,100 men for 112 days, and butter, cheese, pease, oatmeal, salt, sherry, brandy, and beer—a quart a day for forty-four days—were transported. This was very different provision to that of earlier times. To pay for these and other recent heavy charges, the Queen had recourse to a forced loan, repayable in six months.[1]

On 2 August the Lord Justices and the Lieutenant-General informed the Privy Council that Sir Henry Bagenal was now ready to march into Ulster, in the first instance to relieve the Blackwater fort. Ormonde himself was returning to the disaffected region of Leinster. The stage was set for the greatest drama of the Irish wars.

[1] *C.S.P. Ireland*, Vol. CCII (Pt. 2), 104, 105. *A.P.C.*, Vol. XXIX, pp. 17, 32, 40.

CHAPTER XV

THE YELLOW FORD

THE Blackwater fort had been built and garrisoned to provide a means of entry into the territory of the Earl of Tyrone by the main route from Dublin through Dundalk, Newry, and Armagh. Though on the near side of the river, it secured the passage because the enemy could hardly entrench the far bank under its fire. From the point of view of garrison, it did not amount to a heavy charge, since it was held by no more than 300 men. Unless, however, there were a genuine chance of invading Tyrone's dominions, the fort lost its strategic advantage and became the heaviest commitment the Government had to bear, all the more so when it was decided to withdraw the garrison of Armagh, the next most advanced strong point upon the route. At the same time, it was clear that Tyrone would use his utmost endeavours to reduce the fort and that no settlement would content him while it was held for the Crown. It was, as Fynes Moryson later noted, 'a great eyesore to him, lying on the chief passage into his country'. The victualling of the garrison thus became a major operation, requiring almost the total mobile resources of the Government.

Sir Henry Brouncker, an old and experienced soldier, who had served in the north with the first Lord Essex a quarter of a century before, put the case even more clearly than Fynes Moryson. 'First', he wrote to Sir Robert Cecil, 'the building of the fort at the Blackwater seemed necessary because it gave an entry into the enemy's country, near the place of his greatest credit and chiefest strength. But, because the place was too little and the garrison too weak, it stands in no more stead than a guard to assure the passage.' Since it could not draw in its own supplies, Brouncker went on, a whole army was needed for the purpose. Anyhow, one garrison, without others supporting it, was of little avail. It had been, he thought, a mistake to abandon Armagh town, not only because the place provided a good depot within easy reach of the fort, but also because its loss freed the open country east of the river for the pasturage of the enemy's creaghts by which he could maintain his forces in County Armagh.[1]

Ormonde himself would have been glad to be rid of the burden of maintaining the fort. It was, he said, 'an excessive charge to Her Majesty'. It had better not to have been built; the earth walls were always falling away, putting the garrison to great labour; Armagh would have been more satisfactory, since there the soldiers might lie dry; the fort was 'never victualled but once (by myself) without an army, to Her Majesty's exceeding charges'. In June 1598 he told the Privy Council that he considered it would be less dishonourable 'to have it razed, or yielded upon composition, than the soldiers to be left to the uttermost danger'. He would have liked to cut his losses.[2]

At the termination of the truce in that month Tyrone had surrounded the fort and completely blockaded it. Thomas Williams inspired his men to a splendid resistance. The rebels would not venture on another assault after the handling they had received in the previous October, when, according to a remark shouted up by Tyrone to Williams, they had lost 400 men, but they determined to starve it out. It was victualled only to the end of June, but the garrison then ate its horses and, according to the report, eked them out with roots and grasses.

At the inquest on the events of 14 August the two Lord Justices, Loftus and Gardiner, tried to shovel off upon the Lieutenant-General responsibility for what had occurred. It appears, in fact, that the Irish Council, with Ormonde present, debated the question of revictualling the fort and decided to send a letter to Sir Henry Bagenal, the Marshal, which he was to convey to Williams, bidding the latter make the best composition he could with the rebels. On receiving this message, Bagenal protested against such a surrender and volunteered to undertake the relief himself with forty companies of foot and such horse as could be raised. He was then sent for to come to the Council from his post at Newry and entrusted with the task, which now appeared practicable owing to the arrival of fresh troops in Ireland. The whole Council signed his instructions.[3]

There remains the question why Ormonde himself, the Lieutenant-General and commander of the troops in Ireland, did not lead

[1] C.S.P. Ireland, Vol. CCII (Pt. 1), 29.
[2] C.S.P. Ireland, Vol. CCII (Pt. 1), 5; (Pt. 2), 19, 72, 76.
[3] C.S.P. Ireland, Vol. CCII (Pt. 3), 68, I.

the expedition in person. Though the Lord Justices were prostrated by the disaster which followed, fearful of the Queen's wrath, and eager to disburden themselves of the responsibility, it is reasonable to believe their plea that they had wanted the Lieutenant-General to go. His prestige was so great that many gentlemen would have been glad to follow him, increasing the cavalry contingent, and this prestige might have exercised its effect upon the minds of the Irish. As a soldier he was far superior to Bagenal. Ormonde declared that his presence was required in Leinster. There the Kavanaghs, O'Byrnes, O'Moores, and O'Connors had been making trouble even before the end of the truce with Tyrone, and at its conclusion he had sent a strong force to aid them. After all, Bagenal was an experienced man, whose post lay upon the border of Tyrone's country, and it was natural enough that he should do the job for which he had volunteered. It is not to be supposed that Ormonde hoped to avoid the responsibility, since that must be his in any event.

Unfortunately for him, this is not the last word. He seems to have been a little mistrustful of Bagenal's competence. He had often warned him of the danger of dispersion against an Irish army.[1] Would he have spoken thus to an old campaigner unless he had thought him prone to such an error? The supposition that Ormonde was consulting his ease may be dismissed, though he was now sixty-six years of age. Yet there remains the possibility that he was thinking of his own estates and that he desired to put himself and the forces under his command between the Leinster rebels and the Butler lands. He was actually at his castle of Kilkenny when he received news of the defeat of the Yellow Ford, a calamity which would hardly have happened had he commanded the northern army.

The force under Bagenal's orders numbered 3,901 foot and about 320 horse, a considerable army by the standards of Irish war. It was also well equipped. An unusually large proportion was Irish, but the English included a detachment of veterans from the Continent, both intermingled in the regiments. On 12 August Bagenal marched from Newry to Armagh, which he entered without opposition. Next day, Sunday, he rested and held a council of war, and on the 14th continued his march towards the Blackwater, with every prospect of having to encounter the full force of the enemy.

The army moved in six regiments, two in the vanguard, two in the battle or main body, two in the rear guard. The intention was that each pair should join hands on coming into action if the ground

[1] *C.S.P. Ireland*, Vol. CCII (Pt. 3), 36.

proved suitable. Most of the comments stress the point that the distance between the regiments was excessive. The main route was strongly held by the enemy. Bagenal advanced a little to the east of it—'a mile on the right side of the common highway'. Almost at once he found himself hotly engaged, Tyrone attacking his left flank while O'Donnell passed round to assail his right. Tyrone's force was covered by a bog, across which his sharpshooters passed with their usual agility. O'Donnell was sheltered by a plantation.[1] The enemy was rather superior in numbers to the royalists, having some 4,050 foot and 600 horse according to Irish accounts and 6,000 to 8,000 by English estimates, and if the Irish were the worse armed their mobility gave them the advantage.

Galled continually by the fire of the Irish from both flanks, the leading regiments pushed on across the Callan brook, passing it at a point known, from the colour of the banks and the bed of the stream, as the Yellow Ford. Shortly afterwards the foremost regiment, under Colonel Richard Percy, found itself confronted by a long trench, five feet wide, four feet deep, and surmounted by a thorn hedge. By this time the whole column was under attack. A saker, the heaviest gun with the force, kept sticking in the boggy ground and delaying the main body, which fell further and further behind. Finally a wheel came off in the ford and the draught bullocks were shot down. Percy's regiment crossed the trench, though not without loss. The garrison of the fort could now perceive the head of the column. Expecting relief and a square meal, the poor souls cheered and threw up their hats.

No such fortune awaited them. After crossing the trench, the regiment came under still heavier fire. Still it struggled on, till it received orders to retreat in order to decrease the gap between the vanguard and the main body. But it was already becoming disorganized by the loss of its musketeers and gaps in the array of pikemen. It wheeled about in disorder, was charged by bodies of Irish horse and foot, broke up, and was destroyed in a few minutes. Bagenal, commanding the whole force and the whole vanguard in particular, was with the second regiment, his own, which he had persisted in leading though told his place was with the main body. He led it forward to the support of Percy, and himself dashed up with a small body of horse; but as he reached the scene of the disaster he was shot through the head and killed. His foot regiment not only

[1] *History of Catholic Ireland*, p. 109. O'Sullivan Bere calls the trees junipers, which do not grow wild in Armagh.

arrived too late to do anything for Percy's, but met the same fate. It was broken up and slaughtered.

Sir Thomas Wingfield, commanding the second regiment of the battle, and the senior officer after the death of the Marshal, decided that retreat was imperative. He rode forward to the leading regiment of the battle, commanded by Colonel Henry Cosby, and ordered it back, at the same time directing the rear guard to hold the ford in order to cover the withdrawal. Cosby, a veteran settler on the English estates in Leix, began to fall back in good order with his regiment intact, but then, in disobedience of orders, went forward again in an endeavour to bring off some remnants of the broken units in front. Wingfield then considered it his duty to lead on his regiment to extricate Cosby, who was now also in serious trouble. His regiment would probably, but for Wingfield's action, have been ruined as completely as those of the vanguard. As it was, it was thrown into confusion, but Wingfield did succeed in bringing off a substantial proportion of it, though he himself lost most of his musketeers.

At about this time—the accounts are not precise as to when the episode occurred—a soldier in the main body, who had expended all his powder, went up to the powder-cart to replenish his supply. A spark from his lighted match dropped into an open barrel. A big explosion followed, killing and knocking out a number of men. The clouds of black smoke which speedily enveloped the neighbourhood, and the enemy's yell of triumph at the sight, added to the confusion. It was probably at this stage that the Irish companies and some of the raw English reinforcements began to run away, the Irish going straight over to their countrymen. In the end there was not much of Cosby's regiment left to take part in the retreat.

Meanwhile, the rear guard, itself fiercely engaged at close quarters, had been unable to perceive what was going on ahead of it and for some time was unaware of the defeat. The leading regiment under Colonel Cuney, the Serjeant-Major, then moved forward to aid Wingfield in his withdrawal. Colonel Richard Billings, commanding the second regiment—that is, the rearmost of the whole force—and his officers give an account of their experience which could probably be applied to other regiments and goes far to explain the defeat. After he had passed the ford, he says, 'the enemy charged us with horse and foot, to the number of two thousand foot and four hundred horse, having long entertained skirmish, and by reason of the great number of the enemy's shot and horse coming so near and fast upon us, we were forced four or five several times to charge with our colours in the head of the pikes, by reason our shot were so beaten, and our new men bringing the rest in confusion'.

To translate into modern idiom, the Irish, after manœuvring about the regiment and galling it with musketry fire for some time, came in with a rush to close quarters in great strength. The musketeers on the flanks had largely used up their ammunition or been dispersed, and the recruits were crumpling under the strain. In view of the strength and speed of the enemy's advance, it was impossible to hold him off with such slender fire power as yet remained, and it was doubtful whether the shaky pikemen would stand the shock of the encounter. The officers therefore repeatedly brought their colours forward to animate the troops and charged at their head.

Where the regiment of Billings was concerned, these methods succeeded, but the incident reveals the weakness of an army of this period, not drawn up in line of battle, but advancing in column of regiments and assailed by such tactics as were here used by the Irish. The 'loose wings' of each regiment—that is, the musketeers and calivermen—were likely to blaze off all their powder and to be caught before they had a chance to take refuge among the pikemen. It would then be a question of pikes only against weapons of all natures, including in this case the spears or javelins which the Irish still used as missiles. If there were wavering in the ranks of the pikemen, the regiment would find itself in an ugly situation. In line of battle the danger was diminished because there pikemen and musketeers were alternated in the formation and afforded each other mutual protection. Here too the royal forces were handicapped because the cavalry was weak—it would have been stronger if Ormonde had been in command, because some of the best Irish horse would have accompanied him.

Billings, as already stated, received orders to secure the ford. As he drew back towards it, he saw a large body of the enemy, horse and foot, flying the colours they had captured from the vanguard, racing to reach it first. Fortunately for the remainder of the force, he got there in time, even saving three pieces of ordnance. Later on he received an order to fall back and make good a hill between the ford and Armagh until the rest came up. While he was executing this operation the Irish cavalry got between him and the town, but he checked its ardour by firing a gun at it. Under cover of the English horse, which behaved excellently throughout, the force reached the shelter of Armagh.[1]

The losses in killed and missing were variously reported as 1,300 and 2,000, but did these, as stated, include some 300 Irish who had deliberately deserted, a number which was added to when more slipped away by night from Armagh? At all events, it was reported later that there were only about 1,500 at Armagh. Two Englishmen took service with Tyrone. They appeared at the wall, like Kipling's deserter from the Aurangabadis, and shouted that Tyrone paid them a bounty of 20s. for their attestation. Some thirty officers were left upon the field, including one of the few northern and native loyalists, young Mulmore O'Reilly of Cavan, killed while displaying great gallantry in striving to rally broken and flying troops. A large number of colours were lost—it must be remembered that an Elizabethan force carried a high proportion because each captain of a company had his own, and Bagenal's force had numbered forty companies of foot. This was, as always, a misfortune morally; what was of more importance materially was that much of the considerable supply of food, intended for the revictualling of the Blackwater fort as well as for the needs of the field army, had been left behind; in fact, the survivors at Armagh had but eight days' supply.

On reaching Armagh it was decided that the horse under Captain Montague—Colonel Calisthenes Brooke having been seriously wounded—should attempt to break through the rebels and make its way to Newry. This was accomplished with little loss, and Montague himself rode on to Dublin to bring the news to the appalled Council. The foot huddled within the shelter of the cathedral church, almost broken in spirit.

Such was the disaster of the Yellow Ford, the worst that has ever been suffered by the English in Ireland. It redounded to the credit of the Irish and of Tyrone as their chief commander. He had employed just the right tactics, keeping his forces from a *corps-à-corps*, in which they were at their weakest, until their success had been thoroughly prepared by fire, and exploiting all their good qualities. Yet the English had played into his hands by bad dispositions, bad leadership, and the employment of untrained conscripts. Ormonde, when he heard the story, declared that the devil must have bewitched them all. He then seized the opportunity to let the Queen and her Privy Council have his views on the enormity of taking

[1] *C.S.P Ireland*, Vol. CCII (Pt. 3), 20, I: 28, II, III; 34, I; 36; 56; 94, I, II, III. *Carew Cal.*, Vol. III, p. 284. *History of Catholic Ireland*, p. 106.

men from the plough and the counter, putting them into uniform, herding them to a port, shipping them over the water, and then expecting them to defeat a foe as tireless and savage as the wolves still lurking in the forests of Ireland. Yes, matters had been made easy for Tyrone. It chanced that the scene of his victory was only five miles from Benburb, where his nephew, General Owen Roe O'Neill, gained an equally striking victory over Monro's Scots in 1646.

The effects of the battle of the Yellow Ford were far-reaching. There had been other reverses, but this had put out of action the main force at the Government's disposal. The local results must be described first of all. The Blackwater fort was obviously doomed. Unexpectedly, the Earl offered relatively easy terms. The garrison of the fort was to quit it, leaving behind colours, drums, and ammunition, and to join the army at Armagh. Then the whole force was to march out to Dundalk, this time taking with it all that it could carry and with colours displayed. The terms were accepted on the spot, but the army actually halted at Newry, probably from nervousness about moving through the Moyry, the pass on the road from Newry to Dundalk. Tyrone had found himself opposed in council over this step, and there were some who urged that the English should not be allowed to escape, but his view prevailed.[1] He told some officers who had volunteered as hostages during the withdrawal that it cost him £500 a day to keep his great force assembled and that he supposed the garrison had food for a month or six weeks. Within that time he expected a landing in Lough Foyle. 'He thought it better to save that charge, to gain the fort of the Blackwater, and to bend himself to hinder the landing of our forces in Lough Foyle, than by lying by us, with so great charge, to hazard so many inconveniences as he feared he might otherwise fall into.'[2]

His information was, as usual, good with regard to the projected landing in the Foyle, but it had not occurred to him that as a result of his victory it would be cancelled and the troops sent to Dublin instead.

The acceptance of the composition with Tyrone about the troops in the fort and at Armagh had not been made by the Irish Council, which knew nothing about it. Unfortunately for themselves, however, the Lord Justices had contemplated negotiations and the Queen had learnt of the manner of them. It is not surprising that Archbishop Loftus and Sir Robert Gardiner should have been perturbed

[1] Four Masters, Vol. VI, p. 2,074.   [2] *C.S.P. Ireland*, Vol. CCII (Pt. 3), 34, I.

by the news which Captain Montague brought them. The only army opposing the march of Tyrone on Dublin had been routed. Their military adviser was absent. Until the force originally destined for Lough Foyle reached them—and the first detachment did not arrive in Dublin until 13 September—they had virtually no troops at their disposal. They lost their heads. On 16 August they addressed to Tyrone the following ignominious letter, to which, besides themselves, the Secretary (Sir Geoffrey Fenton), the Treasurer at Wars (Sir Henry Wallop), and the Master of the Ordnance (Sir George Bourchier) appended their signatures:

'We have taken knowledge of the late accident happened to part of Her Majesty's forces employed in Ulster, only for victualling of the Blackwater, and that many of them are retired into Armagh, where they now remain. We thought good upon this occasion to send to you on their behalf, though we think that, in your own consideration, you will let them go without doing them any further hurt. We are to put you in mind how far you may incense Her Majesty's indignation towards you, if you shall do any further distress to those companies, being as you know in cold blood; and, on the other side, how far you may move Her Majesty to renew a favourable conceit of you by using favour to these men. And besides, your ancient adversary the Marshal being now taken away, we hope you will cease all further revenge towards the rest, against whom you can ground no cause of sting against yourself, being employed by Her Majesty in these Her Highness's services. Thus much we thought good to signify unto you, by way of caution to admonish you to avoid to provoke so mighty a Prince upon such a matter as to distress her servitors in cold blood. To this end we have sent this bearer, the pursuivant, by whom we expect your answer.—At Dublin, 16th August, 1598.'[1]

A copy, the only version in existence, was despatched to England. In a postscript to the covering letter addressed to the Privy Council, it was stated that the original had been sent to Tyrone by the pursuivant, who had been directed to find out the true state of the troops, and that this was the chief reason for sending him to Tyrone.

Queen Elizabeth did not condemn compromise. Indeed, there had been occasions in the past when her dealings with Tyrone might have been stigmatized as weak. She was, however, a proud monarch and prouder than ever in adversity. The scathing indignation of her rebuke could hardly be excelled, and the bitterest part of it lies in

[1] C.S.P. Ireland, Vol. CCII (Pt. 3), 20, II.

the allegation that the minds of the writers of the appeal had been crazed by panic and that now, having had time to think matters over, they must realize what craven fools they had shown themselves to be.

'We may not pass over this foul error to our dishonour, when you of our Council framed such a letter to the traitor, after the defeat, as never was read the like, either in form or substance, for baseness, being such as we persuade ourself, if you shall peruse it again, when you are yourselves, that you will be ashamed of your own absurdities and grieved that any fear or rashness should ever make you authors of an action so much to your Sovereign's dishonour and to the increasing of the traitor's insolency.'

'Our cousin of Ormonde', of course, was not included in this burning condemnation. He had done nothing shameful. Yet he also merited and received sharp reproof. 'It was strange to us', wrote the Queen, 'when almost the whole forces of our Kingdom were drawn to head, and a main blow like to be stroken for our honour against the capital rebel, that you, whose person would have better daunted the traitors, and would have carried it with another manner of reputation and strength of the nobility of the Kingdom, should employ yourself in an action of less importance, and leave that to so mean a conduction.'[1]

Later the Council put forward a story, suspiciously like that of a cock and a bull, that the pursuivant was sent only as an agent to discover the state of the troops, that he was not to deliver the letter unless he were intercepted, and that then it would serve as a passport, for which purpose it had been deliberately framed in cringing style; in fact, it had been brought back unread by Tyrone. If so, it is odd that it disappeared, seeing how carefully documents were then preserved; but there is no evidence of its having reached Tyrone. Hearing this news, the Queen put a postscript to her letter quoted above to the effect that she was glad he had not read the message, but that this fact had not altered her opinion of the writers.

Tyrone missed a golden opportunity to strike at the capital, the heart of royal rule. Yet his inaction did not conflict with his character. The Earl was patient and pertinacious rather than determined. He was prone to morbid fits of hesitation and timidity. He believed that he could still at any time patch up a favourable peace and obtain the pardon of the Crown. His sternest foe, Burghley, had died a few days before the battle, which brought comfort to Philip

[1] *C.S.P. Ireland*, Vol. CCII (Pt. 3), 64.

II of Spain on his deathbed. Tyrone was already master of all Ulster but Newry and Carrickfergus. If the Spaniards came, he would be master of all Ireland—probably without letting them into Ulster—but it remained to be seen whether they would fulfil their promises under Philip's successor. So Tyrone waited in Ulster, directing others to do his work.

What they did was formidable enough. O'Donnell established himself in almost complete control of Connaught. He had set up Theobald Burke as the MacWilliam. The latter had over 2,000 followers, while his loyal kinsman, Tibbot ne Long, was forced to take refuge in one of the vessels which gave him his title.[1] Sir Conyers Clifford, the Governor, maintained himself in Athlone and victualled Boyle, Tulsk, and Roscommon, but the garrisons of the three last-named amounted only to fifty-four men and he had in Athlone only 120 English, having sent 300 men to join Bagenal's fatal expedition. In Leinster the O'Moores flung themselves upon the estates of the settlers in King's County and Queen's County, and killed many of the families, though no savagery is reported such as was to occur in Munster. The exertions of Ormonde saved something out of the wreck.

In Munster the case was far worse. The province was already seething when Owen ('Owney') MacRory O'Moore and Richard Tyrrell, Tyrone's best professional commander, burst into it with over 2,000 men by way of Limerick. Tyrone had decided to start a new Desmond rebellion, and he had a tool ready for the task. This was James Fitzthomas Fitzgerald, nephew of the last Earl of Desmond and actually of the elder line, though the seed of a marriage treated as null and void. Some of the Geraldines did not acknowledge the nullity; at all events, with Tyrone's blessing, the descent was considered good enough, and James Fitzthomas was accepted as Earl of Desmond. He has come down to history as the Sugane ('straw-rope') Earl.[2]

Spreading out on all sides and gathering strength as they went, the Ulster and Leinster invaders carried fire and sword through Munster. Naturally, the settlers on the escheated Desmond estates suffered most. Few of them made any defence. Those who were not caught in their homes fled, for the most part to Cork, Youghal, and Waterford, but many were intercepted and killed on the way. Some had their tongues cut out or their noses cut off. Chief Justice Saxey

[1] C.S.P. Ireland, Vol. CCII (Pt. 3), 133. 'Ne Long' means 'of the ships'.
[2] C.S.P. Ireland, Vol. CCII (Pt. 3), 96 and 112.

of Munster tells of 'infants taken from the nurse's breast and the brains dashed against the walls; the heart plucked out of the body in the view of the wife, who was forced to yield the use of her apron to wipe the blood off from the murderer's fingers'.[1] Castle after castle fell into the hands of the Irish, to be either garrisoned by them or demolished. Such Irish loyalists as remained were not spared. The rebels burnt fifty-four 'towns', or native hamlets, on the Barry lands, and took nearly 10,000 cows, nearly 5,000 horses, and nearly 60,000 sheep and hogs.

The whole elaborate structure of the Munster plantation had collapsed at a stroke. Among those who escaped was Edmund Spenser, but according to tradition one of his boys was burnt to death in the flames of his castle at Kilcolman. He had settled in Munster after having been Secretary to Lord Grey, the viceroy, and it was the background of forest and ravine, haunted by outlaw and wolf, which had inspired the scenes of his immortal poem. Another poet, Sir Walter Raleigh, suffered in the same way, but only in pocket, since he was an absentee landlord.

For some or most of the reverses the Queen and Privy Council were hardly responsible, but they had certainly muddled the question of governance and military command. Here was a country in almost universal rebellion, yet it was left without a viceroy for eight months after the disaster of the Yellow Ford and nearly eighteen months after the death of Burgh, all because Elizabeth could not make up her mind about his successor. The two Lord Justices, at the head of the Government, were old men and in her judgement cravens. The military commander, Ormonde, was still vigorous, but he was sixty-six and at odds with the Lord Justices. And when she had to replace Bagenal as Marshal, the second military appointment in the Kingdom, she sent a failing man of seventy, no other than the former Governor of Connaught, Sir Richard Bingham, recently imprisoned on charges of oppression and extortion in that province, but now restored to her confidence.[2] The veteran, burning to strike another blow against his old foes, made but one short expedition from the walls of Dublin—and that too late to prevent a traitorous constable from delivering Athy to an O'Moore kinsman—before he died. Dublin itself was none too

---

[1] *C.S.P. Ireland*, Vol. CCII (Pt. 3), 127 (26 October 1598).
[2] *C.S.P. Ireland*, Vol. CCII (Pt. 3), 64. The Queen herself wrote to the Lord Justices, and in case there should be any doubt about Bingham's position, told them that he was returning 'with our favour and gracious opinion'.

safe. A plot to seize the Castle and admit the rebels was discovered just in time.

Ormonde was not remiss or lacking in vigour. With the resources available, he did what he could. Returning to Dublin after the defeat, he marched soon afterwards with a bare handful of men, mainly 600 newly arrived, to the Ulster borders and took all possible measures for the protection of the Pale. He waited until the people of Meath and Louth had reaped their harvest, saw it housed in castles and strong places, garrisoned these, and left in command Sir Samuel Bagenal, brother of the late Marshal. Bagenal, recently knighted by Essex in the Cadiz expedition, had been the commander of the force which was to have occupied Lough Foyle, but had received instructions, on news of the reverse, to go instead to Dublin. The first 600, mentioned above, were the detachment from Chester. The remainder, 1,300, embarked at Bristol, but bad weather drove the ships into Waterford and Youghal, where Sir Thomas Norris with some justification laid hands upon a company of 140 before sending them on by sea. The slender dam held, but the Queen's bad luck with her leaders persisted; for Bagenal's horse fell with him, and this experienced soldier lay for some time incapacitated.

As regards Ulster there was nothing more that the Lieutenant-General could do except await reinforcements, and, as has been hinted, his own property was always very much on his mind. He went south again in early October. On the 4th he was at Naas, on the 5th at Carlow, on the 6th at his castle of Kilkenny, where he remained but one night with his 'sweet lady'. On the 11th he met Norris, the President of Munster, who had marched up from Cork, at Kilmallock, which was revictualled. On the 14th he reached Mallow, on the 17th Cork, where he put in some fresh troops. On the 20th he put a company into Youghal and scolded the citizens into doing something for their own defence. Then he turned back into Tipperary, where he defeated and hunted a rebel force and recovered some of the spoils of the Munster settlement. At the end of the year he revictualled Maryborough, in Queen's County, with his own cattle. In March 1599 he heard that there were some treacherous Irishmen in the place, so marched again, drove the besiegers out of his path, revictualled Maryborough for nine weeks more, and put in safe men instead of the suspects.[1] Besides the places mentioned, he maintained Ross, Thomastown, Clonmel, Cashel, Fethard, Callan, and the fort of Duncannon.

[1] *C.S.P. Ireland,* Vol. CCIII, 101.

Even in this period of defeat and miserable lack of strength the renown of English arms was not quite extinguished. In Ormonde's perambulations the rebels seldom ventured to attack him in force; if they did he broke through them and continued on his way. Tyrone had warned them to fight only in passes, forests, or bogs, and Ormonde was too old a soldier and too well served in reconnaissance by his horsemen and his gallowglasses to march blindly into such country. Yet, as soon as his back was turned, the Irish flowed in behind him like a tide. He fought under every conceivable handicap. If he revictualled a garrison, he could not therefore conclude that it was safe, because, as has been seen, Irish soldiers might deliver it to the enemy. His own kinsmen, as had happened before, fell away from him, and two Butler magnates, Lords Cahir and Mountgarret, consorted with the rebels. Whatever the sympathies of the observer, it would be ungenerous in him to withhold admiration from this stern and bleak figure, in great part isolated from his own people by his Protestantism as he was separated from the English in Ireland by his nationality, with a vision and ideals for Ireland higher than those of either, almost living in the saddle, but beginning to falter now as age gripped his once tireless frame, yet still as staunch and steadfast as he was wary, faithful to the line he had always followed, and above all intensely loyal and devoted to the Queen who was his contemporary and at whose feet he had sighed when they were both young, when she was indeed the bewitching Gloriana. Ormonde spared no effort, and in actual achievement he left a far better framework of strength for the new viceroy than might have been expected.

Fresh troops were coming in too—in fact, reinforcements without which there would have been complete collapse. A levy of 1,300 men was ordered on 26 August and sailed in October.[1] On the 28th of that month orders were issued to raise 2,000 more from the West Country and the southern Midlands who were to sail from Plymouth, Bristol, Weymouth, Southampton, and Fowey or Padstow to Munster. The arrival of these troops, 1,600 at Cork and Kinsale and 400 at Waterford, was reported by Norris on 9 December in a message which he sent to England by the hand of the ruined Edmund Spenser. He said that the Cork and Kinsale contingents were pretty well equipped, though raw, and that he was taking

[1] *A.P.C.*, Vol. XXIX, p. 94. The original call was for 1,700 from nineteen counties, of whom only 1,000 were sent, and 400 from London, later reduced to 300. The Londoners mutinied on the road to Chester.

their training in hand; Ormonde had drawn off the Waterford contingent. The old companies with Norris numbered 790.[1] A force of 4,090 men would have sufficed to subdue all Ireland only a short while earlier, but times had changed.

Then, on 29 November, another levy of 1,000 men was called for from Berkshire, Bedfordshire, Worcestershire, Oxfordshire, Dorset, Wiltshire, Leicestershire, and Warwickshire. The Privy Council was sensible of the strain and the dislike of these growing demands. Its message to the Lieutenants and Commissioners for the Muster was almost apologetic in tone. There was no need, it wrote, to point out 'how sparingly Her Majesty hath always proceeded to make any levies of men but in causes of greatest necessity'. Now the affairs of Ireland were so bad that the Queen, 'both for the honour of her princely calling and of the realm, is to apply these speedy and effectual remedies that may be able to cure so grievous a disease'. The circular letter, however, ended with the customary warning that the men must be of better quality than before and well equipped. This contingent, commanded by Sir Arthur Savage, was to aid Clifford in Connaught. It arrived in Dublin about 31 January 1599, and at once marched to Athlone.[2]

In December 1598 Sir Francis Vere, the English commander in the Low Countries, was bidden to send over 2,000 seasoned soldiers, who would be replaced by recruits from England, and another levy was ordered to provide these men. Scalding reproaches were launched against Vere because his contingent was short by 500 and deficient in arms, the balance having to be made up in England.[3] Two more big levies were ordered, one for 3,000 in January 1598, and another for 2,000 in February; but these do not affect the period of the interregnum and were for the service of the new viceroy. Vast contracts were entered into with English clothiers and purveyors, one of them with Marmaduke Darrell, the Surveyor of the Victuals for the Navy, and John Jolles, a London merchant, to supply 10,000 men in Ireland with meat, biscuit, butter, and cheese, for three months. As 3,000 men were destined for Lough Foyle, where they would find no utensils of any sort, a stock was provided, including kettles, fifty-three dozen buckets, twenty-six dozen platters, 100 frying pans, dishes, spoons, scales, and measures. Also in the schedule were bricks for ovens, lime, fishing nets, lanterns, and

[1] A.P.C., Vol. XXIX, p. 245. C.S.P. Ireland, Vol. CCII (Pt. 4), 15.
[2] A.P.C., Vol. XXIX, p. 312. C.S.P. Ireland, Vol. CCIII, 31.
[3] A.P.C., Vol. XXIX, p. 621.

candles. Thirty butts of sack, not forgetting taps, borers, and funnels, were added. A supply of liquorice and aniseed to make drinks supposed to ward off or cure fever was included, with iron pestles and brass mortars to powder it.

A regular postal service to Ireland, by way of Holyhead for Dublin and the north and of Bristol for the south, was established, riders and horses being maintained in stages. Those of the former route were as follows: the Court, London, Barnet, St. Albans, Brickhill, Towcester, Daventry, Coventry, Coleshill, Lichfield, Stone, Nantwich, Chester, Rhuddlan, Conway, Beaumaris, Holyhead. The daily payment for each stage was generally 1s. 8d., but might amount to 2s. A packet hired at Holyhead cost £10 a month. The sum total per annum amounted to £634 18s. 4d. The stages of the Bristol route were the Court, London, Hounslow, Maidenhead, Reading, Newbury, Marlborough, Chippenham, Marshfield, Bristol. No sailing packet was engaged on this route, so that the mail must have been carried by such ships as were plying to Ireland. In this case the annual cost was £273 15s. A sum of over £900 for the Irish mail alone was considerable for those days.[1] Never before had so much energy or so much good organization been put into the business of the Irish wars. If they had taken a long time about it, the English had learnt their lesson in Ireland. But again all this was for the new viceroy.

He was to be the foremost figure in the country, the Earl of Essex, Earl Marshal of England. The Queen had hesitated long, partly because she did not want him to quit her side, partly, it may well be, because she doubted his fitness for the task. On 10 December 1598, however, Cecil wrote to Clifford: 'I think Her Majesty is now resolved of her General to be the Earl Marshal, and he shall have a good army of 12,000 or 14,000 foot and 1,000 horse.'[2] There had been other prominent candidates, but Essex had insisted upon being chosen, lest any other should eject him from his place as the greatest man in the kingdom. If the risks were enormous, so were the prizes of renown and glory—and if he had succeeded he would to-day be accounted almost as great a man as Francis Drake. He rejoiced at having overcome his rivals. 'I have beaten Knollys and Mountjoy in the Council, and by God I will beat Tyr-Owen in the field; for nothing worthy Her Majesty's honour hath yet been achieved', he wrote to his friend Harington. Says the modern historian of Elizabethan Ireland: 'It is not in such boastful mood that great men are

---

[1] *A.P.C.*, Vol. XXIX, p. 591.   [2] *C.S.P. Ireland*, Vol. CCII (Pt. 4), 17.

wont to put on their armour. And, besides all this, Knollys was his uncle and Mountjoy his familiar friend.'[1]

He was to be Lord Lieutenant, the first to hold that exalted title since it had been bestowed on Sussex, when the Queen was young and Essex was unborn. He left London on 27 March 1599, riding through a double lane of citizens four miles long, who called down the blessings of Heaven upon him. Delayed by a contrary wind, he did not reach Dublin until 15 April.

[1] Harington, *Nugae Antiquae*, Vol. II, p. 30. Bagwell, *Ireland under the Tudors*, Vol. III, p. 315.

CHAPTER XVI

ESSEX IN IRELAND

ROBERT DEVEREUX, Earl of Essex, had a hereditary interest in Ireland. His father, the first Earl of the Devereux creation, had been in charge of the ambitious Ulster colonization scheme of the 'seventies and had bequeathed to him, with other Irish property, the Barony of Farney, in Monaghan, from which he may have drawn a little revenue in quiet times, such as those of Fitzwilliam's second viceroyalty, after the defeat of the Armada. A group of great families, strangely interlinked, had at the same time close connections with Ireland. They were the Dudleys, the Sidneys, the Devereux, the Knollys, the Walsinghams, and the Blounts. Three of the men—Sir Henry Sidney, the younger Essex, and Charles Blount, Lord Mountjoy—became viceroys. Walter Devereux, the elder Essex, was Captain-General, and virtually independent Governor, of Ulster. Sir Francis Walsingham was often drawn into Irish affairs and was the father-in-law of a viceroy and of a President of Connaught. Robert Dudley, Earl of Leicester, had much to do with Irish policy and was connected in one way or another with all the other families named. Thomas Knollys was at one moment all but designated viceroy. Christopher Blount was Marshal of the Army in Ireland under Essex.

The complex links were those of marriage and also of unsanctioned love. The wives of the two Earls of Essex each married three times. Lettice Knollys, wife of Walter Devereux and mother of Robert, married after the former's death the Earl of Leicester, and after his death Sir Christopher Blount, a cousin of Mountjoy's. Frances Walsingham married, first, Philip Sidney, Sir Henry's son and (by a Dudley mother) Leicester's nephew; secondly, Robert Devereux, Leicester's stepson; and, thirdly, Richard de Burgh, Earl of Clanrickarde, Lord President of Connaught in the reign of James I. Robert's sister, Penelope Devereux, started her adventurous career as the adored—perhaps the mistress—of Philip Sidney and the Stella of his poems; after her marriage to Lord Rich, later Earl of Warwick, she became Mountjoy's mistress; finally, after a divorce from Rich, she was married to Mountjoy in circumstances of doubtful legality. It was all thus something of a family party. The Queen did not care for family parties in Ireland, nor for political parties; and this was the old Leicester party, as opposed to that of Sussex, now the Essex party, as opposed to that of Cecil.

Almost the sole qualifications of Essex for the arduous task which he had undertaken were his great vitality and energy—though they did not save him from premature discouragement—and a certain tactical competence in the field. So far as the handling of an army went, he understood that well, and there is much to be praised in his handling of the Cadiz expedition. He lacked, however, the strategic insight which distinguished his successor, Mountjoy; he was not a great leader of the school of Sidney, Burgh, Ormonde, Bingham, Carew, and Mountjoy again; his organization was indifferent, and he wore out and disgusted his best troops while accomplishing nothing. Yet his reputation was so imposing that, even after his failure and execution, some trace of it lingered on in Ireland.

He attracted to the Irish war a number of volunteers from the group of his adventurous and hot-headed friends and contemporaries. Young bloods of this type were an asset to an army in an age when there was little systematic training except on the battlefield or on the line of march, so that the forces with which they served benefited by their ardour and zeal to distinguish themselves without being saddled with their inexperienced leadership as officers. They could, however, be dangerous if not kept in their proper place, and many of those who wished well to the expedition were 'vexed to see so many raw youths press for the greatest charges'.[1] In the following of Essex were two men of some military experience and of uncontrolled ambition, and it must be a matter for opinion whether their influence upon him or his upon them was the more harmful. Essex on the one hand, Sir Christopher Blount and the Earl of Southampton on the other, did each other no good. The first two were to perish on the scaffold. The third, lover of art and learning, patron of Shakespeare, and as brilliant a figure as Essex himself, was but narrowly to avoid that fate.

The new Lord Lieutenant received the sword on 15 April 1599, when Thomas Jones, Bishop of Meath and afterwards Archbishop of Dublin, preached a notable sermon. The first question to decide was in which direction to launch an offensive against the rebels.

[1] *C.S.P. Dom.*, 1598–1601, p. 151.

The advisers Essex had brought with him were not of high calibre and the Irish Council was weak and timid. Tyrone and his Ulster forces manifestly represented the main root of the revolt. If that could be cut, the rest would be subdued by a relatively slight effort. Yet there were difficulties about a northern journey until pasture was available, because the army was short of transport. After long consultations, it was decided, in the words of Essex himself, to 'shake and sway the branches' before attempting to cut the root—in other words, to go south. It does not appear that Essex needed much persuasion to make him choose the easier course, but the English Privy Council did not disapprove.[1]

The army in Ireland numbered by the list 16,000 foot and 1,300 horse. It was intended to send 2,000 reinforcements every three months to fill up the ranks, in itself a grim commentary on the prospect of surviving sickness, since it was unlikely that Irish warfare would involve anything like that number of battle casualties. It need hardly be said that only a relatively small proportion of the force given above was available to act as a field army under the Lord Lieutenant. If he turned his back on the Pale, he had to assure its safety. Sir Arthur Chichester had 500 foot at Carrickfergus, Sir Samuel Bagenal eight companies at Newry, Lord Cromwell four companies at Dundalk, Lord Audley eight companies at Kells, Sir Henry Harington and Sir Alexander Radcliffe seven companies in Wicklow, Sir Warham St. Leger 550 foot at Monasterevin, and Sir John Shelton 350 men at Ardee. Sir Edward Herbert, with six companies, was to leave the line of march and to garrison Offaly. A company was left in Dublin itself. The defence of the Pale thus accounted for the better part of 5,000 men. Then there were the forces under Norris in Munster, and Ormonde, now at Kilkenny, and the garrisons of the south. In Connaught Sir Conyers Clifford had or was to be given a strength of 3,000 men.

No army ever established in Ireland had better prospects of being adequately maintained. A new Treasurer at Wars, Sir George Carey, crossed with Essex, his veteran predecessor, Sir Henry Wallop, dying on the day of their arrival. He was well furnished with cash. The Privy Council enjoined him, the Master of the Ordnance (Sir George Bourchier), the Muster Master (Sir Ralph Lane), the Commissary of the Victuals (George Beverley), to send returns every two months of estimated charges, receipts of money from England and what little could be collected in Ireland, debts,

[1] *C.S.P. Ireland*, Vol. CCV, 38 and 52.

the quantity of munitions on hand, exact muster rolls of the army, and receipts for victuals sent from England or obtained in Ireland. This time it meant to see where it was going. It had made big contracts for food and clothing, and though Essex grumbled, he was far better off than any of his predecessors had been. The reply to one of his demands was typical. He asked for 200 English draught horses before 1 June, when he proposed to move against Ulster.[1] The Privy Council told him that the Queen had refused, not on principle but because he had not yet done anything notable against the rebels. Whether or not the Queen was as miserly as is pretended, she wanted results for her money and some results before she increased her initial expenditure.

The enemy's armed strength was estimated to be 19,997—a suspiciously exact figure, the artificiality of which is proved by a later guess of 30,000. In Leinster the number was given as 3,230, in Ulster 8,922, in Munster 4,555, and in Connaught 3,290. But before Essex set out from Dublin his intelligence service warned him that Tyrone was about to move into Munster. O'Donnell had already moved into north Connaught. Tyrone had in fact written to one of the revolting Geraldine chieftains in Munster, the White Knight, that he hoped to be with him in May.[2] The Earl did not keep his promise, but O'Donnell soon made his presence felt in Connaught.

Essex left Dublin on 9 May to join the main body of his expeditionary force, about 3,000 foot and 300 horse, near Kilcullen in Kildare. On the 11th, after some trifling skirmishes, the castle of Athy was surrendered to him, and he put a small garrison into it. He then crossed the Barrow by the castle bridge, and came upon Ormonde in camp with 700 foot and 200 Irish horse. Ormonde brought in his kinsmen, Lords Cahir and Mountgarret, who had not deeply committed themselves to rebellion and had decided not to do so more seriously. They fell on their knees before the Lord Lieutenant, were admonished, and handed over to the Provost Marshal. The army now halted for two days to await a scanty train, bringing up supplies thenceforth to be carried by the troops or on packhorses, and also for Herbert's Offaly force and for the garrison of the fort of Maryborough.

On the march to Maryborough the enemy showed himself in the defile at Blackford, near Stradbally, but did not venture to attack. The fort was duly revictualled. Then the rebel commander, Owen

---

[1] *C.S.P. Ireland*, Vol. CCV, 33, 34, 35, 36, and 38.
[2] *C.S.P. Ireland*, Vol. CCV, 19.

MacRory O'Moore, sent in a challenge to match fifty of his men against fifty English with sword and target. Essex accepted, but the Irish did not come to the rendezvous. Ormonde, who had long ago had to remonstrate with Perrott when the latter had proposed to take part himself in a contest of this kind, must have wondered when the English would abandon this medieval mummery, especially when Essex decided to march on by the pass of Cashel, which afforded the rebels every advantage, rather than make a detour.

However, there was nothing amateurish about the march. Essex was at his best on such occasions. The road led through a thick wood, and at one point was cut by a trench, on either side of which the trees were plashed—that is, branches were bent down and woven into an obstacle. Neighbouring bogs gave the Irish further facilities for advance or retreat on the flanks. In front of the vanguard marched the usual forlorn hope, in this case consisting of forty shot and twenty swordsmen. The calivermen were to move straight up to the trench to within point-blank range. Then the swordsmen were to jump into the trench on the flanks, while the vanguard, passing through the calivermen, attacked it frontally. The vanguard itself was flanked by bodies of shot mixed with a few pikemen. They were kept in sight by the main body or battle, which was prepared to support them as required. Between the vanguard and the main body marched the baggage, with a cavalry escort. The rest of the horse moved between the main body and the rear guard, except for thirty men who brought up the rear. The vanguard rushed the trench and pressed quickly through to open country beyond the defile, when it was ordered to halt until the whole column had rejoined it in the plain.

Essex is described as 'flying like lightning' from one part of the army to another, leading, directing, and following the vanguard, battle, and rear guard. The Irish claimed to have cut off a number of his men and say that the defile was called 'the pass of the plumes' in memory of the captured plumed hats or helmets. The English admit the loss only of a handful. Both sides are likely to have made the best of their respective stories, but those of the English come from eyewitnesses, whereas those of the Irish were written a generation later, largely from hearsay. On the 18th Essex marched through another pass to Mountgarret's castle at Ballyragget, but in this case resistance was slight. He put 100 men into this place and then moved on to Kilkenny, Ormonde's town. Here he was nobly received, the townsfolk greeting him with orations and bestrewing the streets with rushes and herbs for his passage.[1]

On 22 May the army set out for Clonmel, where it arrived next day: more demonstrations and orations, heady wine for a man of the Lord Lieutenant's temperament. So far he had done nothing and was leaving Leinster entirely unsubdued behind him; now he decided to plunge into Munster. But first he had to deal with Cahir Castle, some ten miles up the Suir from Clonmel. Lord Cahir was anxious that it should be given up, but though he was sent to persuade his younger brother, who held it for the rebels, to surrender, the garrison decided to fight. Supplies and some cannon had been sent up to Clonmel from Waterford by boat, but no draught horses had been provided, a typical instance of the mismanagement of the expedition. A couple of cannon were dragged to the site by the much-enduring soldiery, and ladders and scaffolding were prepared.

The castle itself was not unduly strong, but it was difficult of approach, since it was built upon an island in the Suir. Moreover, it could be attacked with safety only from one bank—the east—because, had the army been split in two by the river, the enemy might have attacked either part in superior strength. Under cover of the artillery, an orchard under the walls was occupied. Most of the garrison then fled, but the White Knight contrived to put in a reinforcement from the far bank. However, before the assault was launched the garrison fled by night, the English cutting down a fair number in the darkness. It was not much of an exploit, but it gratified Essex, and he made the most of it.[2]

He had known many brilliant days, but he was fated to see few more as satisfactory even as that of the taking of Cahir Castle. During the brief remainder of his life one misfortune after another was to befall him. While he was dealing with Cahir Castle the first disaster of his viceroyalty occurred. Sir Henry Harington had, as related, been left with seven companies to watch the O'Byrnes, one of the most dangerous communities in one of the most difficult districts in all Ireland, but on deciding to go into Munster Essex had cut down the force. Partly to reconnoitre some new works thrown up by Phelim MacFeagh O'Byrne—son of the Feagh

[1] *C.S.P. Ireland*, Vol. CCV, 63, I. Four Masters, Vol. VI, p. 2,113. Harington, *Nugae Antiquae*, Vol. II, pp. 31–8. (The account in Dymmok's *Treatice of Ireland*, p. 32, is almost word for word the same as Harington's.)

[2] *Carew Cal.*, Vol. III, p. 302. Harington, *Nugae Antiquae*, Vol. II, p. 39.

MacHugh slain by Russell in 1597—in the valley of the Avonmore, near Rathdrum, partly to train his raw troops, Harington marched out from Wicklow with 450 foot and fifty horse and camped outside the glen on the night of 28 May. It is alleged that the site of the camp was ill chosen; at all events, the rebels fired volleys into it during the night, not the best medicine for a force on its first expedition. Phelim MacFeagh sent a message that he desired to negotiate, either for the purpose of rendering the English less alert or just possibly for that of getting into touch with the Irish troops in Harington's force. Next morning Harington reconnoitred the glen with his cavalry, and then, finding that the rebels were assembling in force, gave the order to march back to Wicklow.

Harington certainly showed no brilliance. He put in the rear guard an Irish company commanded by Adam Loftus, son of the Archbishop of Dublin and Lord Chancellor, men of doubtful reliability whom he himself described as having for the most part come lately from the rebels. The O'Byrnes hastened in pursuit, galled the retreat for a couple of miles with musketeers flitting about in the woodlands, and then closed in as the English forded a brook which crossed the road. Loftus did what he could, but received a wound from which he died at Wicklow. His lieutenant, Piers Walshe, who had never dismounted from his cob, wrapped the colours round his body and shamefully fled with them, afterwards telling a fine story about having saved them. The men of the Irish company broke and ran, not stopping till they reached Wicklow. But the main body of the English foot made no better showing. The musketeers uncovered the pikemen and the latter pressed forward in blind panic. It was indeed a panic of an extraordinary kind. The men were dazed with fear. Captain Allerton afterwards reported that he rode up and found the rebels cutting them down from behind, while they did not attempt to defend themselves or even turn round. He shouted to them that they had only to face about to save their lives, but they took no heed and hurried on. He charged and drove off the rebels for the time being, but the flight continued, and when the country opened up the men broke and ran in all directions, throwing away their arms. It was a catastrophe on a small scale, but complete, and one more proof that only the very best leadership, lacking on this occasion, would hold together raw English recruits and unstable Irishmen against the rebels in close country.[1]

[1] *C.S.P. Ireland*, Vol. CCV, 75, 108.

Meanwhile, the Lord Lieutenant marched again, heading north-west towards Limerick. He left his sick—probably numerous, since the weather was foul—in Clonmel. He repaired the bridge at Golden over the upper Suir and passed on to Tipperary. Here he received a message from the President of Munster, Sir Thomas Norris, that he had been wounded by a pike in chastising a small body of the Burkes, and Essex with a cavalry escort rode over to see him where he lay in hospital. Norris afterwards rejoined the viceroy, but he died in the following August. Essex reached Limerick on 4 June, and again had to listen to orations. 'I know not which', remarks the impish John Harington, 'was the more to be discommended: words, composition, or oratory, all of which having their peculiar excellences in barbarism, harshness and rustical both pronouncing and action.'[1]

After a few days' rest Essex determined to revictual Askeaton, threatened by the Sugane Earl of Desmond. On the 8th he marched to Adare. The rebels appeared with 2,000 or 3,000 men, but did not dispute the bridge over the Maigue. Next morning he got through a defile at the cost of twenty-six casualties, claiming to have killed 100 of the Connaught bonaghts under James Fitzthomas. Yet the weary troops showed no enthusiasm, and their commander re-proached them for their hesitation. He then went on to Askeaton to witness the arrival of the provision boats from Limerick, which had sailed down the estuary of the Shannon and into the mouth of the Deel.

The progress continued. Essex decided to visit James Fitzthomas's castle at Conna, near Lismore, with the object, it appears, of 'giving the rebel an inexcusable provocation'. Marching past a wood, the English were sharply attacked, but drove off Fitzthomas's men. Sir Henry Norris was wounded and his leg was amputated on the spot. He died a short while after, so that three of these famous fighting brethren, John, Thomas, and Henry, ended their lives in Ireland. Essex camped at Croom on the night of the 11th, then moved on to Bruff, on the Morningstar. He and Ormonde rode over to Kilmallock for a conference with Thomas Norris. In short, he wanted to know what to do next. It was decided he should go on to Conna and home by a roundabout route, the choice of which was governed by the prospect that Norris would produce him food and his promise of a convoy of munitions to be sent from Cork by boat to Fermoy or Castle Lyons. On Sunday 17 June, when he was

[1] Harington, *Nugae Antiquae*, Vol. II, p. 42.

at Fermoy, Lord Barry sent him a message that he had brought the convoy to Castle Lyons, but that the enemy was at hand in some strength. Essex showed prudence in 'deferring the sermons till the afternoon' and took a force to bring the supplies in. The expedition to Conna was fruitless, since Fitzthomas had burnt his own castle.

A council of war was now held in the Lord President's tent. Asked what force he required to pursue the war in Munster, Norris replied that he needed 1,000 foot and 200 horse. Essex, ever large-minded, gave him his brother's company of horse, one of the best in the army, and 100 more foot than he had asked for, and marched without incident to Waterford, where he arrived on 21 June. This time the orations were in Latin. He inspected the harbour and the fort of Duncannon, while boats were collected to ferry the army across the Barrow into Wexford. It was a slow business, since the army was now encumbered by a mob of servants and horseboys more numerous than the troops themselves, as well as sick and wounded. It is not difficult to imagine the sufferings of these unfortunates or the questions asked by now as to what good this expedition was supposed to be doing.

The direct road to Dublin would have been through central Wicklow, but Essex could not march through woods and glens swarming with rebels with his painfully reduced force and his throng of camp-followers. He therefore headed through Gorey to the coast at Arklow. Four miles short of that place, the rebels were found holding the line of a river, which must have been the Clonough. Southampton, who in fact commanded the horse, though the Queen had forbidden any such appointment, got across by a bad, deep ford; Ormonde, marching wide on the right, crossed by a better one on the shore. The rebels gave way after a stiff fight, and, whenever they afterwards threatened in the open country now reached, either Southampton or Essex himself, with as few as half a dozen horsemen, would turn upon them and see them off. Phelim MacFeagh made some proposals to treat, but nothing came of them. Essex re-entered Dublin on 2 July.[1]

He had quitted the capital all but two lunar months earlier, on 9 May. What had he accomplished in this zigzag progress through the south of Ireland? The capture of Cahir Castle, the victualling of a few other places; perhaps we may add, if we desire to be as kindly as possible, the display of the Lord Lieutenant's goodly and impressive person to the Queen's relatively loyal subjects in Clonmel,

[1] *Carew Cal.*, Vol. III, p. 308.

Limerick, Waterford, and some other places. Nothing else is dis-
coverable. He had not obtained a single submission. Even Cahir
and Mountgarret, who were hardly rebels in the real sense, had
submitted, not to him, but to their kinsman, Ormonde, before
Essex arrived on the scene. No district had been subdued. No
attempt had been made to break up the Geraldine confederation in
Munster by seeking the weak places in its armour, the half-hearted
supporters. On the other hand, the army was worn out and mur-
muring. Essex himself was sick, in mind as much as in body, since
he could not disguise from himself what a muddle he had made of
the whole affair. The Queen left him in no doubt of her views and
her reproofs were scalding. Beyond taking 'an Irish hold from a
rabble of rogues'—thus she described the poor man's achievement
at Cahir—he had done nothing that Norris in Munster could not
have done without him, and had not improved the situation that
Ormonde, with so much smaller resources, had bequeathed to him.
She urged him now to put the axe 'to the root of that tree which
hath been the treasonable stock from which so many poisoned
plants and grafts have been derived'—that is, Tyrone and the North.[1]

By bitter experience English commanders in Ireland had learnt
that expeditions in which large forces carried out many long
marches were extremely costly in men, that armies melted away
from sickness and fatigue. Such major enterprises should therefore
be undertaken as seldom as possible and with the most clearly
defined objects in view. Garrisons should be planted at strategic
points, but only when they served a real purpose and could be
revictualled with reasonable certainty, and excessive numbers of
troops should never be locked up in them. Opportunity should
constantly be taken of approaching men who were discontented by
the exactions of the Irish leaders, often even heavier in war than
those of the English. In Munster the situation was actually more
favourable than it looked because the gentry and their people were
growing disgusted by the presence of the mercenaries from outside.
The province, wrote an English captain, Francis Kingsmill, to Cecil,
was groaning under the bonaghts, and gentleman and churl alike
longed to be rid of them after experiencing the strain of supplying
4,000 at 30s. the quarter, food and drink and a cow apiece, besides
illegal exactions.[2] That he was right was proved by Sir George
Carew, successor to Norris as President of Munster. Essex had

[1] *C.S.P. Ireland*, Vol. CCV, 113 (19 July 1599).
[2] *C.S.P. Ireland*, Vol. CCV, 148.

disregarded or failed to appreciate these considerations, which had become the commonplace of Irish warfare.

First of all he dealt fiercely with the poor tools who had failed him in Wicklow. Harington himself, as a member of the Privy Council, could not be tried, but he was confined during the Queen's pleasure and presently restored by her. Piers Walshe, the lieutenant of Adam Loftus, was condemned and executed—justly, it would appear, since he had certainly played the coward and probably played the traitor. The other officers of the foot were cashiered. The soldiers who had broken and fled, or such as survived, were condemned to death, but actually only decimated, the rest being ordered to serve henceforth as pioneers.

Essex now felt that he must do something in King's and Queen's Counties, and set off there on 25 July. The establishment of the army was 16,000 foot and 1,300 horse but the actual strength had dropped to 11,250 foot and 925 horse. There appeared no prospect of launching the expedition to Lough Foyle, which had been so long discussed, but it seemed possible that the Lord Lieutenant could muster some 4,000 men for an expedition to Ulster as soon as he had dealt with the O'Moores and O'Connors. The forts of Maryborough in Queen's County and Philipstown in King's County were once more revictualled, the former by Sir Christopher Blount, the latter by Essex himself. The Lord Lieutenant now achieved a measure of success, after a sharp fight with Richard Tyrrell, the Anglo-Irish soldier of fortune hired by Tyrone to lead a force of bonaghts. Sir Conyers Clifford, Governor of Connaught, affected a junction with him near Tullamore. The O'Connors seem to have been surprised, and had no time to hide their corn, which Essex burnt, 'so that all the county was on fire at once'. He also penetrated some thick woods in search of cattle, and one party alone, under Sir Christopher St. Lawrence, took 500. However, he could not bring the main body of the rebels to battle, so he gave up the attempt, dismissed Clifford to his post, and marched quietly back to Dublin.[1]

Despite her angry letters, the Queen was reasonable enough. She would make any effort if only she got a respectable return for it. The Privy Council informed Essex that, little as Her Majesty liked raising or paying for more troops, she would assent to his demand for 2,000 for the northern expedition. But she continued to rail. She blamed the Council for advising the long Munster tour. Why

[1] Harington, *Nugae Antiquae*, Vol. II, p. 10. Dymmok, *A Treatice of Ireland*, p. 42.

was nothing done about Lough Foyle? Why should not Essex and Clifford simultaneously invade Ulster?[1] Her reproaches were stinging, but her own mind was bitterly troubled. Nothing ever seemed to go right in Ireland. We have one moving picture of her, though it was painted a little later than this, when the abominable conduct of Essex in London had frightened as well as soured her and had added to the strain of the bad or doubtful news from across the Irish Sea. 'She walks much in her privy chamber, and stamps with her feet at ill news, and thrusts her rusty sword at times into the arras in great rage.' Yet her courage did not flag, as that of her Lord Lieutenant had begun to.[2]

[1] *C.S.P. Ireland*, Vol. CCV, 129 and 131.   [2] Harington, *Nugae Antiquae*, p. 65.

CHAPTER XVII

ESSEX AND TYRONE

WHETHER or not Essex would have been induced to take action against Tyrone by the Queen's goading alone must be matter for surmise. However, just after his return from his expedition to Offaly he received a shocking piece of news which forced him to do something. Sir Donogh O'Connor, O'Connor Sligo, was one of the most notable adherents to the Crown of the old Irish chieftains. He had been with Essex in Munster and had returned to his castle of Collooney. There O'Donnell, on his entry into Connaught, besieged him. It was important that this western loyalist should not go unsuccoured, and Essex had therefore ordered Clifford to relieve him. Incidentally, this move might be expected to distract Tyrone and afford the Lord Lieutenant a better opportunity to enter Louth or even Armagh.

Clifford marched to Boyle, in Roscommon, with what troops he could muster without denuding his towns and forts. The numbers are variously given, but the official figures are probably the best. He had 1,496 foot and 205 horse, the latter mixed English and Irish. On 5 August, about four in the afternoon, he stood at the foot of the Curlieu Hills. The troops were tired and hungry. The officers suggested that they should halt for the night before attempting the passage, but the Governor had heard that the enemy was weak in the Curlieus and was anxious to put the hills behind him. He told the troops, who protested that they wanted their dinners, that there would be plenty of beef for them that night, and ordered the march to continue. Clifford was no novice. He was a gallant and experienced soldier, well liked by his men and popular even with the Irish. He was, however, impetuous and headstrong, as he had shown in the affair of Ballyshannon two years earlier.

He placed Sir Alexander Radcliffe in command of the vanguard, with 186 pikemen and 385 shot; the battle—which cannot be called the main body, since it was the weakest of the three divisions—165 pikemen and 256 shot, was led by the young Lord Dunkellin, son of the Earl of Clanrickarde and destined to be one of the greatest figures in Ireland; Sir Arthur Savage had the rear guard, with 160 pikemen, and 344 shot. The horse under Sir Griffin Markham, with the lively and informative John Harington in command of one company or squadron, was left at the foot of the pass with the baggage, to follow when the way was clear.

Brian Oge O'Rourke, taking his orders from O'Donnell, had in fact been watching the pass and was prepared to defend it. Near the mouth he had established a barricade, but the Irish abandoned this after firing a single volley. The road now passed between two bogs, one of them fringed by a belt of woodland. Radcliffe drove the Irish out of this, but a fire-fight then began and lasted an hour and a half, by the end of which time the vanguard had expended its powder. The troops became demoralized. It was the story of the Yellow Ford over again; the great increase in the proportion of musketeers, incapable of defending themselves when their powder was finished, had thrown an undue weight upon the pikemen. The vanguard wheeled about in panic and collided with the battle, whereupon both broke and fled, soon followed by the rear guard. Radcliffe, fighting valiantly, and leading a charge with such pikemen as would follow him, was mortally wounded. The Governor strove desperately to re-form the troops, but without success, and sank exhausted into the arms of Sir John MacSweeny, an officer of the famous old gallowglass family. MacSweeny and another tried to drag him away, but he presently broke from them, rushed at the enemy, and fell with a pike through his body.

Meanwhile, Markham with the cavalry at the foot of the pass observed that there was disorder in the English ranks, though the trees prevented him from seeing how bad it was. He led the horse up by another way to the left of the road, 'if', says Harington, 'it may be called a way that had stones in it six or seven feet broad, lying above ground, and plashes of bogs between them.' This charge temporarily drove back the enemy and saved the routed foot from destruction, since the Irish had now begun to slaughter their foes. The broken remnant of the force streamed back to the abbey of Boyle. O'Rourke cut off Clifford's head and sent it back to O'Donnell, who did not reach the Curlieus in time to take part in the battle. The trunk was, however, decently buried in the famous monastery of Lough Cé. The Irish probably exaggerated the losses of the vanquished, which are given by themselves as ten officers and 231 rank and file killed, twelve officers and 196 rank and file wounded, a total of 449, or nearly one-third of the force. But the moral effect was very great. Essex wrote to Dunkellin and Savage,

whom he afterwards appointed to joint command until a new
governor should be sent, that the men should be divided up among
garrisons as only fit to hold walls.[1] Yet these were not raw troops.

The political result was no less unfortunate. O'Connor Sligo
submitted to O'Donnell: he could not well do otherwise. He now
became a member of the northern confederation of revolting chiefs
and valuable to it by reason of his prestige, though in secret he looked
for an opportunity to return to his allegiance. Essex also found that
the desertion rate of his Irish soldiers increased.

On 21 August he held a council of war of all the lords and colonels.
The unanimous decision was that it was impossible to put a force
into Lough Foyle that year; the spirit of the army was too bad and
there was too much sickness to permit the planting of any northern
garrisons; for the same reason the council advised against any
distant northern journey. The Lord Lieutenant could, however,
muster over 3,500 foot and 300 horse whom he considered reliable.
A week later he set out with vague intentions. 'I am even now
putting my foot into the stirrup to go to the rendezvous at the
Navan', he wrote to the Privy Council, 'and from thence I will
draw the army so far, and to do as much, as duty will warrant me
and good will enable me.'[2] Not, it must be said, a notable plan of
action.

His first scheme was to plant a garrison in his own barony of
Farney, which rather savoured of a private war. This project he
abandoned on a consideration which should have been as apparent
when he started as it was now: that it would be impossible to keep
the garrison victualled in country devastated by war and grazed
bare by the Irish creaghts. On 3 September he marched to Ardee,
in Louth. Tyrone showed himself in great strength, though the
English estimate that he had 10,000 foot and 1,000 horse can be no
more than guesswork and is probably an exaggeration. At least he
had a two-to-one superiority.

An envoy was sent to Tyrone to treat for the release of a recently
captured English officer, and the Earl sent back a message that he
would be glad to make submission. For this purpose he asked Essex
to receive his Constable, Henry O'Hagan, who came in on 5
September to demand a parley. 'If thy master', said Essex, 'have any

---

[1] C.S.P. Ireland, Vol. CCV, 130, 136, and 138. Harington, Nugae Antiquae,
Vol. II, pp. 10, 21. Dymmok, A Treatice of Ireland, p. 44. History of Catholic
Ireland, p. 126.

[2] C.S.P. Ireland, Vol. CCV, 155.

confidence either in the justness of his cause, or in the goodness and number of his men, or in his own virtue, of all which he vainly glorieth, he will meet me in the field so far advanced beyond the head of his kerne as myself shall be separated from the front of my troops, where we will parley in that fashion which best becometh soldiers.' One cannot even call this knight-errantry, since Tyrone was fifty-four, old enough to be the father of Essex.

Next day Essex drew up his army in the form of a St. Andrew's cross, with horse on each flank and in rear. His one hope was that the Irish would attack him on open ground, whatever the odds; but Tyrone had no intention of doing so. An English council of war concluded that an attack might be met with confidence even if the Irish superiority were two to one, but that on no account should the Irish be attacked. On the 7th O'Hagan appeared again and suggested that Essex should meet Tyrone on the Lagan at the ford of Bellaclinthe, the project being that they should converse across the water. The place proved too wide, but Tyrone rode into the stream up to his horse's belly, while Essex remained on the bank. Tyrone, whose manners were good and who always bore himself with humility in the presence of a viceroy, representative of a sovereign whom he had not officially disavowed, saluted Essex with reverence. Thus for half an hour they talked alone.

It is not easy for the modern mind to measure the enormity of the Lord Lieutenant's folly in conversing with Tyrone without witnesses. Elizabeth was highly suspicious, with a good deal of cause where he was concerned, and in any case Irish viceroys were expected to consult their Council on all matters of importance. Mountjoy, the successor of Essex, was so punctilious in this matter that on his second northern expedition he split his Council and took four members of it with him. Essex had enemies at home, and it would have been common prudence to provide himself with evidence against the insinuations they would be sure to make when they heard of this meeting.

A conference followed, Tyrone being accompanied by his brother Cormac, by his sons-in-law Hugh Maguire of Fermanagh and Hugh Magennis of Iveagh, by Ever MacCooley (MacMahon) of Monaghan, by Richard Owen, an Irishman by birth but a visitor from Spain, and by his secretary and most trusted adviser, Henry Ovenden. Essex brought Southampton, Sir Warham St. Leger, Sir William Constable, Sir William Warren, Sir Henry Danvers, and Sir George Bourchier. Again the Irish rode into the water in token of respect. It was agreed that there should be a cessation of arms of six weeks, and arranged that commissioners should meet next day to conclude its terms. One of them who took part on the English side was the celebrated Sir Henry Wotton, private secretary to Essex. The articles finally drawn up may be thus summarized:

(1) The Irish confederates to hold all they then possessed; (2) no garrisons to be placed in new stations; (3) free passages to be assured; (4) all English garrisons to be apprised of the cessation; (5) Essex to give a written assurance; (6) commissioners for the borders between the English and Irish zones to be appointed; (7) any Irish confederate refusing to be bound by the agreement could be prosecuted by the Lord Lieutenant; (8) the cessation could be continued from six weeks to six weeks, or broken by fourteen days' notice; (9) justice to be done regarding all spoils taken during cessation; (10) Tyrone to take an oath for the performance of the articles.

An attempt was, it will be noted, made to save the dignity of Essex by the provision that his signature to the articles sufficed, whereas Tyrone was required to take an oath upon them. Nevertheless, the convention was humiliating. A modern historian must be held to have exaggerated this aspect when he writes: 'Tyrone retired with all his forces into the heart of his country, having gained without fighting a victory greater than that of the Yellow Ford. Bagenal was defeated, the Earl of Essex was disgraced; one had lost his life, the other his reputation.'[1] Yet Tyrone had conceded nothing after all the expenditure incurred on the English side. He still believed in the possibility of a Spanish expedition, and, if it were to come, his best policy was to husband his strength until its arrival, provided that he lost none of his gains by waiting. Here nothing was lost.

After a few days' rest at Drogheda—for he was in bad health— Essex returned to Dublin. The Queen was displeased when she heard of the negotiations, though not as angry as she might well have been. Regarding the private conversation with Tyrone, she was indeed gentle; having entrusted Essex with a kingdom, she said, she was far from mistrusting him with a traitor, but his action was undignified and unwise. She complained that she could form no definite opinion about his meeting with Tyrone, 'but by divination',

[1] Bagwell, *Ireland under the Tudors*, Vol. III, p. 342. For the expedition of Essex, *C.S.P. Ireland*, Vol. CCV, 143, 145, 155, 162, 164, 172. Dymmok, *A Treatice of Ireland*, p. 48.

because he had not told her what passed between them. She had not then heard of the truce and ordered that none should be signed. She also forbade the grant of a pardon to Tyrone without further instructions from herself.[1]

Essex now took an action even more stupid than his dealings with Tyrone. He had been told by the Queen early in August that he was not to quit his post without leave, and this may have aroused in his mind the suspicion that his enemies wanted him kept in Ireland while something to his disadvantage was arranged at home. Now, on receiving the Queen's letter mentioned above, he summoned the Council, appointed Archbishop Loftus and Sir George Carey Lord Justices, directed that Ormonde by virtue of his commission should command the army, and an hour later took ship, on 24 September. Riding post-haste to London, he found that the Court was at Nonsuch, and pressed on there, hurrying into the presence of the Queen covered with mud, before her toilet was completed and while her hair was about her face. It seems to have been his hope that the influence he possessed over her would wipe out the memory of his errors and that he would once more sun himself in her favour, rid of the accursed country which had been the scene of such galling failures. This is the most probable explanation of his desertion of his post, the more charitable being that he considered he must make a personal explanation of the truce with Tyrone. For a little while the Queen appeared not unfavourable, but the more she reflected upon the matter the uglier his conduct appeared. It may well be that she was fearful of a *coup*, since Essex had several truculent friends with him. On 1 October he was committed to the custody of Sir Thomas Egerton, the Lord Keeper. His subsequent fate, one of the most famous in history, affects Ireland in so far only as it affected his successor, Mountjoy, so that any further reference to it may be postponed until his viceroyalty is reached.

In Ireland neither side was in a hurry to return to ordeal by battle. The Queen told the Lord Justices and Ormonde that, though she misliked the truce, it must not be broken.[2] Sir William Warren, on behalf of the Council, had already gone to Armagh and sent a message to Tyrone at Dungannon in hope of arranging an extension of the cessation when the first six weeks came to an end. Tyrone had refused to agree until he had consulted O'Donnell, who was believed to have reproached him for giving too much away. He

---

[1] Devereux, *Lives and Letters of the Devereux*, Vol. II, p. 73.
[2] *Carew Cal.*, Vol. III, p. 339.

promised, however, to expostulate with the O'Connors for crimes committed in Offaly, and even went so far as to say that he would chastise them himself if he were permitted to pass through for the purpose. Fenton informed Cecil that there was some value in the cessation, despite the trouble in Offaly, since the people of the Pale had got in their harvest and were now sowing their seed.[1]

On 16 October Warren saw Tyrone near Dundalk. After some discussion, they met again next day. The demand for an extension of the cessation came entirely from the English side and must be considered a fresh humiliation. Tyrone took a high hand. First of all he said he would not extend the cessation, as he had still no word from O'Donnell. Then, as a favour, he extended it for fourteen days. He told Warren he did not like doing so because he supposed that Essex was mustering more men in England. Finally, a message arrived from O'Donnell, giving him a free hand, whereupon he extended the cessation for another four weeks—that is, agreed to a fresh period of six weeks commencing 21 October.[2]

It is to these negotiations that is owed the best picture of Tyrone and his camp. The clever John Harington, having already put posterity in his debt by his accounts of the progress of Essex in the south and the defeat of Conyers Clifford in the Curlieu Hills, was present on this occasion too. He had accompanied Essex to Ireland and had been directed to follow him back to England, but, finding all the shipping occupied either by sick soldiers or the numerous horses of the Lord Lieutenant, he eagerly accepted the invitation of his friend, Sir William Warren, to accompany him to the north and see the arch rebel face to face. He did not arrive till after the first day's meeting and absented himself from the negotiations, but had much talk with Tyrone.

The Irishman received him as a great nobleman would receive a man of lesser but still of honourable station; for Harington was the Queen's godson. He 'began debasing his own manner of hard life, comparing himself to wolves, that fill their bellies sometime, and fast as long for it'. He apologized for not remembering his visitor, whom he had met at Lord Ormonde's house in London, 'saying these troubles had made him forget almost all his friends'.

When Tyrone and Warren dealt with affairs of state, Harington amused himself by talking to the Earl's two sons and their tutors, one of whom was a Franciscan, Father Nangle, who was supposed to

[1] *Carew Cal.*, Vol. III, p. 337. *C.S.P. Ireland*, Vol. CCV, 204 (Fenton's letter).
[2] *Carew Cal.*, Vol. III, p. 341. *C.S.P. Ireland*, Vol. CCV, 214.

have been in the plot to surprise Dublin Castle in 1598. The boys he found 'of good towardly spirit, their age between thirteen and fifteen, in English clothes like a nobleman's sons, with velvet jerkins and gold lace; of a good cheerful aspect, freckle-faced, not tall of stature, but strong and well set, both of them speaking the English tongue'.

These boys were Hugh, Lord Dungannon, who was to predecease his father in exile in Italy, and Henry, who was to be killed in Spain. Harington gave them his English translation of Ariosto, of which he was very vain. They took it to their father, who swore that his boys should read all the book over to him.

When they returned to business, Tyrone called Harington to him and bade him tell the Lord Lieutenant—not knowing that Essex was already in confinement—that, against the will of his confederates, he had agreed to a longer cessation than he would have countenanced but for his confidence in his fair dealing. '"For," saith he, "now is my harvest time; now have my men their six weeks' pay aforehand, that they have nothing to do but fight. And if I omit this opportunity, and then you shall prepare to invade me the mean time, I may be condemned for a fool."'

Harington noted too that when the written terms were handed to him the Earl signed as 'O'Neill'—the forbidden princely appellation—and that it required all the firmness of Warren to induce him to substitute 'Hugh Tyrone'. That being done with, the party picnicked, sitting on fern forms at fern tables, and Tyrone was merry during the meal. He drank to the health of Essex, bade Harington tell him that he loved him, and acknowledged that the cessation had been honourably kept. It is to the credit of Essex that, for all his failure, he left a favourable impression upon most people who encountered him in Ireland. Tyrone also protested solemnly that he was not ambitious, but sought only safety for himself and freedom of conscience, without which, he said, he would not live, though the Queen would give him all Ireland. Liberty of conscience has a brave sound, but when Tyrone wrote to the Spaniards he talked of the extirpation of heresy.

'His guard', writes Harington, 'for the most part were beardless boys without shirts, who, in the frost, wade as familiarly through rivers as water-spaniels. With what charm such a master makes them love him I know not, but, if he bid them come, they come; if go, they do go; if he say do this, they do it.'[1]

---

[1] Harington, *Nugae Antiquae*, Vol. II, pp. 1-7.

The Queen now gave Ormonde a commission under the Great Seal to deal with Tyrone. She was inclined to compromise in order to end the calamitous war, 'though we dispense with some outward things that ought to be stood for'. As for his religion, that might be left to God. Essex had meanly tried to shuffle off responsibility for his Munster march upon Ormonde, and the Queen chided the latter for encouraging him to make it.[1] Ormonde had no difficulty in refuting this charge. He pointed out that he was not in Dublin when Essex set out and that even after he met him he had no inkling of any intention on the Lord Lieutenant's part to move beyond the Suir.

At first the Lord Justices and Ormonde considered it would be undignified as well as useless to meet Tyrone again. He had sent Ormonde a letter in which he described the Lord Justices as enemies to God and man, and a 'damnable libel', full of 'horrible treasons' had been brought in by an Anglo-Irish knight, Sir Patrick Barnewall, who had visited his camp. It had evidently been intended for circulation, since Barnewall had seen seven copies.[2] No copy of this 'damnable libel' exists, but the document may have borne some likeness to a list of 'articles intended to be stood upon by Tyrone' which appears to have been drawn up after Essex had been interrogated upon his conversation with the rebel at the ford. There were twenty-two of these articles, the most important, and presumably damnable, being the following: The Roman Catholic faith to be openly preached and taught throughout Ireland; the Church to be governed by the Pope; cathedrals and churches to be returned to the Catholics; priests to be permitted to pass freely between Ireland and the Continent; no Englishman to be a churchman in Ireland; a Roman Catholic university to be supported by the Crown rents; the Lord Chancellor, Lord Treasurer, the Council of State, the Justices, Governors of Connaught and Munster, Master of the Ordnance, and half the officers and soldiers to be Irish; O'Neill, O'Donnell, and the Earl of Desmond to enjoy all the lands and privileges of their predecessors; all Irishmen to be free to travel abroad without acquainting the Queen's officers of their movements.[3]

This cannot have been more, at most, than a rough summary of what Essex recalled of his talk; he could not have recalled precisely the nature of twenty-two articles. On the other hand, it cannot be supposed that it was invented, and it probably represents broadly

[1] *C.S.P. Ireland*, Vol. CCVI, 10.   [2] *C.S.P. Ireland*, Vol. CCVI, 33.
[3] *C.S.P. Ireland*, Vol. CCVI, 55.

Tyrone's bargaining points. If so, it is astonishing that Essex should have agreed to a truce immediately after the talk, however bad his position. To a nation at war with the Catholic King, a nation whose sovereign had been excommunicated by the Pope, a nation which had seen priests of the Roman Catholic Church prominent in every plot and machination, the religious proposals were as monstrous as they were absurd. No less fantastic were those connected with foreign travel, which would have permitted visits to Spain in time of war. But the worst of the articles was that which laid down that the house of Desmond should be restored to its lands, escheated for treason and rebellion and placed in other hands. If the Earl of Desmond, why not all those who had forfeited lands and rights?

However, the last cessation, starting on 21 October, would end on 1 December, so that there must either be a renewal or a return to open war. Ormonde was not ready for war because the army was wasted to a shadow by desertion. Already Lord Delvin, with a little force near Trim, was scared—and the Council almost equally so, but in their case lest he should go over to the enemy. He was urged not to run away or parley, but to trust in succour from Ormonde. Something had to be done.

Ormonde mustered the available forces at Navan. The strength on the list was 1,900 foot and 430 horse, the number on parade 1,132 foot and 291 horse. The men were ragged, short of weapons, food, and transport. The 'rising out' of the Pale was a farce. Lord Howth brought in 200 men, but so bad that Ormonde sent them away to hold towns and forts; other lords and gentlemen brought in scarcely any, and in some districts the men said they would rather be hanged in their doorways than killed in action. Tyrone was believed to have 6,000 men on or within the borders of the Pale alone. So another parley was held, again on the Lagan, on 30 November and 1 December, when it was agreed to extend the cessation for yet another month. Ormonde thought it was well worth while, and ordered the revictualling of forts, the building of defences round bridges, and the blocking of fords. Yet he issued a warning that there was no hope of a settlement. Temporizing must come to an end, 'seeing the sore is grown to another nature than to be cured by such kind of medicines'.[1]

On 15 December Tyrone wrote to Warren, complaining of breaches of the cessation, of which there had been some on both sides, though of a paltry nature. In January 1600 Fenton's spies,

[1] *C.S.P. Ireland*, Vol. CCVI, 44, 57, 63, 68.

including an Irish priest at Dungannon, sent information that the Earl was preparing to move south; he had equipped 300 horse in the English fashion, with light lances—and presumably saddles with stirrups. On the 24th he marched from Cavan with a relatively small force, under 2,000 strong, into Westmeath. Here he ravaged Delvin's lands in the barony of that name, then those of the Dillons in the western part of the shire. The chiefry of the O'Carrolls, with whom he had a blood feud, he left with 'ashes instead of its corn and embers instead of its mansions'. He next advanced towards Holy-cross, in Tipperary. Ormonde got there first, and Tyrone was compelled to pass by the place, but the sacred relic after which it was named was brought forth to bless his mission. In Cork he was held up for a time by the flooded Blackwater, but passed the river on 18 February. Ormonde did not venture to attack him and could not save the lands of the loyalist Barrys, which were burnt. Then Tyrone camped between the Lee and the Bandon, and from all hands the nobility and gentry came in to offer their adhesion and to leave hostages in his hands for their fidelity. He had come to blow upon the flames of rebellion. There was no doubt of his attitude now. He was signing proclamations as 'O'Neill', and before starting he had addressed a letter to Philip III of Spain, to which he subscribed himself 'Your Majesty's most faithful subject'.[1]

While Tyrone was in Munster two men, the most formidable combination to which the Irish had ever found themselves opposed, arrived upon the scene. They were Charles Blount, Lord Mountjoy, the new Lord Deputy of Ireland, and Sir George Carew, the new President of Munster. They landed at the Head of Howth, on the north side of Dublin Bay, on 26 February 1600. Two days later Mountjoy took the sword and began his memorable viceroyalty.

[1] *C.S.P. Ireland*, Vol. CCVI, 95; Vol. CCVII, 65, 114.

CHAPTER XVIII

MOUNTJOY TAKES THE FIELD

LORD MOUNTJOY had been talked of as viceroy in 1599, when the Earl of Essex had been preferred to him, or rather had insisted upon going to Ireland. Essex had pretended that Mountjoy was not only too much of a bookworm but lacked experience for the task; yet he had in fact seen a good deal of service. He was now thirty-six years of age and had already made some progress in the rehabilitation of his old but decayed family which had been his ambition since childhood. He had not commanded large bodies of troops in the field, and in several respects had to buy his experience. His instructions were brief and simple. His army would number 12,000 foot and 1,200 horse—of which the greater proportion were old levies already in the country—and he was expected to reform the musters. He was to plant garrisons in rebel countries, but not to establish too many in forts. He was to forbid the sale of gunpowder. He was warned not to be duped by rebels who professed repentance.[1]

At about the time when these instructions were issued to Mountjoy, in January 1600, the Lord Treasurer, Lord Buckhurst, drew up a series of notes also intended for his guidance. Each captain was in future to keep a journal of his actions—we should say a war diary—in duplicate, sending one copy to the Lord Deputy. The company clerks were to be sworn Her Majesty's servants, which would make them liable to more severe penalties for fraud or gross error than when they were but the employees of the captains. An indenture was to be drawn up between the Treasurer at Wars and each captain, giving details of the weapons and armour in the company's charge, and the captain had to keep the record up to date by monthly returns. The Master of the Ordnance was required to produce a list of munitions in store. None but governors, generals, and colonels were to wear silks or silver or gold lace. No public tables were to be kept except by governors. The colour, marks, and age of every horse were to be registered. The stud of Essex was to pass to Mountjoy. Soldiers were to pay for any powder which they drew, except on active service, to discourage them from wasting it. Store-houses

[1] *Carew Cal.*, Vol. III, p. 356.

were to be provided for the victuals which were to be landed in Lough Foyle. Only reliable vendors were to be allowed to sell powder or arms. There exist numerous instances of a similar common-sense forethought in regulations, enough to refute convincingly the allegation that Elizabethan administration was generally weak and always improvised, though it may be acknowledged that most of them are to be found in the latter part of Elizabeth's reign and were the fruit of bitter experience.[1]

A faithful and observant secretary has afforded posterity much information about Mountjoy's personality and methods. In the first place he suffered, or believed he suffered, from poor health, and deliberately mapped out his existence so that weakness or illness should interrupt his activities as little as possible. One might say that he fussed over himself, had not the results been so satisfactory. When on campaign he took an afternoon sleep in his tent. He swaddled himself, wearing as many as three pairs of silk stockings and in winter woollen ones over them and under his high linen boot-hose, and on cold days three waistcoats. He ate the most carefully chosen food and drank the best wines. He smoked a great deal, tobacco being then considered, possibly with truth, a preventive against the colds and other diseases of a moist climate. He bore the strain well, but periodically suffered from fierce headaches.[2]

From the moment of his arrival Mountjoy set himself to restore discipline and raise the spirit of the troops. He revived religious worship in the field, which had of late been neglected. He made use of his personal charm to win the confidence of his men. He strove to contrive for them relatively easy successes in the early stages in order to revive their belief in themselves. He constantly exposed himself to encourage them, with unhappy results for his immediate followers. His horse was shot under him; his gallowglass, carrying his helmet, had it hit while it was in his hands; his greyhound, trotting at his stirrup, was shot dead. One of his chaplains was killed and another had his horse killed under him. One of his secretaries was killed, and Fynes Moryson, the narrator, was hit in the thigh. One of the gentlemen of his chamber was killed, a second wounded, a third unhorsed.

He planted his garrisons so well that the local rebels were afraid to move far away to aid others, and so their co-operation was broken up. He kept the field for longer periods than his predecessors,

[1] C.S.P. Ireland, Vol. CCVII (Pt. I), p. 7.
[2] Moryson, An Itinerary, Pt. II, p. 47.

and, since the secret of his plans was always well preserved, was thus able to throw himself suddenly upon any one rebel, 'while he kept all the rest like dared larks in continual fear, as well of himself as of the garrisons adjoining'. Having behind him an improved administrative machine, he preferred winter expeditions to those of summer, and all the winter through spent some five days a week in the saddle. The enemy's cattle were wasted by being driven to and fro. The stored grain was sought out and burnt. The seed could not be sown. The Irish were driven into woods now bare of leaves. These winter campaigns, says Fynes Moryson, broke their hearts. Whenever he marched through a defile he cleared it of trees, so that it should be easier to pass through on the next occasion.

He gave pardons more sparingly than had been the custom and only to those who had struck blows against their former associates. He forbade conferences and parleys, which had led to treachery and sometimes to corruption on the English side. He listened with unfailing patience to the complaints and petitions of the Irish, and always made a point of ensuring that no warrant of his should be used for extending the power of the nobility over the common people.[1]

Mountjoy had the advantage of excellent subordinates. The new President of Munster was Sir George Carew, a Devonshire man who had served in Ireland more than once. He was given full authority to impose martial law in the province, but only when and where the ordinary administration of justice was impossible. His Council, or any three members of it, he himself being one, was empowered to proclaim in the Queen's name 'any thing or matter tending to the better order of Her Majesty's subjects within the precincts of their commission'. Compositions, fines, and punishments were to be administered at its discretion.[2]

Carew was an able soldier, but a still more astute politician. His long campaign against the rebels of Munster was largely conducted by the Irish themselves. Leader after leader was brought into his orbit and set to work his passage by action against former associates. Though a far from scrupulous man, he stood by the repentant and saw to it that his promises to them were fulfilled. His relations with the Lord Deputy were curious and unsatisfactory. It was the custom of the age for subordinates to communicate over the heads of their superiors directly with the Lord High Treasurer or the Secretary, but the correspondence between Carew and his close friend, Sir

[1] Moryson, *An Itinerary*, Pt. II, p. 49. [2] *Pacata Hibernia*, p. 3.

Robert Cecil, comes into a special category. Cecil was intriguing to get Carew back to his side and striving to bring it about that Mountjoy, in ignorance of the plot, should recommend his being sent home. The plan was over-subtle, like some other proceedings of Cecil, and events in Ireland defeated it. Mountjoy realized that Carew possessed the friendship and confidence of Cecil to a greater degree than he did himself and was chagrined by such parts of the correspondence as came under his notice. 'My lord, these are great disgraces unto me', he wrote to Carew on discovering one flagrant example of the latter's dealings. 'I know you are dear to one whom I am bound to respect with extraordinary affection.' Yet the matter was personal only. In his actions Carew gave of his best. Neither he nor Cecil ever failed the Lord Deputy.[1]

In a more subordinate position at this stage, but throwing himself into his task with enormous, one may say, savage, energy, was Sir Arthur Chichester, Governor of Carrickfergus in the room of his brother, Sir John, killed in action against the Scots.[2] The great period in the career of Chichester belongs to the succeeding reign, in which, as viceroy, he carried out the Plantation of Ulster; but from now until the suppression of the rebellion he played a notable part on Tyrone's flank, continually harrying and threatening him. Mountjoy's other chief assistant was Sir Henry Docwra, the commander of the force which he established in Lough Foyle. Docwra pursued the same policy as Carew in winning the support of Irish chiefs, but he made more mistakes, which exposed him to heavy criticism from England, and he was all too easily gulled, the last accusation which could be brought against Carew. His achievements were, however, remarkable, and they were gained against the principal and most wholehearted rebels, Tyrone and O'Donnell, whereas Carew had to do with Munstermen who had in many instances been dragged forcibly into revolt and were thus more easily detached.

Sir Oliver St. John, a future viceroy, Sir Oliver Lambart, a gallant and hard-fighting soldier, and Sir Richard Moryson, brother to Fynes, were among the officers of the army. Sir Arthur Savage proved an efficient Governor of Connaught in succession to Clifford. He, like Carew, Lambart, and Samuel Bagenal, had served in the expedition to Cadiz. Of the Irish, Ormonde was at last dropping into the background, though not laying aside his armour. Two young western magnates, Lord Dunkellin, son of the Earl of Clanrickarde, and the Earl of Thomond, promised well, though the latter preferred the court to the field.[1]

Mountjoy began his viceroyalty with a piece of good fortune. Sir Warham St. Leger, nephew of Ormonde's old adversary, and Sir Henry Power, Commissioners for Munster pending the arrival of Carew, were out riding with a small escort near Cork when they came upon Hugh Maguire, followed by a few horsemen. The two parties charged one another. In the encounter St. Leger shot Maguire with his petronel, or cavalry pistol, through the body, but the Irishman drove his lance into his opponent's skull. Both died of their injuries. From the English point of view, the loss of St. Leger was a small price to pay for the death of Maguire, who was one of the bravest and most determined of the rebel chiefs and one of the most popular figures in Ulster.[2]

Tyrone had never intended to make more than a temporary stay in Munster; the north called him, and the rebellion there could not long be maintained at full strength without his presence. However, the death of his son-in-law brought about his precipitate departure, though perhaps news of Mountjoy's arrival contributed to it. He appears to have been completely overcome and is recorded to have suffered from 'giddiness of spirits and depression of mind . . . and this was no wonder; for he [Maguire] was the bulwark of valour and prowess'.[3]

Ormonde learnt of Tyrone's intended march, and being now strong, with over 5,000 men at his disposal, determined to intercept him if possible. He concluded that the rebel would cross the Suir at Golden and the Shannon at Killaloe, below Lough Derg. He entrenched the fords and other defiles. He called in Thomond to his aid, but the disaffected mayor of Limerick refused horses to the latter, so that he was unable to move, and Ormonde had to repair in person to Limerick to raise supplies. Tyrone, marching at top speed, evaded him, and then evaded Mountjoy, who had moved out to Trim on 13 March in the hope of catching him.[4]

Tyrone left behind him in Munster about 1,000 Connaughtmen and 800 of his own men to assist the Sugane Earl of Desmond. He had also created Florence MacCarthy the MacCarthy More. This was a strange figure upon the Irish stage. Florence was no fighting

[1] Moryson, *An Itinerary*, Pt. II, p. 41.
[2] *C.S.P. Ireland*, Vol. CCVII (Pt. II), 9, 11. *Pacata Hibernia*, p. 22.
[3] Four Masters, Vol. VI, p. 2,165.
[4] *C.S.P. Ireland*, Vol. CCVII (Pt. II), 22, 39. *Carew Cal.*, Vol. IV, p. 7.

man, but a clever schemer. Son of the MacCarthy Reagh, the second of the MacCarthy chiefs (the third being the MacCarthy of Muskerry), it was his ambition to become the MacCarthy More, the first. This title was held by the Earl of Clancarty, whose daughter Ellen, a great heiress, Florence had married in 1588. Since he was already under suspicion as the close friend of Sir William Stanley, who delivered Deventer to the Spaniards in 1587, this marriage, most unwelcome to the Government, had led to his imprisonment in the Tower, from which he was freed on the intercession of Ormonde. Clancarty died in 1596. Two years later a base son of his took advantage of the disturbed state of the country to assemble 500 bonaghts and proclaim himself the MacCarthy More.

Florence had ingratiated himself with the Cecils, spoke good English, and appeared disposed to loyalty; so it was decided to make the best of his marriage and use him to aid in the pacification of Munster, where the power of the MacCarthys had greatly increased since the extinction of that of the Desmond branch of the Geraldines. It was agreed that he and his wife should hold the lands of the late Earl of Clancarty. His first act was to gather together a force of bonaghts and close his inaccessible county to all-comers. When Tyrone left Munster Florence, though he had accepted the title of the MacCarthy More at the Ulster rebel's hands and had taken over 600 of Tyrone's bonaghts, informed the English authorities that he remained loyal to the Queen.[1]

Without awaiting Carew's arrival at Cork, the Commissioners somewhat ill-advisedly sent a force of over 1,000 men into the MacCarthy country and despoiled it, thus putting themselves in the wrong, since Florence had so far committed no overtly disloyal act. As this force was returning, Florence laid an ambush for it between Kinsale and Cork on 21 April. Fortunately for the English, they saw the glint of the sun on the morions of his bonaghts, who were lying down. A sharp and fluctuating fight followed, but the Irish fell back in the end, and a number of them were cut down by the English horse. On Carew's arrival, he showed what he thought of this policy by inviting Florence to an interview. Florence, a timorous man, plucked up his courage to come, though in fear and trembling. Carew rebuked him for his past conduct and exhorted him to behave better in future. In the talk which followed Carew learnt how great were his ambitions. He would, he said, send his son to Cork as a pledge if the Queen would convey to him the great

[1] MacCarthy, *Life of Florence MacCarthy*.

Desmond estates and make him the MacCarthy More. In a word, he wanted the title, the lands of the Geraldines, and what more he could obtain, and was prepared to take them from either side, whichever was the stronger.[1]

Before Mountjoy had been able to regroup his forces, largely concentrated in the south owing to Tyrone's incursion into Munster, the kidnapping of the Earl of Ormonde caused a sensation in Ireland. On 9 April Carew, on his way to Cork and accompanied by Thomond, arrived at Kilkenny to spend the night with Ormonde. He told his visitors that he was going to parley next day with Owen MacRory O'Moore, one of the rebel leaders. They said they would accompany him and suggested bringing their escort, a squadron of 100 horse, which had been billeted in the neighbourhood by his officers; but this he refused.

Next day Ormonde rode out on a little hack, unarmed but for his sword, accompanied only by seventeen of his Irish horsemen and some merchants of Kilkenny. He took a company of 200 foot, but dropped this two miles short of the rendezvous. Owen MacRory appeared at the head of a regiment of the best Irish pikemen Carew had ever seen, 500 strong. Carew and Thomond disliked the look of the place, level heath fringed with bog and wood, in which kerne might lurk unseen. Ormonde, for his part, did not believe that anyone would dare to lift a hand against him on his own soil. It would be a sort of *lèse-majesté*, even in a rebel.

After long and fruitless discussion, the Earl desired to speak with a famous Jesuit whom he knew to be with the Irish, Father James Archer. A discussion began, soon degenerating into a quarrel. Ormonde bitterly reproached the Jesuit for drawing Her Majesty's servants into rebellion under pretence of religion. By this time the party was surrounded by Irishmen who kept edging closer. Thomond called to Owney MacRory to order his men back, and Carew urged Ormonde to come away. As Ormonde turned his pony's head, a number of men threw themselves upon him and dragged him to the ground. They tried to do the same thing with Carew and Thomond, but they were not weighted with years and were riding great horses. Even then Carew might have been taken, but Thomond thrust his horse upon Owney MacRory and forced him to relax his grip. 'We had more hanging upon us than is credibly to be believed', wrote Carew and Thomond, and on the edge of the *mêlée* pikemen were thrusting at them. Thomond was wounded in

[1] *C.S.P. Ireland*, Vol. CCVII (Pt. II), 130; (Pt. III), 6.

the back, but the two broke clear and got away amid a shower of flung skeans.

They called on Ormonde's troopers, who had scattered to graze their horses, to make a charge in order to rescue their master, but there was no response. Indeed, any such action would have been useless and might have led to the killing of Ormonde. Carew and Thomond therefore rode back to Kilkenny, leaving the Earl in the hands of the rebels.[1]

The capture of Ormonde was more dangerous than it would otherwise have been because his sons had died young and there was some doubt as to the succession owing to the position of attainted lines being obscure. At his age, Ormonde might easily die in captivity, even if he were not killed, and some of the claimants to the earldom were unreliable. His daughter was a great heiress, and there was the possibility that she would be carried off and wedded by force. To protect her, Carew and Thomond remained at Kilkenny until English reinforcements, sent by Mountjoy, arrived to relieve them of their responsibility.

Mountjoy's first comments upon the incident were ungracious and unworthy. He said that he did not know whether to take it as good news or evil. He hinted, and Secretary Fenton followed his lead here, that it was odd to find so wary and experienced a man letting himself be kidnapped tamely by a young wood-kerne. Carew told some preposterous story about Ormonde having told Owney MacRory that if he would leave Ormonde's lands in peace Ormonde would not molest him. Later, after Ormonde had been set at liberty, Mountjoy took a line which did him more honour. 'I cannot', he wrote to Cecil, 'but bear a kind of reverence for so ancient a servant to Her Majesty and a compassion to the miserable fortune he was in.'[2]

After being led from cabin to cabin in the greatest discomfort, Ormonde was confined in a castle in Queen's County. Here he was well treated and allowed his own cooks, but Owney MacRory threatened to kill him with his own hand if a rescue were attempted. Heavy pressure was brought upon him to renounce the Protestant faith and to throw in his lot with the rebels, in which case he was told that the King of Spain would make him Earl of Leinster and perhaps King of Ireland. He remained steadfast. His greatest danger was that of being handed over to Tyrone, from whose hands he

[1] *Pacta Hibernia*, p. 25. Four Masters, Vol. VI, p. 2,167.
[2] *C.S.P. Ireland*, Vol. CCVII (Pt. II), 99, 100, 126; (Pt. IV), 5.

would probably not have issued alive. Tyrone wrote to him with accustomed respect, but tried hard to get him into his custody. The Leinstermen, however, had their own interest in mind and looked with suspicion upon Tyrone and his schemes, which included the marriage of the Butler heiress to one of the young O'Neills. To their credit, some of the Jesuits exerted themselves to secure Ormonde's safety, and even urged, against the advice of Archer, that he should be set free, since he had been taken by treachery. He was liberated in June, but with a mill-stone round his neck. He had been compelled to hand over a number of hostages to the rebels as sureties against his taking revenge upon the O'Moores. Here also he was eventually freed. Owney MacRory was shortly afterwards killed, and Ormonde contrived gradually to release or ransom the hostages.[1]

After his release the Queen addressed to him the affectionate letter of which mention has already been made. 'We are sure', she wrote, 'that there need not be many words from us to make you know how great contentment the news of your delivery hath brought us, who were much more deeply wounded to apprehend the perils of your own life, when it depended upon the savage humours of faithless rebels, than for any other particular that concerned ourself, though there could nothing have happened, in many respects, more prejudicial to our service. Concerning the conditions which we have seen, to tell you true, we were so fully pleased with the contentment of your safety as we have little troubled ourselves to examine the particulars, making this one ground for all, that nothing hath passed the thought of our faithful Lucas which was unworthy of his constant and loyal professions, howsoever the same might be assailed with lewd and vile temptations.' After a word of reproach that he should have given such a wretch as Owney Mac-Rory the triumph of holding the Lieutenant of her Army at his mercy, she went on: 'And yet, for all that parenthesis, let Lucas comfort himself that he, which is our *hasta la muerte*, shall never deserve more trust than we will give him nor desire more happiness than we do wish him and his.'[2] The man who received such a letter from Queen Elizabeth had small reason to worry his head about the unworthy suspicions of her servants. Yet what Mountjoy and others wrote about the greatest and most honourable of Irish

---

[1] *C.S.P. Ireland*, Vol. CCVII (Pt. II), 101 (i), 141 (i), 142; (Pt. III), 27 (ii), 110.

[2] See p. 103. *C.S.P. Ireland*, Vol. CCVII (Pt. IV), 36.

loyalists exemplifies one of the worst of English weaknesses in Ireland.

The forces at Mountjoy's disposal or on the way numbered nominally 1,200 horse and 14,000 foot. This was 2,000 more foot than he had originally been allotted, the Queen having at his entreaty decided to maintain the number of companies and bring them up to strength by drafts. The reinforcements arrived in August.[1]

Of this 14,000 foot, 3,000 were to sail from England to Lough Foyle, assembling at Carrickfergus, and the garrison was to be made up to 4,000 by Mountjoy sending another thousand from Dublin by sea; but 1,500 of these were afterwards to be despatched to Ballyshannon. The other Ulster garrisons, Newry and Carrickfergus, absorbed 700 and 450 foot respectively. To Connaught under Sir Arthur Savage were allotted 1,400, to Munster under Carew 2,950, and to Leinster 4,500. From the Leinster garrison the Lord Deputy could take 3,200 foot, together with 325 horse, for a campaign against Tyrone. But when 'dead pays' and what would now be called lines of communication troops had been deducted, the figure fell to 279 horse and 2,102 foot. Then there would be the sick, who might become numerous. These are the calculations of the Lord Deputy's secretary, who doubtless did not desire to make his master appear too well furnished, and after the arrival of the reinforcements Mountjoy actually led nearly 3,500 foot to the north.[2]

At last the time had come for the accomplishment of the great venture, the planting of a garrison in Lough Foyle. The fleet carrying Docwra and his main force reached Carrickfergus on 25 April, but that carrying the Dublin force did not join him until 6 May. This was a bad beginning, since he had to break into the stores carried for consumption on reaching his destination. Mountjoy now set out for the north in order to distract the attention of Tyrone while Docwra was effecting his landing. On 16 May he moved towards the Blackwater, unmolested by Tyrone. He then heard that the Earl of Southampton and others were waiting at Dundalk with a small party, including the Earl's gentlemen volunteers, and some baggage. He sent back a force of fifty horse and 500 foot to convoy them through the Moyry Pass, and then himself moved some distance down to meet them. It was well he took the precaution. They were attacked by Tyrone in the pass and had some smart fighting before Mountjoy appeared, just as Tyrone's main body was coming on the

---

[1] *C.S.P. Ireland*, Vol. CCVII (Pt. IV), 75.
[2] Moryson, *An Itinerary*, Pt. II, p. 59.

scene. The enemy then drew off. It was a neat little engagement and a good augury.[1]

And, though dissidents in the Pale seized the opportunity to come out and do some burning, the expedition was entirely successful in its object. On 15 May Docwra landed at Culmore, near where the river Foyle enters the lough, with no opposition from Tyrone's powerful forces and little from the local inhabitants, and began to build a fort round the remnant of a castle demolished by its former garrison. The worst that happened was a skirmish with O'Donnell's men while the troops were cutting wood. On the 22nd he reached Derry, his future headquarters, now showing little or no trace of the brief occupation in Sidney's day and marked mainly by the ruined cathedral. He began quarrying stone and making lime from cockle-shells, but probably only for the barest necessities. When Derry was taken in the next reign by Sir Cahir O'Dogherty, we know that it was nearly all timber and was burnt to ashes except for the stone chimneys and fireplaces of the houses. Docwra worked hard to get shelter for his troops before the coming of winter. Mountjoy had taken the weight off him at the dangerous moment, and now he appeared to be firmly established.[2]

While awaiting the reinforcements from England and partly to keep his troops in practice, Mountjoy determined to march against the rebels of Leinster who had raided the Pale when he was in Armagh. He was well satisfied with the restoration of discipline and of the spirit of his forces, and wrote confidently to Cecil: 'And now that, with being a nurse to this army as well as a general, I have given it more health and strength, you must hereafter look to hear of deeper blows that we shall either give or receive.' He thought that by the time at which he wrote, 19 June 1600, he could have already broken the back of the rebellion, had he not lacked experience when he arrived. The last hope of the rebels, he said, was Spanish aid.[3]

Here, however, he had cause for anxiety. An agent had, in April, brought news of the arrival of two Spanish ships loaded with calivers, pikes, and powder at Killybegs. In June he obtained the report of Richard Brady, Master of the *Prosper* of Drogheda, who had been seized by the Spaniards to serve as their interpreter. Aboard one of the ships was a prelate sent by Tyrone to the Ulster princes as an ambassador, Mathias de Oviedo, titular Archbishop of Dublin.

[1] *C.S.P. Ireland*, Vol. CCVIII (Pt. III), 51, 63 (i).
[2] Docwra, *Narration. C.S.P. Ireland*, Vol. CCVII (Pt. III), 57.
[3] *C.S.P. Ireland*, Vol. CCVII (Pt. III), 118.

Through him Philip III promised that a force of 5,000 to 6,000 men, commanded by Juan de Aguila, should be sent to Ireland. Tyrone, for his part, had sent his second son, Henry, to Spain. The information from Brady, who had escaped by swimming ashore, was unusually precise and appeared reliable. On the other hand, the Queen was making strong complaints about Mountjoy's expenditure, which was indeed very high, and bidding him remember that he was a governor as well as a soldier.[1]

His expedition to Leix and Offaly in the latter part of July was successful. He cut down the corn and lifted a number of cattle, but it was a lucky bullet fired by one of the soldiers of his lieutenant, Sir Oliver Lambart, on an independent mission, which proved most effective. Young Owney MacRory O'Moore, kidnapper and gaoler of Ormonde, was mortally wounded, and his people at once dis-dispersed.[2]

A more important undertaking lay ahead. Mountjoy was determined to reoccupy Armagh and plant a garrison there. This would not only restore the threat to Tyrone's dominion from the south, but also, now that Docwra was well established on the Foyle, serve as a first step towards creating a direct link with him by land. But, from the manner in which Mountjoy conducted his operations, it would appear that he deliberately courted a trial of strength with Tyrone. The main Ulster rebel army was now so strong and well found that it had to be beaten before the establishment of new garrisons would have the effect desired by the Lord Deputy. And if he desired a trial of strength, he got it. More sensational engagements took place, but in the whole length of Elizabeth's reign there was no such prolonged, dogged, close fighting as was to follow. It might be said that the Moyry Pass, on the minute scale of Irish warfare, was Mountjoy's Somme, with a like calamitous effect upon the side which stood on the defensive. And only his restoration of the army and the confidence with which his leadership had inspired it made it adequate for the grim task.

He had hoped to be ready by 1 September, but the victuals promised did not arrive in time, so that he had to postpone his start until the 15th. Like Burgh before him, he ordered a general hosting (at the Hill of Tara), but did not take with him the levies of the Pale, who were required to defend it, only making them turn over to the use of the army a proportion of their transport horses. His force

[1] C.S.P. Ireland, Vol. CCVII (Pt. II), 143; (Pt. III), 118 (i); (Pt. IV), 34.
[2] C.S.P. Ireland, Vol. CCVII (Pt. IV), 59.

numbered by the list 375 horse and 3,450 foot. In Leinster he left Ormonde, who still held the appointment of Lieutenant of the Army, with 157 horse and 2,700 foot, besides the Palesmen.[1] When Mountjoy marched he knew that Tyrone was holding the Moyry Pass. He reached Dundalk on 17 September, and on the 20th, after a day's delay due to bad weather, moved forward to Faughard, in contact with the enemy in the Moyry Pass. Next day he was again held up by a storm, with torrents of rain. On the 25th and 26th he reconnoitred the fortifications, fighting one sharp and effective rear-guard action as he withdrew, but was then again compelled to lie in camp until 2 October in continual rain. Tyrone stood at the head of some 3,500 men. Across the track through the pass and in the woodlands on two steep and rocky hills which flanked it he had cut a number of trenches, in front of which he had put up obstacles of stone and thorn. To prevent their being turned, he had plashed the trees at either end of the works. Those on the hillsides lay within caliver range of the bottom of the valley, so that cross-fire could be brought to bear upon it.[2]

The weather improving, on 2 October Mountjoy launched an attack on the foremost trenches of the rebels. The struggle lasted two hours, at the end of which he had gained an entry into the pass, but had suffered 120 casualties, a large number by the standards of Irish warfare. Next day he renewed the attack. His progress was as bitterly contested as before. He drove the enemy out of all the works and inflicted heavy loss upon him, but lost another 110 men. His total losses were about fifty killed and 200 wounded, and he estimated those of the Irish at 500. He made no effort to advance, but on 10 October retired to Newry to rest his troops, worn out rather by the weather than by the enemy's resistance. Tyrone had had enough, and drew back to Armagh. On 18 October Mountjoy levelled the enemy's entrenchments in the pass and cut down the trees on the flanks, and on the 26th marched to Newry. The improvement made by Tyrone in the fighting quality of the Ulster forces and their increasing skill in fortification could not have been better exemplified. Even in the days of the Yellow Ford they could hardly have stood up to an English army at close quarters as they did on this occasion.[3]

[1] *C.S.P. Ireland*, Vol. CCVII (Pt. IV), 109; (Pt. V), 15. Moryson puts the list strength at 700 higher, perhaps because the 700 Irish troops whom he includes are not counted in Mountjoy's report.

[2] *C.S.P. Ireland*, Vol. CCVII (Pt. V), 25, 65 (i).

[3] *C.S.P. Ireland*, Vol. CCVII (Pt. V), 74, 79, 83 (i), 88, 121.

The delay in the despatch of the victuals and then the storms which kept the ships from reaching Carlingford had in part defeated Mountjoy's ends, and the sickness in the Lough Foyle garrison was on such a scale that it had prevented Docwra from co-operating with him as he had been bidden. Mountjoy now decided that he could not advance to the Blackwater, or even to Armagh, where he heard that the grass had been eaten by Tyrone's herds, at present. Instead he would build a new fort between Newry and Armagh, from which the latter place could easily be victualled after it had been occupied. On 3 November a site was selected, about eight miles from Newry on the way to Armagh. The basis was an old round earthwork, made, it was believed, by the Danes. The work of construction was interrupted by Tyrone's attacks, but a double-ditched fort, capable of holding 400 to 500 men, was completed, and 400 were left in it under command of Captain Blaney. Mountjoy named it Mountnorris because Sir John Norris, whom he regarded as his tutor in war, had contemplated building a fort at this point. He marched back by way of Carlingford instead of through the Moyry and had a sharp engagement on the way, in which his troops behaved as well as ever and drove the enemy out of their path.[1]

The expedition had not been a complete success, though it was not, as the Irish annalists suppose, the resistance of Tyrone, formidable though that had been, which had prevented Mountjoy from reaching the Blackwater. The lateness of the start, due to the late arrival of food and money, followed by the exceptionally bad weather, had constituted the heaviest handicaps. If the distance beyond Newry along the route into Tyrone controlled by the royal troops were the criterion, Mountjoy would have been in a worse situation than Burgh, since he held this route up to the Blackwater. But Mountjoy had a force in the north, based on Derry, and before his own expedition had been concluded he received news that it had gained outstanding successes, which will be described later. That transformed the situation. Over and above it stood the continued improvement of the army in skill, fighting spirit, discipline, and administration. Despite their trials and losses, the troops returned to the Pale in good heart.

With the Queen Mountjoy was still on the defensive. He was accused of giving companies to small men and drones who desired to prolong the war, of failing to abolish abuses in the musters, of

[1] Moryson, *An Itinerary*, Pt. II, p. 81. *C.S.P. Ireland*, Vol. CCVII (Pt. V), 121; (Pt. VI), 19, 29. Four Masters, Vol. VI, p. 2,223.

allowing too many officers to go on leave, of letting recruits run away and return to England, of letting Irish troops live on their lands and at the same time draw the Queen's pay, and other alleged shortcomings. This hurt and worried him, especially when he had to answer the charges on campaign, with his tent being blown down at intervals. He was reproached with taking counsel of young favourites, the men aimed at being his friends, Sir Henry Danvers, Sir Richard Moryson, and Sir William Godolphin. He retorted that they were all older than Alexander the Great when he conquered the world. Yet, however wounding and distracting were these messages, he was better supported than any of his predecessors had been, and it was not to be long before the Crown and Privy Council realized his worth.[1]

[1] Moryson, *An Itinerary*, Pt. II, p. 81.

CHAPTER XIX

THE WAR IN ULSTER AND LEINSTER

THE force under Sir Henry Docwra, which had entered Lough Foyle and established itself at Derry, did not march off into the heart of Ulster. If it had done so, there is a possibility that it would have brought the rebellion to a speedy close, but it is more probable that it would have been hopelessly handicapped by the lack of communications and possible that it would have incurred a disaster. Its commander had no intention of acting in this way. His object was not to move unless he could lay hands upon a strong place suitable for a garrison which could generally live upon the surrounding country but would be within reach of his arm if in need of aid and sustenance. At the same time he intended to make local friends both for the sake of obtaining cattle for his main body at Derry and for help in establishing and feeding these projected outside garrisons. The prospects of obtaining Irish allies were good. The chieftains on either side of Lough Foyle, O'Cahan to the east and O'Dogherty to the west, 'urriaghts' of Tyrone and O'Donnell respectively, were known to be anxious to escape the dominion of their overlords and even to dispute its legality. In County Tyrone the descendants of Tirlagh Luineach O'Neill were in general unfriendly to the Earl; in County Tyrconnell the supporters of the elder line of the O'Donnells, represented by Neill Garve, might be expected to be jealous of the younger, represented by Hugh Roe, which had elbowed them out of the supreme power. There was promising material to Docwra's hand if he could use it.

As already recorded, the establishment of his force was 4,000 in foot alone, greater than that allotted to the whole of Munster and actually greater than the Lord Deputy himself could lead into the field. On the other hand, he had a great deal to do with it and wastage was to be expected. He therefore disliked the prospect of parting with 1,500 men to garrison Ballyshannon as proposed, and was relieved when in June 1600 he was instructed by the Privy Council to postpone this feature of the plan.

He had not long to wait for signs of local dissatisfaction with Tyrone and O'Donnell. On 1 June, only a fortnight after the expeditionary force had landed at Culmore, Art O'Neill, son of Tirlagh Luineach, came in to him with forty men, pursued by Tyrone's brother, Cormac. Art O'Neill almost at once took part in a number of skirmishes with the forces of Hugh Roe O'Donnell and Cuconnaught, younger brother and successor to Hugh Maguire, who had fallen in Cork. About 9 June O'Donnell left the scene with a large force to march through Connaught and invade Thomond as vengeance against the Earl of Thomond for his loyalty.[1]

Taking advantage of O'Donnell's absence, on 1 July Docwra made another bound forward, seizing Dunnalong, several miles up the Foyle. Here he built a fort into which he put six companies, subsequently reinforced with fifty horse. By the 29th O'Donnell returned and inflicted upon the English commander a humiliation which the Irish magnified into a great victory, while even the Queen attributed to it more importance than it was worth. The Irish laid an ambush for the English cavalry horses which used to be brought out to graze each morning, and captured, according to their own account, 200. Docwra pursued with such horsemen as he could collect, but was smitten down by a javelin thrown by one of O'Donnell's kinsmen and was carried back by his men, who thereupon abandoned hope of recovering the horses. There was a certain prestige involved in this *coup*, but perhaps the Irish were especially gratified by it because the superior size and bone of English horses made them a genuine prize.[2]

Docwra's troops now began to go sick by hundreds, and he lost a certain number by desertion to the enemy, so that the 570 reinforcements who reached him on 1 October represented but a drop in the ocean. He had, however, been encouraged by Art O'Neill to expect the assistance of his friend, Neill Garve O'Donnell, at present serving with the rebels under his cousin and brother-in-law, Hugh Roe. Secret negotiations took place in August. Neill Garve's terms were high: he was to have all Tyrconnell; he was to be accorded liberty of conscience; during the war he was to keep 500 foot and 150 horse in the Queen's pay; he was to be allowed to make his choice of a sheriff of the county, promising to choose one 'as near as he could' to the Deputy's liking; and, finally, he was to have a pardon for himself and his followers. Liberty of conscience was a

---

[1] *C.S.P. Ireland*, Vol. CCVII (Pt. III), 130, 133. Four Masters, Vol. VI, p. 2,193.

[2] Docwra, *Narration*. Four Masters, Vol. VI, p. 2,206. *C.S.P. Ireland*, Vol. CCVII (Pt. IV), 49.

tender subject, and Docwra did not venture to promise more than
that the Irishman should not be molested with respect to his religion.
He would also say only that he hoped to obtain the money for the
troops. But to the other three points he agreed. The first, the
cession of Tyrconnell, was immeasurably the most important, and
Docwra's undertaking on this, as on the others, was confirmed by
Mountjoy.[1]

At the beginning of October Neill Garve came in with three
brothers. He had taken the opportunity of Hugh Roe's absence on
another expedition into Connaught, during which he himself had
been left in command of the force watching Derry, to slip away.
His purpose had, however, been made known to the Irish by a spy
in one of Docwra's garrisons, so that he had to hurry to Derry two
days sooner than he had intended and without completing his plans.
He brought with him a force of only 200 foot and thirty horse,
which was smaller than it would have been had he been granted
those two extra days. But he was boiling with energy and eager to
get to work at once before Hugh Roe returned to interfere. It must
have been difficult for Docwra to make up his mind how far he
could be trusted with English troops, and he had little time in which
to examine the question. It is, however, obvious that Neill Garve
possessed a remarkable personality. Docwra was convinced, handed
over to him a force of 500 foot and thirty horse, and bade him go
and occupy Lifford.[2]

So one of the outstanding characters of the Irish wars entered
English service, a man who was to do extraordinary service and to
be cruelly defrauded in the end, not through malice, but for reasons
of policy, which have since brought a similar fate on many inconvenient friends of the English in various parts of the world. It need
not be said that Neill Garve was out for himself, but it is only fair
to add that he had inherited from his father, grandfather, and great-
grandfather a tradition of co-operation with the English. The
grandfather was Calvagh, who had been so hardly treated by Shane
O'Neill and had later aided Sidney at Derry. It is hardly correct to
describe Neill Garve as a vulgar traitor, though he is usually so
treated.

The title 'Garbh' ('the Rough', generally anglicized as Garve)
indicates his nature. He was haughty, peremptory, hard, acquisitive,

[1] C.S.P. Ireland, Vol. CCVII (Pt. V), 2 (i). Docwra, Narration.
[2] Docwra, Narration. C.S.P. Ireland, Vol. CCVII (Pt. VI), 9. History of Catholic
Ireland, p. 186.

and high-tempered. Yet he was also one of the foremost fighting men of his time and race, who could lead a considerable body of troops and at the same time bear himself like one of the Homeric champions. His personal courage astonished his English allies and followers. 'As valiant and hardy as any man living', Docwra said of him.

In the following year Docwra found it necessary to defend himself against the charge that he had been deceived by his Irish allies and had spent an inordinate sum of money upon them. The charge drew from his pen a notable sketch of the chief of them.

'For Neill Garve', he wrote, 'I cannot compare him to anything more like than a quince. Let him be sugared and dressed with much cost and he will be good for somewhat, but undoubtedly, to speak truth of the man, I am of opinion that the Queen must of necessity bestow more upon him than his body is worth before she shall reap any good of his service; although the man is valiant, of reasonable account in the country among some men of quality, and in the taking of the Lifford only did undoubtedly a singular good piece of service, and may do much more, being tempered and kept in subjection according to the quality of his unbridled nature, which is apparently prone to tyranny where he may command, to proud and importunate beggary where he is subject, to extreme covetousness whether he be rich or poor, and unseasoned by any manner of discipline, knowledge, or fear of God.'

He spoke some broken English and was in Docwra's eyes less savage than his brothers, having perhaps received a better education as head of his branch of the house of O'Donnell. He was about thirty years of age and was married to Nuala, sister of Hugh Roe; but she left him after he went over to the English. His son Nachten he had handed over to Mountjoy as a pledge of his fidelity.[1]

Lifford was taken without trouble, the garrison of its fort running away. Hearing the bad news, Hugh Roe O'Donnell, already on his way back from his raid, posted on quickly with a mounted force, but arrived only in time to find the new occupants of Lifford digging earth-works to defend it. As soon as some of his infantry had arrived on the scene, he made an attack, which, like most Irish attempts upon even the weakest of fortresses, amounted to little more than a demonstration and was easily repulsed. He then drew off a little. Realizing that he was keeping but a careless guard, Neill Garve persuaded the English captain to attack, and himself led the

[1] *C.S.P. Ireland*, Vol. CCVIII (Pt. I), 126.

van. A sharp cavalry engagement took place, in the course of which Neill Garve drove his lance through the body of Hugh Roe's younger brother Manus, who afterwards died of the wound. Another brother, Rory, the future Earl of Tyrconnell, thrust at Neill Garve, but the latter caused his horse to rear, so that the lance entered its body instead of striking its rider. Apart from that, Neill Garve was thrice struck on his mail shirt. Hugh Roe's men were driven off and resigned themselves to a fruitless blockade. Docwra was delighted: first, because of the importance of Lifford, a bridge-head over the Foyle on the main road into Tyrconnell and providing good winter quarters; and, secondly, by the fact that Manus had been killed by Neill Garve's own hand, thus creating a blood feud between the two branches of the ruling family and rendering it impossible for Neill Garve to return to his former condition of allegiance to his cousin, Hugh Roe. A bullet-proof barge was built to keep Lifford supplied by the river.[1]

While these affairs were in progress John O'Dogherty, chief of Inishowen, made some overtures, but did not venture to come to Derry because his son Cahir was a hostage in the hands of Hugh Roe O'Donnell. And then Docwra had a slice of luck. O'Dogherty died at the beginning of 1601, and Hugh Roe, as overlord of Inishowen, nominated as chief Phelim Oge O'Doherty, a brother of the deceased, passing over his son Cahir, who was still a boy. By so doing he incurred the bitter resentment of the MacDavitts, Cahir's foster-brothers, and especially of the two eldest, Hugh Boy and Phelim Reagh, who were the holders of the real power in Inishowen. These young paladins, whose prowess and charm were to exercise a great effect upon Docwra, had taken a leading part in the war. Only just before they had been trying to bribe the commander at Culmore to deliver the fort to them. The love and loyalty which Irishmen gave to a foster-brother of a princely house, the closest of all ties in Irish life, completely changed the attitude of the brothers. They rescued the boy Cahir and brought him in to Derry, where Docwra proclaimed him chief of Inishowen. The people cheerfully acknowledged him as such, 'and from that day forward we had many faithful and singular good services from them, their churls and garrans assisting us with carriages, their cattle, with plenty of fish, meat, and Hugh Boy and Phelim Reagh with many intelligences and other helps; without all which, I must freely

[1] *C.S.P. Ireland*, Vol. CCVII (Pt. VI), 10. Docwra, *Narration*. Four Masters, Vol. VI, p. 2,217.

confess a truth, it had been utterly impossible we could have made that sure and speedy progress in the wars that afterwards we did'.[1]

It was providential to have secured control of this rich country, unravaged by war, but its occupation carried Docwra into the mazes of Irish politics. Neill Garve was already discontented and sulky because he did not consider that his achievements had been sufficiently rewarded. His services had indeed been invaluable, including victories in several combats not here recorded and aid in obtaining supplies. His friend Art O'Neill had died, according to English evidence, from a combination of drink and fever, and the latter's brother Cormac, who took his place in Docwra's camp, had accused Neill Garve of plotting to betray Derry and Culmore to Hugh Roe O'Donnell. Now, as prospective chief of Tyrconnell and esteeming himself overlord of Inishowen, Neill Garve proposed to cess his soldiers on that country. Hugh Boy MacDavitt, speaking for his young master, Cahir O'Dogherty, denied his right to do so, and to Neill Garve's fury this view was upheld by the Deputy and his Council, who decided 'that the O'Donnells could by Irish law and tradition claim no more than a head rent from the O'Doghertys, and had no right to quarter troops upon their country.[2]

However, the work continued and Neill Garve did not cease to take part in it. In March Docwra entered the country of MacSweeny Fanad, west of Lough Swilly, and reduced it to submission, though he had some further trouble with it. In April, in company with Neill Garve, he marched up from Lifford to the relief of Dogh Castle, held by a friendly MacSweeny and besieged by O'Donnell's forces, drove off the besiegers and captured a great quantity of cattle. On his return he left behind Neill Garve with 150 English and 300 Irish troops to secure the country west of Lough Swilly. Hugh Roe O'Donnell, who had acquired a large number of muskets brought to Lough Swilly in January in two Spanish ships, moved against him in overwhelming superiority of numbers. For once Neill Garve lost heart and crossed the Swilly to tell Docwra that he could not maintain himself west of the lough. Docwra directed him to return. He went unwillingly, but his performance was as good as ever. With no tools, he fortified Rathmullan, and Hugh Roe dared not

[1] Docwra, *Narration. C.S.P. Ireland*, Vol. CCVII (Pt. VI), 77. Four Masters, Vol. VI, p. 2,237.
[2] Docwra, *Narration. C.S.P. Ireland*, Vol. CCVIII (Pt. I), 47.

attempt to storm it. Later on Docwra allowed Neill Garve to return, leaving one of his brothers in command.[1]

The next incident is typical of Irish warfare as waged by the most energetic of Irish raiders and one of the ablest of English tacticians. The peninsula of Inishowen, O'Dogherty's country, was invaluable to Docwra, his granary and pasture, on which some 16,000 cattle were now grazing. Its southern base, from Lough Foyle to Lough Swilly, was only about seven miles wide, and this neck was a marsh with but half a dozen crossing-places. Docwra fortified these and stationed companies in the two most important. As a second precaution, he drove the cattle into the tongue of land in northern Inishowen and put Phelim Reagh MacDavitt in command of a little Anglo-Irish force with orders to fortify the approaches. He took out a further insurance policy by forcing the leading men among his Irish allies to put kinsmen or children into his hands as hostages. On 26 May O'Donnell advanced with a large body of Donegal men and 800 of Tyrone's best bonaghts—1,500 were counted by Docwra himself, but there may have been as many as 2,000.

Finding the passages barred, Hugh Roe resorted to the usual method of crossing bog or marsh in Ireland. He got over on a causeway of hurdles between two English posts. Now he was at large in Inishowen and thought that the prey was at his mercy.

Next day he marched north, to find his path barred by the position behind which the cattle lay. Thrice the rebels charged, and on the third occasion broke in and planted their colours forty yards behind the trench. Then a counter-attack expelled them with a loss of fifty men. They had been balked by Docwra's prescience and Phelim Reagh's gallantry; they had missed the prey, except for about 100 cattle which had not been driven into the refuge; and they had found English and Irish standing shoulder to shoulder with invincible tenacity. O'Donnell managed to slip out along the strand of Lough Swilly at low tide and so save his force, but he had suffered an undeniable check.[2]

The reason why Docwra had not met him in the open was the weakness of the English at Derry owing to the dispersion of their forces in garrisons and the incidence of sickness. Ships with 800 reinforcements arrived in Lough Foyle on the very day of O'Donnell's repulse. Almost simultaneously another success was

[1] C.S.P. Ireland, Vol. CCVIII (Pt. II), 19, 58.
[2] Docwra, Narration. C.S.P. Ireland, Vol. CCVIII (Pt. II), 69, 103; (Pt. III), 12.

gained. On 27 May Docwra sent Neill Garve towards Lifford to raid Tyrconnell in Hugh Roe's absence. On the march, however, Neill Garve learnt that Tyrone, whom he had hitherto believed to be in Armagh, awaiting a new expedition by Mountjoy, was actually lurking in O'Cahan's country, east of the river Foyle. Neill Garve turned and attacked him, scattering his force and capturing a number of his newly acquired Spanish muskets. He personally pursued the fleeing Tyrone, shouting to him to turn and strike one blow if he were a gentleman, and at one moment the supreme rebel leader was within a lance's length of death. In July Neill Garve took Castlederg, in Tyrone, and on 2 August seized Donegal Abbey, right in the heart of O'Donnell's country.[1]

The Government had sent to Derry one Captain Humphrey Covert to check the musters, and this official had an unhappy time of it. The great decline in strength due to sickness and desertion afforded the captains an admirable opportunity to pocket large sums of money by concealing the losses and drawing the pay of the dead and the absent. When they found that this peculation would be exposed by Covert's strictness and honesty, they became infuriated against him. 'The captains, with their officers', he wrote to Cecil, 'are most violently bent against my proceedings in the musters, and daily myself and such as in this employment for Her Highness's service I use are boldly threatened to have our throats cut.' To his discredit, Docwra showed displeasure with Covert. It would not be fair, however, to assume without evidence, of which there is none, that the Governor was dishonest. He wanted to sweeten his captains and keep them in good heart, and it did not appear to the average Elizabethan soldier a crime to achieve this by passing swollen musters. Leicester in the Netherlands 'did mitigate or pardon the checks'—that is, forbade too inconvenient investigations—but there is no proof that it was to enrich himself.[2]

It was not the number of killed in battle which had so reduced the Lough Foyle force, but desertions and deaths from sickness. Docwra had established a hospital in the old cathedral on his arrival at Derry, but it did not suffice to take in more than a small proportion of the sick. By June 1601 the strength by the list or establishment

---

[1] Docwra, *Narration. C.S.P. Ireland*, Vol. CCVIII (Pt. II), 103; (Pt. III), 12. The dates of Phelim Reagh's and Neill Garve's actions are taken from the letters of Captain Humphrey Covert from Derry, as likely to be more accurate in this respect than the *Narration*.

[2] *C.S.P. Ireland*, Vol. CCVIII (Pt. II), 17, 71. Neale, *E.H.R.*, Vol. XLV.

was 3,000 foot, with 2,135 effective; but these figures do not reveal the extent of the losses already suffered. Mountjoy had in the previous October cassed 1,000 foot, which does not mean that he had transferred them to other commands or sent them home—though some of the seriously ill were commonly sent home—but that he had struck off the list companies equivalent to these numbers because no men remained to fill them. Since then, at least 1,500 reinforcements had arrived, so that there were only 2,135 effectives to show for 5,500 sent in all.[1] By October 1601, the effective strength had dropped to 1,343, with 629 sick, a percentage of nearly 32 of the total of 1,972 present.

Only a limited amount of information can be derived from these figures because we do not know the number of dead from disease, the number of sick sent home, the number who deserted on returning ships, or the number of deserters to the enemy. Again, the deserters on shipboard were not all lost, because many were apprehended at the English ports and sent back again, though probably not to the same stations. In April 1600 the Privy Council informed Mountjoy that the force then waiting at Chester would have been greatly depleted by desertion had it not been for the 'runaways' from Ireland who were used to fill up its ranks.[2]

Lough Foyle has been spoken of, by the few who have ever discussed it, as particularly fatal to English troops; but in fact 32 per cent. of sick is the highest incidence recorded in that garrison, the lowest being 13, whereas the percentage of sick of the British Army in the Peninsula in January 1813 amounted to between 33 and 34.[3] The two most useful generalizations to be made about sick wastage are, first, that in old wars troops in camps or bivouacs always suffered much more heavily than those quartered in well-built towns; and, secondly, that no care could prevent sick wastage being high on campaign, or loss of life among wounded heavy, before the invention of the antiseptic, the anæsthetic, the antitoxin, and the various sanitary measures used in the field, the majority of which have been evolved within living memory.

Meanwhile, from his headquarters at Carrickfergus, Sir Arthur Chichester had been carrying out a policy similar to that of Sir Henry Docwra at Derry. He had early in 1601 driven Tyrone's nephew, Brian MacArt O'Neill, out of Upper Clandeboye, the country west of Strangford Lough, and temporarily divided it

---

[1] *C.S.P. Ireland*, Vol. CCVII (Pt. V), 119; Vol. CCVIII (Pt. III), 16 (i).
[2] *A.P.C.*, Vol. XXX, p. 263.   [3] Stewart, *Journal of the R.A.M.C.*, Vol. XCI.

between two rival claimants of the Clandeboye O'Neills. In Lower (northern) Clandeboye he had made much the same arrangement. He had entered into negotiations with James MacSorley MacDonald, who was too scared to come to him in person because he had caused the death of Chichester's brother John.[1] James MacSorley died soon afterwards, and his brother Randal appeared to usurp his Antrim lands from his son. Another James MacDonald, of Dunnyveg, who had been in Tyrone's camp, came into Antrim with a handful of men and was attacked and captured by Randal, who locked him up in Dunluce Castle. The whole story cannot be unravelled without reference to the tangled, obscure, and repellent politics of Clan Donald in Cantyre, which the reader may be spared, as only their results affect the Irish wars.[2]

The bonaghts whom Chichester had established in Upper Clandeboye thrived. When Brian MacArt returned with a force of 400, they set upon him with gusto. The casualty list was substantial, but all Irish. 'It was good service on both sides; for never an honest man was slain', wrote Chichester, with his typically sardonic humour.[3]

Chichester could be savage and terrible as well as sardonic. His account of his operations carried out west of Lough Neagh is one of the grimmest of many grim passages surviving from the Irish wars. 'I have launched the great boat', he wrote to Mountjoy in May 1601, 'and have twice visited Tyrone with her, and oftener with lesser [boats]. We have killed, burnt, and spoiled all along the lough within four miles of Dungannon, from whence we returned hither yesterday; in which journeys we have killed above one hundred people of all sorts, besides such as were burnt, how many I know not. We spare none of what quality or sex soever, and it hath bred much terror in the people, who heard not a drum nor saw not a fire there of long time. The last service was upon Patrick O'Quin, whose house and town was burnt, wife, son, children, and people slain, himself (as is now reported unto me) dead of a hurt received in flying from his house, and other gentlemen which received blows in following us in our return to the boat; and Tyrone himself lay within a mile of this place, but kept himself safe, sending 100 shot to know the matter, which he seemed to marvel at.'[4]

[1] See p. 208.

[2] If the reader be curious about them, he can obtain information from Hill, *Macdonells of Antrim*, and Hayes-McCoy, *Scots Mercenary Forces*.

[3] *C.S.P. Ireland*, Vol. CCVIII (Pt. II), 68.

[4] *C.S.P. Ireland*, Vol. CCVIII (Pt. II), 91 (i).

Mountjoy had returned to Dublin at the end of November 1600, after his campaign in Armagh. He remained inactive for less than a month. Before his next expedition he received a generous and lively letter from Queen Elizabeth. In one letter he had petulantly spoken of himself as a scullion. On 3 December the Queen began her reply in these words:

'Mistress Kitchenmaid,—Comfort yourself therefore in this, that neither your careful endeavour, nor dangerous travels, nor heedful regards to our service, could ever have been disposed upon a prince that more esteems them, considers, and regards them than she for whom chiefly, I know, all this hath been done.'

She pointed out that no man in his position could hope to avoid some errors, but that she knew of none who had committed fewer. She warned him not to confuse admonitions with accusations, and subscribed herself, 'Your Sovereign that dearly regards you'.[1] Those who served Elizabeth had much to put up with, but none knew better than she how to compensate them, and bind them to herself, with kindly words. Sometimes, it is true, these were all they got.

Wicklow still remained an open sore, and, like Russell before him, Mountjoy had to deal with it in intervals between campaigns against the main rebels in Ulster. He now announced that he would spend Christmas at Monasterevin, in Kildare, where there was a castle belonging to the Queen, and sent tapestries and provisions there to confirm his intention. It was given out that he would harry the O'Moores of Leix and the O'Connors of Offaly. On 22 December he met the Leinster garrisons assembled at Naas and sent most of his household to Monasterevin. Then he turned left-handed and marched with his bewildered troops over the hills in falling snow, resting only three hours in about thirty, to Ballinacor, the stronghold of the O'Byrnes. They were completely surprised. Phelim Mac-Feagh escaped naked out of a back window; but his son was taken, his Christmas dinner was eaten, his drink was drunk, and then his house was burnt. Mountjoy remained in the Glens till late January, burning houses and barns and driving off cattle. He then visited Leix, and did not return to Dublin until April 1601, leaving several garrisons in the disaffected areas.[2] In his absence Phelim MacFeagh surrendered in Dublin.

It was while he was in Westmeath, in February, that news arrived

---

[1] *Carew Cal.*, Vol. III, p. 481.
[2] Moryson, *An Itinerary*, Pt. II, p. 87. *C.S.P. Ireland*, Vol. CCVII (Pt. VI), 103.

of the outbreak of Essex and of his imprisonment in the Tower. This was a time of acute anxiety for Mountjoy. He had been the familiar friend of Essex and of another nobleman deeply involved, Southampton, who had served under him in Ireland. He was the cousin of a third plotter, Sir Christopher Blount. He was the acknowledged lover of the sister of Essex, Lady Rich. Worse still, he was accused in the confessions of the plotters of intercourse with them at least bordering on treason. They had, said one of them, Henry Cuffe, sent an emissary over to him at Christmas. Southampton testified that he had written to the King of Scots asking him to bestir himself to keep the government out of the hands of enemies to his succession; Mountjoy himself would help, 'duty reserved to Her Majesty'. Sir Charles Danvers stated that Mountjoy had promised to send an army to England to assist the enterprise of Essex.[1]

All the men named above except Southampton died on the scaffold. Mountjoy was never even questioned, though his secretary believed that, if summoned to England, he would have fled to France. The evidence given by the accused was not considered reliable, and it appears that the Queen and Cecil were not disposed to impute to Mountjoy anything worse than extreme rashness. Besides, his success and the hopes based upon him served to safeguard him. He wrote at once to Cecil to say that the army was free from all infection, and there the matter dropped.[2]

He had a disagreeable task to carry out in May, the debasement of the Irish currency as a means of economy, but it does not seem to have worried him, and the new almost worthless silver was received by the troops with a rather better grace than might have been expected.[3]

Mountjoy was certainly a cool hand. The rebellion in Ireland was nearly extinguished, but it might burst into a great flame once more if the Spaniards landed. And they were now almost certain to come in the near future. Yet the Lord Deputy would not await them in Munster or keep the forces idle in expectation of their landing. No; he proposed to take away 1,000 of Carew's troops in Munster for Connaught and to march himself into Ulster once again. Even

[1] Camden Soc., *Correspondence of King James VI with Sir R. Cecil*, pp. 89, 96, 100. For Sir Christopher Blount, see note at end of chapter.

[2] *C.S.P. Ireland*, Vol. CCVIII (Pt. I), 54. Moryson, *An Itinerary*, Pt. II, p. 89.

[3] *C.S.P. Ireland*, Vol. CCVIII (Pt. II), 79. This story is set out in Bagwell, Vol. III, p. 395.

Carew, whose nerves were good also, was a little shocked. Mountjoy told the Privy Council that if the Spaniards came thousands of troops would have to be sent over, and he proposed that these should be kept in readiness. He was not going to allow the threat to impose idleness upon him.[1] But he was growing rather tired of the life. Writing to Carew in April, he expressed the hope that God would send them both a quiet return and a happy meeting 'in the land of good meat and clean linen'.[2]

On 22 May Mountjoy went to Drogheda and on 8 June reached the familiar Moyry Pass, which was not held. The old trouble, lack of supplies from England, detained him, but he went into Lecale, south of Strangford Lough, and there posted Sir Richard Moryson with 500 foot. Chichester came out from Carrickfergus to meet him and was given another 200 men. Sir Henry Danvers—lucky to remain in the service after his brother's treasonable association with Essex—was placed with 750 foot and 100 horse in Armagh, mainly to cover the grazing, which had been the perquisite of Tyrone and his creaghts the previous year; but Mountjoy had to make a second march to stock the place with provisions. This time, on 14 July, he forced the passage of the Blackwater, which was strongly fortified. He expected serious loss, but a few rounds from two small cannon on the previous day had their effect, and the enemy ran away in face of an assault before dawn. With 800 foot and sixty horse, Mountjoy penetrated to Benburb, inside the Tyrone border. There on the 16th he had a sharp fight lasting three hours, which was highly successful, but cost him over 100 casualties. He had been hoping that Docwra would join hands with him, but Docwra was held by lack of match for his muskets. Even Mountjoy's daring did not permit a deeper penetration; the consequence of his being pinned down in Ulster when the Spaniards came upon the scene would be too serious. He decided to move nearer Munster, but still leaving strong forces in Ulster.[3] On 12 August Cecil learnt that English pinnaces had encountered fifty Spanish sail, probably bound for Ireland. Then the fleet temporarily disappeared. It had been driven back by a storm. But it resumed its course, and on 14 September Carew, at Cork, learnt that it was drawing close to the Irish shores.

[1] C.S.P. Ireland, Vol. CCVIII (Pt. II), 11.   [2] Carew Cal., Vol. IV, p. 41.
[3] Moryson, An Itinerary, Pt. II, pp. 106, 113. C.S.P. Ireland, Vol. CCVIII (Pt. III), 79, 83.

NOTE ON SIR CHRISTOPHER BLOUNT

It has been possible to clear up the relationship between Lord Mountjoy and Sir Christopher Blount. In *The Dictionary of National Biography* Christopher is described as probably a younger brother of Mountjoy's. Other historians have clearly avoided the issue and make no suggestions. The Irish correspondence is full of negative evidence against this relationship, but no positive evidence has been advanced till now.

On 21 February 1600 Mountjoy, on his way to Ireland, wrote to Cecil that his cousin, Sir Edward Blount, had come to say goodbye to him at Lichfield, but had been persuaded to accompany him to Ireland. On 28 February Sir Geoffrey Fenton wrote to Cecil: 'The 26th of this month the Lord Deputy arrived at the Head of Howth. ... Sir George Carew and Sir Henry Danvers were the two men of note that are come with his lordship, besides Sir Edward Blount, brother to Sir Christopher Blount.' If Edward was Mountjoy's cousin and Christopher was Edward's brother, then Christopher was Mountjoy's cousin.

This opens up another question, of no concern with the present book, but of some interest. If Christopher had been Mountjoy's brother, as Sir Sidney Lee (author of the notice in *The Dictionary of National Biography*) supposed, then he would have been younger than Mountjoy and therefore in the year 1589 less than twenty-six years of age. In or about that year he married Leicester's widow, mother by her first husband of Robert Earl of Essex. The lady is often sneered at for taking such a juvenile husband. But now that Christopher is established as Mountjoy's cousin his age becomes uncertain; he may in fact have been several years older than Mountjoy. He was manifestly a great deal younger than his wife, but the gap between them may not have been scandalous or ludicrous, as has been alleged upon unsound evidence.

CHAPTER XX

THE WAR IN MUNSTER AND CONNAUGHT

WHEN Sir George Carew reached Shandon Castle, near Cork, in his province of Munster, his first message to Cecil, on 2 May 1600, bore a rather pessimistic air. He had 3,000 foot by the list; but from this number there had to be deducted 300 'dead pays', the same number of sick, and the garrisons of Youghal, Kinsale, Kilmallock, Mallow, and some smaller places. He was left with 1,740 foot to take the field. He estimated that there were 7,000 rebels in arms in Munster. Small wonder then that he temporized with Florence MacCarthy; he could not, he explained, fight him and James Fitzthomas (the Sugane Earl of Desmond) at once.[1]

After receiving some submissions and doing his best to insure that Cork should remain quiet until his return, Carew marched on 24 May towards Limerick with all his available field force. At Kilmallock he gained a great prize, the submission of one of the most important of the Geraldine chieftains, Edmond Fitzgibbon, the White Knight. At Limerick he mounted an old gun found in the store to batter the castle of Lough Gur; but the commander of the garrison, hearing of this activity, delivered the place into his hands. This was an invaluable acquisition, as its garrison and that of Bruff—also occupied without a fight—protected the castle of Kilmallock. The incident, the surrender of a fort of masonry on the mere hint of a cannonade, is typical of the Irish wars.[2]

As he looked about him the President became convinced that the Munstermen had little heart in the war. What kept it going above all was the large force of Connaught bonaghts following the standard of James Fitzthomas or fighting under a man of their own province, Dermot O'Connor. The wily Carew was as good a warrior as any, but he preferred diplomacy to war. He was already keeping Florence MacCarthy quiet by diplomacy. Could he square either of the other two of the trinity of great men in Munster? Not Fitzthomas; his ambitions were boundless, and he would be satisfied with nothing less than the earldom of Desmond, which the Queen

---

[1] *Pacata Hibernia*, p. 32. *C.S.P. Ireland*, Vol. CCVII (Pt. III), 6.

[2] *Pacata Hibernia*, p. 44. *C.S.P. Ireland*, Vol. CCVII (Pt. III). 113.

would assuredly not bestow upon him. O'Connor was of another breed. The nationalist cause attracted a few men who were purely soldiers of fortune—including even an Englishman or two—and Dermot belonged to this class. He had begun the war as what Carew called a Connaught kerne, a man of two ploughlands, though actually a gentleman born, of the house of the O'Connor Don. He had risen by sheer ability and strengthened his position by marrying the former Earl of Desmond's daughter, Margaret. A mercenary might be bought. Dermot was bought.

With extreme cunning, Carew wrote a letter to the address of James Fitzthomas, in terms suggesting that he was already a collaborator and promising him good conditions if he would bring in O'Connor dead or alive. This he gave to O'Connor, who was to pretend he had intercepted it and use it as an excuse for action against Fitzthomas. And in mid-June O'Connor contrived to seize Fitzthomas. Unfortunately for Carew, a hitch occurred. On 26 June Lady Margaret O'Connor came to receive the £1,000 promised for the person of Fitzthomas, but there had been some delay, which gave the prisoner's friends time to set him free.[1]

The other rebels now turned upon O'Connor. He took refuge in Ballyallan Castle, where he was besieged. On 29 July Carew moved from Limerick to relieve him. Then the comedy, so typical of Ireland, took another turn. If Dermot were rescued, the besiegers reasoned, he would again serve Carew. On the other hand, they despaired of taking him. A brilliant solution of the problem was to forgive him, restore him to his command, and so balk the Saxon. This was arranged, and Dermot's services were lost to Carew. His end was, however, tragic. He did not regain his prestige and presently led his bonaghts back to Connaught. In December, on his way with a safe-conduct to see Carew, he was waylaid by an ally of the English, Tibbot ne Long Burke, over a blood feud, captured, and hanged. Carew was deeply indignant, because the death of Dermot reflected upon himself and because he held Tibbot ne Long to be a useless hanger-on who had never done anything to earn his pay.[2]

In the account of affairs in Ulster it has been recorded that Hugh Roe O'Donnell left the Lough Foyle area for the purpose of raiding Thomond. He marched down through Roscommon and arrived

[1] *Pacata Hibernia*, pp. 36, 54. C.S.P. Ireland, Vol. CCVII (Pt. III), 129. *History of Catholic Ireland*, p. 133.

[2] *Pacata Hibernia*, pp. 59, 103. *Carew Cal.*, Vol. III, p. 490.

in the county on 21 June. Scientifically thorough as always in these matters, he burnt everything that would take fire. Enormous clouds of smoke enveloped the country. With the touching sympathy which they always display towards the plunderer, if a poor man, the annalists relate that many a feast fit for a lord was eaten by a party of four or five men in the shelter of a shrubbery. Carew sent the Earl of Thomond 800 foot and sixty horse, with whose aid, he claims, O'Donnell was pushed out, though according to the Irish account he withdrew in his own time and at his ease. Returning through Connaught, he used his torches again in the Clanrickarde territories.[1]

All the Irish successes in Munster, though they looked well, were pinpricks, whereas there was solid advantage in those of Carew. On 5 July he arrived with the Earl of Thomond in front of the strong Glin Castle, on the Shannon, where a ship with artillery awaited him. The demi-cannon brought ashore proved to be so 'cloyed' that it could not be fired. The President, an expert in these matters, bade the gunner elevate the muzzle as high as possible, give her a full charge of powder, roll in a ball, and then fire the charge from the mouth. This resulted in clearing the touch-hole—a drastic remedy and perhaps an unenviable duty for the gunner. A breach was made quickly, but fighting within was ferocious, from floor to floor, the last defenders being thrown from the top of a tower into the river. Carew then repaired the castle and put in a garrison. This capture led to the surrender of Carrigafoyle, lower down the Shannon—again the familiar process by which the fate of one castle and its garrison terrified the garrison of the next into giving it up.[2]

At the end of July Carew learnt that the rebels, despairing of holding their castles in Kerry, were about to destroy them. This he was anxious to prevent, but a wet summer had made the direct route from Limerick impassable by wheels. He therefore marched down the north bank of the Shannon to Kilrush, where the river is four miles wide. Boats provided by the Earl of Thomond carried a force of 1,050 foot and seventy-five horse over to Carrigafoyle. Carew's lieutenant, Sir Charles Wilmot, pushing on at top speed, recovered Lixnaw, which he found prepared for burning. He then led on fifty horsemen to Tralee, the old castle of the Denny family where the survivors of the Armada had been slaughtered, and got right into the midst of a company of James Fitzthomas's soldiers who

[1] C.S.P. Ireland, Vol. CCVII (Pt. III), 129. Four Masters, Vol. VI, p. 2,197.
[2] Pacata Hibernia, p. 66. C.S.P. Ireland, Vol. CCVII (Pt. IV), 26.

were destroying it. The Irish fled, leaving twenty-two dead and the arms of another 100 lying on the ground. Another prominent Geraldine, the Knight of Kerry, came in and submitted to mercy, and nearly all the freeholders showed a tendency to follow suit. Everything was going well. The English soldiers, accustomed to victory in these small affairs whatever the odds might be, were fighting with supreme confidence and daring. One slight accident served only to emphasize their superiority. The treachery of a guide brought on a fight between troops of Carew's ally, the White Knight, and a party from his garrison of Kilmallock. The numbers were just 300, including 160 musketeers, on the Irish side, and under 100 on the English, but the Irish broke and ran after suffering heavy loss. The President was distressed that the combat should have taken place, but consoled himself by reflecting on the admirable bearing of his men.[1] Dermot O'Connor's mercenaries cleared off into Connaught in August, and most of the remainder had been killed or received into submission. Only about 1,200 men in all still followed the Sugane Earl, the Knight of the Valley, the Baron of Lixnaw, and Florence MacCarthy—and the last-named of these had avoided open acts of rebellion.

On 16 September occurred a little affair which proved to be Carew's crowning mercy in Munster, though he cannot have guessed at the time that it would. Hearing that James Fitzthomas was moving into the great woodland of Aharow, many square miles in extent, where it would be most difficult to come to close quarters with him, Captain Richard Graeme came out from Kilmallock with a handful of men in the hope of intercepting him. He failed in his attempt to surprise the Irish, whose scouts gave warning of his presence. Confident in their great superiority of numbers, apparently about 350, they came on. To begin with, Graeme had but thirty-six horsemen, and his foot did not come up until the end of the action, but he cut to pieces their horse and skirmishing musketeers and captured their transport. Fitzthomas himself led the main body on foot, and he was seen to beat with a cudgel captains of bonaghts and deserters from the English army who were trying to parley. He restrained them from doing this, but they managed to send a message to Graeme that they would serve him if they could. Fitzthomas drew off, leaving sixty dead on the field and 300 laden garrans in the hands of the English. Though he brought off intact the main body of his force, he was never able to draw it together

[1] *Pacata Hibernia*, pp. 70, 73, 78. *C.S.P. Ireland*, Vol. CCVII (Pt. IV), 88.

again. His prestige was gone. A week later Carew reported to Cecil that he was now no better than a wood-kerne, wandering none knew where.[1]

After his dealings with Dermot O'Connor earlier in the year Carew had come to the conclusion that what attracted the rebels in James Fitzthomas was the shadow of the beloved earldom of Desmond. What if he could produce for them a real Earl instead of the Sugane Earl? The material was to hand in a luckless individual known generally as 'James of the Tower', Dermot O'Connor's brother-in-law.

It will be recalled that twenty years before, during the Desmond rebellion, the Irish leader's wife had handed over her little son to English keeping.[2] He had been brought up in the Tower, but in fair comfort, and his correspondence suggests that he had been well educated. Cecil persuaded the Queen to send him over, and with him she sent a patent restoring him in blood and honour. That is to say, he became Earl of Desmond as his father had been; nothing was said about the estates, granted after the escheat to undertakers, who had in their turn been driven out by the Irish. His despatch to Ireland was an experiment, brought about by the friendship of Cecil for Carew, from whom the project sprang.

The young man, with a grim but kindly guardian, Captain Price, landed on 15 October at Youghal, where he was received with enthusiasm and kissed by the old women. He went overland to Cork, but there he was treated coldly and even rudely by the mayor. He then went to Mallow, where the President awaited him, and afterwards to Kilmallock. Here his reception was a triumph. Visitors from all round the countryside had flocked into the little town. When he left his lodgings to dine with Sir George Thornton the troops tried to form a lane for him, but it took him half an hour to make his way through. Blessings were called upon his head and handfuls of wheat and salt were thrown at him, in token of the prosperity which the crowd desired for him. Carew's scheme seemed to be going well.

Next day was a Sunday, and the young lord walked to church. The crowd implored him not to enter the building, but he disregarded them. When he reappeared their temper had changed. Now they railed at him for deserting the faith of his fathers. The visitors left Kilmallock in disgust. From that day Desmond's

---

[1] *Pacata Hibernia*, p. 82. *C.S.P. Ireland*, Vol. CCVII (Pt. V), 31 (i), 40.
[2] See p. 128.

attraction and influence dropped almost to vanishing point. A Butler in Kilkenny and Tipperary, with the personality of Ormonde, might carry the handicap of the Protestant faith with success, but not an unknown Geraldine in Cork or Kerry. The President and his Council still waited to see whether Desmond would establish himself even on a moderately good footing, and no word came from England to put any power into his hands. Two months later he wrote to Cecil that Carew was treating him kindly, but that he was contemptible to the country because he had no command. He rendered the English one piece of service in negotiating the handing over of the fort of Castlemaine, but as a whole his mission proved a failure. He does not seem to have been a man of character—perhaps that could hardly have been the case in view of his upbringing. The murder of Dermot O'Connor scared him. In March 1601 he returned to England disappointed. Cecil sent him a friendly note and talked of marrying him to a charming heiress; but 'the Queen's Earl', the last Earl of Desmond, died not long afterwards.[1]

Carew had thus failed in both his schemes, to kidnap the Sugane Earl and to exploit the Queen's Earl, but all else went well with him. Florence MacCarthy came in on 29 October 1600, promising to be Her Majesty's true man, and was given a safe-conduct. In December Listowel Castle, the last in Kerry to hold out, surrendered to Wilmot. By January 1601 Carew was able to cass 500 men and send 1,000 into Connaught. In April he underwent some alarm because he heard that fresh attacks from the north were impending and that the seafaring O'Malleys and O'Flaherties proposed to transport a force from Thomond into Kerry. But the project came to nothing. A merchantman and some smaller craft were armed and sent to lie off the estuary of the Shannon, with the result that the Connaughtmen did not venture to put to sea. Carew sent a force into Thomond to aid the small garrison there and himself moved to Limerick in case further support were needed; but a single skirmish in Thomond broke up the rebel body which had entered the county. It fell back across the Galway border, was pursued, and driven in confusion over the Suck, where, according to Carew's information, some 200 were drowned. Carew was particularly gratified that a number of Irish lords had mustered men to meet the threat. He could not deal with Connaught, and its own garrison was too weak

[1] *Carew Cal.*, Vol. III, p. 409; Vol. IV, pp. 33, 49. *Pacata Hibernia*, pp, 85–92. C.S.P. *Ireland*, Vol. CCVII (Pt. V), 104. Bagwell, *Ireland under the Tudors*, Vol. III, p. 379.

for the moment to carry out the task, but his province was subdued and almost peaceful. Mountjoy admitted that Connaught was in the worst state of the four provinces, but he considered that it would be the easiest to pacify.[1]

Still Carew had not laid hands upon James Fitzthomas, the Sugane Earl, though he was known to be reduced to the last extremity, with no followers at his heels, and with no hope but to avoid capture until the Spaniards landed, if land they ever were to. He was believed to be in the White Knight's country and that chieftain was called upon to prove his loyalty by finding him. In fact, some of his followers knew the fugitive's hiding place, but probably believed that their lord was playing a deep game and did not intend to take him. On 29 May one of them asked if he really desired to find him and, on hearing that he did, led him to a deep cave—apparently one near Mitchelstown, still well known—where the fugitive lay hidden. The Sugane Earl was sent to Cork, and later on to England. Carew advised against his execution, in case his brother John should assume the title of Desmond, and James died in the Tower in the next reign. Carew was as well pleased with the White Knight as the remaining rebels were disgusted.[2]

The one other anxiety of Carew was the conduct and behaviour of Florence MacCarthy. This man possessed patience and skill in intrigue which had kept him, if not just within the law, at all events not far beyond its borders. Some of his correspondence, however, smacked of treason. But Carew worried above all over his probable action if the Spaniards should land. Less than three weeks after the capture of James Fitzthomas he arrested Florence. Fourteen days of the period during which he was protected under the Great Seal remained unexpired, and by the standards of the time this was a grave act of treachery. Carew excused himself by the plea that the prisoner had been guilty of double-dealing and also by the casuistical argument that he had meant to set out that very day on an expedition which would have left him little time to return and put in sureties so that his protection might be extended. Carew's action has been condemned by history, but it was accepted without comment by the Government. Florence MacCarthy was sent over with James Fitzthomas and with him lodged in the Tower. Cecil,

[1] *Carew Cal.*, Vol. IV, p. 46. *C.S.P. Ireland*, Vol. CCVII (Pt. VI), 2, 60; Vol. CCVIII (Pt. II), 35. *A.P.C.*, Vol. XXXI, p. 129.

[2] *C.S.P. Ireland*, Vol. CCVIII (Pt. II), 103; (Pt. III), 7. *Pacata Hibernia*, p. 136. Four Masters, Vol. VI, p. 2,261.

on interrogating the two, found the latter more sensible and moderate than he had expected and the former what he had expected, a vain, malicious fool.[1] If he was that then, he would seem to have become a benignant old man, with a touch of scholarship. He lived to a great age, with several periods of confinement in the Tower or the Marshalsea, and died not long before the outbreak of the English Civil War.

No other event of great importance occurred in the Munster Presidency before the arrival of the Spanish expeditionary force. Carew had received one reinforcement of 350 men in October 1600, whose arrival in Cork afforded the mayor an excuse for the bad accommodation he allotted to the young Earl of Desmond. This reinforcement, Welsh in composition, was intended to be larger, but a ship from Bristol with 200 men was driven into Milford, where about half the local men, being 'lewdly disposed', ran away. After sending to Connaught the force already mentioned and cassing another 500, his list strength was reduced to 1,350 foot and 200 horse by July 1601.[2]

He could not regard the situation with equanimity. He had indeed learnt that another 2,000 men were to be sent to him in August, but, to his disquietude, these troops were delayed, and did not begin to land until 4 September, only just before the arrival of the Spaniards. As an example of how complex the despatch of reinforcements had become and how much organization was required to carry it out, the list may be given in full on this occasion:

Devon, 100; Hants, 100. To embark at Barnstaple, August 6th. Glouc., 100; Northt., 100; Somerset, 100; Warw. and Salop, 50 each; Leicester and Caermarthen, 50 each; Worcester and Hereford, 50 each; Wilts, 100. To embark at Bristol, August 9th. Denbigh, 30; Flint, 20; York, 50; Cheshire and York, 50 each; Notts and Derby, 50 each; York, 100; Lancashire, 100. To embark at Chester, August 9th. Total, 1,400.

(All the above were in companies, commanded by their captains, whose names were given. The remaining 600 were to be taken over by conductors, to join existing companies.)

---

[1] MacCarthy, *Life of Florence MacCarthy*, p. 329. *C.S.P. Ireland*, Vol. CCVIII (Pt. III), 24. *Pacata Hibernia*, p. 161.

[2] *C.S.P. Ireland*, Vol. CCVII (Pt. V), 113; Vol. CCVIII (Pt. III), 34 (i). *A.P.C.*, Vol. XXX, p. 728.

Dorset, 50; Cornwall, 25; To embark at Barnstaple, August 6th. Cardigan, 25; Pembroke, 40; Glamorgan, 50; Brecknock, 25; Radnor, 25; Monmouth, 30. At Bristol, August 9th.

Stafford, 50; Huntingdon, 50; Rutland, 25; Carnarvon, 40. Out of York, 100; Montgomery, 40; Merioneth, 25. At Chester, August 9th.

It will be observed that 300 men were sent from Yorkshire and that they were divided as follows: fifty in one company, linked with fifty from Denbigh and Flint; fifty in a company linked with fifty from Cheshire; 100 in a wholly Yorkshire company; and finally 100 among the 600 taken over by conductors. Out of these 600, fifty each were to go to Carew's own company and that of Lord Thomond, and he was asked to agree to Thomond's desire that his fifty should be men from Cornwall and Dorsetshire, an interesting choice on the part of an Irish nobleman. The rest were for captains already in Munster, so that Carew should not be deprived of patronage by having new men brought in in place of those who had served him and whom he wished to reward.[1]

There was some speculation as to whether the Spaniards would make for Galway, but Carew was convinced they would land in his province. It would not be, he thought, at Waterford, because that would be too close to English ports, but at Cork or Limerick, and Cork rather than Limerick. Mountjoy told him that his one duty now was to hold these two towns, an instance of the clear and simple directives which he issued to subordinates. The Lord Deputy would be responsible for the rest, with the aid of the Queen and the Privy Council.[2]

What Carew had accomplished had been done without outside aid, though of course the action of Mountjoy in keeping Tyrone in Ulster had alone rendered it possible. Carew had fought few actions. He had enjoyed the support of one vigorous assistant in the Earl of Thomond, but he had lately gone to England and was now at court, refusing to give a direct answer to Cecil's questions as to what he wanted, apart from the separation of Thomond from Connaught and its embodiment in Munster. Cecil suspected that, despite his dislike of Connaught, he desired to become President of that province and was of opinion that this post would go to Clanrickarde. Richard de Burgh, who had succeeded his father Ulick in May 1601

---

[1] *Carew Cal.*, Vol. IV, pp. 116, 117, 142.
[2] *C.S.P. Ireland*, Vol. CCVIII (Pt. III), 30, 56.

THE WAR IN MUNSTER AND CONNAUGHT   291

at the age of about twenty-eight, was indeed to become President, though not until after the death of Elizabeth.[1]

The sum of Carew's achievement was great. He could not well have done more to make his province inhospitable to an invader. The back of the rebellion in it was broken. The Sugane Earl and the MacCarthy More were in the Tower. The Connaught and Ulster mercenaries had nearly all gone. Most of the other leaders had submitted. Not a single strong place remained in rebel hands. English prestige had been restored. The means employed had not always been pretty, but the general policy had been based on the assumption that this was not Munster's war and that few Munstermen, despite the exhortations of Father Archer and others, were more than lukewarm about it, while many needed only a stern warning and promise of protection to bring them over. That assumption had proved to be correct.

[1] *Carew Cal.,* Vol. IV, p. 77.

CHAPTER XXI

THE SPANIARDS IN MUNSTER

THE energy, however ill directed, and the determination, however rash, displayed by the Spaniards in this, to all intents and purposes the last venture against England in the course of the war, were surprisingly strong. They certainly came as some surprise to England. The Treaty of Vervins, concluded in 1598, had freed Spain of the burden of the war with France and for the time being there was no serious threat from the Turks—in any case not, since the rout of Lepanto, the danger they had been in the western Mediterranean. Otherwise the Spaniards had plenty on their hands, especially in the Netherlands. The all-powerful Duke of Lerma, however, came to the conclusion that there would never again be such an opportunity as existed in Ireland and that it was worth while supporting the Irish rebels by a powerful expedition. In his appreciation he was correct; his action was taken dangerously late and on a dangerously small scale.

Perhaps the success of the expedition to Cadiz had rendered the English over-confident and careless. Early in 1598 there had been a scare about invasion, and it was then discovered that nothing was ready to meet such a threat. Actually the Spanish forces, relatively small in numbers, were reinforcements for the Netherlands, but the lesson might have been learnt. It was so little learnt that when there was another scare in 1599 things were no better. Now again there was unreadiness in the Narrow Seas, though when action became a matter of life or death great promptitude was shown in recovering the lost ground.

The Spanish fleet assembled at Lisbon. There was a difference of opinion about its destination. Commentators have criticized the decision to land in Munster and asserted that the expedition should have made for a northern harbour. In fact, the Spaniards, though unaware to what an extent the rebellion had been extinguished in Munster or that the Sugane Earl was a prisoner in the Tower, realized that the main strength of their friends lay in Ulster. From the naval point of view, Cork was preferable to an Ulster harbour, and it is to be noted that Carew never even considered the possibility of a landing outside his own province; but the organizers of the expedition were not blind to the fact that a landing at Cork left a dangerous amount of ground between the landing force and its Irish allies. After the landing, the Adelantado of Castille, Don Martin de Padilla, in a letter to the King, boldly and even scornfully criticized both the landing place and what he considered the inadequacy of the force. This he stigmatized as a general weakness of Spanish military policy. He hoped that a really big reinforcement would be sent to finish off the business quickly, not driblets like sips of broth.[1]

French official opinion, the Venetian Ambassador in France wrote to the Doge and Senate, was inclined on hearing of the landing to think that the force might be thrown away because it had arrived at the opposite end of Ireland to that of Tyrone's strength. The French suspected that the motive of the Spaniards was not conquest, but rather to obtain a footing in Ireland so as to be able to intervene in the matter of the succession on the death of Elizabeth.[2]

The Admiral, Don Diego Brochero, sailed with thirty-three vessels. He was carrying 4,464 foot, six pieces of artillery to be employed ashore, with arms and munitions for the Irish. The Spaniards in Elizabeth's day seldom enjoyed luck with the weather, and now the flagship and eight other ships were separated from the fleet by a gale and entered Coruña. This was a serious matter. In these nine ships were Pedro de Zubiaur, 650 troops, and apparently a large proportion of the stores, leaving the main force short.[3] The senior military commander was Don Juan de Aguila, an experienced soldier, though perhaps not one of the most vigorous in the service. With the force at his disposal, 3,814 men after the detachment of nine ships, and some shortage of stores, he was engaged in a difficult and highly risky enterprise because he would be heavily outnumbered on the spot. He could not hope for success unless the Ulster leaders hastened to his support and substantial reinforcements reached him from Spain at an early date.

Mountjoy had moved to Trim, in Meath, at the beginning of September 1601 to be nearer Munster. On the evening of the 14th he reached Kilkenny, where he was the guest of Ormonde. He had been informed that another 2,000 men—that is, in addition to the force which had just landed at Cork and Waterford—were to come to him from Chester and had demanded from the Privy Council

[1] C.S.P. Spanish, Vol. IV, pp. 676, 690.
[2] C.S.P. Venetian, Vol. IX, pp. 477, 483.   [3] C.S.P. Spanish, Vol. IV, p. 692.

yet another 2,000 foot and 200 horse. On the 22nd, when Carew had joined him, he heard from the mayor of Cork that the Spanish fleet was off the Old Head of Kinsale and apparently making for Cork Harbour. Next day, in the midst of a council of war, a messenger rode in from Sir Charles Wilmot, whom Carew had left as Governor of Cork, that the Spaniards had not after all made for Cork, but had anchored in the haven of Kinsale. Ormonde and the Marshal, Sir Richard Wingfield, advised Mountjoy to return to Dublin to assemble his troops, but the psychologist Carew urged him to go forward even if he had no follower but his page, so that the inhabitants should not see the Lord Deputy turn his back on the enemy. Mountjoy was concerned by the shortage of victuals at Dublin. Carew reassured him on this point; he had for the past six months cessed the troops on the country and was now well stocked. Mountjoy sprang up from his chair and embraced Carew in gratitude for his foresight.[1]

On the 24th Mountjoy sent away Wingfield and other senior officers to bring down the forces from the Pale and Armagh. He himself set off for Cork, by way of Clonmel, with no greater escort than a squadron of 100 horse. Before his departure he wrote a confident letter to Cecil. Owing to a delay in the arrival of reinforcements, he was compelled, he said, to weaken the northern garrisons further than was desirable, but the Spaniards represented the decisive objective. 'If we beat them, let it not trouble you though you hear all Ireland doth revolt, for (by the grace of God) you shall have them all return presently with halters about their necks; if we do not, all providence bestowed on any other place is vain. . . . I apprehend a world of difficulties with as much comfort as ever poor man did, because I have now a fair occasion to show how prodigal I will be of my life in any adventure that I shall find to be for the service of my dearest Mistress, which, when I have done, I will sing *Nunc dimittis*.'[2]

The Spaniards had, in fact, intended to enter Cork Harbour, where the town itself would have provided an invaluable prize as a base, though they would have a great deal of trouble in securing it. Just as they reached the entrance the wind fell off, whereupon the fleet tacked and made for Kinsale. This was an insignificant place by comparison with Cork, but, on the other hand, they did not have to fight for it. The garrison of one company quitted it in accordance

[1] *Carew Cal.*, Vol. IV, pp. 147, 149, 179. *Pacata Hibernia*, p. 196.
[2] Moryson, *An Itinerary*, Pt. II, p. 135.

with orders; the townsmen opened the gates; and the sovereign, with his white rod of office in his hand, found the invaders their billets with more solicitude than if they had been the Queen's troops.[1]

The Spaniards did not find Kinsale, though it was walled, a really strong place; but they set about adding to its fortifications. They also garrisoned Castle Park, on the west bank of the Bandon, and the castle of Rincurren, on the east side, perhaps in the hope of preventing English ships from entering the harbour. Aguila and Mathew de Oviedo, the Spanish titular Archbishop of Dublin who had accompanied him, wrote to Tyrone and O'Donnell, bidding them hasten into Munster and bring with them horses, the chief need. Aguila also issued a proclamation, probably written by the Spanish priest, that he would never seek to draw any man from his allegiance to his lawful prince, but that Elizabeth had been deposed by the Pope; thus every Irishman who aided the Spaniards was not failing in due obedience, but rather obeying God's word, uttered by the Pope, his mouthpiece on earth. There was no conception here of Ireland as a nation, but an attempt to prove that Elizabeth was not its lawful sovereign.[2]

On Sunday 27 September Mountjoy reached Cork, and on the 29th reconnoitred Kinsale. The Spaniards were greatly handicapped for lack of cavalry because they could not prevent the English horse from approaching the walls. Most of their shipping had already put to sea, and the rest was about to do so. Mountjoy was eager to attack before Irish forces from Ulster arrived on the scene, but for the moment there was nothing he could do but await his troops. It was at least comforting to find that, so far, Munster remained quiet and virtually none of those who had submitted to Carew relapsed. The troops began to arrive on 3 October and by the 27th the list strength of the field army assembled was 6,900 foot and 611 horse. Mountjoy, however, did not wait until the whole force had concentrated or for the arrival of ships with artillery and tools from Dublin. It appeared to him preferable to take the field early rather than disclose his deficiencies by doing nothing, so on the 16th he encamped within half a mile of Kinsale, on the flank of a hill called Knockrobin, even though he had not the means to entrench.[3]

On 22 and 23 October the shipping arrived. Mountjoy now moved to the Spittle Hill, north of Kinsale, and began to open

---

[1] *Pacata Hibernia*, p. 189. [2] *Pacata Hibernia*, pp. 198–200.
[3] *Carew Cal.*, Vol. IV, p. 198. Moryson, *An Itinerary*, Pt. II, p. 127.

parallels. He had at his disposal an experienced engineer or 'trench master' in Captain Josiah Bodley, brother of the celebrated Sir Thomas. He determined first of all to capture Rincurren, held by 150 Spaniards, because this fort, a quarter of a mile from the town, inconvenienced his shipping. Before the artillery opened up, Aguila attempted to relieve or reinforce the castle by means of boats, but fire from one of the supply ships drove them back. The bombardment by two and eventually three pieces was interrupted, as constantly happened, by the breaking of carriages. Aguila did what he could to interfere by bringing guns out from the gate of Kinsale and firing into the camp. He killed two men beside Mountjoy's tent and burst two hogsheads of his beer. He also made a further effort to get boats to the castle, but again they were stopped by fire. Next he sent out 500 men to attempt to reach the place by land, but they were forced back into the town after hand-to-hand fighting. Carew, whose speciality was gunnery, considered that the English artillery was being mishandled. He therefore laid the pieces himself, taking the level with his quadrant, so that fire could be maintained by night as well as day. The Spaniards finally beat a parley and on 1 November surrendered the castle with promise of their lives. It was a good start.[1]

The speed with which Mountjoy had closed upon Kinsale contrasted with the dilatory proceedings of Tyrone. The withdrawal of so many troops from Ulster, Connaught, and Leinster made it certain that he and O'Donnell would be able to march south to the aid of the Spaniards. O'Donnell was the first to move. He raised the siege of Donegal Abbey in September, assembled his forces at Ballymote in Sligo, and marched south through Roscommon. He was ferried across the Shannon at Shannon Harbour, and from thence moved into Tipperary. For three weeks he camped north of Templemore, 'plundering, burning, and ravaging the country'. The excuse was that the people had submitted to the English, but raiding was a pastime to O'Donnell and it did not occur to him to try any other form of persuasion, though the victims were his fellow countrymen and co-religionists.[2]

Hearing of his approach, on 7 November Mountjoy held a council of war, at which it was agreed by a majority that a force should be sent into Tipperary to intercept him. Carew dissented from this decision in the belief that the Irish would, as usual, prove too quick-

---

[1] *Carew Cal.*, Vol. IV, pp. 179, 182. *Pacata Hibernia*, pp. 204–9.
[2] Four Masters, Vol. VI, p. 2,277.

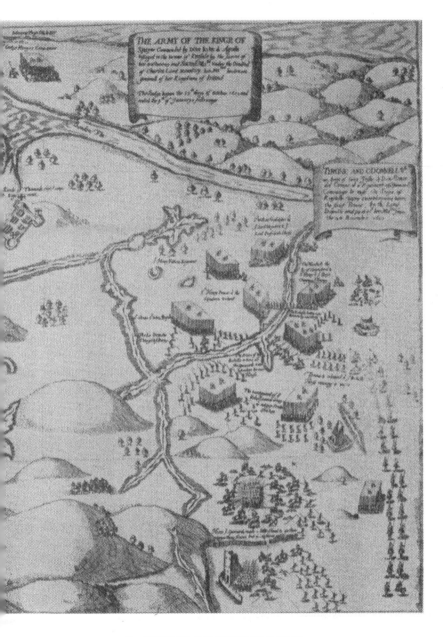

7   THE SIEGE AND BATTLE OF KINSALE

Various scenes covering the whole period of the siege, from 17 October 1601 to 9 January 1602, are shown simultaneously; but the English advance across two boggy streams can be followed and the battle is clearly shown (*Pacata Hibernia*).

footed for the royal troops. Mountjoy, however, agreed with the finding of the majority and designated Carew to undertake the task of interception, as the commander best acquainted with the country. He was allotted two regiments of foot, nominally over 2,000 strong, but, according to his own account, not above half that figure, and 250 horse. In addition, Sir Christopher St. Lawrence, who was moving from the Pale into Munster with his regiment, was ordered to join him.

Carew marched at once and took up a position at Ardmayle, on the Suir. Here he was only a few miles from the Irish outposts, at Holycross, but the main body lay in a fastness of wood and bog, and he was uncertain as to its exact position. However, he was standing right across O'Donnell's road to the south, and the alternative route across the Slievefelim Mountains into Limerick was impassable to pack-horses by reason of heavy rains. A sudden very sharp frost, a rare occurrence in southern Ireland at this season, gave O'Donnell his opportunity. Breaking camp in darkness, he marched over the mountains into Limerick, and over the Maigue in the centre of the county. Carew had at once realized the significance of the frost and had drawn back to Cashel in the hope of intercepting the Irish as they emerged from the mountains, but they had passed before he could reach the point at which he aimed. He then pursued at top speed to Kilmallock, but there was no hope of catching O'Donnell, who outpaced him through west Cork and finally arrived on the Bandon. Carew therefore marched back to Kinsale, in justified confidence that he would reach it before O'Donnell, since the English were on the direct road, whereas the Irish had to make a wide detour to the west. As matters turned out, O'Donnell did not close on Kinsale, preferring to await the arrival of Tyrone. It was estimated that the enemy had covered thirty-two Irish miles (just over forty English) in virtually a single march and in bad country, the greatest feat of marching of which Carew had ever heard. Nor is there any account of stragglers from an army of some 3,000, though a good deal of baggage was abandoned. Carew reached the English camp on 25 November.[1]

The Spaniards were not long unaware that a large proportion of Mountjoy's force had marched away under Carew. On 10 November they made a sortie in strength from Kinsale. The small advanced guard which approached the English camp was, however, driven

[1] *Pacata Hibernia*, p. 210. O'Clery, *Life of O'Donnell*, p. 305. *History of Catholic Ireland*, p. 144.

back. A rearward position had been entrenched for its support, but a force of English musketeers took this in enfilade and compelled the defenders to abandon it. The advanced guard was thus deprived of succour and had to continue its retreat post haste to the gate of Kinsale. Aguila, it was reported, was infuriated with the leader of the sortie, whom he accused of bad judgement and want of resolution.[1]

On this day Mountjoy learnt that Lord Thomond, coming from England, had been blown out of his course and had entered Castlehaven with 1,000 foot and 100 horse, and that the remainder of his contingent, the total of which was 2,000 foot, had arrived at Waterford. On the 12th came more good news. Admiral Sir Richard Leveson had arrived at Cork with ten ships of war and a further contingent of 2,000 men, including trained gunners and artisans, and a consignment of munitions. Queen, Privy Council, officials, soldiers, and sailors had acted with great promptitude, and the Earl of Nottingham (the former Lord Howard of Effingham), was justified in his complacency when he boasted that 'there never was such a fleet of the Queen's ships so suddenly sent out by any Admiral before'. Leveson was bidden to come to Kinsale and arrived on the 14th, but the weather was so foul that it was impossible to begin landing the troops until next day. They were raw men, much upset by the voyage, and on the very first night a number of them died. Mountjoy sent about 1,000 of them to Cork to rest and pass the time until hutments could be prepared for them.[2]

Having won Rincurren, Mountjoy's next task was to take Castle Park. The fleet joined in the bombardment, and on 17 November a storm was attempted, so that the anniversary of the Queen's coronation might not pass without some action of note. A 'sow' was pushed up to the wall, but the Spaniards smashed it by dropping stones upon it from the top of the tower. So a return was made to battering the place. The attempt to relieve it by boats from Kinsale was defeated, as had happened in the case of Rincurren, and on the 20th the seventeen Spaniards in the fort surrendered. It is certain that Aguila would not have tried to hold so small a place had he not expected the Irish to come to his aid sooner than they actually did.[3]

Hitherto little had been accomplished against Kinsale itself beyond investing it. The arrival of reinforcements and munitions and the capture of the outlying forts enabled Mountjoy to take positive

[1] Moryson, *An Itinerary*, Pt. II, p. 151.
[2] *Carew Cal.*, Vol. IV, pp. 158, 164. *Pacata Hibernia*, p. 214.
[3] *Carew Cal.*, Vol. IV, p. 186. *Pacata Hibernia*, p. 215.

measures. Reinforcements in new companies and drafts for the old had brought his list strength up to 11,800 foot and 857 horse, but this number was greatly diminished by sickness, and some were Irish levies, not well suited to siege warfare. He could, however, now close upon Kinsale and begin a methodical bombardment. He formed a 'flying squadron' of 1,050 foot in list, freed from all watches or direct part in the siege, the sole duty of which was 'to answer alarms'. The day after the capture of Castle Park, 21 November, he opened fire on Kinsale with a cannon and a demi-cannon mounted on a platform. The Spaniards, to save their provisions, sent out of the town a number of Irish women and children, who were allowed to pass through the English lines. Four more pieces were brought into action on the 22nd and next day another three culverins began firing from the waterside in the region of Castle Park.[1]

On the return of Carew's force from its attempt to intercept O'Donnell, it was posted on the west side of Kinsale to prevent Spaniards and Irish from joining hands. Thomond was placed in command of this secondary camp because Mountjoy desired to keep Carew and Clanrickarde by his side. The culverins were brought over from Castle Park to a hill overlooking the town. The Spaniards fired with some success on the ships, hitting the flagship twice, but finally the demi-cannon doing the damage was put out of action. On the 28th a trumpet was sent to summon Kinsale to surrender, but Don Juan sent back the answer that he was holding it, first for Christ, and next for the King of Spain, and would defend it *contra tutti inimici*. On 1 December a reconnaissance in force discovered that a breach close to the gate was still impracticable for assault. Next evening the Spaniards made their greatest effort. The frost had given way to cloud and rain, and it was very dark when a force of 2,000 men issued from the gate. They brought with them tools to pull down the gabions and spikes to put the English guns out of action. They came on with great resolution and overran the trenches, three English companies being driven out in a flight which an observer calls shameful; but the danger-point was strongly reinforced by Mountjoy and the enemy drew back into Kinsale with a loss of fifty killed, that of the English being nearly as heavy. The Spaniards succeeded in spiking only one gun, and that was afterwards repaired.[2]

[1] Moryson, *An Itinerary*, Pt. II, pp. 160-2.
[2] *Carew Cal.*, Vol. IV, p. 188. *Pacata Hibernia*, p. 221. *C.S.P. Ireland*, Vol. CCIX, 243A.

Meanwhile Pedro de Zubiaur, who had, it will be recalled, been compelled to put back into Coruña, had sailed again with ten ships. He had but 829 soldiers aboard and carried chiefly food and stores—biscuits, wheat and rye flour, oil, arms, and powder. Once again the weather favoured the English, though that was a probability at this late season in the Bay of Biscay. Three ships of the fleet became detached, but the rest benefited by fortune when weather forced them into Castlehaven, instead of Kinsale, where the English fleet lay. One of the ships did enter Kinsale. This was a Scottish vessel, and its role of transport for the Spaniards does not suggest a neighbourly spirit on the part of its crew. However, the skipper promptly handed over to the English the eighty Spaniards aboard. It is notable how the various fleets missed each other, as so often in the days of sail. Thomond was lucky that he got clear of Castlehaven before Zubiaur came in, and on the other hand Zubiaur, whose ships were small and nearly all merchantmen, was lucky that he did not encounter Leveson. The remaining six ships arrived at Castlehaven on 1 December, according to the Spanish account, but if this is correct it is curious that the news did not reach the English until the 3rd. The Spaniards landed the troops carried in these ships and five cannon, as well as the stores.[1]

On 5 December Leveson sailed for Castlehaven with the *Warspite*, *Defiance*, *Swiftsure*, *Merlyn*, a merchantman, and a carvel. He arrived next morning and at once attacked. Very hot fighting lasted several hours, the Spaniards being reinforced by bands of local Irish. The Admiral's report that he sank one Spanish ship and drove another ashore agrees with the Spanish account; but Mountjoy afterwards credited an Irish story, almost certainly false, that all but two of the Spaniards were finally sunk. The Spaniards claimed to have sunk an English ship, which is also untrue unless it were the merchantman or the little carvel. Yet it looks as though Leveson made a good story out of what was in fact a reverse, and that he was driven off. He admits that he had to endure a heavy pounding, his hulls and sails being repeatedly hit before the weather abated enough for him to warp out of the harbour—and he certainly left Spanish ships in it.[2]

The landing at Castlehaven raised the spirits of the Spaniards in Kinsale and those of O'Donnell. It also brought about the first

[1] C.S.P. Spanish, Vol. IV, pp. 692, 700.
[2] Carew Cal., Vol. IV, p. 190. Pacata Hibernia, p. 115. C.S.P. Spanish, Vol. IV, p. 700. History of Catholic Ireland, p. 142.

serious hostile action on the part of the local Irish in west Cork and Kerry. The almost simultaneous arrival of Tyrone encouraged their tendency to revolt or relapse. The castle at Castlehaven, commanding the harbour, was delivered to the Spaniards. Sir Fineen O'Driscoll, who had been a loyalist all his life, handed over to them two castles covering the entry to Baltimore. O'Sullivan Bere gave them Dunboy, on the north side of Bantry Bay. All these were garrisoned by Spanish troops, the magazine or base remaining at Castlehaven. The strength brought by Zubiaur is variously given, but does not appear to have exceeded 700.[1]

Tyrone had, as has been stated, dallied, either because of habitual hesitation or because of his embarrassments in Ulster. He did not start until the early part of November, at least six weeks after the landing of the Spaniards at Kinsale and indeed after O'Donnell had crossed the Shannon. Even then Tyrone's progress was a crawl. To encourage loyalists in the western part of the Pale to join him, he plundered and burnt their lands, but without winning them over. The first news that he was at hand reached Mountjoy on the evening of 6 December, the day on which he heard the English and Spanish artillery in action at Castlehaven. It is hard to estimate Tyrone's strength. About 6,500 for the combined forces, including some Munster allies and 200 Spaniards who had landed at Castlehaven, was a figure given subsequently. O'Sullivan Bere states that each of the Ulster leaders brought 3,000 men, to which would have to be added the Munstermen who joined them in Kinalmeaky, north-west of Kinsale.[2]

Now the crisis was come. On both sides there was heavy strain and cause for deep anxiety. Aguila was holding a wretched little town continually battered with cannon behind walls beginning to crumble. His troops, though fighting stoutly, had achieved no real success in numerous sallies. He had little but biscuit and some rice on which to feed them. The Irish showed no signs of relieving him or directly co-operating with him. In a letter dated 28 December (O.S. 17th) he reproached Tyrone and O'Donnell for not having closed upon Kinsale. The enemy, he said, were sick and weary, and could not man a third of their trenches. If the Irish would attack he would guarantee to give the besiegers enough to do on his side.[3]

Mountjoy was, indeed, in many respects worse off than the

---

[1] *Pacata Hibernia*, p. 224.
[2] *Carew Cal.*, Vol. IV, p. 189. *History of Catholic Ireland*, p. 144.
[3] *Pacata Hibernia*, p. 227.

Spaniards. He told the Privy Council in a letter of the 13th that since the arrival of Tyrone he had strengthened his camps and slackened his bombardment, since he dared not now attempt a storm with so powerful an enemy outside the walls and at his back. He asked for further reinforcements because his strength was melting. He had lost a number by death and had many more incapacitated by sickness. The drain of desertion was also serious. Men were fleeing to Cork, Youghal, and even Waterford and Wexford, from which by one means or another they got passages to England. He had posted police parties at these ports, and at Waterford alone they had rounded up 200 deserters whom they hoped to send back. For the sick he had provided a guest house in Cork, where they were given increased rations and could buy in the market from their 'lendings'. In the camp the officers were contributing £50 a week for comforts, including hot broth, as a result of which a number of men had recovered. Yet his 11,800 foot in list had dwindled to 6,595 men on their feet, not counting the sick, wounded, and deserters; and the only way the recaptured deserters or supplies could reach Kinsale was by water, since he was now cut off from the other ports. His horses were near starvation, and he was debating whether to order his cavalry to cut its way out. In a sense he, the besieger, was now besieged. With magnificent determination, he maintained the investment and kept on firing upon the walls, making big breaches in them. This might bring Tyrone and O'Donnell upon him, which was what he most desired; if not, the breaches might prove useful in themselves. In these few days Mountjoy reached the summit of his grandeur as a man and a soldier.[1]

Tyrone did not want to attack. He knew all too well the weakness of the Irish in open country. It appeared to him that the English could be worn out by a continuation of his present strategy until, at the worst, they would have to abandon the siege, and, at the best, they could be reduced to so low an ebb that they might be overwhelmed and annihilated. It offended his Fabian doctrine to risk such happy results by putting the issue prematurely to the test. But this reasoning did not take account of the situation or feelings of the Spaniards in Kinsale. They might find it impossible to hold out, and might even come to terms with the English if it appeared to them that they were being left in the lurch by their allies. The younger and higher-spirited O'Donnell urged him to maintain the honour of Irish arms, and this counsel eventually prevailed.

[1] Moryson, *An Itinerary*, Pt. II, pp. 170–5.

Messengers could still slip through the investing forces by night, and a simple plan was agreed upon. The Irish would advance to the attack at a designated point, and simultaneously the Spaniards would issue from Kinsale with all possible strength and fall upon the besiegers.[1]

Mountjoy was watchful. When, on 21 December, the Irish in force approached Spittle Hill from the north, he quickly mustered adequate strength to meet them; but they drew off under cover of darkness. Then treachery in the Irish camp gave him warning of the date on which the combined assault was to be delivered, a great advantage for a man facing odds of at least three to two. With Tyrone was Brian MacHugh Oge MacMahon, the unsuccessful candidate for the chieftaincy of Monaghan during the second vice-royalty of Fitzwilliam. This commander had run out of whiskey, and now, on 22 December, sent a boy to Captain William Taaffe, begging him to ask Carew, in whose service his eldest son had been a page in England, to send him a bottle for old time's sake. Carew sent it. Next day the same messenger brought Taaffe a letter, conveying his love to Carew, thanking him for the aquavitae, and bidding him stand upon his guard that night. MacMahon declared that he had been present at a council of war when it was resolved to assault the English camp before daybreak, the Spaniards having undertaken to sally forth in strength at the first alarm. Mountjoy promptly strengthened the guards and put the army in readiness. He further directed that at the setting of the moon the flying squadron, under the orders of Sir Henry Power, should take up a position west of the camp, close to the main guard of the cavalry.[2] After that he could only wait.

[1] Four Masters, Vol. VI, p. 2,283.   [2] *Pacata Hibernia*, p. 232.

CHAPTER XXII

THE VICTORY OF CHRISTMAS EVE

THE night of 23 December 1601 was dark, wild, and thunderous. Cavalrymen on outpost duty afterwards reported that the lightning flamed on lance-heads like lamps. Mountjoy, who was now in the habit of staying up all night and sleeping by day, had summoned Carew and Wingfield to a conference in his hut. Half an hour before dawn a trooper came to the door and called out to him: 'My Lord, it is time to arm; for the enemy is near unto the camp.' Immediately afterwards another man arrived from Sir Richard Graeme, who commanded the guard of horse that night, to report that he could see the glow of the matches of the Irish musketeers. This time the enemy came from the west. Mountjoy at once mounted. He first pushed forward Graeme's cavalry and the flying squadron of foot to a passage over boggy ground impassable by cavalry at any other point and commanded by artillery from Thomond's camp. He then stationed five regiments to hold the main camp (his own, Carew's, Lord Clanrickarde's, Lord Audley's, and Sir Richard Moryson's), and four to hold Thomond's (Lord Thomond's, Sir Richard Percy's, Sir Charles Wilmot's, and Sir Christopher St. Lawrence's). His first intention, in view of his inferiority in numbers, was to start the battle against the Irish on the defensive, and, having ridden out to examine the ground, he decided that the most favourable position would be the passage over the bog, which was already fortified. He ordered the Sergeant-major, Sir John Berkeley, to draw out the regiments of Sir Henry Follyot and Sir Oliver St. John and bring them over to this position. Their combined strength was probably not 600, and that of the flying squadron under Power under 500, so that he was matching less than 1,100 foot against over 5,000 Irish and leaving about 4,000 foot to face a Spanish force now reduced to about half that strength in fit men.

It was now broad daylight. While the English regiments of foot were moving into position the Irish were observed to fall back beyond a second stretch of boggy ground, likewise traversed by only a single sound passage. The whole conduct of Tyrone's army had been miserably inefficient, and it was paying the penalty which must be paid by any force whose commander does not know his own mind, disbelieves in his own plan, and cannot enforce obedience upon his subordinates. O'Donnell thought himself as good a man as O'Neill, and his men of Tyrconnell were jealous of the men of Tyrone. The two chieftains began with a wrangle about which contingent should lead the attack. The 'nobility of mind and pride of strength of both' prevented either from yielding. The long discussion delayed the start of the approach march and so made it impossible to launch the attack at the hour agreed upon with the Spaniards. To add to the trouble, O'Donnell missed his way in the dark, an extraordinary accident to befall an Irish force in friendly country, and further delayed the operation. The army finally advanced in three massive 'battles' in line: Tyrone and his Ulstermen, O'Donnell with Tyrconnell and the Connaughtmen, and a third consisting of Tyrrell's mercenaries and Munster contingents, with 200 Spaniards from Castlehaven under Captain Alonzo del Campo. The last-named, seeing the weakness of the English advancing to meet the attack, told Tyrone that he now had a golden opportunity to overthrow them and urged an instant assault. Tyrone, however, preferred to stand on the defensive and, as has been stated, drew back beyond a bog. It may have been only then that O'Donnell joined him.

Wingfield sent back a message to Mountjoy that in the course of this withdrawal the Irish had fallen into some confusion, and urgently demanded permission to attack. Clanrickarde then galloped up to add his entreaties that a charge should be launched. Mountjoy was not the man to balk a thrustful subordinate. He first asked men who knew the country whether there were in the vicinity any ground peculiarly suited for defence. He was told that there was none and that the country was 'a fair champagne'. He then sent Carew back with some of the horse, ordering him to take command of the forces in both camps and to watch for a sortie from Kinsale. Then he directed Wingfield to cross the passage and gave him full liberty to act at his discretion. Power followed with the flying squadron.

The horse pushed on for the better part of a mile till it stood facing the Irish in their new position, and Power quickly joined it. The Irish threw out a number of musketeers to dispute the causeway over the second bog, behind which the Irish were now posted. Wingfield ordered out 100 musketeers to oppose them, under the command of an expert in the tactics of skirmishing, Lieutenant Cowel, who wore a red cap so that his troops should always be enabled to locate him. The English shot were first of all driven back, but on being reinforced advanced again to the attack, drove back the Irish, and cleared the causeway. Wingfield secured it with infantry and passed over with Clanrickarde, Graeme, Taaffe, and Fleming, with their horse. Mountjoy, who had ridden up on to a hill to obtain a long view, now ordered Sir Henry Danvers to support Wingfield with the Lord Deputy's and Lord President's regiments of horse, which he had hitherto kept in reserve, and directed Berkeley to lead forward the two regiments of foot at top speed.

Meanwhile, Wingfield with the horse at his disposal launched a charge on the 'battle' commanded by Tyrone, estimated at 1,800 strong. For cavalry to charge home against unbroken pikemen was madness, especially when the infantry outnumbered the horse by six or seven to one; but against troops who might prove shaky it was worth while to bluff, in the hope that the enemy would waver and open a way through the forest of his pikes. This time, however, the Irish pikemen stood firm. Using tactics in which cavalry were then trained, Wingfield wheeled round at the last moment and drew off, the Irish greeting this withdrawal with a yell of triumph. At this moment the reinforcements of cavalry, led by Sir Henry Danvers, and the two regiments of foot, led by Berkeley, reached the scene of action. Wingfield drew up Mountjoy's and Carew's horse beside his original force. He, with Clanrickarde and Danvers, put himself at the head of the whole body of cavalry, still only 400 strong, and charged once again, this time directing himself not only against the same Irish 'battle' but against the enemy's horse as well, his front being now broad enough to cover the two. Power's flying squadron supported him closely. This time he achieved an amazing success. The Irish horse immediately broke and fled. The Irish infantry, discouraged at the sight, and, according to one account, opening its ranks to let some of the fleeing horse-men through, was immediately afterwards itself pierced and broken. It fled in confusion, pursued by the cavalry, hacking and hewing.

The vanguard of the Irish army under Tyrrell meanwhile stood firm on the right flank. Mountjoy had drawn up part of his foot within musket-shot of it. Observing that it began to close on the centre as if to support Tyrone's runaways, he sent a company to attack it in flank, whereupon it moved off, still in close order, and took up a position on a neighbouring hillock. The third Irish formation, the rear guard, was now also in flight, and all the English cavalry was in pursuit.[1]

There remained to account for Tyrrell's vanguard, reputedly composed of the best Irish troops and including the little Spanish contingent. It did not take long to deal with this force, which had already fallen into disorder. Soon after the launch of the attack the Irish melted away, leaving del Campo's 200 standing alone. The Spaniards redeemed their reputation for steadiness and fought until three-fourths of them had been killed. The commander, two captains, and forty-seven other ranks finally surrendered.

The cavalry horses had suffered so severely from lack of forage that the pursuit could not be pressed for more than a mile and a half; otherwise the loss of the Irish might have been very much heavier. As it was, the English claim that 1,200 bodies were left upon the field. The Four Masters state that the loss was not great, but an Irishman afterwards gave Mountjoy the names of fourteen captains killed and reported that of the 300 MacDonald Redshanks who had accompanied Tyrone to Munster only thirty-one got away alive. In any case, the remains of the Irish army broke up, each section making for its own home at top speed. The northward flight of Tyrone's men was itself a disaster. The route was left littered with the bodies of men and horses, and some of those whose houses and goods had been burnt in the advance of the Ulstermen now enjoyed the sweet pleasure of revenge upon them in their retreat, throwing them into bogholes and treading them down. O'Donnell decided to go to Spain and seek further aid from Philip III. He handed over command of his contingent to his brother Rory, who led it back through Connaught, and himself went aboard a Spanish ship and sailed from Castlehaven.

The English losses were trifling. One officer was killed, Graeme's cornet. Sir Henry Danvers, Sir William Godolphin, and Captain Henry Crofts, the Scout-master, were slightly wounded, together with some half a dozen soldiers. Many horses were, however, killed in an action fought mainly by the cavalry. Clanrickarde had been foremost in the fight, killing some twenty men with his own hand and shouting to the troops to spare no rebels. His clothing was pierced by bullets and pikes, but he came off without a wound.

---

[1] In armies of the period three formations drawn up in line would continue to be called 'vanguard', 'battle', and 'rear guard' or 'rear'.

After the battle, having given thanks for the victory, Mountjoy knighted him amid the dead bodies.[1]

As time slipped by without the Irish launching their attack as planned, Aguila in Kinsale had concluded that for one reason or another they had called off the operation. He therefore did not stir, and indeed he might not have accomplished anything of note if he had, since Mountjoy had heavily insured against a successful sortie by leaving superior numbers to face it. On his return to the camp, Mountjoy ordered a volley to be fired in celebration of the victory. The Spaniards, thinking that Tyrone was at last assaulting, issued forth from the town; but, finding themselves opposed by the full strength of the English, no Irish in sight, and above all seeing captured Spanish colours waved in triumph by the besiegers, they drew back. On Christmas Day they sallied out again, without any success. Again at 9 p.m. they came out in strength in an endeavour to capture a new trench begun by the English, and maintained the fight for two hours. On the night of the 26th they sallied once more from the west gate and this time, advancing most determinedly, overran the trench, killing or wounding a number of its occupants. They were, however, held up by the fire of a fort in rear, and after that drew back into the town.[2]

Though the relieving army was dispersed, the Spaniards were still strong in Kinsale. Mountjoy was prepared to storm the place if necessary, but he feared that the loss would be very heavy. In early November he had reminded Cecil that Sir John Norris had lost nearly 1,500 men in an attack on a fortress in Brittany, held by about 200 Spaniards. A walled town held by good troops was likely to break the army that assaulted it, even if the storm were successfully carried out. The English troops were exhausted by the winter siege, and sickness continued to rage. It was possible that a further Spanish expedition was even now on the way, and he urged that a powerful fleet should be maintained upon the coast. It can therefore be well imagined that he was not in unbending mood when, on the last day of the year, Aguila offered a parley, sending his drum-major with a letter and suggesting that an English officer should come into Kinsale to negotiate with him, he for his part sending to Mountjoy a Spanish officer of similar rank, as pledge for the envoy's safety.

[1] C.S.P. Ireland, Vol. CCIX, 256. Moryson, An Itinerary, Pt. II, pp. 170–8. Pacata Hibernia, pp. 232–5. Four Masters, Vol. VI, p. 2,283. O'Clery, Life of O'Donnell, p. 313. History of Catholic Ireland, pp. 144–7.

[2] Moryson, An Itinerary, Pt. II, p. 179.

Mountjoy selected his friend Godolphin to go, and Aguila sent to the English camp Pedro Enriquez.

Aguila informed Godolphin that he had found the Lord Deputy an honourable foe, if a bitter one. His Irish allies, on the other hand, appeared to him weak and barbarous, if not perfidious. He was now prepared to make terms which might be profitable to England, with the least prejudice to the Crown of Spain, by delivering Kinsale and the other places held by the Spaniards. He demanded, however, that the force should be allowed to depart on honourable conditions, befitting men who were prepared to bury themselves rather than submit to any that were not. Godolphin brought this message to Mountjoy, who sent him back to say that he was ready to entertain the offer, but that the terms must take into account the advantage already gained by the English.

Despite these sentiments on both sides, agreement was not easily reached. Mountjoy began by demanding that the Spaniards should leave behind them their treasure and artillery, as well as the Queen's natural subjects, to be disposed of at Her Majesty's pleasure. This the Spaniard flatly refused, as beneath his honour. He claimed that he had over 2,000 fit men, mostly veteran troops, in the garrison; they were comfortably and warmly housed, whereas the besiegers were in misery. He did not believe that Mountjoy would succeed in storming the town, but even if he did that would not put the other harbours into his hands, and the King of Spain would send reinforcements to them. As for himself, he had been sent by the King his master to assist the Condes O'Neill and O'Donnell, who were to join him within a few days. He had long awaited them, holding off the while the viceroy's army. When they had come at last he had seen them broken by a handful of men and blown asunder: O'Donnell into Spain, O'Neill to the furthest north. Now there were no Condes *in rerum natura*. He considered himself relieved of his mission.

Mountjoy and his Council decided to agree to the Spanish terms. The greatest inducement was to his mind the prospect of the surrender of the forts commanding the other three harbours. At the same time his own situation was worse than even Aguila guessed. The Queen's ships would shortly have had to leave the harbour for want of provisions. He had only six days' food and could mount only one battery, five of his guns being out of action; besides which, he was short of powder.

Here it may be revealed that one unknown Spaniard at all events attributed to Castlehaven and 'Valentimor', as he wrote Baltimore, a potential importance even greater than that ascribed to them by Mountjoy. An elaborate appreciation was drawn up in March 1602 about the results to be expected from the fortification of the two harbours as a Spanish base in Ireland. The writer begins with a religious consideration, that such a base would enable the Faith to be preserved throughout Munster and the sacraments to be freely administered. Then he comes to more mundane affairs.

England would be in the first instance compelled to strengthen the forces maintained in the country, and the greater the number sent to Ireland the less the damage that the English could do elsewhere. Spain would not have to consider a defensive war that year, because if the base were established about April English forces would be concentrated in Ireland and would conclude that the aim was to admit the Spanish fleet then fitting out to that country. Allowing six weeks for the fortification to be carried out and for the Queen of England to assemble a large army in Ireland, the Spanish fleet should then sail for England, which would thus lie open to attack. When this took place, it was to be supposed that the greater part of the English force would be withdrawn from Ireland. Then Ireland could easily be freed by the Irish themselves, with some aid from the Spaniards in the Castlehaven-Baltimore base. It is an ingenious though hardly a practical scheme, which if successful would indeed have liberated Ireland, but would also have concentrated the greater part of the resources of England against the Spanish expedition which was to land in that country.

Holding this bridgehead, the Catholic King would be able to recruit infantry in Ireland; Aguila, it was pointed out, had had 200 Irish under his orders and they had behaved to his entire satisfaction throughout the siege of Kinsale. The base would provide valuable intelligence from England and Scotland. A dozen warships could be stationed at it, and they might establish in it an advanced store and depot for the fleet carrying out the invasion of England. In fact, thought this invincible optimist, the squadron would require to be supplied with food only, pay and other expenses being made a charge upon the booty which it would capture.

The base would in part pay its way. Irish, English, and Flemish ships, carrying the produce of their countries, might be admitted to the harbours, while refused direct access to Spanish ports, and the King would be able to provide funds for the base out of payment for salt, wine, oil, raisins, figs, sugar, and spices, which would be transported to it and bought by the owners of the foreign ships.

'These ports', the writer concluded, 'would shelter any fleet or ships of His Majesty driven out of their course by storms or other accidents, as might happen to a fleet sailing from Spain to England, or sailing to or from Flanders; and if a fleet sailed this year from Spain to the Channel and could not secure its objective on the coast, it could still put into these ports and undertake the conquest of all Ireland, so that all the cost of the expedition would not be lost.'[1]

It requires no great knowledge of the principles of strategy to discover the factor left out in this appreciation. It is command of the sea. It would have been impossible to maintain such a base against an English blockade, and to break this the full power of the English naval forces would have had to be broken also. Yet there was a fruitful germ in the conception. A base close to a hostile power provides the best means of intercepting its shipping. A generation earlier the able Spanish naval commander and shipbuilder, Pero Meñiendez de Avila, had—it is true at a time when English naval power was not as formidable as in 1602—put forward a plan to seize the Scilly Isles, establish a base there, and afterwards open communications with disaffected Irish with a view to securing a port or ports in their country. Like the author of the scheme just quoted, Meñiendez advocated keeping on the station a special squadron; in his case it was to consist of from fifteen to twenty of the fast, small galleons of his own design which had made such a name for themselves.[2]

On 2 January 1602 articles of surrender were drawn up in English, Spanish, Latin, and Italian, Fynes Moryson acting as translator. Kinsale, Castlehaven, Baltimore, and Berehaven were to be handed over. The Spanish forces were to be shipped to Spain, in one echelon if possible, if not in two. Aguila pledged himself that they should not bear arms against the Queen, even if reinforcements should arrive, until they reached Spanish soil. They were permitted to take with them their colours, artillery, money, and other possessions. If contrary winds drove them into any English or Irish harbour, they were to be treated as friends and allowed to buy provisions. There was to be a truce at sea during the passage home. Aguila himself was to stay in a place designated by the Lord Deputy, and if two shipments were required to send the troops home he would await the second.[1]

[1] Arch. Gen. de Simancas, L.2847.
[2] Corbett, *Drake and the Tudor Navy*, Vol. I, p. 204.
[3] Moryson, *An Itinerary*, Pt. II, p. 184.

That afternoon Aguila came out and dined with Mountjoy. Next day Carew, Leveson, and Godolphin dined with Aguila in Kinsale to make arrangements about the English shipping required to carry the force home and the victuals, for which the Spaniards were to pay ready money. Carew brought out three captains, who were to remain in English hands until the shipping returned from Spain. One of these was Pedro Morijon, whose name greatly interested Fynes Moryson. The Spanish hostage afterwards accompanied Mountjoy to Dublin, and Fynes, in talk with him on the road, found that he was descended from an English gentleman who had followed the Emperor Charles V in his wars and had been granted an estate in Spain.

On 4 January a Spanish ship was seen 'hovering' off the Old Head of Kinsale. Mountjoy sent out a boat with a message that he and the Spanish commander were now good friends and that the ship might safely enter the harbour. The captain, however, on receiving this information, pulled the boat and its crew aboard and made off. Carew, while regretting that these men had fallen into Spanish hands, comforted himself, in telling the tale, with the belief that the messages had had a good effect. The Spaniards had learnt of the defeat of the Irish army, but their first news of the surrender of Kinsale came from this ship, and Carew professed to have learnt that it slackened their preparations for the dispatch of reinforcements.[1]

On 9 January Mountjoy rode with Aguila and some of the senior Spanish officers to Cork, the bulk of the Spanish force remaining at Kinsale. On the following day he issued orders for the dispersal of the army into winter quarters. He also directed Captains Roger Harvey and George Flower, with several companies, to go by sea and take over the castles at Castlehaven, Baltimore, and Berehaven from the Spaniards. This part of his programme was, however, long delayed, principally by westerly winds, so that the first castle, at Castlehaven, was not occupied by Harvey until 12 February. Mountjoy was accepting a certain risk, in case another Spanish expedition should arrive before the garrison of Kinsale had been repatriated and while it still retained its arms. Writing to his friend Carew in February, Cecil expressed anxiety on this point. Supposing another Spanish force landed, would the fact that Don Juan and other officers were hostages in Cork restrain the Spaniards at Kinsale from aiding it? Might not the commander of the second force come with orders to disavow the unsuccessful commander and leave him

[1] *Pacata Hibernia*, p. 248.

to his fate? Cecil was not a scrupulous man; neither was his correspondent. The former first hinted strongly that the pledge to the Spaniards should be broken and then assumed arrangements had been made to secure the Kinsale force 'so suddenly (though with breach of some formal article) as no new descent shall make these spiders dare to crawl'. English honour was not put to the test, since this letter was not received until after the Spaniards had all reached Coruña.[1]

Mountjoy and Carew practised upon Aguila one piece of trickery which can be defended in the circumstances. About 10 February they learnt that a Spanish pinnace had arrived in west Munster, and that a courier was coming overland to Cork with letters for the Spanish commander. They had the man waylaid on the road, robbed of his packet, and then released. When the messenger reached Aguila he made a protest to Mountjoy, but the latter replied that the documents must have been stolen by deserters and offered a reward for their recovery. The letters were from the King and others. News had been received of the Irish disaster, but Aguila was enjoined to hold out and await reinforcements and supplies, which had actually been shipped, though the number of men mentioned was small. Before he departed Aguila was shown copies of these messages, which were said to have been recovered.[2]

Negotiations with Tyrone were begun. In Kinsale with the Spaniards was a certain Richard Owen who, like other Irishmen serving with their forces, was exempted from English vengeance by the terms on which Aguila had honourably insisted. Owen had assisted the renegade Sir William Stanley to hand Deventer over to the Spaniards, had been with Tyrone for the past three years, had conducted his son to Spain, and had returned to Ireland with the expedition. He stated that Tyrone, the morning after the defeat, had directed him to repair to the Lord Deputy and report that he was 'willing and desirous to become a subject'. Owen was given leave to make his way to Ulster and came back a month later, on 4 February. He brought a message from Tyrone, who expressed regret that he had caused so much blood to be shed and his country to be ruined and said that he would be glad to be received into the Queen's mercy. His grief and humility were, says Carew, 'farced' with exorbitant conditions, but Mountjoy considered it worth while to continue negotiations, if only because they were likely to

---

[1] *Pacata Hibernia*, p. 249. *Carew Cal.*, Vol. IV, p. 215.
[2] *Pacata Hibernia*, pp. 252–63.

exercise an effect on rebels of inferior standing. He therefore sent Captain George Blount to him with a guarded message that he might be received to mercy, but on strict terms. Though nothing came of this correspondence, it was significant of the state to which Tyrone had fallen and of his readiness to seek a settlement when affairs went wrong. He had done so in the past, but now he was freed from the influence of his former ally, Hugh O'Donnell, always in favour of fighting, and the latter's brother and successor as commander of the men of Tyrconnell and Connaught was a milder and less resolute man.[1]

When Captain Roger Harvey reached Castlehaven on 10 February he was hospitably entertained by the Spanish commander, Pedro Lopez de Soto. He learnt that the O'Driscolls had recently by a ruse obtained an entry into the castle and seized it. The Spaniards were actually undermining it to retake it from their former allies, but on sight of the English ships the Irish surrendered it to de Soto on condition that they might depart in safety. Leaving his brother Gawen in command, Harvey, accompanied by de Soto, then sailed to Baltimore, where the two castles were handed over to him on 26 February. On 2 March the Spanish garrisons were shipped to Spain. From Baltimore Captain George Flower sailed for Berehaven with two companies, but was driven back by contrary winds and lost no less than fifty soldiers from sickness. So Dunboy Castle was not recovered, and remained to be a thorn in the flesh of Carew in his final pacification of Munster, as will presently be related.[2]

In his talks with Mountjoy Aguila broached the subject of the possibility of peace between England and Spain, but the Lord Deputy, while reporting what he said, felt himself constrained to reply only in general terms. At the same time conversations of the greatest interest took place between Roger Harvey and de Soto, who became warm friends during the three weeks of their intercourse. The Spaniard frankly acknowledged the strain imposed upon his sovereign by the war with Elizabeth and suggested that there was no cause why it should continue. He promised Harvey a passport for himself or a nominee to visit Spain. A junior officer was eventually sent, with orders to acquaint the Spaniards with the contents of an intercepted letter from O'Donnell in which he admitted that he was deceiving the Spaniards about the state of affairs in Ireland in order to induce them to send another expedition. The emissary did not in fact return until after the death of Elizabeth,

---

[1] *Pacata Hibernia*, pp. 254–8.   [2] *Pacata Hibernia*, p. 266.

but these exchanges are symptomatic of a desire for peace in both countries, a desire speedily fulfilled after the accession of James I. Harvey, apparently a brilliant young man, who was Carew's kinsman and treated by him as a son, but was in the black books of Mountjoy over a matter of discipline, died before the war was over, to the deep grief of the Lord President, who thought that his death was due to a broken heart.[1]

On 20 February the first Spanish contingent, twenty captains and 1,374 others, sailed from Kinsale. On their arrival at Coruña the English crews were well treated, and it was observed that several vessels lying in the port were shortly afterwards unloaded instead of sailing for Ireland. On 8 March, the second contingent being embarked and the wind being favourable, Don Juan went aboard. The wind, however, changed again, so that the fleet could not sail until the 16th. Mountjoy did not await its departure. Eager to be back in Dublin, he set out on 9 March. The number of Spaniards repatriated was about 3,500, not including 200 prisoners already sent to England. The deaths in the two contingents must have numbered about 800, heavy enough loss, but in lesser proportion than in the English army. Mountjoy's troops continued to be ravaged by sickness. A 'kind of plague' developed, probably a very violent type of influenza, from which there died such great numbers that the final toll amounted to several thousand. To replenish the ranks, 2,000 reinforcements were dispatched, and on reaching Waterford Mountjoy found that five good companies had already arrived at that port, together with food and munitions.[2]

Aguila did not fare well in his native land. To begin with, no charge was made against him; in fact, it was considered that the terms he had got represented a master-stroke on his part. In this period he wrote a friendly letter to Carew, sending him a present of wine, oranges, and lemons. This arrived when Carew was at the siege of Dunboy and by mistake was forwarded to the Lord Deputy in Dublin. Mountjoy, in happy mood, wrote a jocular letter to Carew telling him that he intended to stick to the goods until the title had been decided. A little later, finding that the fruit was rotten and the wine not all it should have been, he moralized on his loss in a passage which might almost have come from a Shakesperian comedy: 'Once before I had a ship, and victualled her out in the laudable traffic of piracy, and lost all my charge, and in the end my

[1] Moryson, *An Itinerary*, Pt. II, p. 205. *Pacata Hibernia*, pp. 274-8, 340-8.
[2] Moryson, *An Itinerary*, pp. 198, 203.

ship; which I took to be God's will to discourage me in seeking to thrive by other men's goods. And since this last cozenage doth thrive so evil with me I will from henceforth forswear all dishonesty.' Carew, though not receiving Aguila's present, sent him in return the best that Ireland afforded, an ambling horse. If Irish horses were only second-rate for the purposes of war, the trained hacks were pleasant rides and much sought after. But Aguila, like Carew, did not receive the gift. On the plaint of the Irish, he had been placed under house arrest, and shortly afterwards he died.[1]

The failure in co-operation between Irish and Spaniards at Kinsale had created bitterness. The foregoing narrative has shown that the Irish were the more to blame, but they laid the responsibility at the door of the Spaniards, as some Irish historians have continued to do. Unfortunately for Aguila, O'Donnell for a time enjoyed great prestige in Spain. Soon after his arrival he had an audience of Philip III, who promised that reinforcements should be sent to Ireland. The King doubtless meant what he said at the time, but after hearing of the surrender of his troops began to change his mind. O'Donnell had been bidden to return to Coruña, and there the unhappy man waited through the spring and summer for the expedition which was never mustered. At last, after being frequently importuned, the King granted him another audience at Valladolid. On his way thither he was taken ill at Simancas, and, sixteen days later, on 10 September (N.S.), he died. He was buried with the highest honours in the chapter of the Monastery of St. Francis at Valladolid. Carew, who knew that an Irishman had gone to Spain with the intention of killing him, thought that he had been poisoned, but this is highly unlikely.

Hugh Roe O'Donnell had not completed his thirtieth year; but he had made for himself an imperishable name. It was said of him that he never suffered wrong, reverse, or insult without taking immediate vengeance, and that he was 'a warlike, predatory, aggressive plunderer of others' territories'. On the other hand, he was a dove in meekness and gentleness to all who did not oppose him—which is, of course, not an altogether difficult standard to attain, but not a common one for a Celtic prince. His morals were pure, an even rarer virtue. In person he was of middle height, with the ruddy hair and skin that gave him his sobriquet, and wonderfully handsome. In speech he was eloquent, and his voice was like

[1] *Carew Cal.*, Vol. IV, p. 248. *C.S.P. Venetian*, Vol. IX, p. 496. *Pacata Hibernia*, p. 326.

the music of a silver trumpet. It is not a wonder that he should have been the idol of the people of Tyrconnell. He was a remarkable young man, with the virtues as well as the defects of his kind sharply accentuated, the fine flower of a society which virtually perished with him.[1]

From Waterford Carew accompanied Mountjoy as far as Kilkenny, where they were entertained by Ormonde. Both of them were smitten by the prevalent fever. Mountjoy was determined to get back to Dublin, but had to travel in a horse-litter. Carew had to take to bed at a house only three miles from Kilkenny, but struggled on next day and reached Cork by easy stages. The delicate Mountjoy, worn out by his exertions, kept his bed for some weeks after reaching Dublin.[2]

The victory at Kinsale is an event of very great moment, one of the greatest military achievements of the reign of Elizabeth. It has already been suggested that, in a sense, it marked the end of the old Celtic culture in Ireland. For the Queen and England it removed a deadly peril. Irish and Spaniards had lost what had been for both a golden opportunity. This was due in part to their mismanagement and in the case of the former to their shameful panic. Yet they had been outplanned and outdared as well as outfought. If we compare the way in which England met this situation with the delays and muddles of earlier days, we shall conclude that the administrative improvement had been enormous. Then the skill of Carew in siege warfare, the enterprise and dash of Wingfield and Clanrickarde at the head of the cavalry, the steadiness and endurance of the infantrymen meeting the sorties of some of the best-trained troops in Europe were powerful factors in the great triumph. That which clinched the success was the able generalship, the masterly handling of the reserves during the siege, the calm and balanced judgement, and the iron determination of the leader, the Queen's Deputy.

Occasionally an effort is made to exalt Carew above Mountjoy and allot to him the chief part. The evidence is all to the contrary, but some may have been led astray by Carew's assertions and hints that he was the soul of the army. His services were outstanding, but he shows himself at this period, as a modern commentator has observed, 'small-minded and self-seeking, envious of the success of a man much younger and incomparably greater than himself'.[3]

---

[1] O'Clery, *Life of O'Donnell*, pp. 323–7.
[2] Moryson, *An Itinerary*, Pt. II, p. 207. *Pacata Hibernia*, p. 280.
[3] *C.S.P. Ireland*, 1601–3, Preface, p. xii.

Mountjoy entered upon this dangerous campaign with the serenity of mind which is one of the first virtues in a commander. Writing to Cecil, after painting the worst possibilities, he declared that he would not hide his confidence of being able to beat the Spanish Dons as he had beaten the Irish Macs and O's. He maintained an admirable balance throughout. Every decision of the smallest importance was his, and his was the full responsibility. If, under the beating rain that flooded his trenches, with his men going sick by the thousand and dying by the hundred, with supplies running out and his horses weak from want of food, with a defiant Spanish army behind the walls to his front and a large Irish army ready, at the time and place chosen by itself, to attack him in the rear, he had raised the siege of Kinsale, which to many would have seemed an act of prudence, he might instead have brought upon his head and upon England a great disaster. His good nerves and reasoned temerity preserved him from disaster and carried him to victory.

CHAPTER XXIII

EXPLOITATION OF VICTORY

ON quitting Munster, Mountjoy left for the prosecution of the war in that province under Carew's orders a force of 325 horse and 4,400 foot in list, which for active service did not number more than about half that strength. A strong body of rebels remained to be dealt with, especially in west Cork and Kerry and above all on the peninsula between the Kenmare river and Bantry Bay. The delay in sending troops from Baltimore to take over Dunboy Castle, overlooking Berehaven, had had unfortunate results. Donnell O'Sullivan Bere, who had free access to his own castle, surprised the Spanish garrison and sent it to Baltimore, keeping in his hands the captain and four or five gunners, whom he hoped to induce to take part in its defence. He wrote to the King of Spain on 20 February (N.S.) to explain his action by the not unreasonable plea that he had delivered the place to the Spaniards for the purpose of the war against England and had every right to take it back now that he knew the Spaniards were about to surrender it. Aguila, in Cork, felt himself deeply affronted by this Irish *coup* and offered to go to Berehaven with his own troops from Kinsale to recover the castle and the Spanish guns, but Mountjoy and Carew, anxious to see his heels, told him not to worry about the matter. They would, they said, deal with Dunboy when he was gone.[1]

Before escorting the Lord Deputy to Kilkenny, Carew directed the Earl of Thomond to march into Carbery with 1,200 foot and fifty horse to burn the corn and take the cattle, and to reconnoitre Dunboy. Thomond moved to Bantry Abbey, and there learnt that O'Sullivan Bere was busily adding to the fortifications of Dunboy, facing the barbican wall with sods to a depth of 18 feet for defence against artillery. He worked with the advice of a Spaniard and an Italian, but it was not intelligent advice. In the first place, the earth covered the slits in the barbican wall, so that the garrison could not fire through them; in the second, if the castle above the barbican wall were knocked down into the space between—only a few feet— a storming party would be able to climb the turf slope and enter the

[1] *Pacata Hibernia*, p. 269.

breech. Thomond saw that at all events the capture of Dunboy would be a major operation. Leaving a force of 700 men on Whiddy Island in Bantry Bay, he returned to Cork. Carew determined to take Dunboy at all costs, and mustered all the field forces in the province except for the regiment under Sir Charles Wilmot, who was then acting against the rebels in Kerry. He thought it absolutely necessary to reduce this castle, still nominally held for the King of Spain, and that its capture or destruction might induce the Spaniards to give up the project of sending a new expedition, if they still entertained it. Friends and advisers in Ireland and England urged caution upon him lest he should incur a serious setback. Old Ormonde, who knew all this country as if it had been the back of his hand, wrote to dissuade him from the attempt. Carew took no heed of the warnings.[1]

On 23 April 1602 he marched out from Cork. On the way to his objective he inspected the castles and garrisons at Castlehaven and Baltimore, receiving supplies by sea in the latter harbour. On the 30th he reached Dunnemark—which he takes pleasure in calling Carew Castle in memory of distant ancestors who built it—near Bantry Abbey. There he awaited his artillery and munitions for the siege and a supply of food, and ordered Sir Charles Wilmot to join him.

Wilmot, one of the most vigorous of the colonels then serving in Ireland and who knew Kerry thoroughly, had enjoyed great success. He had marched right up to the Shannon and left a garrison in the old castle at Carrigafoyle, though it was now more or less a ruin. Then he had turned south, crossing the Cashen—where he had to swim his horses—so quickly that the intention of the rebels to oppose him was frustrated. The strong castle of Lixnaw had been surrendered to him; the Dingle peninsula had been cleared; the Knight of Kerry had been defeated in a desperate little combat near Castlemaine and had soon afterwards surrendered on terms. Now Carew could safely call Wilmot in to him, knowing that no enemy of any account remained in his rear. Wilmot, who had the appointment of Governor of Kerry, bore the reputation of being a less hard man than most of his contemporaries among the English commanders, and this served him well. Donnell MacCarthy, illegitimate son of the late Earl of Clancarty and so brother-in-law to Florence, who had lately been in revolt, but only because the English cause

---

[1] *Pacata Hibernia*, pp. 287–92. *Carew Cal.*, Vol. IV, p. 239. Four Masters, Vol. VI, p. 2,307.

had appeared hopeless, came to Sir Charles without protection, bringing with him a vast herd of cattle, sheep, and horses. The Governor, 'hereby perceiving his loyal simplicity', let him go free and gave him such countenance as he could. Wilmot also had some dealings with William Burke, who stood at the head of a body of Connaught mercenaries. Burke stated that he would never betray the lives of any of his associates, but that he would undertake to lay hands on all the cattle in the Desmond country and hand over half to the garrison, provided that he were allowed to depart into Connaught with the rest. This last negotiation, however, bore no fruit immediately.[1]

Wilmot, in order to join Carew, had to march by Killarney and over Mangerton, described as 'a most hideous and uncouth mountain', and expected to have to fight his way, since the track had been fortified by the enemy. At the last moment, however, the courage of the rebels failed them and the junction of the two forces was accomplished without a blow. On the same day, 11 May, ships with food and munitions arrived from Cork, and on the 12th a hoy came in with the cannon.

Carew now held a council of war, at which it was decided that the overland passage to Berehaven, through mountainous and boggy country, was impracticable for transport and would in any case involve serious loss in the defiles held by the enemy. The force would have to be ferried across Bantry Bay. About 1,000 men might be encountered, the most formidable being a body of 500 bonaghts under Tyrrell, who were maintained by Donnell O'Sullivan Bere and were living on his creaghts. Tyrrell, who was beginning to see the red light, opened negotiations with Thomond, as an Irishman easier to deal with than Carew himself, but did not come to the rendezvous. Throughout the latter part of May the force was held in camp by foul weather, much to the disgust of Carew, who wrote to Mountjoy that the country of Bere was full of witches.[2]

On 31 May fine weather returned. The army broke camp, leaving the many sick under a guard on Whiddy Island, and marched down the southern shore of Bantry Bay towards Sheep Head to a point opposite Bere Island, some four miles across the water. Thomond's regiment was carried over to the island without opposition next day, and the remainder followed. The Constable of Dunboy Castle, Richard MacGeoghegan, came across and had an interview with Thomond. The Earl urged him to take his last

---

[1] *Pacata Hibernia*, pp. 292–8.

[2] *Carew Cal.*, Vol. IV, pp. 239, 242. *Pacata Hibernia*, pp. 299–301.

chance to surrender on terms, but he replied that he had come only out of the affection which he entertained towards him to dissuade him from crossing. 'I know,' said he, 'you must land at yonder sandy bay, where before your coming the place will be so trenched and gabioned as you must run upon assured death.' MacGeohegan was rowed back, nothing having come of the talks except that a piece of useful information had been acquired by Carew.

That wily man carefully reconnoitred the coast in a pinnace. He saw that the sandy bay in front of the castle was indeed entrenched. He also observed another point where a landing was feasible, and that this was concealed from the sandy bay by high ground. He now landed two guns and his two leading regiments on the little island of Dinish, between the Bere Island and the mainland, with orders to keep the defenders of the sandy bay well occupied by their fire and make it appear that a landing was to be carried out from this point. Next the shipping returned and embarked two more regiments. The skippers feinted to land them also on Dinish, but carried on past it and landed them on the mainland on the beach selected by Carew. The Irish failed to reach the scene until the landing force was established, and they were then driven off with heavy loss. All this was pretty tactics.[1]

The arrival in the Kenmare river of a Spanish ship with munitions, several thousands of pounds in gold, and carrying a priest named Owen MacEgan, described as the Vicar Apostolic, heartened the garrison of Dunboy. In response to extravagant promises of speedy and powerful aid from Spain, these deluded men determined to hold out to the last. Carew was confident that the last would not be long. On 12 June a force of 160 foot, including a few friendly Irish, captured Dursey Island, at the toe of the peninsula, where the enemy had intended to make his last stand if he lost Dunboy. The unfortunate garrison were executed in the usual way. By the 16th the work of entrenchment and the building of platforms for the guns was finished. About dawn next morning a demi-cannon, two culverins, and a demi-culverin opened fire. Within four hours one turret, in which a falcon had been mounted, collapsed, burying most of its defenders. A messenger came out, offering to surrender the place if the garrison might depart with their arms, but the Irish kept up their fire all the time. Carew hanged the messenger. Soon the breach was practicable and the storming party went forward. A fierce and bloody fight followed. The defenders fired into the

[1] *Pacata Hibernia*, pp. 303-5.

thick of the assaulting troops from a tower which flanked the breach until a shot killed their gunner. From above they dropped cannon balls and stones. Finally, the garrison were driven into the cellars and the remainder of the castle was captured. Again the defenders offered to surrender on promise of their lives, but the plea was refused. A few who tried to escape by water were killed from boats which Carew had kept manned all the time.

Next morning twenty-three surrendered unconditionally. Mac-Geohegan having been seriously wounded, Thomas Taylor, a man of English birth, was chosen as his successor. Carew now began a new bombardment of the vault in order to bury the defenders in the ruins, but they soon compelled Taylor to surrender. When the English officers went in to bring them out, MacGeohegan, desperately wounded though he was, contrived to get to his feet and staggered towards an open barrel of powder with a lighted candle in his hand. Captain Power seized him and held him in his arms, intending to take him prisoner, but the soldiers stabbed him to death. Taylor and the rest, about forty-two in number, were then brought out. Their pluck might well have earned them some mercy from Carew, but he accorded them none. Fifty-eight were executed in the market-place of the camp. Fifteen were respited in case they should afford some acceptable service, but eventually met the same fate. What was left of the castle was destroyed with the Spanish gunpowder provided for its defence.

The storm of Dunboy Castle was the hardest-fought affair of its kind in the reign of Elizabeth in Ireland. 'So obstinate and resolved a defence had not been seen within this kingdom.' The garrison had numbered 143 souls; every man was either killed in battle, buried in the ruins, or executed afterwards. O'Sullivan Bere asserts that the defenders both of Dunboy and Dursey Island were promised mercy, but the more reliable Four Masters make no such allegation.

The English losses are not given exactly, but appear to have numbered at least eighty killed and wounded, a vivid contrast to the dozen or so casualties of the battle of Kinsale. Carew would not have stormed the place had he not felt himself pressed for time, in view of the possibility of another Spanish landing, in which he still believed. The defeat at Kinsale had prevented the rebellion in Munster from remaining a danger, except in such a case. The loss of Dunboy broke its back.[1]

[1] *Pacata Hibernia*, pp. 306–20. Four Masters, Vol. VI, p. 2,309. *History of Catholic Ireland*, pp. 153–6.

Little more remained to be done in the province. On Carew's return from Berehaven, Mountjoy sent Colonel Sir Samuel Bagenal to Cork to withdraw from him all his troops in excess of the old Munster establishment, about 1,000 by the poll, leaving his own force only some 1,500 strong. It was Mountjoy's original intention to station Bagenal at the central point of Westmeath, but the continued rumours of a fresh Spanish expedition induced him to send him back to Limerick, where he could either operate in Connaught or aid Carew in Munster as required, and later to Cork again. Carew's companies had been worn to a shadow, but he found at Cork 1,000 reinforcements to be distributed among them.[1]

One by one such strong places as remained in the hands of the rebels were recovered. The last actions in the province were fought in the depth of winter. Carew having gone to Galway to meet Mountjoy, Sir Charles Wilmot was in command. Hearing that he was concentrating all the forces that could be spared from the garrisons, the rebels broke up into three bodies. O'Sullivan remained in Bere with 700 men. The MacCarthys assembled 400 in Carbery. Tyrrell was to have gone into Kerry with the 500 that remained under his orders. But Tyrrell was a mercenary and was sick of the business in Munster. He had already been given a drubbing by Sir Samuel Bagenal in October, when he had fled in his shirt. Now he deserted his allies and marched off at top speed into King's County. Wilmot concentrated his forces on 27 December and on the last day of the year marched swiftly into the enemy's fastness. He laid hands upon thousands of cattle, on which the rebels were subsisting, but had to fight fiercely for six hours to bring his prey back to camp.

The power of the enemy to continue the struggle was not yet entirely broken, but his will was. Captains of bonaghts began to surrender to Wilmot. The Connaughtman William Burke fled to Connaught, declaring that he would no longer remain with O'Sullivan in Munster, and the latter, brave and determined as he was, decided that there was nothing left for him but to break out and join Tyrone in the north. He set forth with 400 or 500 fighting men and a throng of sutlers and women, but almost at once his following began to melt away. Marching from twenty to thirty miles a day, beating off attacks by Irish levies in the Queen's service, he reached the Shannon at Portland, near the northern end of Tipperary. The boats had been removed to prevent his passage, but he made a big

[1] *Carew Cal.*, Vol. IV, pp. 257, 268, 285, 298. *Pacata Hibernia*, p. 323.

curragh of osiers, over which the skins of eleven horses were stretched and which would carry thirty men at a time. A number of soldiers got over to the Galway bank, but then the local inhabitants fell upon the camp on the near or Tipperary bank, killing the sutlers and driving terror-stricken women into the river.

On went O'Sullivan, still fighting his way, putting to flight a force brought by Sir Thomas Burke, Clanrickarde's brother, which tried to intercept him at Aughrim, but continually losing and abandoning men and horses. After crossing the Curlieu Hills, he came in sight of the friendly Leitrim Castle, belonging to O'Rourke. He now had with him thirty-five persons—eighteen soldiers, sixteen horseboys, and one woman—out of about 1,000 who had set forth with him. A few more stragglers came in later, but the rest had all been killed, had dropped out from exhaustion, or had found some refuge after leaving the column. 'I am astonished', writes Philip O'Sullivan, 'that Dermot O'Sullivan [O'Sullivan Bere's kinsman], my father, an old man near seventy, and the woman of delicate sex, were able to go through these toils, which youths in the flower of age and height of their strength were unable to endure.' O'Rourke received the fugitives hospitably, and O'Sullivan Bere eventually made his way into Glenconkeine in March 1603 to join Tyrone; but by this time the rebellion was over.[1]

Meanwhile Carew, on his road north to Galway, had sent Captain Taaffe, with his troop of horse, forty foot, and 400 Irish kerne, to harry the MacCarthys in Carbery. On 5 January Taafe attacked them. Owen MacEgan, the Vicar Apostolic and titular Bishop of Ross, led a counter-attack at the head of 100 men, a drawn sword in one hand, his beads and his portus or breviary in the other. He was cut down, and his men thereupon took to flight. His death exercised a moral effect, but in any case the rebellion in Munster was now almost stamped out, the surviving partisans lurking in the bogs and thickets in small parties. The MacCarthys themselves speedily submitted.[2]

We have now to return to the doings of Mountjoy and of his lieutenants Docwra and Chichester in the north. The last incident recorded in Docwra's command was the seizure of Donegal Abbey by Neill Garve O'Donnell in August 1601. Here he was besieged by his cousin, Hugh Roe. He was, however, in no danger until, in

[1] *Carew Cal.*, Vol. IV, p. 403. *Pacata Hibernia*, pp. 362–6. *History of Catholic Ireland*, pp. 160–76.
[2] *Carew Cal.*, Vol. IV, p. 406.

mid-September, a fire broke out in the abbey and thirteen barrels of gunpowder blew up, almost completely wrecking the place and killing twenty-nine men. The Irish at once assaulted, but even then they were repulsed, the defenders clinging bravely to a corner of the building where the walls stood up. Neill Garve had done some gallant service already, but here he surpassed himself.[1]

This was an unlucky autumn for Docwra in other respects. He had sent a little English force under Captain Atkinson to occupy a castle at Newtown (to-day Newtownstewart) and with him a body of kerne under a well-tried Irish freelance named Tirlagh Magylson. Suddenly this man threw himself upon his allies, captured Atkinson, and cut the throats of every one of his men. Yet he did not seek a composition with Tyrone, whom he had deeply offended. Docwra found the Irish temperament hard to understand. Soon afterwards the same thing happened at Castlederg, though in this case the lives of the English soldiers were spared. Chichester also had a revolt to deal with, that of Con O'Neill, whom he had set up as chieftain in Upper Clandeboy, and this occurred weeks before the Spanish landing. The effects of the coming of the Spaniards were mixed. On the one hand, Hugh Roe O'Donnell speedily disappeared, marching with the bulk of his followers to Munster and leaving Docwra more liberty of action. On the other, men were inclined to go over to Tyrone, who, it will be remembered, remained for some time in the north. Randal MacSorley MacDonald, either out of simplicity or effrontery, told Chichester that he could no longer resist the pressure and asked his permission to change sides. He did accompany Tyrone to Kinsale, but the days were gone when great bodies of Redshanks could be raised for this service, and the small force which Randal took with him was cut to pieces.[2]

Both the English commanders carried out winter expeditions. Chichester marched north from Carrickfergus on 17 November, penetrating almost to the mouth of the Bann and sparing neither human beings nor goods found on his path. About this time a curious event occurred at Dunluce, where, it will be recalled, James MacDonald was imprisoned by his kinsman, Randal. In Randal's absence in Munster, James secured possession of his own gaol, though on Tyrone's return to the north he was persuaded to give it back. Chichester would have liked to get Dunluce into his hands, but it was too inaccessible. Docwra marched to Donegal

---

[1] *C.S.P. Ireland*, Vol. CCIX, 110A. Dowcra, *Narration*.
[2] *C.S.P. Ireland*, Vol. CCIX, 66, 109, 154. Docwra, *Narration*.

Abbey, and, finding the garrison too numerous in view of the damage done by the explosion, took part of it on to Asheroe, where he established a really strong force, including Neill Garve's Irish, within a stone's throw of Ballyshannon Castle. However, the long-desired castle, talked about for thirty years, could not be secured until a cannon was brought to the scene.[1] Docwra afterwards raided O'Cahan's country, east of the Foyle.

The cannon arrived on 20 March 1602, and on the 25th Bally-shannon Castle was secured. About the same time Docwra settled accounts with Tirlagh Magylson. The outlaw was now all alone, hunted from place to place. It was discovered that he evaded capture by lighting a fire at night to mark the place where it would be supposed that he would sleep, then slipping away to another, and perhaps repeating the process several times before settling down for the night. An Irish boy was sent to track him, and at last he was seen to take off his trousers and lie down. Four men went to seize him. He sprang up and struck a terrific blow at the first. The man inter-posed his target, in which the sword of Magylson made an incision so deep that it seemed incredible mortal man could have smitten so hard. Then he was killed and beheaded.[2]

Meanwhile, Mountjoy was preparing for his next campaign in the north. He could not start until the spring provided him with forage, but even if an expedition had set forth earlier he could scarcely have commanded it in person. In the latter part of May he wrote to Cecil that his health was improved, but that he was still far from strong and suffered greatly from headaches. He had, in fact, but another four years to live, and it may well be that the strain of the Kinsale campaign fatally undermined his constitution. He arrived at Newry on 10 June. The force with which he intended to operate had already assembled there and numbered by the list 506 horse and 3,650 foot. It may have amounted to three-quarters of that strength. Berkeley, the Sergeant-Major, was already engaged in revictualling Armagh.[3]

On 14 June Mountjoy marched to the Blackwater, reaching it at a point some five miles east of the old Blackwater fort. He pushed Sir Richard Moryson's regiment across to form a bridgehead, and under its cover built a bridge and another fort to guard the passage. This fort he named after his own Christian name and title Charle-mount (which became Charlemont) and left to garrison it the

---

[1] *C.S.P. Ireland*, Vol. CCIX, 196, 219; Vol. CCX, 2, 64.   [2] Docwra, *Narration*.
[3] *C.S.P. Ireland*, Vol. CCXI, 61B. Moryson, *An Itinerary*, Pt. II, p. 211.

company of Captain Toby Caulfeild, a name since linked with the
Charlemont peerage. Six miles away at Dungannon Tyrone's castle
and the cluster of buildings about it called a town were seen to be
on fire, proving that he was taking to the fern. Mountjoy moved
forward and occupied it. In a sense he was possessed of the enemy's
capital, and he wrote happily to Sir George Carey, the Treasurer at
Wars: 'We have drunk your health in Dungannon. Tyrone is turned
a wood-kerne.' On 26 June Docwra, who had on his march thrown
a garrison into the strategic point of Omagh, met him. Next day
Chichester came across Lough Neagh to join them in conference.
'The axe,' says Docwra, 'was now at the root of the tree.'[1]

The Queen still intended to prosecute the war to the final extremity and hoped that it would be ended that year. Tyrone had, she
wrote, no hope but rumours of Spanish aid, and that she had taken
care to render impossible, first by aid to the Dutch States, and
secondly by sending a fleet to cruise off the coast of Spain. She bade
the Deputy receive to mercy subordinate chiefs whom he could not
otherwise lay hands upon. He was given full powers in this respect,
save only as regards the pardon of 'the Arch Traitor'. Cecil, however, hinted that Mountjoy might at least entertain negotiations,
even with Tyrone.[2]

Mountjoy could not maintain his army indefinitely where he
was. Ordering Docwra from the west and Chichester from the east
at Toome to harry Tyrone in his present refuge of Glenconkeine,
he himself moved into Monaghan to revictual, taking on the way a
few strong places held by the enemy. A casual shot from one of them
killed Berkeley, who was replaced by Sir Henry Danvers. Finding
that the MacMahons stood upon 'proud terms', he despoiled the
barony of Dartry. He also established Connor Roe Maguire, known
as 'the Queen's Maguire' as opposed to the Irish champion, Cuconnaught, in a castle of the MacMahons on the border of his native
Fermanagh, as a step towards securing it. At the end of July the
Deputy returned to Newry to rest his troops. From there he wrote
to the Privy Council, still discussing the possibility that the Spaniards
would return.[3]

On 20 August he advanced again. His aim now was to induce the
gentlemen of Tyrone who would receive the Queen's mercy to
come south across the Blackwater with their followers and dwell

[1] C.S.P. Ireland, Vol. CCXI, 63A. Docwra, Narration.
[2] Moryson, An Itinerary, Pt. II, p. 219.
[3] Carew Cal., Vol. IV, p. 282. Moryson, An Itinerary, Pt. II, p. 225.

there for the time being, while he laid waste the country to the north. Then, when the Earl of Tyrone returned from Fermanagh, to which he had now moved, he would find no subjects, no resources, nothing but the Queen's garrisons. With this end in view, Mountjoy crossed the Blackwater on the 29th and made Dungannon defensible. He destroyed all the corn of the countryside. He went to Tullahogue, the place where the successive chiefs of the O'Neills were proclaimed, and smashed the stone chair in which they seated themselves for the ceremony. He put a garrison into the castle of Augher. For the present he could not follow Tyrone into south Fermanagh, where he lay in the midst of a forest. But Tyrone was now a nuisance rather than a danger. His army had disappeared and he had only about 600 men with him. Cuconnaught Maguire had left him, gone to Sir Henry Follyott at Ballyshannon, received the Queen's protection, promised to restore Enniskillen Castle and hand it over to the Queen, and agreed to submit to a division of Fermanagh between himself and his kinsman, Connor Roe. The end was drawing near. Ordering Docwra and Chichester to proceed with the wasting of Tyrone and the destruction of all supplies not needed for their garrisons, Mountjoy recrossed the Blackwater and on 9 September established in the undevastated country to the south of it two old sons of Shane O'Neill, Henry and Con, with their creaghts.[1]

In Connaught some success had been gained. The Governor, Sir Oliver Lambart, marched from Galway at the beginning of June. He found the Moy so high that he could not cross without boats, but the Burkes provided him with a couple. Rory O'Donnell, O'Rourke, and O'Connor Sligo—the last-named virtually a prisoner since Clifford's defeat in the Curlieus had thrown him into the power of the O'Donnells[2]—attempted to oppose his advance to Sligo, but without avail. He found the town, such as it was, burnt, but made a defensive position for his baggage. Then he turned on the rebels, who were passing their creaghts over the Curlieus, and caught a few of the cattle. He bought a galley, rowed with fifteen oars a side, to clear the coast and the islands of those longshore pirates, the O'Malleys and O'Flaherties. He was disappointed in Sligo itself. It would make, he considered, 'a dainty dwelling for a gentleman', but could not be made strong because commanded from the neighbouring hills and situated too far back to defend the anchorage. He built a fort over the cellars of the ruined abbey.[3]

---

[1] Moryson, *An Itinerary*, Pt. II, pp. 234-7.   [2] See p. 244.
[3] *C.S.P. Ireland*, Vol. CCXI, 61c, 81.

The last Irish victory of the war was won in Connaught, at the very place in which Clifford had been defeated and slain. Early in August Clanrickarde and Sir Arthur Savage, marching from Boyle across the Curlieus and reaching the great bog on the summit, found themselves opposed by 400 musketeers commanded by Rory O'Donnell and O'Connor Sligo. A brisk engagement followed, which at first appeared to be going well for the Queen's troops. Suddenly, however, the pikemen of the vanguard were smitten by panic and turned tail. The remainder of the force promptly broke and fled, fiercely pursued by the Irish, who cut down many of them.[1]

However, the collapse of the Irish fortunes was too complete for them to be restored by a minor success of this character, and the resolution of their foremost leaders was falling. News of the death of Hugh Roe O'Donnell in Spain induced his brother Rory to sue for peace. He and O'Connor Sligo made terms with Lambart, who in December brought them to Athlone to meet Mountjoy. O'Connor had a good case, in that he had been a loyalist until the defeat and death of Clifford in 1599 had compelled him to submit to Hugh Roe and fight in his cause. Rory's story did him no credit. He harped upon the ancient loyalty of the O'Donnells, including his father, and asserted that he had secretly promised Clifford to serve against his brother, but that his plot had been discovered and he had been kept in irons. Mountjoy and his Council stated that they knew this plea to be true.[2]

There exists, however, only too good reason to fear that Mountjoy was far from being disinterested in his policy towards Rory. He saw in him a man of inferior calibre to that of his cousin, Neill Garve. The latter was too strong a personality to be entrusted with the whole of Tyrconnell, though that had been promised him. Besides, his haughty bearing and his insolence to Docwra had been growing intolerable. Mountjoy concluded that it would be well to divide the country and accord the greater part of it to the weaker man, Rory, and in the end Neill Garve, the principal architect of the successes of the Lough Foyle force, got no more than his original lands in the Finn valley. Rory, on the other hand, was ennobled by King James I as Earl of Tyrconnell and obtained nearly all the remainder of the county.

The ugliest feature of the affair is that Docwra was egged on to

[1] C.S.P. Ireland, Vol. CCXII, 4. Four Masters, Vol. VI, p. 2,333.
[2] C.S.P. Ireland, Vol. CCXII, 90, 114. Four Masters, Vol. VI, p. 2,335.

give adverse evidence about the conduct of Neill Garve and declare him to be unfit for great power. The headstrong Ulsterman was his own worst enemy. He had himself proclaimed as the O'Donnell at Kilmacrenan, where the supreme chiefs of the O'Donnells were always elected, as were those of the O'Neills at Tullahogue. On the death of Elizabeth, Docwra laid hands on him and put him under restraint, but he broke out again. In the revolt of Sir Cahir O'Dogherty in 1608 he served the Crown, but was arrested for treachery and lodged in the Tower, where he was confined until his death.

Docwra freely admitted in after years that Neill Garve had been hardly treated, driven into treason, and that he himself had been made a catspaw in the process. His repentance is indeed marked by exceptional frankness. He writes of the two cousins, Neill Garve and Rory:

'I will only say this of him in general words (and I think my Lord Deputy and Judges that were in that time will bear me witness I say true), that there were no vices in poor Neill Garve, that had done us many good services, but the same were in him and more, in a far more pernicious degree, that had never done any; and then I confess it made me see clear mine own error and the wrong (I may call it) I had done to Neill Garve. Not that my conscience accuses me to have done anything towards him with malicious or corrupt intentions (no, thereof I take God to witness my heart is clear), but that with simplicity I suffered myself to be made an instrument of his overthrow, under the pretence of those misbehaviours that were plainly tolerated, yea, and allowed of, in another.'[1]

Here is indeed a heavy indictment of Mountjoy, but it is not the man so much as the policy that is accused. From the sixteenth on to the twentieth century England on many occasions sacrificed Irish friends for the sake of professedly repentant foes, or even to buy foes not promising repentance. The custom was variously described as recognition of realities or magnanimity, and became so popular that in later days it was extended to many parts of the world. Mountjoy doubtless meant well, as have others who have followed his example; but a common result has been the destruction, the despair, or the hatred of the deserted friend and the contempt of the foe who was to have been appeased.

From Athlone Mountjoy marched to Galway, where he received a number of submissions. The only rebel of any importance now

[1] Docwra, *Narration. C.S.P Ireland*, Vol. CCXI, 16.

out in Connaught was Brian O'Rourke in Leitrim, and even he was contemplating coming in. Carew had, as already recorded, gone to meet Mountjoy, and his service was nearly at an end. His intrigue with his friend Cecil to be recalled at last bore fruit, and on returning to Dublin he was summoned to court. He was in fact held up by unfavourable winds till 20 March, by which date Mountjoy had taken the familiar road again and gone to Drogheda.[1] His avowed object was to receive the surrender of Tyrone.

If the Queen had decided to pursue the issue to the end, as had for long been her intention, Tyrone would have shared the fate of Desmond and would shortly have been hewn to death in some corner of Glenconkeine, to which he had returned from Fermanagh. It has been asserted that he was saved by Elizabeth's death, but that interpretation of events is absurd. It may be that approaching death softened the Queen's heart. As early as 17 February she had authorized Mountjoy to go beyond his original instructions and to offer the rebel life, liberty, and pardon upon certain terms in order to bring this miserable war to a conclusion. Tyrone had been seeking mercy, so it seemed certain that a composition would be reached, though Mountjoy remarked with candour that if he saw a chance to get his head without engaging the Queen's word for his safety, he would do so. On 25 March he directed his friend, Sir William Godolphin, and his host, Sir Garret Moore, owner of Mellifont Abbey, where he was now staying, to go to Tyrone with a written safe-conduct and bring him in.

If the drama of these days is to be appreciated, it must be realized how far-reaching was the effect of the death of the Queen upon the offer made by Mountjoy to the great rebel who had so long withstood her rule and power. Elizabeth had in fact died on 24 March, the day before the emissaries were sent to Tyrone. With her life the house of Tudor, and with it an epoch, had come to an end. London was in the grip of excitement. Carew heard the news on reaching Chester, but in Ireland none knew what had happened. Mountjoy himself, one of the partisans of the Stuart succession, was as much in the dark to begin with as the rest. His authority was gone. He had been appointed the Queen's Deputy in Ireland and his mission depended upon her and her alone. He had no longer the right to accept the surrender of Tyrone, and if he did so it would not necessarily bind the Queen's successor.

While Mountjoy awaited Tyrone's coming the servant of a

[1] *Pacata Hibernia*, p. 390.

gentleman volunteer in his entourage got a quick passage to Ireland and reached Mellifont during the night of 27 March with a report of Elizabeth's death. The gentleman at once brought his servant to Fynes Moryson, the Lord Deputy's secretary, who pledged him to secrecy and advised the master to go to Mountjoy's room and inform him alone of what had occurred. Mountjoy could not be certain that the report was true, though there was little likelihood that it was not. If it were, some disturbance might occur and Tyrone might hang back in order to acquire prestige by having refused to submit to the Queen; if it were not, no harm would be done by hastening Tyrone's coming. He sent a messenger to the Blackwater to that purpose.

Tyrone arrived on the afternoon of the 30th. On reaching the threshold of the room in which Mountjoy awaited him he went down on his knees and made submission in all penitence. Mountjoy then bade him approach. Again he knelt, this time at the feet of Mountjoy, and for a full hour made his protestations of repentance and loyalty. Next day he put his submission into writing. He appealed to the princely clemency of the Queen. He asked that she should mitigate her just indignation because, he vowed, the first motive of his unnatural rebellion had been fear for his life, which he believed to be threatened. If the Queen would restore him to his dignities, he would ever afterwards remain her loyal subject. He absolutely renounced the style and title of 'the O'Neill'. He abjured all foreign power and dependence upon any potentate other than the Queen, especially the King of Spain. He swore not to interfere with the 'urriaghts'. He resigned all title to any lands except such as should be granted to him by Her Majesty's letters patent. He promised, as a subject, to be advised by the Queen's magistrates and aid them in anything that might tend to the advancement of her service and the peaceful government of the Kingdom, such as the abolition of barbarous customs.

This submission he presented to the Lord Deputy and Council, again on his knees. Then Mountjoy in the Queen's name promised pardon to him and his followers and his restoration to the earldom. He would be given new patents for the lands previously granted to him, excepting the holdings of two O'Neill magnates to whom rewards were due, Henry Oge O'Neill, Shane's grandson, on the Blackwater, and Sir Tirlagh MacHenry O'Neill, his own half-brother, in the Fews of central Armagh, and 300 acres each to maintain the forts of Mountnorris and Charlemont.

On 3 April Mountjoy rode with Tyrone to Drogheda. Next day they reached Dublin. On the 5th Sir Henry Danvers arrived with letters from the Lords in England, announcing the Queen's death and that James I had been proclaimed King, and bidding Mountjoy make a similar proclamation in Dublin.

Tyrone wept when the news was announced. For all his craft and subtlety, he was an emotional man. His memory could span the whole of the momentous reign that had now closed and he had ever professed for the Queen a respect which may be accounted genuine. It would seem unwarrantable to deride his own explanation, that he was deeply affected by the passing of so great a figure. Fynes Moryson, however, the author of the scheme to withhold the news from him and bring him in under false pretences, saw his grief in another light, as exasperation over the opportunities he had missed. 'There needed no Oedipus to find out the true cause of his tears. For, no doubt, the most humble submission he had made to the Queen he had so highly and proudly offended much eclipsed the vainglory his actions might have carried if he had held out till her death.'

On 6 April the Council, in accordance with constitutional precedent, elected Mountjoy to the office of Lord Justice, temporary governor of the country until it should please the new King to appoint him or another Lord Deputy. Tyrone had to make a new submission to James, in the same form as that which he had made to the dead Elizabeth. He also wrote to the King of Spain to inform him that he had submitted and would continue faithful to James I and to request that his son should be sent back to him. Henry O'Neill in fact entered the Spanish service, and never returned.

Mountjoy now ordered Danvers to go to England and render to the King a record of recent events. He omitted all mention of the report brought by the gentleman's servant, on the ground that this was merely a piece of private intelligence, on which he could not safely build. He was able to inform the King that there was now not a rebel in Ireland who had not sued for mercy. His intention was to bestow it upon the majority of those who had not yet received it, but to reserve some few for prosecution to utter ruin, as an example to other ill-affected subjects; but therein he desired to know His Majesty's pleasure. The great rebellion, 'Tyrone's rebellion', was over.[1]

[1] Moryson, *An Itinerary*, Pt. II, pp. 275–84. *C.S.P. Ireland*, Vol. CCXV, 9.

CHAPTER XXIV

AFTERMATH

THE history of Elizabeth's Irish wars manifestly concludes with the death of the Queen and the termination of the wars, which were simultaneous. Certain events which followed may suitably be mentioned as winding up the account, before a final review of the whole field, but need only be briefly recorded. After the ceremony in Dublin the Earl of Tyrone returned for a few weeks to his miserable country. The regions of Ulster most fought over were largely depopulated. The survivors were starving; the habitations were burnt; the cattle had been driven off. Corpses lay on the highways, the mouths stained green with the grasses with which the wretched men and women had striven to sustain themselves. Fynes Moryson tells of a band of old women who enticed little girls into their company, killed them, and ate their flesh. Wolves pulled down grown men in daylight. The kites alone were fat. Great numbers of people had fled south of the Blackwater, even as far as the Pale, to find food. The districts which had suffered worst were Down, south Antrim, and east Tyrone. North Antrim and Coleraine were not seriously affected, and Tyrconnell, Fermanagh, Cavan, Monaghan, and west Tyrone had escaped complete famine and devastation. What has been said of Munster after the Desmond rebellion must, however, apply here too. A pastoral and agricultural community recovers fairly quickly even from such horrors as this, and the Ulster lands did in fact soon become repopulated and recultivated.

Mountjoy was eager to quit the country, but he found a last unwelcome task to perform. The towns of Ireland had remained loyal throughout the rebellion and indeed, with a few unimportant exceptions, throughout all the troubles of the reign. When Elizabeth had ascended the throne, nearly half a century before, there had been remarkably little disturbance, but the succession of a monarch was always likely to be associated with unrest, and that of a type peculiarly affecting the towns. The present occasion seemed suitable for an attempt to recover full religious freedom. A rumour was spread, doubtless deliberately, that the new King was a Roman Catholic.

It is not likely that many priests believed this; in fact, some of them based their opposition to him on the plea that he was a heretic. If they missed with the edge of the blade they could hope to strike with the flat.

The extraordinary religious fever which now broke out was complicated by two other influences, the distress and disgust created by the base money of 1601, which was only now coming to a head, and a widespread belief that the moment was favourable for acquiring increased municipal freedom. The agitation was confined to the towns and did not extend to all. Dublin was untouched, and Galway is not mentioned. By far the most serious case was that of Cork. Yet even Drogheda, the most loyal town in Ireland, caused Mountjoy a certain anxiety, though, since the municipal authorities were prepared to take action, he took none.

All over Ireland, in town and countryside, Roman Catholic services, to which the Government turned a blind eye, had for some time been held. They took place for the most part in private dwellings, but sometimes also in small semi-public chapels. Now a number of priests came out into the open. They began to celebrate Mass in the town churches, and when they could not get possession of them otherwise, broke in forcibly, often aided by the municipal officials. Whereas, however, the mayors of towns commonly professed loyalty to James I and pretended astonishment that their actions should be considered unwelcome to him, the priests and congregations often took a stronger and more rebellious line. In Waterford the Recorder was pulled down from the market cross when he tried to proclaim the King. In Cashel the one English Protestant citizen had his house burnt and was threatened with the flames himself until he professed to have been converted to Catholicism. Cork declared officially that the authority of the commissioners left by Carew to carry on the presidential government ceased with the demise of the Crown and that the Corporation became sovereign within its own liberties. It shut its gates against Wilmot, the senior commissioner, who had been absent and engaged in extinguishing the last sparks of revolt in Kerry. For some time it utterly refused to proclaim the King, though this was finally done. The priests reconsecrated the churches, and some of them preached that the claim of the Spanish Infanta to the throne was better than that of James.

Mountjoy marched south on 27 April. He was met by Ormonde, who had faced defiance in his own town of Kilkenny, but had proclaimed the King in the little town of Carrick, where he also had a great house. As a soldier, Ormonde had dropped out, but he was useful in an affair of this sort and he provided boats which enabled Mountjoy to cross the Suir and deal with Waterford. Ormonde pleaded for mercy for the offenders, but he seems to have been pushing an open door. Many an Englishman of that age would have set up a gibbet in every troublesome town, but Mountjoy's outlook was wider. It is clear that he realized the problem at once. The Government could not continue without the support of loyal towns and townsmen. But for them the English would have been driven into the sea long ago. Therefore they must be brought back to loyalty. Persuasion would now be more politic than coercion. As for religion, he was perfectly content that the Mass should be celebrated quietly, so long as it was not in the churches, and hoped that the King would not lay down a policy too sharply defined and severe. Mountjoy's view, remarkable for his time, was that persecution increased the strength of any faith, and that conversion could be hoped for only through good example.

His handling of the affair was masterly. He was one of the rare men in such a position who could combine affability with dignity. A scholar and something of a theologian, he argued with priests and, at least to the satisfaction of his entourage, refuted their arguments. He was firm on essentials, and let the rest go. The only penalty enforced upon Cashel was the rebuilding of the Englishman's house which the people had burnt. Several towns quietened down directly he arrived in Munster. Severe measures nowhere proved necessary. He was not called upon to deal with the question of the currency, that matter being left to his successor, Sir George Carey, the Treasurer at Wars. Mountjoy was able to leave the country, his work accomplished, on 2 June 1603. He had been raised to the office of Lord Lieutenant of Ireland, the title borne by Sussex and Essex alone of the Elizabethan viceroys, but in his case under an arrangement for which there was no recent precedent: his office was to be exercised in England, and Carey was to be Lord Deputy in Dublin.

Mountjoy took with him the two principal pardoned rebels, the Earl of Tyrone and Rory O'Donnell. They sailed in the pinnace *Tramontana*, which had done valuable service on the coasts and was to do more in the later revolt of O'Dogherty. Having escaped all the dangers which beset an active commander in the Irish wars, Mountjoy came near to ending his career there and then and drowning in company with his former foes. The weather was foggy. Suddenly the *Tramontana* was surrounded by a multitude of screaming gulls. A moment later eyes, sharpened by the warning, sighted the black rocks of the Skerries just ahead. The helmsman contrived to save the ship, but she passed so close to the nearest rock that a boat slung in the stern struck it. She put in to Beaumaris Bay. On the road to London Mountjoy had to protect Tyrone from Welsh women who had lost sons and husbands in the wars and who pelted him with stones and mud.

At Hampton Court Mountjoy received his reward. He was created Earl of Devonshire, sworn to the Privy Council, and later appointed Master of the Ordnance. He received grants of money and of lands in Ireland. As Lord Lieutenant he was given full superintendence of Irish affairs, with two-thirds of the Deputy's salary. In 1604 he was one of the commissioners to arrange a treaty with Spain, against whose fleets and armies he had constantly fought. His last years were marked by a striking and famous incident. He had for some time been the lover, not openly, but accepted as such by the people of his own great world, of Penelope, Lady Rich, the sister of Essex, who had borne him children. Suddenly she left her disagreeable husband, who obtained from her a divorce *a mensa et thoro*. In December 1605 Mountjoy induced his chaplain to marry him to her, in circumstances of more than doubtful legality. The chaplain was William Laud, the future Archbishop of Canterbury, who was afterwards obsessed by a consciousness of sin for having performed this ceremony. Mountjoy died suddenly of pneumonia in April 1606.

Tyrone was well received by the King. His pardon and the restitution of his lands were confirmed. Rory O'Donnell was created Earl of Tyrconnell, but had to resign his claims to O'Dogherty's Country, the peninsula of Inishowen.

The great experiment of setting up Tyrone and Tyrconnell once more in the north as lords of territories granted by the King failed to work. A number of factors, including an outburst of persecution of leading Catholics, vague promises of Spanish aid, indulgence in vaguely treasonable talk which the Government was believed to have heard of, claims of Protestant clergy to Church lands, loss of fisheries, resentment over the behaviour of garrisons, but most of all the realization that the day of great independent Celtic chiefs was done, resulted in the summer of 1607 in that astonishing and tragic event, the Flight of the Earls. Tyrone and Tyrconnell, with Cuconnaught

Maguire, their families and chief followers, and various other members of the Ulster aristocracy, sailed from Lough Swilly, reached France, visited the Spanish Netherlands, and finally made their way to Rome. In Italy all the most important except Tyrone— that is, Tyrconnell, Maguire, Tyrone's son, Lord Dungannon, and Tyrconnell's brother Cathbar—died swiftly of fever. Tyrone survived until 1616. A few years before a spy had reported to the English Ambassador to Venice that when he was *vino plenus et ira,* as he usually was each night, he would declare that it was his purpose to die in Ireland. He was a shrewder and longer-sighted man than his principal ally, Hugh Roe O'Donnell, and a better organizer; but he lacked the other's singleness of vision and of purpose. His caution and subtlety were not far removed from persistent indecision. If Hugh Roe had lived and enjoyed as much good fortune as Tyrone in the year 1603—or as his own brother Tyrconnell—he might have come to be recognized as the greater man.

The Flight of the Earls was followed by the Plantation of Ulster, carried out by Lord Deputy Chichester, the colonization of the northern province with English and Scots settlers, an event which has profoundly affected Ireland ever since and the results of which have in modern times provided one of the most important of political problems. Unlike the Marian and Elizabethan plantations, this took deep root, and though twice almost exterminated, has never ceased to grow stronger.

The victories gained by Mountjoy and his lieutenants were decisive. The one revolt recorded by history in the years that followed was that of Sir Cahir O'Dogherty in 1608, and that was over in a few weeks. A rising was planned in Ulster in 1615, but the Government got wind of the plot and it came to nothing. There were always a few wood-kerne, dispossessed men or old bonaghts of the wars, in the forests and glens, and more in Ulster than elsewhere. Yet the next great rebellion did not occur until 1641. And, though it was connected with the Ulster Plantation, it is not likely that it would have occurred at all but for the influence of the disturbance and resistance to the King in England, which were so soon to lead to civil war. With that civil war the Irish rebellion became inextricably mingled. It can thus be said that Mountjoy's settlement endured for thirty-eight years, and that it was ended by exterior forces.

CHAPTER XXV

A RETROSPECT

AN attempt has already been made at the commencement of this narrative to point out the importance of the Irish wars and the strength of the menace to English power represented by an alliance between rebellious Ireland and Spain. In this final review the main object is to consider the methods employed and the reasons for their success. For successful they were up to the death of Lord Burgh and completely so in the end, after a phase in which the English suffered heavy reverses and appeared to be on the point of losing control altogether.

Even though the policy pursued was not often clearly and was sometimes perhaps only half-consciously expressed, it is apparent that Queen Elizabeth and Burghley sought the substance rather than the shadow. There was, it appeared to them, after the death of Shane O'Neill, no case for a war to the death against Tirlagh Luineach because, whatever his pretensions, he was never likely to set himself at the head of Ireland in revolt. It was better to put up with a little defiance, to close the eyes to this and pretend not to hear that, than to stir up trouble by adopting too logical an attitude and taking up a position too strictly in accordance with theory. When, however, a situation arose which threatened grave danger, they were prepared to make great and prolonged efforts, to call for great sacrifice of the country's blood, and to pour out its money in order to restore security. It may well be argued that the Queen, who hated spending money, got herself and the country into unnecessary trouble by refusing to take precautions in time—as indeed in all her warlike operations—but the magnitude of the exertions undertaken when the struggle became one of life and death must be acknowledged. Nor must it be overlooked that, hampered by an obsolete financial system, Elizabeth avoided bankruptcy, which Philip II may be said to have incurred.

The first reason why these efforts did not fail in face of great difficulties and temporary humiliations was the strength and temper of the Elizabethan state. Materially, for the material business of waging war, it belonged to a modern and advanced civilization, despite weakness in finance and military organization. At the same time England under Elizabeth was young and vigorous. It could take knocks and endure adversity. It possessed confidence enough in itself and its destiny to persevere. There is an analogy between its spirit and that of its representative, Mountjoy, when, with the Irish army at his back, he refused to raise the siege of Kinsale. Doubts and questionings may come to such sanguine and vehement states, but they are brushed aside.

Strategically, the English employed four methods of dealing with rebellion, the three first invariably, the fourth in serious situations where the others did not suffice, in which case it was combined with the other three. They were the seeking out of the enemy to bring him to battle and break his force into fragments; the maximum use of Irish aid; the installation of garrisons, in general surprisingly small to modern eyes, in castles or more rarely earth forts at strategic points to cover river crossings, protect anchorages, deny pastures to the enemy; and in the last resort the devastation of the country-side to render it impossible for considerable hostile forces to live upon it. All proved effective, but the last inflicted terrible hardship and frequently starvation upon the whole population of the district.

If the rebellion were a strong one a battle was always needed, though often hard to bring about. The next method was probably the most valuable after a battle had been won. It took advantage of rivalries and dissensions among the Irish, but it also exploited certain traditions of loyalty and friendship which are often over-looked in hasty or prejudiced examination of the various rebellions. The author of the *History of Catholic Ireland* attributes the defeat of the Munster phase of Tyrone's rebellion mainly to this factor. He is manifestly torn between pride that the Irish were not—and, he claims, could not have been—subdued except by Irishmen, and regret that Irishmen should thus have betrayed the national cause. It must be recalled that he himself had left Ireland as a boy, had been brought up in Spain and entered the Spanish service, so that he looked upon Irish affairs as a whole from a standpoint almost unknown among his countrymen at home. To them the conception of a national cause was extremely unusual, if not unheard of.

He argues that the English policy was to be tender to the Irish when their assistance was needed, to make them fine promises, and then to discard them or even fall upon them and accuse them of treason. Cases of base ingratitude for services rendered do indeed · appear in the records, but on the whole the English authorities kept their promises to those to whom they were thus indebted. Sir George Carew was a hard and unscrupulous man, but he pleaded strongly for confirmation of his settlements with men who had returned to allegiance and also pressed for rewards for their services. Docwra, years after the events in question, was still shocked and hurt by what seemed to him a particularly scandalous affair, the breach of promises made to Neill Garve O'Donnell, in which he had been in some sort involved.

The value of Irish allies was very great. In engagements in the field it was often considerable, but not at its highest. The district of a loyal chief was roughly policed, especially if he possessed a strong place. He would keep his cattle out of rebel hands if he could, and provide beef for the royal forces. He would help to hunt down a rebel who had already been defeated and was on the run. He would furnish light forces which could operate where regular troops found themselves in difficulties. He would produce boats to convey these regular troops across rivers, horses for their transport, guides and scouts on their marches. Above all he would bring in intelligence, not only of the designs, whereabouts, and movements of the enemy, but also of the temper of the countryside. At the lowest, if he kept his kerne at home they would not serve in the enemy's ranks.

Castellated districts were districts in which the enemy must move with great circumspection. The wards tended to keep the wavering from passing over to the rebel cause. They distracted chiefs in revolt, sometimes prevented them from leaving their own country for places where their presence would have been less welcome to the Government, and, if they did venture to march away, compelled them to leave a proportion of their forces at home. They facilitated the marches of the royal army. On the debit side in time of adversity they might involve unwelcome responsibility, but the balance was highly favourable.

Needless to say, what applied to the castle or fort applied on a greater scale to the walled town, which would hold a larger garrison, would provide accommodation in winter, possessed a market, and could be used to store cannon, tools, reserves of arms, powder, and miscellaneous equipment. It was almost unknown for a walled town to be lost, and none of the greater ever was lost in the course of Elizabeth's reign. Athenry was burnt by the Burkes; Kilmallock was burnt and looted by Fitzmaurice; Youghal was sacked and partially destroyed by Desmond; Kinsale was secured by the Spaniards; but Galway, Limerick, Cork, Waterford, Wexford,

Drogheda, Newry, Athlone, and some of the smaller inland towns of Leinster and Munster were the strongholds and foundations of English rule.

Devastation was a double-edged weapon. If it weakened resistance, it made the passage of royal forces more difficult and diminished the value of allies. When, however, it was employed against a rebel commander maintaining large forces from his vassals or hiring large bodies of mercenaries it became an overwhelmingly efficient form of warfare. The organization painfully and skilfully built up by Tyrone, which had provided him with a permanent trained force to meet the English on equal terms, was dealt a deadly blow by the defeat of Kinsale, cracked and dislocated by the garrisons stationed throughout Ulster, further weakened by the defection of subjects and their followers, and finally brought to ruin by the burning of grain in field or barn and the raids on the creaghts. This furnishes an example of the combination of all the methods employed by the Government against rebellion.

Despite the genius attributed by some historians to Shane O'Neill, Tyrone, and Hugh Roe O'Donnell, it is clear that the English forces enjoyed in general the better leadership. Some of their commanders were very fine soldiers. If Mountjoy was the greatest, Sidney, Burgh, Ormonde, Gilbert, Drury, Pelham, Malby, Bingham, Docwra, Arthur Chichester, Brooke, Richard Wingfield, Wilmot, and Graeme, on their several scales, constitute a company of great fighting men. For all the differences between continental and Irish warfare, the experience which nearly all had gained on the Continent—some of the earliest in the days of the Spanish alliance, the later in those of hostility to Spain—was invaluable. Their knowledge of tactics might not ensure victory, but it did render defeat unlikely, and, after all, very few defeats, great or small, were suffered in nearly forty-five years, while innumerable victories were won.

The second factor in success was the superiority of English weapons. It is true that the Irish made great strides in the use of firearms and often became better shots than the royal troops. At the same time, it was only in their best companies that the musketeers reached as high a proportion of the whole as they did in the English. The short lance of the English light horseman was a superior weapon to the Irish horseman's spear and, as has previously been pointed out, the Irishman, riding without stirrups, had no chance against the English trooper in shock action.

Where the Irish were weakest of all was in artillery. A gun or two was captured, and the Spaniards supplied a number in the last phase; otherwise the Irish forces never possessed any. This was a heavy handicap. It meant that no castle held by the English need ever fall unless it were betrayed, surprised, or starved out, whereas practically no castle could be maintained by the Irish, provided the English could reach the scene with cannon of adequate weight. That was the difficulty, as is vividly illustrated by the case of Dunboy, for which Carew set out from Cork on 23 April 1602, and which he took on the morning of 17 June about twenty-four hours after beginning his bombardment—fifty-four days to get to close quarters and mount the guns; one day to make a breach and storm the castle.

Carew's artillery was brought to Bantry Bay by sea, as was almost always the case when artillery had to be moved for any considerable distance. Sea power served the English well as regards the movement of supplies, which was more important than that of cannon. They made constant use of the indentations of the coast and of the navigable rivers to bring seaborne supplies deep into the country. Lough Foyle, Belfast Lough, Carlingford Lough, Waterford Harbour and the Barrow, Cork Harbour and the Bandon, Bantry Bay, the Kenmare River, Dingle Bay, the Shannon and the Fergus, Galway Bay, provided shipping with channels penetrating far within the coast and enabled land forces to reach their supplies by relatively short marches accompanied by relatively little transport.

Throughout the whole period, with a short and doubtful interlude, the superiority of English discipline and steadiness was very marked and enabled English commanders to undertake expeditions and accept battle at a disadvantage in numerical strength which would otherwise have confined them to inaction and a rigid defensive. Despite desertion, occasional bad behaviour, and a few instances of downright panic, the English soldier proved himself a wonderful fighting man in these campaigns. When he met the Spaniard in the sorties from Kinsale he lived up to his form and paid an incidental tribute to the Irish troops who had on countless occasions given him trouble and on some defeated him. The company was, as already explained, the administrative, and until near the end, the fighting, unit. Many companies created and preserved a fine *esprit de corps*. The regiment was perhaps too new an organization to do so.

Here there may be mentioned a feature of Irish warfare which has not been to any great extent illustrated in the narrative because that would have called for too much detail in the accounts of the smaller combats. They resembled Homeric or Virgilian encounters by reason of the deeds of heroes or champions on either side. There appear frequent accounts of the achievements of half a dozen of 'our best men', or claims that the enemy had lost a similar number of 'his best men'. A few troopers charging at the heels of a dashing—but it must also be noted, a well-armoured—commander, a Bingham or a Southampton, often achieved amazing results. When Docwra was smitten to the ground near the camp at Derry, the blow is said to have been dealt by a member of the princely house of O'Donnell. Neill Garve killed his cousin with his own hands. Rory O'Donnell drove his lance into the head of Neill Garve's horse and brought him down. Neill Garve personally chased Tyrone. Serjeants or private soldiers, not famous men flattered as such, are reported to have performed prodigious deeds against the Spaniards at Kinsale. Warfare was still very much a personal matter, constantly marked by acts of individual prowess. This was recognized abroad in much greater campaigns, where the pikeman of the front rank was a *doppelsöldner*.

These wars were merciless. The Irish in revolt were nearly always treated as traitors to their sovereign and, if they fell into the hands of the royal troops, whole or wounded, killed on the spot. On the other side the kerne made almost a ceremony of beheading prisoners and wounded on the battlefield. Women, children, and the aged as often as not shared the fate of the fighting men. In other respects each side accused the other of bad faith, but it would seem that an undertaking to allow a besieged garrison to march out in safety was generally observed. It is, however, to be noted that in all contractual engagements the stronger side always, and both sides sometimes, took pledges or hostages, liable to be executed on failure to fulfil the conditions. Dealings in these matters were technical and often skilful. A chief would be accounted to have scored heavily and proved himself an astute man if he had palmed off on an English commander third-rate pledges, perhaps worthless cousins in whom he took no interest and for whose lives he did not care a groat. Then, if he wanted to break his undertaking, he could snap his fingers and bid his opponent hang the wretches if it gave him satisfaction to do so. If the pledges were of more interest to the pledger, he might have to liberate them by bribery or cunning before he found himself free to act as he desired, as occurred to Ormonde when he was liberated by those who had kidnapped him near Kilkenny. The system of taking pledges was practised by all.

This narrative is in the main military. Political and moral issues are not, it is hoped, completely neglected, but they play, as they are intended to, a secondary part. Perhaps enough has been said to indicate that a higher degree of statesmanship might have secured a different and happier future for the relations between the two countries. It is legitimate to speculate upon such matters, but the speculator must beware of one error into which it is all too easy to fall: that of judging by standards which do not belong to the age and had not even been conceived, except perhaps among a handful of theorists whose ideas carried no practical weight.

The Elizabethan wars in Ireland involved the collision of two civilizations, in which the older went down. Both sides fought according to their lights. It is as idle to argue that the Irish should have welded the opposition to English rule and the Protestant faith into a single national and Catholic force as it is to regret that the English were not inspired by national, political, and religious toleration. They followed their destinies in either case. The wars, however, were not purposeless or preposterous. There existed good reasons why they should have been fought, and good reasons why they should have ended as they did.

BIBLIOGRAPHY

THE authorities listed below are fairly numerous, but by far the most important is that of the State Papers, Ireland, of the reign of Queen Elizabeth. It would probably be possible to write a better history of affairs in Ireland during this period, from the English point of view, from this source alone than from all the others put together.

The printed calendars of these Elizabethan State Papers begin as little more than a catalogue of the subjects of the documents and develop from 1585 into a series of transcripts of the most important documents. I will not go so far as to say that it would be affectation to consult the originals all through, but I consider that it would be waste of time for one who is getting on in years and who hopes to accomplish some other work of research in his lifetime. Even as it was, the perusal of eleven volumes of the Irish calendar, averaging perhaps 500 large pages apiece, proved a formidable task, not only in time, but also as regards eyesight. To do the same thing with the originals, in the often difficult Elizabethan script, would have taken several years at the same rate of progress per year.

This explanation is called for partly in order to make clear the system of reference. Starting off with the originals, I naturally numbered these as they are numbered on the pages in the Public Record Office. These numbers are appended to the entries in the calendar, and I have thought it convenient to continue to use this system for reference, it being just as simple as it would be to give the page numbers of the calendar. Thus, if I give a reference to the *Calendar of State Papers* (*C.S.P. Ireland*), as, let us say, Vol. LXVII, 28, this refers to the volume and number of the original document, whereas a reference to the *Spanish State Papers*, such as Vol. III, p. 425, refers to the volume of the calendar and its page. The reference can be checked as quickly in one way as in the other. The only other manuscript source which I have consulted, and that only during the briefest of visits or by photographic or manuscript copies since obtained, is the Spanish Archivo General de Simancas.

The second great English source is the State Papers, Carew, at Lambeth Palace. Here originals are followed pretty closely throughout in the calendar, and I have not consulted any of them. The historian Bagwell, who wrote just after the publication of this calendar, suggested that it would not again be necessary to go to the originals, and he was both a leisured and a conscientious man, who read all the official State Papers in manuscript. The third important English source is the Acts of the Privy Council.

The Irish records are disappointing. The best from my point of view is the *Annals* of the Four Masters. The *Annals of Lough Cé* do not cover the whole of the reign of Elizabeth and are otherwise less satisfactory for a military study. O'Clery, who wrote a life of Hugh Roe O'Donnell, was one of the Four Masters, and as most passages relating to O'Donnell are almost word for word the same in the two works the biography has no great value. *The History of Catholic Ireland (Historiae Catholicae Iberniae Compendium)* has some value because the author talked with older men who had taken part in Tyrone's rebellion, but must be used with caution even for that, and more carefully still for earlier affairs, first, because he had few if any documents, and, secondly, because he invented shamelessly.

Fortunately, modern Celtic scholarship, as exemplified in the works of Professor Eoin MacNeill and in *Scots Mercenary Forces in Ireland* by Dr. G. A. Hayes-McCoy, supplies much that would otherwise be lacking. There must be more to do in this field, and few skilled enough for the task. Dr. Hayes-McCoy breaks virgin soil. I can only say of his book that, whatever the value of my own study, it would have been much less had I not had the benefit of this remarkable work and indeed that without it I might not have attempted my present task.

There is little modern English work of high importance touching my subject, which is almost as new as that of Dr. Hayes-McCoy. Archbishop Mathew's *The Celtic Peoples and Renaissance Europe* contains fascinating character sketches. An article by Professor Neale in the *English Historical Review* was most valuable, though not concerned with Ireland. His great work on the Elizabethan House of Commons unfortunately appeared just too late for me to profit by it. Mr. C. G. Cruickshank's *Elizabeth's Army*, though wholly administrative, provided a number of pointers. Relatively few references are made to *Ireland under the Tudors*, by Richard Bagwell, but his volumes have always been beside my hand, as they must be beside the hand of a writer dealing with any aspect of Tudor Ireland.

MANUSCRIPT

State Papers, Ireland (Public Record Office).
Archivo General de Simancas (Spain).

CALENDARS AND ORIGINAL ENGLISH PAPERS

Calendar of State Papers, Ireland.
Calendar of State Papers, Carew.
Calendar of State Papers, Domestic.
Calendar of State Papers, Roman.
Calendar of State Papers, Spanish.
Calendar of State Papers, Venetian.
Calendar of Border Papers.
Calendar of Scottish Papers.
Calendar of Scottish Papers (Thorpe).
Calendar of Treasury Papers.
Calendar of Patent Rolls, Philip and Mary.
Acts of the Privy Council.
Digges, Sir D.: *The Compleat Ambassador.*
Galloglas, The Rate of the Wages of the (Irish Arch. Soc. Tracts, Vol. II.).
Historical MSS. Commission, *De Lisle and Dudley Papers.*
—— *Rutland Papers.*
—— *Salisbury Papers.*
—— *Various Collections.*
James VI, Correspondence of with Sir Robert Cecil (Camden Society).
Maxwell, C. (Editor): *Irish History from Contemporary Sources* (excerpts).
Morley, H. (Editor): *Ireland under Elizabeth and James* (excerpts).
Navy Records Society: *The Defeat of the Spanish Armada.*
Sydney (or Sidney) Papers (Collins).

IRISH RECORDS

Annals of Lough Cé (Rolls Series).
Four Masters: *Annals of the Kingdom of Ireland.*
O'Clery, Lughaidh: *The Life of Red Hugh O'Donnell* (translation).
O'Sullevan, P.: *Historiae Catholicae Iberniae Compendium* (part translated as *Ireland under Elizabeth* by M. J. Byrne).

CONTEMPORARY (OR NEARLY CONTEMPORARY) ENGLISH ACCOUNTS

Birch, T.: *Memoirs of the Reign of Queen Elizabeth.*
Camden, William: *Annales.*
—— *History of the Life and Reign of Elizabeth* (translation of Vol. II of *Annales*).
Cox, Richard: *Hibernia Anglicana.*
Derricke, T.: *Image of Ireland, with a Discourse of Woodcarne* (Small).
Docwra, Sir H.: *Relation of Service done in Ireland* (Celtic Society Miscellany).
—— *Narration of the Services done by the Army ymployed to Lough-Foyle* (Celtic Society Miscellany).
Dymmok, J.: *A Treatice of Ireland* (Irish Arch. Soc. Tracts, Vol. II).
Harington, Sir J.: *Nugae Antiquae* (Ed. 1779).
Hooker, J.: *Irish Chronicles* (in Holinshed).
Moryson, F.: *An Itinerary* (Ed. 1617).
Pacata Hibernia (Ed. 1633).
Pynnar, N.: *Survey of Ulster* (in Harris, Walter: *Hibernica*).
Spenser, Edmund: *View of the State of Ireland* (see Morley).
Strype: *The Life of Sir Thomas Smith,* 1698.

CONTEMPORARY WORKS ON WAR

Digges, T.: *An Arithmetical Warlike Treatise.*
Londoño, S. de: *Disciplina Militar* (Ed. 1943).
Markham, F.: *Epistles of War.*
Osorio: *Vida y Hazanas de Don Fernando Alvarez de Toledo, Duque de Alba* (Spanish translation by José Lopez de Toro from original Latin, 1945).
Rich, Barnaby: *A Pathway to Military Practice.*
Styward, T.: *The Pathway to Martial Discipline.*

LATER WORKS

Alba, Duke of: *The Great Duke of Alba as a Public Servant.*
Armamento de los Ejércitos de Carlos V en la Guerra de Alemania (Spanish Servicio Histórico Militar, 1947).
Bagwell, R.: *Ireland under the Tudors.*
Butler, W. F. T.: *Gleanings from Irish History.*
Cheyney, E. P.: *History of England, 1588-1603.*
Corbett, Julian S.: *Drake and the Tudor Navy.*
—— *The Successors of Drake.*

Cruickshank, C. G.: *Elizabeth's Army.*
Devereux, W. B.: *Lives and Letters of the Devereux.*
Falls, Cyril: *The Birth of Ulster.*
Fortescue, Sir J.: *History of the British Army.*
Gregory, D.: *History of the Western Highlands.*
Grose, F.: *Military Antiquities.*
Hayes-McCoy, G. A.: *Scots Mercenary Forces in Ireland.*
—— "Clontibret" (*Irish Historical Studies*, June 1949).
Hill, Rev. G.: *Historical Account of the Macdonnells of Antrim.*
Hume, Martin: *The Great Lord Burghley.*
Joyce, P. W.: *A Social History of Ireland.*
MacCarthy, D.: *The Life and Letters of Florence MacCarthy.*
McKenna, Rev. J.: *Devenish (Lough Erne).*
MacNeill, Eoin: *Celtic Ireland.*
—— *Early Irish Laws.*
—— *Phases of Irish History.*
Maine, Sir H.: *Early History of Institutions.*
Maitland, F. W.: *The Constitutional History of England.*
Mathew, David: *The Celtic Peoples and Renaissance Europe.*
Neale, J. E.: 'Elizabeth and the Netherlands' (*English Historical Review*, Vol. XLV).
Oman, Sir C.: *A History of the Art of War in the Sixteenth Century.*
Read, Conyers: *Mr. Secretary Walsingham.*
Ronan, M. V.: *The Reformation in Ireland under Elizabeth.*
Routledge, F. J.: 'Journal of the Irish House of Lords in Sir John Perrott's Parliament' (*English Historical Review*, Vol. XXIX).
Stewart, D.: 'Sickness and Mortality Rates of the English Army in the Sixteenth Century' (*Journal of the Royal Army Medical Corps*, Vol. XCI).

INDEX

AGARDE, FRANCIS, 117

Aguila, Juan de, commands Spanish expedition, 293; calls Tyrone to his aid, 295; his difficult situation, 301; unaware of battle of Kinsale, 308; makes terms with Mountjoy, 308; discusses peace with England, 314; his fate in Spain, 315

Albert, Archduke, 195

Allerton, Captain, 236

Alva, Duke of, 38, 44, 105

Apsley, Captain, 147

Archer, Father, 259, 291

Argyll, 4th Earl of, 81

Armada, Spanish, off Ireland, 9, 164; preparations to meet, 49; sighted, 162; its relation to Ireland, 163; its losses off Ireland, 167; the 'Second Armada', 196

Asturias, Prince of, 195

Atkinson, Captain, 326

Audley, Lord, 232

Austria, Don John of, 124, 238, 240

Azores, expedition to, 196

BACON, SIR NICHOLAS, 117

Bagenal, Sir Henry, retreats before Scots, 155; his hatred of Tyrone, 173; defeats Maguire, 176; his removal recommended, 180; accuses Tyrone of treason, 184; revictuals Monaghan, 187; reports Burgh's death, 207; prepares to relieve Blackwater fort, 212, 214; defeated and killed at Yellow Ford, 215

—, Sir Nicholas, 160

—, Sir Samuel, 211, 225, 324

Ballina, English reverse near, 191

Baltimore as Spanish base, 309

Baltinglas, Viscount, 134, 146

Barnewall, Sir Patrick, 250

Berkeley, Sir John, 304, 306, 327, 328

Berwick, troops for Ireland from, 95

Billings, Richard, 217, 218

Bingham, Francis, 170

—, Sir George, 171

—, Captain George, 188

—, Sir Richard, on Irish levies, 41; 72, 138; Governor of Connaught, 154; routs Scots on the Moy, 158; leaves Ireland temporarily, 160; his report on the Armada, 164; kills the survivors, 166; his harshness, 170; fails to retake Sligo, 191; revictuals Ballymote, 193; imprisoned, 197; death of, 224

Biscuits, Ford of the, 72, 182

Blackwater fort, 186, 204, 207, 213, 220

Blaney, Edward, 266

Blount, Sir Christopher, 231, 240, 279; identity of, 281

—, Sir Edward, 281

—, George, 314

Bodley, Josiah, 296

'Bonaghts' (Irish mercenaries), 68

Bourchier, Sir George, 137, 221, 245

Brady, Richard, 263

Brehon law, 31, 86

Brewitt, Miles, 162

Brochero, Diego, 293

Brooke, Sir Calisthenes, 205, 219

Brouncker, Sir Henry, 213

Buckhurst, Lord, 253

Burgh, Lord, enlists Irish, 41; on Tyrone's methods, 75; Lord Deputy, 200; bad health of, 202; energy of, 203; builds Blackwater fort, 204; garrisons Cavan, 206; death of, 207

Burghley, Lord, 9; supports Ormonde, 101, 149; 106; encourages Pelham, 131; told of misery of troops, 172; advises recall of Russell, 199; death of, 222

Burke, Theobald, 223

—, Sir Thomas, 325

—, Tibbot ne Long, 223, 283

—, William, 321, 324